Rod Rolle

Nelson Lichtenstein is one of the country's leading experts on labor and politics and the editor of a much-cited collection of essays on Wal-Mart. A professor of history at the University of California, Santa Barbara, where he directs the Center for the Study of Work, Labor, and Democracy, he is also the author of several highly regarded books on American history, including the award-winning *Walter Reuther: The Most Dangerous Man in Detroit*.

THE RETAIL REVOLUTION

THE
RETAIL
REVOLUTION

HOW WAL-MART
CREATED A BRAVE NEW WORLD
OF BUSINESS

NELSON LICHTENSTEIN

PICADOR

A METROPOLITAN BOOK
HENRY HOLT AND COMPANY
NEW YORK

For George Cotkin
Historian and Friend

www.picadorusa.com

Picador® is a U.S. registered trademark and is used by Henry
Holt and Company under license from Pan Books Limited.

For information on Picador Reading Group Guides,
please contact Picador.
E-mail: readinggroupguides@picadorusa.com

Designed by Kelly Too

ISBN 978-0-312-42968-3

First published in the United States by
Henry Holt and Company

CONTENTS

INTRODUCTION

FROM BENTONVILLE
TO GUANGDONG

Shopping has become the most important thing we do to keep America's $13 trillion economy humming. It is the retailers, Wal-Mart first among them, who have become the key players in the worldwide marketplace of our time. They are the new business giants fueling the China boom, building huge container ports on every continent, and transforming the metropolitan landscape at home. Controlling more than half of all world trade, they make the markets, set the prices, and determine the worldwide distribution of labor to produce that gigantic stream of commodities that flows across checkout counters in every major industrial country.

All this is graphically apparent upon a visit to the two most dynamic nodes of transnational capitalism today. It is easy to get to Bentonville, Arkansas, where Wal-Mart has its world headquarters in an unimpressive, low-slung building nearby the company's original warehouse. There are lots of direct flights from Denver, Chicago, New York, and Los Angeles to this once remote town in the far northwestern corner of Arkansas; Beijing and Hong Kong are but one stop away. Bentonville is still not very big. Between Fayetteville, the university town twenty miles to the south, and the Missouri line just north of Bentonville there are hardly more than three hundred thousand people. But it is now one of the fastest-growing metropolitan regions in the country. The parking lots are full, the streets are crowded, and new construction is everywhere. There are dozens of subdivisions full of oversized houses, scores of freshly built motels and hotels, new country clubs and churches, and even a mosque and a synagogue. And the Walton family presence is everywhere: there's a Sam Walton Boulevard in Bentonville; a Bud Walton Arena and a Walton College of Business at the University of Arkansas; a terminal building named after daughter Alice Walton at the airport; and an ambitious, family-funded art museum in the offing.

Most important, Bentonville and nearby Rogers are now home to at least 750 branch offices of the largest Wal-Mart "vendors" who have planted their corporate flag in northwest Arkansas in the hope that they can maintain or increase their sales with the world's largest buyer of consumer products. Procter & Gamble, which in 1987 may well have been the first company to put an office there, now has a staff of more than 250 in Fayetteville; likewise Sanyo, Levi Strauss, Nestlé, Johnson & Johnson, Eastman Kodak, Mattel, and Kraft Foods maintain large offices in what the locals sometimes call "Vendorville." Walt Disney's large retail business has its headquarters not in Los Angeles but in Rogers, Arkansas.

These Wal-Mart suppliers are a who's who of American and international business, staffed by ambitious young executives who have come to see a posting to once-remote Bentonville as the crucial step that can make or break a corporate career.[1] If they can meet Wal-Mart's exacting price and performance standards, their products will be sucked into the stream of commodities that flows through the world's largest and most efficient supply chain. For any goods maker or designer, it is the brass ring of American salesmanship, which explains why all those sophisticates from New York, Hong Kong, and Los Angeles are dining at the surprisingly large number of good restaurants that have sprung up in northwest Arkansas.

If Bentonville represents one nerve center of retail's global supply network, Guangdong Province is the other. Located on the southern coast of China, its sprawling factories link a vast new Chinese proletariat to the American retailers who are putting billions of Chinese-made products on a million U.S. discount store shelves every day. With more than 15 million migrant workers, tens of thousands of export-oriented factories, and new cities like Shenzhen, which has mushroomed to more than 7 million people in just a quarter century, Guangdong can plausibly claim to be the contemporary "workshop of the world," following in the footsteps of nineteenth-century Manchester and early-twentieth-century Detroit.

This was my thought when I taxied across Dongguan, a gritty, smoggy, industrial sprawl located on the east side of the Pearl River between Guangzhou (the old Canton) and skyscraper-etched Shenzhen. We drove for more than an hour late one Sunday afternoon, along broad but heavily trafficked streets, bordered by bustling stores, welding shops, warehouses, small manufacturers, and the occasional large factory complex. This is how the cities of the old American rust belt must have once looked, smelled, even vibrated.

Because of its proximity to Hong Kong, as well as its remoteness from the capital, the Chinese government in Beijing chose Shenzhen as a special economic zone in 1979. A few years later the entire Pearl River Delta became part of this zone, with low corporate taxes, few environmental or urban-planning regulations, and the increasingly free movement of capital and profits in and out of the region. The results were spectacular. Gross domestic product in the Pearl River region leaped from $8 billion in 1980 to $351 billion in 2006. Shenzhen's population rose twentyfold. Guangdong Province itself, which covers most of the Pearl River Delta, produces a third of China's total exports. And 10 percent of all that finds its way to Wal-Mart's U.S. shelves.[2]

Although Wal-Mart owns no factories outright, its presence

is unmistakable. Its world buying headquarters is now in Shenzhen, it has already put more than a dozen big stores in the
province, and Wal-Mart is feared and respected by everyone
involved with any aspect of the export trade. That is why the
executives at the Yantian International Container Terminal in
Shenzhen, now the fourth-largest port in the world, give top
priority to Wal-Mart-bound cargoes. "Wal-Mart is king," a port
official said when I visited there in 2005.

But the Pearl River Delta is not merely an export platform
like the border region of northern Mexico or the free trade
zones of the Caribbean. In Guangzhou, Shenzhen, and their
environs, well-paved roads pass through a staggeringly crowded
landscape of factories, offices, dormitories, apartments, and
streams of migrant labor. Governments at both the provincial
and national levels are making huge infrastructure investments; likewise thousands of foreign investors from Taiwan,
Hong Kong, South Korea, Japan, and the United States are
building production facilities of increasing complexity and capacity. This makes it possible to transform raw materials into
containerized consumer goods in just a few weeks. Nike managers at the huge Yue Yuen factory complex in Dongguan bragged
that they could fill an order from the United States in just two
months. Container ships are loaded in half the time it takes in
Los Angeles.

The Retail Revolution puts all this into world history. It explains how Wal-Mart, America's largest and most controversial
company, roared out of an isolated corner of the rural South to
become the vanguard of a retail revolution that has transformed
the nature of U.S. employment, sent U.S. manufacturing abroad,
and redefined the very meaning of globalization.

For decades neither economists nor politicians gave retailing the respect it deserved. Shopping was what we did once all
the heavy lifting had been sweated out of us: after the steel had
been poured, the automobiles assembled, the skyscrapers built,

and the crops harvested. This was certainly the way the editors of America's most august business magazine saw the world. *Fortune*'s famous list of the five hundred largest American corporations consigned even the biggest retailers to second-class economic citizenship. The publisher Henry Luce had inaugurated the Fortune 500 in 1955 when the top five U.S. firms were General Motors, Standard Oil of New Jersey, Ford, U.S. Steel, and Chrysler. His editors at *Fortune*, reflecting the views of economists and businessmen in general, thought the mere selling and transport of consumer goods a derivative, subordinate, dependent function within the more important and far larger industrial, factory-based economy. So the retailers were not considered for the Fortune 500 list, even if they were billion-dollar chains like Sears or Woolworth.

But by the 1990s this perspective was clearly at odds with economic and social reality. Manufacturing was "dematerializing" in an economy of "digitization and deregulation," asserted a new generation of *Fortune* editors. This was "fuzzing up the line between manufacturing and service activities."[3] Were companies like Nike and Microsoft manufacturing companies or design and marketing powerhouses? Likewise, a new and innovative set of great retailers were not just huge employers with an enormous stream of revenue, but their connections with a global manufacturing network were practically incestuous. They might not own the Asian or Central American factories from which they sourced all those big-box consumables, but their "vendors" were linked to them by a "supply chain" that evoked the iron shackles subordinating slave to master.

Thus when *Fortune* inserted retailers on its list of giant corporations, Wal-Mart immediately popped up as number 4, measured by sales revenue, right behind GM, Ford, and Exxon Mobil. Sears, Roebuck was number 9 and Kmart number 15. Indeed, by 1995 sixteen of the top one hundred firms on the Fortune 500 list were mass retailers. Wal-Mart, which also displaced General Motors as the largest private employer in the nation, moved to number 1 on the Fortune 500 list in 2002, and it has held that rank ever since, except for the year 2006 when the spike in oil prices put Exxon Mobil at the top. Today, the retail trade employs some 15.5 million workers, more than in all manufacturing. Wal-Mart alone employs almost twenty times the number of workers as the biggest oil company.[4]

Founded less than fifty years ago by Sam Walton and his brother Bud, this Arkansas company is today the largest private-sector employer in the world, with nearly 2 million workers, 1.4 million of whom are in the United States. It operates more than six thousand huge stores, doing more business than Target, Home Depot, Sears Holdings, Safeway, and Kroger combined. It imports more goods from China than either the United Kingdom or Russia. Though Wal-Mart and the other mass retailers seem low-tech, these big-box stores may actually be the most consequential and effective users of computer processing power in our time. Their lofty place on the Fortune 500 thus signals a tectonic power shift within the structure of the economy, both in the United States and around the world.

The retailers, Wal-Mart above all, have set the standard for a new stage in the history of corporate capitalism. When Peter Drucker, the founder of modern management studies, wrote the pioneering analysis of a modern business, *The Concept of the Corporation*, in 1946, it was the General Motors organization from the Flint assembly lines to the executive offices in Detroit and New York that he thought exemplified corporate modernity in all its variegated aspects. Sixty years ago GM was the world's largest corporation, with sales that amounted to about 3 percent of the U.S. gross domestic product, making it an even larger economic presence than Wal-Mart is today. "The automobile industry," wrote Drucker, "stands for modern industry all over the globe. It is to the twentieth century what the Lancashire cotton mills were to the nineteenth century: the industry of industries."[5]

Other powerful enterprises have been hugely influential of course, the template enterprises of their time, embodying an innovative set of technological advances, organizational structures, and social relationships. At the end of the nineteenth century the Pennsylvania Railroad declared itself "the standard of the world." U.S. Steel defined the meaning of corporate power and efficiency for decades after J. P. Morgan consolidated the first billion-dollar company in 1901. In the mid-twentieth century General Motors symbolized bureaucratic management, mass production, and the social enfranchisement of a unionized, high-wage, blue-collar workforce. In the 1960s and 1970s IBM seemed an information-age version of General Motors, but in more recent years, Microsoft, Google, and the other Web-based innovators have seemed the model for a digital economy that has transformed the production and diffusion of knowledge around the globe.

Wal-Mart today commands the respect and influence once wielded by the manufacturing giants of the twentieth century. The company's innovations in logistics, merchandising, and labor relations have become part of the core curriculum at Harvard and other business schools, and not only for those with their eyes on an executive post in retail.[6] Just as industrialists and social savants were mesmerized by the "machine age" power of Ford's first assembly lines nearly a century ago, so today we live in a time when the supremacy of the mass retailers, in culture, politics, and ideology, as well as logistics, manufacturing, and merchandising, seems to define so much of our contemporary world.

In business, information is the raw material out of which market power is built. Before Wal-Mart, the bar code was but a grocery store innovation, useful for quickly scanning cans of soup and cartons of milk. But Sam Walton made the lowly bar code sing: he demanded that all Wal-Mart vendors slap a bar code on every product they shipped to his stores, and then he built a mammoth "digital warehouse" in Bentonville to slice and dice all the information that now poured across Wal-Mart's checkout counters each day. This enabled Wal-Mart, as opposed to the manufacturer, wholesaler, or distributor, to capture, manipulate, and respond to the raw sales data generated by billions of individual transactions each week. Sam Walton and his successors understood that this kind of knowledge gave them an enormous competitive advantage, which they deployed to vastly increase the efficacy of what the biz school professors now labeled the "retail supply chain." Wal-Mart now wields the tools to relentlessly squeeze every cost out of both its worldwide system of supply as well as the millions who work for the Bentonville giant, directly in its stores and warehouses or at the workbench of the sixty thousand vendors who are dependent upon the American retailer.

Wal-Mart began as an Arkansas upstart, but its enormous commercial success created a business template that reshaped the nation. It is the architect of a social order here in the United States that reflects its origins in the rural South of a half century ago. Unlike so many other twentieth-century titans of American business, Wal-Mart began its stupendous growth in a region that was distinctively provincial, even fundamentally at odds with the economic structures and political expectations that had nurtured commerce in the great northern tier of industrial states that stretched from Boston to Chicago and Minneapolis. America's manufacturing belt was a region of ethnic and racial heterogeneity, home to an increasingly skilled workforce and, after the reforms of the New Deal and the Great Society eras, a potent union movement and an extensive welfare state.

In contrast, the Ozarks of northwest Arkansas and southern Missouri were poor, white, and rural. Neither the New Deal nor the civil rights impulse had really come to that region when Sam Walton began to assemble his chain of small-town stores in the 1950s and 1960s. But the agricultural revolution of the early postwar era was in full swing, depopulating the farms and sending tens of thousands of white women and men in search of their first real paycheck. Walton took full advantage of these circumstances.[7]

Indeed, one hidden key to the Wal-Mart success story is Mr. Sam's capacity to capitalize upon the social and cultural "backwardness" of his region in order to build an organization of exceptional flexibility and efficiency. Walton's folksy paternalism was not a new management style, but he carried it off with brio, expressing a barely veiled contempt for the federal laws and Yankee business practices that sought to reshape the South. Like so many other employers of his time and region, Walton played fast and loose with minimum-wage regulations and overtime standards, not to mention the new laws governing race and gender equality in the workplace. And of course Walton was a bitter foe of any union effort to organize his stores.[8] In the place of all this governmental regulation, Wal-Mart created a self-contained corporate culture, an ideology of family, faith, and folk communalism that to this day coexists in strange harmony with a Dickensian world of low wages, job insecurity, and pervasive corporate surveillance.

Even as Wal-Mart expanded beyond the Ozarks, the company consciously targeted the kind of low-income customers with which it had started. In the process it reproduced the distinctive entrepreneurial culture and grinding labor policies that Walton had worked for decades to construct. Wal-Mart's growth after 1980, when the chain had 276 stores,[9] was nurtured by the transformation of the economic environment ushered in by Reagan and his conservative successors. It relieved employers, especially the retailers and fast-food restaurants, of hundreds of billions of dollars in annual labor costs. Real wages at Wal-Mart actually declined in the years after 1978, tracking the 30 percent fall in the real value of the minimum wage during the next three decades.[10]

Wal-Mart's expansion during that era, into the Midwest, the Rocky Mountain states, and many of the struggling rust belt cities of the old manufacturing heartland, paralleled the Republican conquest of much of this same territory. Wal-Mart and the GOP worked symbiotically to roll back the wage standards and welfare systems established since the New Deal, while promoting a Protestant, evangelical sense of social morality, the deunionization of labor, and the global expansion not only of U.S. economic power but of American cultural authority as well.

Today the commercial and political influence of this giant corporation enables Wal-Mart to rezone our cities, set health insurance and wage standards for millions of Americans, determine the popular music many teenagers can buy, channel trade and capital throughout the world, and conduct a kind of international diplomacy with a dozen nations. In an era of weak government regulation, Wal-Mart management may well have more power than any other entity to "legislate" key components of American social and industrial policy. The Arkansas-based giant is well aware of this leverage, which is why it is spending millions of dollars on TV advertisements that tout how its stores revitalize communities, employ happy workers, and generate an outpouring of philanthropic good works.[11]

Wal-Mart and its defenders emphasize the extent to which the company and its emulators have been in the vanguard of a revolution that has squeezed billions of dollars out of a once-bloated system of manufacture, transport, distribution, and sales, thus contributing decisively to a cheaper market basket for millions of hard-pressed shoppers.[12] But not everyone is convinced that this Wal-Mart bargain is either beneficial or long for our world. The evisceration of U.S. consumer goods manufacturing has been largely completed, yet the fate of the hundreds of thousands of entrepreneurs and the tens of millions of workers in Central America and East Asia is hardly settled. The commodities produced by this vast new working class are the lifeblood of the retail revolution, but it would be a mistake to count forever upon this torrent of cheap and sweated products. China, the most dynamic economy in the world, is also an exceedingly unstable place, plagued and energized by tens of thousands of strikes, protests, marches, and demonstrations each year.

The market-minded Communists still in control of that meganation vacillate between repression and accommodation, while Western investors have jacked up both wages and prices at the same time as they search for new lands and new hands with which to fill the insatiable supply chains that feed the big-box universe. History teaches us that rapid industrialization cannot be sustained for long on the backs of an impoverished and unfree working class. From the mines and mills of Victorian Britain to the shipyards and shoe factories of contemporary East Asia, the search for a higher standard of living and a more democratic society has often disputed and displaced business practices and plans that once seemed rational and efficient. The revolt of these millions may yet represent an insoluble challenge to the world Sam Walton built.

In the United States the stakes are different but still compelling. When Wal-Mart locates one of its grocery-selling Supercenters in metropolitan America, it asserts the legitimacy and power of a brand of capitalism that is antithetical to the regulated marketplace and the high-wage nation that was built by reformers and unionists during the middle decades of the twentieth century. The company is therefore constantly defending itself against a set of class-action lawsuits—some involving race and gender discrimination, others charging company violation of state and federal laws governing overtime pay, lunch breaks, and health and safety standards—filed by those who seek not only compensation for their clients but reform of Wal-Mart's internal pay and promotion practices.

Likewise, Wal-Mart finds itself in the midst of a permanent political campaign, promoting its expansion plans before scores of zoning commissions, city councils, and county supervisory boards all across blue-state America. Here local merchants, environmentalists, liberal activists, and labor partisans have drawn the line against Wal-Mart's effort to impose its alien business model on their home turf. And with the Democrats now in power in so many state legislatures and at both ends of Pennsylvania Avenue, it is certain that Wal-Mart and every other employer of low-wage labor will become embroiled in a fierce political battle over the cost of an expanded health insurance system, an increase in the minimum wage, the definition of free trade, and the effort to make unionization once again possible for millions of U.S. workers. Wal-Mart's omnipresence in commerce and culture has therefore drawn a new set of fault lines within American politics, creating the conditions for a day of reckoning, both at home and abroad, that is likely to affect almost every aspect of its far-flung operations. A battle royal is upon us, the outcome of which will shape American life for a generation.

CHAPTER ONE

SAM WALTON'S WORLD

Many titans of American business have had humble origins in out-of-the-way places. But their path toward wealth and power normally leads to and through the big cities, with their dense set of commercial networks and business opportunities. Not so with Sam Walton, who was born and raised in small-town Missouri and who built his retailing empire in one of the most rural and economically underdeveloped sections of the United States, the Ozark plateau comprising portions of Oklahoma, Arkansas, and Missouri. Ironically, Walton's mid-twentieth-century success owed much to the social and cultural peculiarities of this part of the country. Walton stole merchandizing ideas from any and all competitors. But his retailing genius arose out of a capacity to turn to his advantage the isolation, poverty, and hostility to Yankee commercial ways that had long characterized the small towns and county seats where he would site his first generation of discount stores. Like all revolutionaries, Mr. Sam created a new world out of the most unlikely material.

MERCHANTS AND MANUFACTURERS

History, Mark Twain once remarked, never repeats itself, but sometimes it rhymes. Wal-Mart's retail hegemony in the twenty-first century therefore echoes the mercantile regime once presided over by the great seventeenth- and eighteenth-century merchant and banking houses of Amsterdam, Hamburg, and the City of London. Wal-Mart's contemporary command of such a large slice of global trade puts it in roughly the same place as that of the eighteenth-century Dutch East India Company, which stood at the center of world commerce and politics, rivaling both the North German Baltic traders and English commercial/imperial ventures such as the Hudson's Bay and East India companies. Writing in 1728, Daniel Defoe might well have been offering an analysis of the Wal-Mart business model when he described the Dutch traders as "the Carryers of the World, the middle Persons in Trade, the Factors and Brokers of Europe . . . they *buy* to *sell* again, *take* in to *send* out: and the Greatest Part of their vast Commerce consists in being supply'd from all parts of the World, that they may supply all the World again."[1]

At the dawn of the American republic a similar, if less imperial-minded, set of seaboard traders, shippers, and bankers dominated much of the political and cultural life of the antebellum United States. In 1830, seven out of ten of the most affluent Bostonians were merchants; likewise a tiny New York trading elite owned most of that city's wealth in the mid-1850s. This coastal ruling class was cosmopolitan and well connected, with trading partnerships that stretched from New York to Bombay, from Boston to Buenos Aires, and from Philadelphia to Liverpool. In a society in which production was highly decentralized and largely that of agricultural commodities, the power of these wholesalers, jobbers, and traders to create a market and manipulate it for their own purposes put them at the center of commerce and society until the Civil War. They leveraged their unparalleled knowledge of the Atlantic trade to make themselves indispensable to a nation of still-isolated planters, farmers, craftsmen, and shopkeepers.

Troth and Company, a Philadelphia wholesale drug importer,

exemplified the power and scope of these early merchant houses. The firm was a jobber that bought large quantities of drugs and medicines from abroad and then resold them in small lots on short notice to the capital-starved pharmacists, physicians, and storekeepers of the American hinterland. The "drugs" of the day were all generic—quinine, ginger, arrowroot, opium, and gum arabic, as well as glass goods, varnishes, and even paint—which meant that the end user of these products had no way of knowing what firm, farm, or factory had actually produced them. Troth and Company therefore stood at the center of what we would today define as the "supply chain" for antebellum medicinals. The Philadelphia firm took responsibility for the quality of the drugs, advanced credit and maintained a flow of information on the financial condition of its customers, arranged for packing and shipping, and performed numerous services, including the supply of skeletons and medical saddlebags for the frontier physicians who were among Troth and Company's most reliable consumers.[2]

The most consequential traders of antebellum America were those who rendered their services to King Cotton. Most of the bankers and merchants of New York, New England, and Baltimore were allies of the Southern cause, "cotton Whigs," who believed the abolition of slavery would destroy the commercial civilization that their own power and prosperity exemplified. They made their fortunes advancing credit to the Slavocracy, buying and shipping cotton for the textile mills of Lowell, Manchester, and the British Midlands, and then selling the cloth in every corner of the globe. They were free trade, low-tariff partisans and opponents of a federal effort to encourage domestic manufacturing.[3]

The Civil War ended the reign of these merchants and their Southern confederates, heralding a Gilded Age America ruled by a new class of iron masters, meatpackers, and railroad barons. It would take more than a century for the merchants, now led by Wal-Mart and other huge discount chains, to once again exercise so much market power and political clout. But in the meantime, the explosive rise of U.S. manufacturing during the late nineteenth century transformed North American capitalism, not only in the mills, mines, and workshops of Philadelphia and Pittsburgh, but also along the tentacles of trade and commerce that moved this man-made abundance from factory to household. The great consumer products corporations that emerged in the late nineteenth century, firms like Procter & Gamble, Armour, Swift, American Tobacco, Kodak, Campbell's Soup, Quaker Oats, Munsingwear, and H. J. Heinz, did not merely command far more revenue and employ far more workers than the old merchant traders. They captured for themselves many of the economic functions and profit possibilities that were once the exclusive province of the antebellum jobbers and wholesalers. In the next century Wal-Mart would have to wage a war with these firms to win back that market power.

This would not be an easy fight because the entire structure of the American economy now sustained manufacturing prowess. For example, G. F. Swift and Company became the largest meatpacking firm in the world by deploying the two great technological innovations of the nineteenth century: the railroads and the telegraph. This allowed Swift to ship millions of head of cattle to Chicago, where highly efficient disassembly lines made salable everything except the squeal. It also led to the destruction of a whole network of preexisting wholesale butchers and regional slaughterhouses. The change was cultural as well as technological, because Swift, followed by the other big Chicago meatpacking firms, had to convince consumers that refrigerated beef and pork, traveling up to fifteen hundred miles by rail, was not just cheaper but as wholesome and flavorful as that slaughtered across town by skilled butchers. By 1899 the revolution was complete. Except for New York City, which maintained a thriving kosher meat industry, local slaughtering was history.[4]

The emergence of the branded product—Ivory Soap, Parker Pens, Wrigley's Spearmint Gum, even the canned Swift ham, and the fixed prices that normally accompanied such packaged goods—also eroded the market-making capacity of the wholesalers. It forged a durable connection between millions of far-flung customers and the products marketed by a specific, multibranded producer. Manufacturers subsequently began to develop their own highly complex distribution networks, their own salesmen and "drummers," their own systems of credit, advertising, research, and in some instances their own network of retail stores. Thus the Singer sewing machine company built a worldwide organization that ran eight thousand stores and employed forty thousand house-to-house salespeople by the 1920s. Likewise Heinz constructed an immense organization to distribute its "57 Varieties." By 1922 it maintained fifty-eight branch offices and warehouses and seventy foreign agencies. Its American sales force employed over a thousand men and women.[5] But even when the manufacturer still used traditional distribution channels, the branding and advertising of a distinctive mass-produced product gave to these firms the marketing leverage that Wal-Mart and other large discounters would claim many decades later. "To the manufacturer who advertises," wrote the pioneering ad man Earnest Elmo Calkins in 1905, "it makes no difference what jobber or what commission man buys his goods. All of them will have to buy them in the end."[6]

For more than a century, from roughly 1880 to 1980, the manufacturing enterprise stood at the commanding heights of the U.S. economy's production/distribution nexus. The government sometimes challenged the more egregious oligopolies, and a few big chains like A&P exerted sufficient leverage to actually bargain with manufacturers on the price of the goods they supplied, but for the most part the mass-production firms administered their price schedule so as to ensure continuous production and a healthy profit. General Motors wanted a 20 percent pretax return on investment, and for more than half of the twentieth century the company got it, during the boom of the late 1920s, the Depression, World War II, and on through the first three postwar decades. U.S. Steel, which Andrew Carnegie and J. P. Morgan had created as the de facto price umbrella for the nation's most basic industry, used an elaborate system of freight surcharges—Pittsburgh Plus—to sustain the valuation of its capital-intensive mills and mines in Pennsylvania and Ohio.[7] Even the manufacturers of food items and light consumer goods, like Hartz Mountain, Gillette, P&G, 3M, Hershey, Kraft, and Coca-Cola, conducted themselves in an imperious manner when they stocked the shelves of the regional grocery and drug chains that sold their wares.[8]

CONSUMPTION IN TOWN AND COUNTRY

How then did people buy the enormous torrent of consumables pouring out of the factories and workshops? Before chains like Penney's and Sears took root in the 1920s, the great department stores of the early twentieth century provided one high-profile solution: Macy's and Gimbels in New York, Wanamakers' in Philadelphia, Filene's in Boston, Marshall Field's in Chicago, Hudson's in Detroit, and Bon Marché in Seattle. They were "department" stores because, under one large roof, and on several spacious floors, they divided the world of goods into a distinct set of selling spaces that offered a wide variety of merchandise at prices that were fixed and ranked according to quality, fashion, and demand. These big-city department stores, writes the historian Neil Harris, "were mass encounters with the art and objects of the modern world, dramatic, persuasive, self-consciously designed to produce a maximum effect." They were huge institutions: Jordan Marsh was the fourth-largest employer in New England in 1900, and in its busy season Marshall Field had ten thousand employees and a quarter of a million customers each day.[9]

Often linked directly to stations serving the new subways and urban trams that New York, Chicago, and other cities had begun building in the years just before the First World War, these urban emporiums cultivated female sociability, status, and glamour. They defined a kind of genteel, urban culture, even as their basements and bargain annexes provided an often chaotic selling space for the mass of immigrant women and men who sought an inexpensive taste of New World abundance. Although suburbanization and the discount revolution would eventually doom these multistory emporiums, no other twentieth-century institution exemplified with such panache the idea that the American dream could be realized through a fulfillment of consumer fantasies.

Far less glamorous were the factory-like warehouses that constituted another of the key distributive mechanisms of a newly industrialized America. Mail-order houses, first Montgomery Ward and then Sears Roebuck, channeled manufactured commodities to the rural hinterland that for decades remained well beyond the reach of the urban department stores. These firms constructed huge distribution complexes in Chicago, the capital city of a vast, rural commodity-producing and trading territory that stretched from Montana to Mississippi and from Ohio to the Mexican border. The railroads, parcel post, rural free delivery, and the steam printing press were the nineteenth-century innovations in technology and organization that made it possible for these mail-order companies to put a dress or a doll at the door of a Kansas farmhouse 20 percent more cheaply than could the proprietor of the nearby village store.

In their commitment to system, speed, volume, and vertical integration, the mail-order houses of the early twentieth century prefigured Wal-Mart, Costco, and other successful discounters. Their closest contemporary equivalent is undoubtedly Amazon.com and the other online retailers, whose Web sites constitute the functional equivalent of the well-illustrated, two-pound catalogs once found in every farmhouse kitchen. And like Sears, Montgomery Ward, and Spiegel's, the modern Web sites of Amazon, Lands' End, and Barnes & Noble are backstopped by an enormous warehouse/transport infrastructure that generates the industrial rhythms and routinized, blue-collar work characteristic of Chicago's bygone mail-order complexes. In 1906, for example, when Sears moved its headquarters complex to a new forty-acre tract in Chicago, all the buildings were connected by pneumatic pipes, underground tunnels, and miles of railroad track. Two thousand people opened and processed more than nine hundred sacks of mail a day; the express delivery companies, railroads, and post office all managed branches on the grounds. And at the height of the U.S. industrial era, Sears proved itself the one merchant whose buying power rivaled that of a latter-day Wal-Mart. It invested in or owned outright scores of supplier firms and used its leverage to win brutally low prices from other manufacturers. Every vendor wanted its wares advertised in the famous Sears catalog, a book that became synonymous with the quest for consumer excitement. With a print run approaching 5 million copies a year, the Sears catalog promised to bring "New York to Your Door." Like the return policy instituted by Sam Walton many years later, all merchandise exchanges were guaranteed, no questions asked.[10]

Urbanization and the automobile doomed the mail-order

house because farmers and small-town folk always preferred to fondle, squeeze, and handle the products they bought, rather than just imagine how they would feel. Both Sears and Montgomery Ward began to build a chain of suburban stores in the 1920s, "white goods"–oriented department stores that often beat the old-line emporiums to the automobile-dependent suburbs. As General Robert E. Wood, the autocratic, long-serving Sears executive who had once commanded the Panama Canal, put it, "Sears made every mistake in the book in retailing except one—it catered to automobile traffic."[11]

In contrast to the downtown department stores, whose German-Jewish owners were often sympathetic to the New Deal and the new labor movement of that era, top executives at Sears and Montgomery Ward tended to be Protestant, native-born Republicans who fought a successful battle to keep the unions out of their warehouses and suburban stores. Montgomery Ward president Sewell Avery, who was famously hoisted out of his executive offices by rifle-toting soldiers during World War II, a consequence of his refusal to abide by a government order that he recognize a newly formed union of his employees, thought the New Deal a political abomination and the prospect of a postwar world of high wages and high consumption an economic delusion. In the decade after World War II he hoarded company cash, stopped building new stores, and prepared for imminent financial collapse. This proved one of the most monumental business miscalculations of all time, sending Avery into a bitterly resisted retirement and his company into a downward spiral that eventually ended in merger and oblivion.

At Sears, General Wood commanded the nation's largest retailer in a far more adroit fashion, even though he was just as conservative as Avery. Under his leadership in the 1950s and 1960s, Sears redoubled its efforts to become a fixture at every new shopping center. The company's high degree of vertical integration, often with supply firms that it kept on a tight contractual leash, foreshadowed the dominant relationship Wal-Mart would establish with its own vendors. But Sears also made a grand miscalculation. Wood and the generation of Sears executives who followed him assumed that the American middle class would enlarge itself indefinitely. And Sears, the quintessential purveyor of middle-brand, middle-quality products for the middle-class family, would prosper right along. But increasing income polarization after 1973 soon transformed the demographics that might have sustained this kind of merchandising. An ever more prosperous upper middle class began to shop at upscale stores like Bloomingdale's and Macy's, now both national chains, while for the vast body of American wage earners—"the working middle class"—income stagnation and insecurity began to take their toll. They needed a new place to shop. Thus Sears found itself in a permanent identity crisis from which it could never escape.[12] Neither Sam Walton nor his Wal-Mart heirs would make this kind of mistake.

Indeed, Walton's career began among the retailers that catered to those consumers who had to watch every penny. They were served by the chain stores that first proliferated late in the nineteenth century. George Huntington Hartford opened the first outlet of the Great Atlantic & Pacific Tea Company in 1859; Frank Woolworth started a string of variety stores selling items priced at no more than five or ten cents in the 1870s. But it was not until the 1920s that the chain store truly came of age. By the end of that decade there were more than 37,000 chain stores. A&P, the leader in the grocery segment, operated an astounding 15,000 stores, although most were small neighborhood markets. In apparel J.C. Penney grew from about 300 to more than 1,400 outlets, while Woolworth, with 2,248 dime stores, had doubled in size during the 1920s.[13] These chains forged close ties with manufacturing supply firms, but there were still plenty of wholesalers left in the U.S. economy, many headquartered in the Midwest or New York, which serviced hundreds of thousands of independent stores and groceries found in every small town and every neighborhood. Butler Brothers, for example, which played a large role in Sam Walton's early business career, purchased its merchandise in large quantities from manufacturers throughout the country and then distributed it from warehouses in Chicago, New York, St. Louis, Minneapolis, Dallas, and San Francisco. By the 1930s this company was the largest wholesale distributor in the United States, supplying medium-priced variety goods to upwards of one hundred thousand retailers nationwide and in several foreign countries. Roughly half of its customers were in towns of ten thousand or fewer.[14]

SAM WALTON'S WORLD

Sam Walton was born in Kingfisher, Oklahoma, in 1918, on the eve of America's great chain store expansion. The Waltons had settled in Missouri and Oklahoma late in the nineteenth century, but like so many erstwhile farmers, they were wedded to the land only so long as it generated an income that could sustain their ambitions. During World War I Walton's parents had planted, reaped, and sold their corn and cotton at record prices, but in the years afterward they were pushed and pulled by the same economic forces that were decimating the family farm throughout rural America. And like the land agent in *The Grapes of Wrath*, the Walton family played their small part to lubricate the financial machinery that depopulated so many rural counties.

In the 1930s Sam's father, Tom Walton, worked for an older brother who was a Missouri agent for the Metropolitan Life Insurance Company, which then held a mortgage or insurance policy on every fifth man, woman, and child in North America.

Metropolitan had its headquarters on lower Broadway in New York City, but it was heavily invested in midwestern farm property, which is why Tom Walton, often accompanied by his teenage son, traveled far and wide throughout the Missouri countryside during those grim Depression years. They were debt collectors. Tens of thousands of farmers were in default, and it was part of Walton's job to assess the property, make the threats, and serve the papers that dispossessed a generation of families from their land. The young Sam Walton got a first-hand glimpse of the social revolution that was sending so many dirt farmers to California, Chicago, Kansas City, and other urban locales. According to Sam, his father tried to do this dirty work with enough sensitivity to leave "those farmers with as much of their self-respect as he could."[15] But the dispossession of so many rural folk was still something close to theft, the brutal climax of America's great enclosure movement, a multidecade eviction that would prepare the cultural and economic ground upon which Sam Walton built his commercial empire.

The states of the old Southwest—Arkansas, Missouri, Oklahoma, and Texas—which would become the Wal-Mart home turf, were almost the last of the nation's farming frontiers.[16] This region of rolling plains and hilly plateaus had filled in and then overfilled in the late nineteenth century as farmers fought for one more chance at the independent, agricultural way of life many Americans had long venerated. The Ozarks of northwest Arkansas, eastern Oklahoma, and southern Missouri were full of small farms well into the twentieth century. Indeed, Benton County, where Walton would headquarter his company and open his first discount store, had the largest proportion of proprietor-run farms in Arkansas. Many were subsistence homesteads, but no matter; they kept their owners connected to the land.[17]

Such farms couldn't last, of course, and after World War I a declining international market for wheat, corn, and cotton, plus erosion, drought, and the beginnings of mechanization, began a great wave of agricultural consolidation. The proportion of all farms with tractors leaped from 20 to 80 percent in the fifteen years after the start of World War II. By 1950, Oklahoma had lost 55 percent of its agricultural labor force, Arkansas 52 percent, Texas 51 percent, and Missouri 47 percent. In the Ozarks the devastation was even greater, with more than two-thirds of all farms disappearing in the quarter century after 1940. And of those farmers who remained, half earned more money in town than from the land.[18] In Arkansas, which had always been one of the most rural states in the nation, population loss continued into the 1960s, when state efforts to lure low wage nonunion employers finally paid off. Then northwest Arkansas, the Wal-Mart epicenter, began a particularly rapid economic expansion, with new income from tourism, retirement communities, industrial-style chicken growing, and light industry. "This part of Arkansas didn't come out of the Depression until the early 1960s," remembered one local developer.[19]

Sam Walton knew this world, and he equipped himself with the tools and resources necessary to conquer it. He was a natural-born striver, a boy who always had a part-time job, an Eagle Scout, a champion high school athlete, and a big man on campus at the University of Missouri, where he graduated with a business degree in 1940. "It never occurred to me that I might lose," Walton told his biographer a half century later. "To me, it was almost as if I had a right to win. Thinking like that often seems to turn into sort of a self-fulfilling prophecy."[20] Walton took his first job, as a management trainee, with J.C. Penney in Des Moines, Iowa. At the time Penney, a well-established national institution, had 1,586 stores, most located in small cities and towns. Often described as junior department stores, they carried merchandise that was a step above the five-and-dimes, largely because Penney specialized in the soft goods and housewares also sold by the big urban emporiums. As with many first jobs, happenstance played its role in pointing Walton toward a career in retail. He wanted a "real" job, he was good at selling things, and he lacked the money to pay for the two years it would take to earn an MBA at his school of choice, Wharton at the University of Pennsylvania in Philadelphia.[21]

Walton stayed at J.C. Penney for almost eighteen months; he was a natural salesman but thought the paperwork and record keeping tedious, a complaint shared by generations of retail merchants who had long found that inventory control of thousands of disparate products was a heavy, profitless burden. Moreover, the war was looming, an affair with one of the store's clerks turned sour, and Walton didn't like working for other people, even when he was good at it. So while awaiting army service, he got a job at a defense plant in Oklahoma and rented a room in nearby Claremore. There he met Helen Robson, the daughter of the town's most prominent citizen, Leland Stanford Robson, a wealthy and savvy banker, rancher, and politician. Walton's 1943 marriage to Helen was the social event of the year in Claremore. And it endured as a stable and essential resource for his business career. To open a store that could sustain a middle-class lifestyle in the 1940s, even in small-town Arkansas, required upwards of thirty thousand dollars, now not far below half a million. Walton did not have that kind of money. His parents, who had clung to a precarious existence, had separated as soon as he graduated from college. His younger brother Bud was energetic and loyal, a ready business partner, but he had no resources either.

Loans for a young man with few assets were scarce; in the agricultural South, even with the wartime boom, most banks remained severely undercapitalized and most bankers still shell-shocked from their Depression losses. In the 1940s and 1950s, Arkansas, Missouri, and Oklahoma were something of an underdeveloped nation. A few big investment banks like Stephens in Little Rock struck it rich speculating in state and local bonds, some of which had defaulted in the Depression, and the federal government pumped in a lot of defense money during the war, but there was little payoff in terms of sustained commercial development. The population of Arkansas actually declined during the 1940s as energetic men and women left for Detroit, Chicago, and Los Angeles. "Unless one owned land or a business," wrote a historian of the state, "those who left Arkansas . . . had little economic reason to return."[22] The branch plants established in the 1950s by many northern employers of cheap labor were just that, branch plants; they remained isolated nodes of female employment plunked down amid the plantations still found in the eastern part of the state or among the marginal farms in the Ozarks to the north and west.

So the business and social connections of the Robson family, into which Sam Walton had married, provided a lifeline. Helen had her own trust account against which Walton borrowed on more than one occasion, but his wife and her powerful father also exercised something close to veto power over how it was invested. For example, in 1945, when Walton got out of the service, he and a college fraternity friend considered the purchase of a modest department store in St. Louis. But Helen said no. She wanted to raise her family in a small town, not unlike Claremore. Moreover, she was opposed to partnerships, having seen a few "go sour." So instead, Walton found a five-thousand-square-foot store in Newport, Arkansas, a cotton-processing town and county seat of some 6,254 souls on the White River, about eighty miles from Memphis. The store, a shoddy, under-performing affair, was a unit of the Ben Franklin chain, part of the Butler Brothers franchise network. For twenty-five thousand dollars the company sold Walton the right to operate the store, but not the property, which was in the heart of town, on a street facing the railroad station and the cotton warehouses.[23]

Butler Brothers got into the franchise business during the 1920s because it wanted to ensure a market for its wholesale merchandise. By 1947 there were more than twelve hundred franchise stores under the Ben Franklin name, most in small southern and midwestern towns. Store owners were obligated to purchase 80 percent of their merchandise from Butler Brothers at a markup of about 25 percent for the wholesaler. In return the Chicago-headquartered firm provided merchandising manuals, training workshops, and advertising material. The wholesaler sought to ensure that Ben Franklin stores were properly stocked, often with Butler Brothers' own private brands, operated according to standard retail business practices, and competed effectively with Woolworth's, S.S. Kresge's, and other chains, whose stores were a bit larger. Butler Brothers offered its clients some sound variety store advice: how to buy insurance, maintain good credit, eliminate stale merchandise, and take inventory. Above all, it pressured stores to turn over their stock as rapidly as possible. To do so the Chicago wholesaler advised store managers to avoid "overbuying," which would leave them with too much dead, unproductive merchandise. Instead managers should "buy small and often." Good advice, at least for an undercapitalized store owner, but also highly profitable for Butler Brothers, which avoided volume discounts on the goods it sold to its tightly leashed franchisees.[24]

Walton learned all of these retailing rules, and then he forged his own path. The first thing he realized was that even within a small town, the size of the retail market could be far more elastic than Butler Brothers believed. In many of these sleepy villages, local merchants had long colluded to avoid competition; since there were rarely more than one or two general merchandise stores, a monopoly or duopoly took hold almost as easily and naturally as the cotton ripened. But from the start Walton was a vigorous competitor, a price hawk who recognized that he could undercut his chain competitors and draw in customers from well beyond the usual trading area if his store won a reputation for cut-rate prices.

In 1945 the United States had too many stores, 1.7 million of them. In the South, hundreds of thousands were little more than shacks situated at the confluence of two dirt tracks. In Arkansas almost nineteen thousand retail stores were open for business, but of these fewer than eight thousand even had a payroll.[25] These were mom-and-pop establishments: country stores of limited stock, dusty shelves, and episodic sales that still required a measure of barter, credit, and charity. But their days were numbered. The rural-road building frenzy, which began in the 1920s and then advanced even more smartly during the era of the New Deal's job creation programs, had paved a lot of Arkansas roads. In the postwar years southern highway commissions were often cesspools of political corruption, but they did lay down ever more asphalt and concrete, enabling farmers to bypass the hamlet general store and drive an additional ten or fifteen miles to the county seat.

In Newport Walton reaped a large portion of this new traffic, even if some of it still arrived on the buckboard of a mule-drawn wagon. In the five years he remained there sales rose rapidly: 45 percent in his first year, from $72,000 to $105,000, then up another third to $140,000 in his second year, and on and on until sales peaked at $250,000 in 1950, which probably made him the leading Ben Franklin store operator, for both sales and profits, in the company's six-state south-central region. Even grander prospects were in the offing as postwar prosperity filtered down into small-town America. The Ben Franklin

winning its share of that business, doubling the
outlets in the decade after 1947. But Walton chafed
at Butler Brothers' tutelage. Its nearest warehouse was in St.
Louis, and its goods were not always the most attractive or the
lowest priced. Indeed, Walton had found jobbers and manufacturers in Memphis and Little Rock that were delighted to
undersell Butler Brothers, especially if he bought a lot, sold it
cheap, and turned his inventory quickly. Why, therefore, should
he buy 80 percent of his merchandise from Butler Brothers,
and at a markup that conceded nothing to Walton and his high-
volume enterprise? Acting on these grievances and opportunities would have to wait, however.

By all accounts the Waltons loved this little trading village
of Newport. They bought a gracious house, Helen gave birth to
three of their four children there, and Sam served as head
of the chamber of commerce. But everything came crashing
down in early 1950, a moment Sam Walton would forever
remember as the "low point" of his life: "I felt sick to my
stomach . . . it was really like a nightmare."[26]

He lost his lease. Walton had been suckered in 1945 because
the five-year rental contract he had signed had no renewal clause.
So the landlord, one P. K. Holmes, whose son was both a genuine war hero and a politically ambitious young man, chose this
moment to bequeath to his heir an amazingly successful store.
"It didn't seem fair," protested Walton. He hired a lawyer, strategized with his father-in-law, offered Holmes even better terms,
but nothing worked. He had to leave town, search for a new
store, start all over again. It seemed, at the time, a disastrous
moment.

Newport in 1950 was a biracial town stirring uneasily at
the dawn of the civil rights revolution. Just a decade before
and not all that far away, desperately poor black and white
Arkansas sharecroppers had downed their hoes and waged a
bitter collective battle against the plantation oligarchy. And

ten years later, in the early 1960s, small-town merchants would find themselves at the epicenter of a civil rights movement they instinctively resisted. Walton could not know, of course, that his expulsion from Newport would have a decisive impact on his entrepreneurial success. But in hindsight it is clear that the growth of his retail business might well have been fatally constrained had Wal-Mart been launched with a home office that stood on the edge of the brooding Mississippi Delta.

Instead, Walton found a new store at the far distant northwest corner of the state, in one of the most remote, rural, and all-white counties of Arkansas. Bentonville is situated at the western edge of the Ozarks, a sixty-thousand-square-mile region of wooded hills and plateaus that includes portions of Missouri, Arkansas, Kansas, and Oklahoma. Bentonville itself, the seat of Benton County, was even smaller than Newport, with just 2,964 people. Thousands of near-subsistence farmers were fleeing the land, many migrating to the North and West. Even more were finding new sources of cash income near home, in the poultry sheds, the shirt factories, and Ozark resorts that lured Chicago retirees south. Indeed, for all its remoteness and marginal farming, Benton County actually had twice the retail sales of Newport's Jackson County, and this even before Walton had ginned up his first store.[27] Moreover, Walton had other reasons to like Bentonville: the town was not too far from Claremore, and because of its location near the borders of Missouri, Kansas, and Oklahoma, he could now purchase four hunting licenses and indulge his passion for quail in multiple states.

Walton quickly made a success of the Bentonville store, a Ben Franklin franchise he opened on the town square. Within a few years he started additional Ben Franklin stores in similar towns throughout Arkansas, southern Missouri, and Kansas: Fayetteville, Springdale, Siloam Springs, Ruskin Heights, Saint

desha, and Coffeyville. Despite Walton's irritation
Brothers' merchandising strictures, he stuck with
... Franklin chain. Walton needed a wholesaler that
could provide him with the hundreds of variety store items on
a regular basis. Butler Brothers was slow, it was expensive, it
was imperious, but it was the only game in town. Walton would
have to enlarge his own small chain and develop entirely new
sources of supply and distribution before he could get out from
under.

One of Walton's great virtues as an entrepreneur lay in his
capacity to borrow, steal, or appropriate good ideas from anywhere he found them: the competing store manager across the
village square, a visiting salesman, an item in the *Wall Street
Journal*, or a far distant retailer like Sol Price, who actually
charged shoppers to buy a "membership" in the warehouse-
like "club" he had opened in San Diego. And by 1960 Walton
had learned three important things about how the retail industry was changing. First, self-service was essential, and not only
for grocery stores. In 1952 Walton took the bus to Minnesota
to see how self-service worked in a couple of Ben Franklins
there. The benefits were obvious: fewer cash registers, a lower
overall payroll, and far less training for each clerk, since branded
products sold themselves. Moreover women, southern middle-
class white women in particular, liked self-service because it cut
down on the sometimes awkward interaction with male clerks
of lower social status. And merchants found that customers, of
whatever class, bought more stuff when they selected the goods
themselves. So from then on all of Walton's stores would be
self-service.[28]

Second, Walton knew that if self-service were to work, a
merchant had to stock his store with well-known brand items
that would sell themselves even in the most spartan environment. Companies like Procter & Gamble, Coca-Cola, and Kraft

Foods spent hundreds of millions each year on advertising to make their products seem distinctive and essential.

And third, the price had to be right, discounted below the price suggested by the manufacturer or mandated by the 1936 Robinson-Patman Act, which sought to protect the small-town merchant from the chain store "menace." Under this federal price maintenance law, as well as the state-level statutes that mimicked it, all retailers had to abide by a uniform manufacturer's price. In the 1920s and 1930s these laws had been particularly popular in the South where the proprietor of the country store made his stand with the fast-vanishing yeoman farmer as a pillar of resistance against all those predatory Yankees whose variety stores had pushed into the South.

These laws were always hard to enforce, and by the 1950s the courts had invalidated two dozen state "fair trade" laws. Walton had violated the Arkansas law with impunity. If he could get a bargain shipment of branded toothpaste or detergent, he knocked down the price, undercut the competition, and watched the product fly off the shelves. Walton's difficulty was that he neither owned nor had access to a system of supply that could cut out all the middlemen—the jobbers, wholesalers, truckers, and warehousemen who added so many costs and insecurities to the supply chain that replenished the merchandise in his collection of remote, rural stores.

E. J. KORVETTE AND THE DARK CONTINENT

Walton's problem was that of the American economy writ large. Post–World War II prosperity created a huge, baby-boom demand for every conceivable kind of consumer product, from furniture to fridges to food processors. Twentieth-century assembly-line technology could certainly churn this stuff out, inexpensively and in huge quantities. However, the distribution system servicing this manufacturing powerhouse was remarkably inefficient and circuitous, in Arkansas surely, but also throughout metropolitan America. From the moment a product came off the production line until it reached the hands of the consumer, it passed through half a dozen separate corporate entities, each with a separate management structure, labor force, billing procedure, and profit target. "Selling and distribution," Thomas Edison told an interviewer in 1910, "are simply machines for getting products to consumers. And like all machines, they can be improved with great resulting economy. But it is the plain truth that these machines for distribution have made the least progress of all machines. They are the same in many instances that they were forty and fifty years ago"[29]

Half a century later, indeed in 1962, the year in which Sam Walton opened his first true discount store in Rogers, Arkansas, Peter Drucker made the same complaint. Drucker was no ordinary professor of management. A witness to the rise of fascism in central Europe, Drucker understood that the stability of American capitalism and the legitimacy of the modern corporation needed continuous ideological and economic renewal in order to command the democratic acquiescence of the populace. Drucker had almost certainly never heard of Sam Walton, but they shared a disdain for the baroque and wasteful channels by which even the most efficient manufacturing corporations put their goods on the retail shelf. When Drucker wrote "The Economy's Dark Continent" for a prescient series on the discount revolution published by *Fortune*, he estimated that 50 percent of each dollar consumers spent in stores underwrote activities that took place after the goods had left the factory. "Distribution," wrote Drucker, "is one of the most sadly neglected, most promising areas of American business." The executive of a manufacturing firm knew the cost of every hour of labor, every pound of steel and plastic that flowed into the final product, but once he cast his eyes beyond the legal boundaries of his own corporation—to the people and institutions that actually distributed and sold their product—ignorance and guesswork took over. Hence the persistent inventory booms and inventory busts that exacerbated so many twentieth-century recessions. "We know little more about distribution today," asserted Drucker, "than Napoleon's contemporaries knew about the interior of Africa. We know it is there, and we know it is big; and that's about all."[30]

The cash-rich opportunities available to those who might explore and exploit this continent had become apparent in the 1950s. Before there was Sam Walton, there was Eugene Ferkauf. Depression-bred like Walton, Ferkauf also felt comfortable and trusting only among his own tribe. In his case these were the Jewish, Brooklyn-born buddies of his youth, ambitious veterans who were too impatient or too poor for college and the long climb into the professions. They worked hard, liked big cigars, married their childhood sweethearts, and gobbled fast dinners at the nearest greasy spoon.

Ferkauf was the son of a Manhattan luggage-store owner. Competition was intense on everything but price, because the Robinson-Patman Act and its state-level cousins remained on the books. These laws extended to branded items, such as electric razors, fountain pens, radios, watches, luggage, and the "white goods" that were now in such demand for all those suburban kitchens.[31]

But in New York, everyone knew, or wanted to know, someone who could "get it for you wholesale." Ferkauf subverted the price maintenance laws by opening something he claimed to be a "membership store" in 1948. Certainly it did not look like much of a retail outlet. The Forty-sixth Street entrance was just a door that led up a narrow set of stairs to a tiny twenty-by-twenty-foot loft on the second floor. There was hardly a sign

and no window display; passersby found out about the "store"
from the salesmen who stood on the street passing out price
lists and membership cards. But prices were 30 percent and
more below those of the big New York department stores, and
since most of Ferkauf's merchandise consisted of well-known
national brands, customers knew they were getting a deal. His
first store was a smash hit, and so too were each of the other
outlets he opened in Manhattan. Ferkauf's hole-in-the wall
operations were always packed; his initial second-story outlet
sold an astonishing $1 million in merchandise in the first year.
During the Christmas rush the salesmen worked through the
night, sleeping on the floor if necessary. Ferkauf called his company E. J. Korvette, after the initial of his first name and that of
an early partner, Joe Zwillenberg, as well as the name of a
Canadian fighting ship, the Corvette, which sounded classy to
him.[32]

Ferkauf could undercut both Macy's and Sears and make
money in the process because he held overall labor cost per
dollar of sales far below his larger rivals. He paid his clerks
relatively well for New York City, but their services cost Ferkauf little since they were so scarce in the self-service aisles.
Thus E. J. Korvette held its labor cost to but 6 or 7 percent of
sales, far lower than the 18 or 20 percent paid by the full-line
department stores. Even more important, Korvette's entire inventory was replaced thirty times a year, in an era when the
department stores thought themselves doing well if merchandise had to be reordered six or seven times per annum. Such
merchandise turnover meant that the capital deployed by E. J.
Korvette was four or five times more productive than that deployed by its multistoried rivals.[33]

Every square foot of shelf space, every salesman, every dollar paid in rent was four times more productive than that
of Ferkauf's competitors. So E. J. Korvette did not in fact need
cheaper sources of supply, low rents, or even inexpensive help

to make a ton of money. That was made abundantly clear in 1954 when Ferkauf opened the nation's first true discount store in Westbury, Long Island. "Korvette City," with some 150,000 square feet, proved a huge success, generating traffic jams and lines that hardly diminished after the Christmas shopping rush. E. J. Korvette soon issued stock, expanded throughout the New York metropolitan area, and made Ferkauf a millionaire. By 1965 his company was the nation's premier discounter, with sales well above half a billion dollars per year.[34]

Ferkauf did a lot of things that would later prove essential to Sam Walton's success. He was a fierce competitor who blithely ignored the Robinson-Patman Act despite lawsuits and legal challenges from Macy's, Gimbels, and some of the brand manufacturers. He visited all of his stores each day; he encouraged store managers to buy into the operation; he rarely advertised; and he kept his inventory limited just to the best sellers, because self-service demanded that a store could stock only what it could actually display. Instead of the familiar department store motto, "Thick on the best, thin on the rest," Korvette operated according to what would become the discounter's credo, "Thick on the best, to hell with the rest." Thus if Macy's carried 129 separate styles of men's white dress shirts, Korvette thought 35 more than enough. And finally, Ferkauf and Walton shared something else. Both encouraged a cultlike managerial culture and a distinctively regional sales-floor atmosphere, even if to a lot of people Brooklyn hustle and Ozark country were equally exotic.[35]

LEARNING FROM THE COMPETITION

Sam Walton knew all about the rise of E. J. Korvette. In 1960 he'd traveled to New York to look over Ferkauf's operation, pry as much information out of the founder as his country-boy, aw-shucks manner would allow, and visit with the heads of other successful discounters, like Spartan's, Zayre, and Mammoth Mart. But no matter how pioneering or inspiring, these exotic New York City discounters were overshadowed by more prosaic heartland firms that were an immediate challenge to Walton's Ozark ambitions. Indeed, Walton's motivation to go into discounting owed a lot to fear that his Ben Franklin chain would be crushed unless he joined the march to much larger, high-volume, low-markup stores that sold a far wider range of merchandise than the typical small unit in a variety chain.

For example, the Gibson Products Company of Dallas began to put a series of franchise discount stores on Walton's home turf during the 1950s and early 1960s. They were austere operations that conformed to the company's operating credo: "Buy it low, stack it high, sell it cheap." Like the latter-day Wal-Marts, Gibson sold lots of branded goods to working-class customers in stores that sometimes reached ninety thousand square feet. By 1964 there were 138 Gibson Discount Centers with total sales of $190 million, fifty times that of all the stores that Sam Walton ran. Four years later those Gibson numbers had climbed to 434 stores and $1 billion in sales.[36]

The Detroit-based discount powerhouse Kmart was undoubtedly Walton's greatest rival and for almost two decades the standard by which Walton measured his own retailing success. By the late 1950s the S.S. Kresge five-and-ten-cent-store chain was at a dead end. Most of its seven hundred variety stores were in downtown areas from which white working-class customers had begun to flee. If the firm were to thrive, it would have to recapture this clientele where they now worked and lived, in suburbia. This was the job of Harry Cunningham, who proved the first real successor to company founder Sebastian Spering Kresge, the nineteenth-century dime-store entrepreneur who had long presided as Kresge chief. Cunningham, who got his start as a Kresge stock boy in a 1920s-era Lynchburg, Virginia, store, was determined to transform the variety chain by selling branded, nationally advertised merchandise at a steep discount.

The company could make this leap because it had an army of experienced store managers, a sophisticated real estate department, and a clear vision of its customers: the blue-collar workers who now lived in the suburbs of the big industrial cities scattered throughout the East and Midwest. Working-class incomes were rising in the 1960s, but money was still tight: the Bureau of Labor Statistics reported that under a "lower-middle-class" standard of living, a family of four could buy a used Chevy every four years, go out to the movies once a month, and purchase two new dresses a year. So the Kresge discount stores would have plenty of customers. Cunningham wanted a different name on the entity, so his new generation of big, freestanding discount stores would be called "K-Mart" (the hyphen was later dropped). Company headquarters moved from downtown Detroit, where Sebastian Kresge had founded his variety store chain in 1899, to one of the nation's quintessential postwar suburbs, Troy, Michigan, in blue-collar Oakland County just outside the motor city.[37]

Then in 1962, when Walton was scraping together the capital to open his initial Wal-Mart in Rogers, Cunningham made Garden City, a Detroit suburb, the site of his first Kmart, opening seventeen more that same year. Kmarts exploded across blue-collar America, providing the model for much of the discount revolution that subsequently swept the country. Almost all of the new stores were freestanding—much cheaper than paying rent to a shopping mall—surrounded by acres of parking. The company sold many brand-name products, but it also pioneered Far Eastern sourcing for a variety of inexpensive products, including toys, dresses, and small kitchen appliances. Unlike department stores, Kmarts had only one set of entrance/exit doors and just a single, centralized checkout area located at the front. As with Korvette in its heyday, low prices were a product of high merchandise turnover. Hence customers pushed their own shopping carts down the aisles, self-service style, still highly unusual for a store that sold no groceries. The success was remarkable: by 1966, Kmart had 162 discount stores, and by the mid-1970s Kmart was opening about a hundred each year, some in Walton's Arkansas backyard. "I was in their stores constantly because they were the laboratory," Walton later told *Fortune* editor John Huey. "I spent a heck of a lot of my time wandering through their stores talking to their people and trying to figure out how they did things."[38]

SAM WALTON'S MIRACLE DECADE

To survive Walton had to get moving, either to expand his chain of Ben Franklin stores or to begin a new discount operation. "I could see that the variety stores were gradually dying because there were giant supermarkets and then discounters coming into the picture," he later recalled. But Walton needed a wholesaler. So he first tried to persuade Butler Brothers to slash its markup on his high-volume purchases by 50 percent, which would have enabled him to generate the traffic necessary to make a large store profitable. "They blew up!" Walton said of his interview with the Butler Brothers executives in Chicago. "They just couldn't see the philosophy."

Next he flew to Dallas to beg an audience with Herbert Gibson of Gibson Products Company. "Do you have one hundred thousand dollars?" Gibson asked. "No," admitted Walton, not ready cash, anyway. "Well, we buy in carload lots. Takes a lot of money to do that," Gibson told him. "You're not fixed to do business with us. Good-bye."[39] That exchange is illuminating: the capital requirements for discount retailing were considerably higher than for a variety store franchise, not necessarily because the stores themselves were that much larger, but because each link in the supply chain had to carry a far larger and costlier stream of goods.

So Walton was on his own, without the backing of a big wholesaler. He did secure a loan from the Republic National Bank in Dallas, which enabled him to buy in volume and build his first discount stores, although his dependency on this bank, as well as on the Robson family, meant that for the next few years Walton's expansion program would proceed with more financial deliberation than he might have wished. Walton never got a big wholesaler on his side, but he solved this problem by erecting his own Bentonville warehouse and distribution center at the end of the 1960s. In the meantime, Walton scrambled to supply his small chain from a catch-as-catch-can set of jobbers and wholesalers in Memphis, Kansas City, and St. Louis. Always on the lookout for a bargain or a deal, Walton also kept his markups, never more than 30 percent, well below those of the small-town competition, counting on volume and turnover to generate the profits.

His first Wal-Mart, in nearby Rogers, was a thirty-five-thousand-square-foot affair that proved an instant hit, but Walton still waited almost two full years before he opened his second discount store in the Ozark town of Harrison. Compared to Cunningham, Gibson, and the other chain discounters, Walton was still a small fry, and a cautious one, opening just a handful of stores each year. By the end of 1969, in addition to his fourteen Ben Franklins, Walton ran eighteen true discount stores, eleven in Arkansas and the others in southern Missouri and eastern Oklahoma, a region Walton would call his "magic circle."[40]

But explosive growth, usually at the expense of the older chain variety stores, was in the offing, heralded by Walton's vengeful return to Newport in 1969, where he gave Larry English, one of his most competitive young store managers, his orders. "Break him," said Mr. Sam of P. K. Holmes, who had snatched Walton's lease twenty years before. In short order English accomplished the task. "You can't say we ran that guy—the landlord's son—out of business," Walton later told his biographer. "His customers were the ones who shut him down. They voted with their feet."[41]

By 1970, when Walton finally took his collection of discount stores and Ben Franklins public, he knew he had a formula for rapid and sustained growth. Indeed, the 1970s were Wal-Mart's miracle decade, in which the firm moved from obscurity and regional curiosity to crack the $1 billion sales mark. Opening as many as fifty new stores each year, Walton saw Wal-Mart revenues soar at an annual rate of almost 40 percent. Employment mounted as well, to more than twenty-one thousand at the end of the decade, but Wal-Mart remained an extraordinarily lean and highly centralized corporation, with Walton reluctantly authorizing each expenditure on new warehouses, stores, and personnel. The *Wall Street Journal* was a bit mystified by the company's "rah-rah style," but nothing could gainsay Wal-Mart's enormous growth, which had already made the little-known regional retailer number 4 among all the discounters in 1981.[42]

How did Walton do it? First, Wal-Mart knew its market. Almost all the stores, no matter how large, opened in towns of ten thousand or under. "We challenged the assumption that you need a large population base to make this type of store successful," asserted Jack Shewmaker, who was Wal-Mart's president at the time.[43] Kmart rarely put a store in any city of fewer than fifty thousand, and Gibson's, which also knew the territory, avoided anything below ten thousand. On the other hand, Wal-Mart executives understood that most country towns, especially those that doubled as county seats, had a market area five times larger than their own population. As Wal-Mart became a one-stop shopping experience, the local competition, such as it was, simply evaporated, leaving the chain with something close to a retail monopoly. "The company's concept is to be the dominant one-stop department store providing a vast assortment of quality goods," asserted Wal-Mart's *1975 Annual Report*. And low prices were particularly powerful in this decade: the oil shocks that spiked the price of gas made shopping in more distant cities expensive, and the chronic inflation of the 1970s made everyone price conscious. A clever pricing stratagem reinforced Wal-Mart's low price reputation: henceforth, Walton banished the number 9 as the last digit on any price sticker. Toys, blouses, and hammers might sell for $3.98, never $3.99. *Discount Store News* soon found that "for people in rural areas where it does business, Wal-Mart is magic." In the 1970s Wal-Mart grew between four and five times as rapidly as Penney's, Kmart, and Woolco, the discount division of Woolworth.[44]

That Wal-Mart was developing a system far superior to that of key competitors became too glaring to ignore. For most discounters, the combination of inflation and recession—stagflation it was called—made for an economic environment that was poison. Clustered in cities and suburbs, they were locked into a fierce, profit-draining price competition, even as wages, interest payments, and shipping costs soared. But Wal-Mart, with most of its stores in small towns and exurbs, escaped this trap. Many of Wal-Mart's rural customers—part of its core consumer base—actually benefited from the burst of 1970s inflation as land and farm commodity prices rose rapidly. Even those without a direct attachment to a farm shared in the bounty. Thus in 1974, at the very nadir of the first oil shock, Wal-Mart sales jumped 41 percent as the chain grew to 104 stores. And Wal-Mart profited even more from the recession of 1979–81 (engineered by Federal Reserve Board chairman Paul Volcker, whose effort to kill off the inflationary virus with a stringent regimen of tight money sent interest rates spiking above 20 percent). For any retailer with substantial debt, these were disastrous times. E. J. Korvette, Mammoth Mart, and Vornado all went bankrupt. Woolworth liquidated its 336-store Woolco discount division, while Kmart and Sears watched in bewilderment as profits shrank even as nominal sales continued to rise.[45]

But Wal-Mart thrived. The chain had little debt and even less real competition. And as Americans became hyper–price conscious, they flocked to the store that promised consistently low prices, without gimmicky sales, rebates, or trading stamps. Although Walton generally eschewed growth through acquisition, Wal-Mart could hardly resist the fire-sale opportunities generated by the bankruptcy of so many of its rivals. Thus the company picked up more than one hundred stores when it bought the Nashville-based Kuhn's Big K chain in 1979 and then some thirty-two of the old Woolco stores in 1983. By then Wal-Mart sales were pushing close to $4 billion a year, and it had well over five hundred outlets, double the number of just three years before.

Wall Street analysts were astounded that Wal-Mart was closing in on Sears and Kmart. "So far, Wal-Mart's rapid growth has been managed with remarkable vision," reported Isadore Barmash, the veteran retail reporter for the *New York Times.* "Wal-Mart is the fastest-growing major retailer in the United States," agreed Stanley Iverson, a Chicago retail analyst. "Its management, motivation, communications and responsiveness to change are unique in the retailing industry."[46] This kind of praise sent Wal-Mart's share price soaring, enabling Walton to split the stock five times in just over a decade. An investment of one thousand dollars in 1970, when the stock was first listed, would have generated a stake of close to half a million dollars in just twenty years. Maggie Gilliam, an analyst for First Boston Corporation, who made an early pilgrimage to Bentonville, became a true believer. "Wal-Mart is the finest-managed company we have ever followed," she gushed in a report from the mid-1980s. "We think it is quite likely the finest-managed company in America, and we know of at least one investor who thinks it is the finest-managed company in the world. We do not expect to find another Wal-Mart in our life time."[47] Yet astonishingly, the company still did most of its business in just over twenty states, mainly in the South and Midwest. A whole continent remained open to the company's expansive ambitions.[48]

CHAPTER TWO

SUPPLY AND COMMAND

Wal-Mart would have remained but a regional sensation had it not set out to solve the vexing problems of supply and replenishment that had so stymied Sam Walton in his years as a dime store merchant with Ben Franklin. Walton would find a solution, but it proved far more than a clever business stratagem designed to put cheap merchandise on the shelves of his middle South discount stores. His success proved consequential because it revolutionized the relationship between merchants and their vendors. Led by Mr. Sam and his Bentonville executive team, Wal-Mart helped empower every chain retailer. He cut out a raft of salesmen, jobbers, and other supply chain middlemen, squeezed the manufacturers by shifting every imaginable cost, risk, and penalty onto their books, and taught the entire retail world how the bar code and data warehouse could finally put real money on the bottom line.

By the early 1970s Sam Walton faced a twofold dilemma. His stores were too small and too remote to take deliveries of merchandise in the pallet-loads manufacturers sent, but the use of intermediary wholesalers and jobbers was no solution. They took their large cut out of the price; even more vexing, most Wal-Mart stores were in towns that were too small and rural for timely delivery. When big metropolitan chains like S.S. Kresge shifted to discounting, they contracted with the same wholesalers and truckers that had been supplying their thousands of variety stores. But Don Soderquist, whom Walton recruited from Butler Brothers for his wholesaling expertise, recalled that "the trucking companies did not have the delivery scheme for dependably sending shipments out to small markets, as opposed to the Memphises and St. Louises; so [our] distribution system, in that sense, was born out of a necessity to get reasonable and dependable deliveries."[1] In his autobiography Walton remembered the whole situation with disgust: "We were out in the sticks with nobody to distribute to our stores, which meant that basically our managers would order from salesmen and then someday or other a truck from somewhere would come along and drop off the merchandise . . . this was totally unworkable."[2]

IN LOVE WITH LOGISTICS

Walton had no choice but to do his own warehousing. He would have to build his own distribution network to service his ever-expanding set of stores. This cost hundreds of thousands of dollars that Walton sorely begrudged, but the payoff came quickly. Operating its own system meant that Wal-Mart spent an average of 3 percent more on distribution than other retailers, but it also resulted in far greater overall savings for the Arkansas-based discounter. Now truck deliveries were more predictable and on a schedule, to and from its stores, that met Wal-Mart's specific needs and not those of the drayage company.

Indeed, purchasing, warehousing, distribution, trucking, what we today call "logistics," have become the core competencies of the corporation. Wal-Mart has rarely relied very much on its capacity to tickle the public fancy, to discover and promote a desire for a particular style or fashion in order to move the mountain of goods that flow across its shelves. Instead, from the early 1970s onward, Wal-Mart deployed a hyperefficient operational arm to put a conventional basket of branded consumer goods before the public in the best possible way. A consistently low price, not periodic sales and promotions, ensured customer loyalty, thus reducing what the Wal-Mart executive and future CEO David Glass called the "peaks and valleys in volumes that drive labor costs through the roof."[3] Unlike most other retail firms, where a background in merchandising or finance was essential to climb high on the corporate ladder, both of Wal-Mart's most important, recent CEOs, Glass and H. Lee Scott, have come out of logistics, and so too have most of the key executives who served directly under them.

"The misconception is that we're in the retail business," a Wal-Mart executive once remarked to a meeting of Wall Street analysts, but in reality "we're in the distribution business."[4] Retailers, like Kmart, who failed to understand this essential reality soon found themselves in big trouble. In the mid-1980s, when Kmart sales were still triple those of Wal-Mart, the Detroit-based discounter became an object lesson about how and why sheer size alone is not enough to make discount merchandising a success. Like E. J. Korvette, Kmart lost its focus. The company bought and then divested itself of several specialty retailers, including Borders, the Sports Authority, and a couple of grocery chains. Five chief executives came and went in little more than a decade.

One of Kmart's greatest problems arose from what it had once touted as a signal strength. Merchants ran Kmart. Its top management arose almost entirely from the ranks of its store managers. Because Kresge had been a variety store in an era of slow mail and slower trucks, the firm, like all mid-twentieth-century retailers, had always had a decentralized structure that gave managers in the field much autonomous room for creativity and salesmanship. Store managers could call a snap sale with their "Blue Light Specials," they often restocked their shelves from local wholesalers, and they advertised extensively in local newspapers. These managers were paid well, stayed put in their communities, and knew what might appeal to regional consumer taste. Many had been with Kresge their entire lives, so anything that threatened to take power out of the hands of these store managers, such as centralized ordering or computer-driven replenishment, was bound to be seen as an attempt by headquarters to strip them of their merchandising creativity. Most Kmart managers thought the solution to almost any sales problem lay in a new round of snazzy marketing. And it could work: the line of Jaclyn Smith clothing and Martha Stewart housewares first vended by Kmart in the late 1980s did send dollars flowing to the bottom line, but merchandising savvy could generate only temporary relief from the structural problems that plagued the discounter.

The company had scattered its stores all across a blue-collar archipelago that proved increasingly difficult to serve from a set of warehouses that were inadequate to the task. Only 30 percent of Kmart goods passed through the company's own replenishment system, while Target distributed 50 percent and Wal-Mart almost 80 percent. This put Kmart at a decisive cost disadvantage. Moreover, Kmart subcontracted its entire trucking operation, so most stores were restocked just once a week. And in the 1990s, when Kmart flooded its stores with heavily advertised merchandise in a vain attempt to undercut Wal-Mart prices, it had no place to store the goods, so in one instance fifteen thousand truck trailers were commandeered to hold on to them. Since the company had but a primitive inventory control system, few store managers knew what had been packed away in all those trailers sitting at the back of their parking lot.[5]

In contrast, Wal-Mart made logistics the heart of its business. At the core of this system stands a set of "distribution centers," not warehouses. And the importance of this distinction can hardly be underestimated. Historically, when the demand for retail goods could be neither forecast nor regulated, when manufacturers ran their lines full bore to ensure productive efficiency, when department stores and variety stores stocked up for the big Christmas season, warehouses served as regulatory nodes of the distribution system, absorbing the surplus or shipping out extra large orders during a busy selling season. In the late 1940s, for example, Butler Brothers purchased goods from more than 7,500 different manufacturers for later sale. As much as 25 percent remained in stock from one to three years![6]

And therein lay the problem. Goods sitting in a warehouse were unproductive capital, a waste of money. Walton was determined to keep his commodities in motion. Wal-Mart stores had relatively small storage areas, suitable merely as a place to open the boxes once they came off the truck. Thus, the series of Bentonville distribution centers Walton financed in the late 1970s were designed not to store—not even for a few days—the goods bought in bulk from the manufacturers, but to quickly repackage and consolidate them into truckloads that would move immediately to the nearest store. As Ron Mayer, the logistics-savvy executive who briefly served as Wal-Mart CEO in the mid-1970s, explained, Wal-Mart stores required "a flexible ordering system for obtaining smaller quantities at a lower cost and with faster delivery." The 150,000-square-foot distribution center the company built in Bentonville "is not intended to be used as a warehouse per se." It was not a storage facility, but in a procedure that would soon be labeled "cross docking," Mayer explained that "merchandise goes directly from the incoming rail cars or trucks to outbound trucks without being stored in the Center."[7] When Wal-Mart built its first entirely new distribution center in Searcy, Arkansas, in 1978, the company boasted of the "revolutionary" conveyor system there, designed "to move freight on an automated belt at the rate of approximately 200 feet per minute."[8]

These DCs have set the pattern for Wal-Mart's continental growth. Until 1978 all new Wal-Mart stores were built or acquired within a single day's round-trip truck drive from Bentonville. Although the company was opening scores of stores each year, the average distance from Bentonville was just 273 miles. This is what made it possible and efficient for Wal-Mart to ship so much of its store merchandise through its own distribution center, far more than most competitors.[9] Thus when Wal-Mart did expand beyond its Arkansas/Missouri homeland in the early 1980s, into Texas, the Deep South, and the Plains states, it first built a distribution center and then filled in the territory with about one hundred fifty new stores, as many as a large DC could handle. With hundreds of employees, miles of conveyor belts, and scores of trucks, the centers were in constant motion, twenty-four hours a day. Few were constructed in a metropolitan region. Instead, most were built deep in the countryside, where wages were low and workers largely antiunion.

For example, the distribution center in Searcy, Arkansas, was designed to serve stores in Tennessee, Mississippi, Kentucky, eastern Missouri, and Illinois. The land was purchased from nearby Harding College, known then and now for its ties to evangelical Christianity, its free market ideology, and its hostility to unionism. Many Harding students worked part-time at the Searcy DC, and a good number of alumni took management posts there.[10] The success at the center, although not without its own labor troubles during the chaotic start-up months, convinced Walton and his managers that the company could replicate the system indefinitely. So a third DC was built in Palestine, Texas, a fourth in Cullman, Alabama, and a fifth in Mt. Pleasant, Iowa. Near the end of the first decade of the twenty-first century, Wal-Mart had located more than one hundred twenty distribution centers all across North America.[11]

Today a typical DC is gigantic, sprawling over 1.2 million

square feet, with roofs that cover the equivalent of fifteen or twenty football fields. Two or three hundred trucks arrive each day, either from the company's suppliers or to pick up a load for the stores. The trucks nestle into one of the hundred or more bays that penetrate each side of the mile-long wall that encloses the distribution center itself. From these semitrailers, thousands of boxes, each labeled with its own identifying bar code and destination address, are quickly fed along one of the many small conveyors—there are more than twenty miles in all—that reach into the building's interior from each loading bay. These riverlike streams of boxes soon converge in four larger tributaries at a "merge center," from which the torrent of boxes streams into a mechanized sorting area. There electronic eyes read the labels after which electric arms reach out and guide the boxes, destined for particular Wal-Mart stores, out of the sorting area and into one of the facility's hundred chutes, which lead onto a waiting truck, all at the rate of two hundred cartons per minute, seven days a week, twenty-four hours a day.[12]

Unlike the great icons of the twentieth-century industrial age, like Ford's sprawling River Rouge complex celebrated in Diego Rivera's heroic murals, or the vast Boeing Assembly building at Renton, Washington, the Wal-Mart DCs build nothing. They are neither inspiring nor grim, merely a functional set of docks and locks for the river of commodities that came from one place and are destined for sale and consumption somewhere else, hundreds of miles downstream. Yet these DCs, and the similar facilities operated by Home Depot, Target, UPS, and Federal Express, stand at the center of the production and consumption network that now girdles the planet. Daniel Defoe's words about the great Dutch traders echo: "their vast Commerce consists in being supply'd from all parts of the World, that they may supply all the World again."

BAR CODE AND POWER SHIFT

If the new distribution centers represented Wal-Mart's muscle and bone, the corporate logistics operation needed a nervous system as well. The home office in Bentonville requires from its stores and vendors a sea of data that the company can instantly translate into a complete picture of its sales, profits, expenses, and inventory. Walton was determined to keep on top of this information; he wanted to know as soon as possible and with great accuracy what was happening out in all the individual units of his burgeoning commercial empire. So all through the 1970s and early 1980s he brought into his organization a series of bright young computer-literate managers who could help him link the home office to the vendors, stores, and distribution centers. They installed a lot of computers and began to create a data center at Bentonville, but communications were still primitive, at least by contemporary standards. Store managers had to manually collect sales data from each cash register, conduct periodic and laborious inventories to see how much remained on the shelf, and keep their own paper tally of all the expenses incurred at each store. In the early 1970s managers were still using the post office to mail in their sales and expense records each week. A decade later, they used the telephone to dial up a central computer in Bentonville, but the information flow was still neither fluid nor entirely reliable.[13]

Walton needed a technological fix, a system that would have the same transformative impact as the telegraph and the telephone a century before. And he got it, courtesy of the grocers, with the arrival of the Universal Product Code. Today the bar code is so omnipresent that we forget that life once existed before almost everything we buy had a UPC symbol affixed, that familiar oblong square of ten white and black computer-readable lines and spaces. The idea for a machine-readable price tag had been around since the 1930s. It became technologically feasible in the early 1960s when lasers were finally perfected. But the real impulse for the development of the bar code, and the cooperation it would demand from both manufacturers and supermarket retailers, came later in that decade. Then product proliferation, inflation, and the upswing of unionism in the service sector led to the creation of an industry-wide effort to establish uniform technological and informational standards, a system that could read not just the price but a whole suite of other characteristics on tens of thousands of separate products. Agreement was not always easy. Manufacturers like Kraft and Heinz wanted handheld scanners because they were cheaper to develop and initially more accurate in practice, but when supermarkets installed scanners at every checkout counter, they insisted on built-in models, since this would leave the clerk with both hands free to speed the merchandise on its way. So today the more expensive but labor-saving bottom scanners are pervasive.[14]

The first item bearing the UPC code, a package of Wrigley's gum, crossed the scanner at a March Supermarket in Troy, Ohio, in June 1974. Thereafter the UPC symbol spread rapidly. Within two years 75 percent of all items in the typical supermarket carried a UPC symbol. The scanners necessary to read the new codes came a bit later, first in the grocery stores and then in the 1980s in many other retail establishments.

Wal-Mart was in the forefront of this UPC transition. As early as 1980, when only 35 percent of all of the merchandise it sold actually had a UPC bar attached, Wal-Mart put a scanner in a Grapevine, Texas, store. Like the supermarkets, Wal-Mart was anxious to find out if it could handle "more goods with less person hours of labor." Soon checkout productivity jumped by 50 percent, and Wal-Mart managers began giving out pins to exceptionally proficient cashiers, those who could scan five hundred items per hour.[15] By the mid-1980s almost all Wal-Mart stores were tied into the UPC system, well ahead of Kmart, Sears, and most department stores. Today, even dusty library books and archaeological finds have a UPC bar code affixed. Bar codes are used to keep track of every piece of equipment that is transferred between space shuttle and the space station, every liter of whole blood, and they are found attached to the toes or wrists of both newborn babies and bodies awaiting identification in the morgue.

The rise of the bar code has had two dramatic and immediate consequences. First, it has enabled stores to manage sales, complexity, and product proliferation without getting paralyzed. From the 1950s through the 1970s the size of the average supermarket remained about the same. Most were about 20,000 square feet, and they carried about 9,000 items. But twenty years after the introduction of the bar code, this new technology enabled the supermarkets, now branching out into cosmetics, videos, toys, and clothing, to stock up to 60,000 items. This made possible the merger of supermarkets and general discounters, which had always concentrated on apparel and hard goods. Without the bar code to speed sales, facilitate instant price changes, and manage inventory, this dramatic retail expansion would have generated gridlock at the checkout counter. Thus could Wal-Mart manage the fivefold expansion in the size of one of its typical stores, from about 40,000 square feet in the 1970s to nearly 200,000 square feet today.

A satellite-based telecommunications system proved essential to the management of this huge flow of information. Here Wal-Mart took the lead, deploying between 1985 and 1987 the world's largest private, integrated satellite communication network, which beamed data, voice, and video communications to and from corporate headquarters and more than fifteen hundred stores, all via a single communications satellite in geostationary orbit 22,300 miles above the equator.[16] As with so many other organizational innovations, Wal-Mart adopted this technology to compensate for and complement the peculiarities of a firm that was still rooted in the rural South. By the early 1980s Wal-Mart's low-income customers were finally beginning to use credit cards at the checkout counter, but this made the lines long, bothersome, and costly. Many customers had poor credit, so before a clerk could ring up a purchase, say at the "floor limit" of fifty or one hundred dollars, she first eyeballed a list of bad credit card numbers and then dialed up the Visa or Mastercard central computer to see if the card was still okay. More time and money disappeared late that evening when the store manager had to use a telephone modem to forward to Bentonville all the sales information generated by his store's UPC scanners. This could take four hours and incur long-distance telephone charges, which in the rural South were still notably higher than in the more metropolitan North and East.[17]

Sam Walton was not enthusiastic about the money—half a billion dollars eventually—it cost to deploy a satellite network; the company founder still thought all such technology merely another overhead expense. But company president Jack Shewmaker convinced Walton that the system would not only save money but enable him to offer daily pep talks and product demonstrations directly to hundreds of thousands of employees via the company's own TV network. That would save the founder, then well into his sixties, a good deal of flying around to visit the stores.[18] This was a nice touch, but the real benefits soon showed up on the bottom line: credit card purchases were now verified in less than four seconds, employee mistakes and theft declined, the cost of phone calls and data transmittal became insignificant, and stores were able to feed the sales tally into corporate headquarters eight times a day. "In every store, every day," boasted Doyle Graham, then Wal-Mart's vice president of business systems planning, "we can capture every transaction . . . the time of day, the register, whether it was paid for by check, credit card or cash, and how many of the items were at reduced price."[19]

When they installed this system, however, neither Wal-Mart nor other retailers were entirely aware of the second and even greater impact that a computer-linked bar code network would have on the way these companies did business. For the bar code was not just a device that eliminated labor costs or increased efficiency within a single firm: it enabled retailers to leverage their enormous buying power against that of the manufacturers and suppliers. Before the deployment of this new technology, manufacturers possessed the best information about sales trends, shifts in demand, even how the competition was doing. An individual retailer might not know the true state of his sales until an end-of-the-quarter inventory, but a manufacturer would get a steady stream of signals from the numerous retailers it served, from market research, and from its own sales force and its wholesalers. Indeed, some vendors restocked supermarket shelves on their own schedule, relying on historic sales figures and their own best estimate of future prospects. But with the automatic, electronic collection of point-of-sale data, information and power thereafter shifted to the retailer.[20]

And the bar code helped in the merchandising itself. All those bar code swipes at the checkout scanner generated billions and billions of bits of information that poured into Wal-Mart's data warehouse, often described as second in size only to that of the National Security Agency. Retailers and vendors now knew when and where to replenish the vacant shelves, but Bentonville could also collect "market-basket data" to find out what products were likely to be purchased together, what kind of customer bought them, and at what time of day, week, and year. Wal-Mart was able to create an information trove so vast and detailed that it exceeded what many manufacturers know about their own products. This "cement[ed] Wal-Mart's power over vendors," observed the *Wall Street Journal*.[21]

It also provided Wal-Mart with the information necessary to stock its shelves so as to generate highly accurate "item affinity" sales that would give the retailer a small but consistent edge against its discount competitors. Little Debbie snack cakes were put next to the coffee; Kleenex tissues were shelved with the cold medicines as well as stocked in paper goods. Measuring spoons were in housewares and also hanging next to the Crisco shortening. At the grocery-selling Supercenters, rather than displaying popular items at the end of an aisle in flashy displays, Wal-Mart often put hot sellers on interior shelves. That brought traffic down the aisle. The vendors wanted to be near the popular items even if it meant displaying their product on a lower shelf instead of at eye level. Much of this seems intuitive, but the Wal-Mart data warehouse could generate tens of thousands of such merchandising insights. In the 1990s, Wal-Mart managers began to use a handheld computer—a Texiron—to scan bar codes on store shelves and get a real-time report on sales, turnover, and inventory. "Everybody thinks they have a feel for what people like," observed a Wal-Mart information officer at the time. "But we keep the data."[22]

PADDLING WITH PROCTER & GAMBLE

The power of this new kind of information, and the uses to which Wal-Mart put it, were demonstrated by the company's successful, two-decade effort to draw into Bentonville's imperial force field America's largest and most venerable consumer product manufacturer. By the 1980s Procter & Gamble had been selling soap for more than a century and saw itself as a merchandiser of a distinctive set of branded household products. When it launched Ivory a century before, it transformed a generic product into a high-value, company-specific consumer good. By World War II, P&G was organized entirely around the promotion and development of such highly identifiable products. The key executives at P&G were the "brand managers" who battled outside competitors and internal rivals to capture market share for their specific product. Ivory, Tide, Crest, and Pampers were so well known, so powerfully attractive, that customers would make a beeline for these products on the retail store shelf.

P&G's gigantic advertising budget—the company practically invented the soap opera, on both radio and TV—meant that no retailer could avoid doing business on the company's terms. Thus P&G abandoned jobbers and wholesalers in the 1920s and began direct sales to the grocery and variety stores of that era. And this system continued into the booming postwar period, when P&G market power gave the Cincinnati soap maker remarkable control over prices, retail display, and credit. "Arrogant," "dictatorial," and "domineering" were some of the adjectives used to describe the company, and in particular its hypercompetitive sales force. "Supermarkets," observed *Forbes* magazine, "feel like helpless pawns in the P&G marketing machine."[23] Sam Walton remembered that P&G, along with Eastman Kodak and some of the other large, established consumer product firms, "would dictate to us how much they would sell us and at what price. P&G gave a two percent discount if you paid within ten days, and if you didn't, man, they took that discount right off."[24]

By 1987, Wal-Mart was P&G's third-largest domestic customer, and P&G was Wal-Mart's single biggest vendor. Both had about the same annual income, $15 billion, although Wal-Mart was growing much faster. Remarkably, Wal-Mart had never hosted a single corporate executive from P&G's Cincinnati headquarters. "We just let our buyers slug it out with their salesmen and both sides lived with the results," remembered Walton. Lou Pritchett, then a longtime P&G sales executive, recalled that "most suppliers, including P&G, looked upon the [trade] customer as a necessary evil—a link between the manufacturer and the end user."[25] There was "no sharing of information, no planning together, no systems coordination. We were simply two giant entities going our separate ways, oblivious to the excess costs created by this obsolete system. We were communicating, in effect, by slipping notes under the door."[26] The situation was so bad that when Walton, hoping to open something of a high-level dialogue, called P&G headquarters in 1985 to say that he wanted to honor the company as its "vendor of the year," no one bothered to return the call, so Wal-Mart picked another supply firm to recognize.[27]

This could not continue, for Wal-Mart had accrued enough market clout to drive its own hard bargain with P&G. The retailer's scanners and bar codes were generating an enormous quantity of information about every aspect of the sale of P&G products. For the first time in the soap maker's history, another entity commanded as much knowledge about its customers as did P&G's own marketing and customer research apparatus. As *Fortune* observed, "P&G could no longer bully its way into the stores, waving figures a retailer couldn't dispute that showed Tide was outselling All and was therefore entitled to more shelf space."[28]

But equally important, the Cincinnati manufacturer had come to realize that an unremitting commitment to brand salesmanship had reached something of a dead end. Marketing costs were getting out of hand, not just from advertising but from the confusion and duplication of effort that arose when P&G sent a regiment of sales reps to take separate brand orders from the big merchants, even from individual store managers. There were eleven different national sales divisions, each hawking a product line such as detergents or foods, but no P&G unit had the same system to take orders, offer discounts, set promotion values, or determine performance requirements. Moreover, the

costs of P&G promotions had ballooned during the economically difficult 1970s and 1980s. But these costly and episodic
price fluctuations threatened to undermine brand value even as
the numerous requirements for retail customers to earn this
money generated much record keeping and not a little confusion and conflict. P&G knew that it had to reorganize its four-
thousand-person sales force, de-emphasize brand marketing,
and reorganize into retailer-specific sales teams.

The P&G/Wal-Mart courtship began in July 1987 during a
now legendary canoe trip in which Walton paddled Lou Pritchett
down the Buffalo River through the Arkansas Ozarks. They
got along. Both had been Eagle Scouts; both hailed from the
South. More to the point, Walton knew that he was in a position to eradicate inefficiency and generate lower prices through
out the entire system—soon to be called a supply chain—that
began in the P&G factories and ended at the Wal-Mart checkout station. Walton told Pritchett that electronic ordering would
make obsolete much of the vaunted P&G sales force; the savings for both vendor and Wal-Mart would be shared because
"the days of automatically passing cost increases through to
the customer are over."[19] For its part P&G had to collaborate
with this rapidly growing retailer if it was to ride the Wal-Mart
tiger to a new level of productivity and profits. Even without
Wal-Mart's prodding, top executives at P&G knew that change
was in the wind. The company played frequent host to W.
Edwards Deming, the American management guru whose lec-
tures on "total quality management" were then all the rage. He
helped popularize and codify the "just-in-time" production techniques developed by Japanese car makers to control inventory
costs and speed up the assembly line. American businessmen
found them particularly efficacious in the de-unionized world
increasingly characteristic of consumer manufacturing, both
at home and abroad.

After Walton and other Wal-Mart executives spent a weekend

at P&G headquarters in Cincinnati, the manufacturer sent a sales team to Arkansas on a permanent basis. The transition proved difficult. (The P&G sales force called Fayetteville, the site of their office, "Fayette-nam.") The principal task was to make the computers in Cincinnati and Bentonville talk with each other, but this proved harder than expected. There were technical problems, of course, but more vexing were the conceptual barriers: "We didn't have systems, measurements, or scorecards that talked the same language in the same timeframe," remembered one participant, "and that made it extremely difficult to solve business problems."[30] The development of a common data-delivery highway consumed a year and a half, and the number of P&G people serving the Wal-Mart account in Fayetteville soon rose from just a handful to 250. But within a few years the two companies were functionally interwoven at multiple points: buying and selling, of course, but also trucking, production, product development, finance, and international logistics. Among the first collaborations were just-in-time ordering and delivery systems for Pampers and Luvs disposable diapers. When the diapers ran low in a store, a computer sent an order by satellite to a P&G factory, which in turn automatically shipped more diapers directly to the outlet. An order and shipment process that once took nearly two weeks was now slashed to three or four days.

Symbiotic collaboration of this sort had an immediate financial payoff: P&G sales to Wal-Mart leaped upward by $250 million in 1989, the first full year in which the data exchange was in operation, and the big retailer increased its profitability on almost every brand that P&G sold through Wal-Mart. Thereafter, P&G increased its total sales to Wal-Mart from about 10 percent of all its output in the late 1980s to as much as 18 percent in the early 2000s.

But P&G executives, like those at so many other supply firms, feared that the autonomy and creativity of their company had been compromised. P&G had to rotate staffers out of northwest Arkansas because after a few years on the account they identified as much with Wal-Mart as with the Cincinnati soap maker. "The people were paid by P&G and sat in P&G's office, but it was like they were working for Wal-Mart and P&G equally," admitted Tom Muccio, who headed the P&G Wal-Mart team until 2004. "The payroll just happened to come from P&G."[31] Even more significant, Wal-Mart had clearly gained the upper hand when it came to pricing, product development, and sheer financial clout. In the late 1970s, P&G sales had been ten times higher than those of the retailer; twenty years later Wal-Mart earned triple the income of P&G and by 2005 it was five times as large. Both of these corporations were giants, but Wal-Mart was larger and was prepared to throw its weight around.

In 1994, for example, Bentonville was quick to take advantage of a P&G miscalculation when the soap maker failed to renew its trademark on White Cloud toilet paper, which P&G had abandoned in favor of upscale Charmin. A private entrepreneur snapped up the trademark and sold it to Wal-Mart, which quickly reintroduced the product, using the valuable market research that P&G had shared with Wal-Mart on the toilet paper market in general and on Charmin's "squeezable" niche in particular. P&G executives felt betrayed, but they simply took their lumps, since every other consideration had to be sidelined when a customer was purchasing nearly $8 billion of their product. Indeed, by the early twenty-first century, P&G could hardly introduce a new sales item without getting Wal-Mart's approval, and the Bentonville retailer sometimes demanded abrupt changes to products already on the shelf. In 2001, when Tom Coughlin, the Wal-Mart vice president who had once been in charge of the Loss Prevention department—the shoplifting police—got wind of the thefts that were eroding profits in the health and beauty category, he summoned Gillette and P&G

executives to Bentonville, demanding that they reconfigure their packaging to make them harder to steal. So P&G changed its Olay package from a box to a clear plastic container with a flat piece of cardboard, known as a "clamshell" because it is so difficult to open. And the company transformed and enlarged the package that held its Crest Whitestrips. Gillette also adopted clamshell packaging for its razor packs. The expense for this repackaging would be borne by the vendors, not Wal-Mart.[32]

All this produced a growing sense of alarm in Cincinnati. P&G was by far the largest consumer products company in the United States; with more than $51 billion in sales in 2005, it stood at number 26 on the Fortune 500 list. And it was remarkably profitable. In good times and bad, people had to buy their toothpaste and detergent. But Cincinnati executives were well aware that their good fortune increasingly depended on Wal-Mart, which explains why in 2005 they bought Gillette, the Boston-based razor and deodorant company with sales of $10 billion. The deal cost P&G $57 billion, but it would be worthwhile if the combination of these two consumer product giants could finally create an entity large and efficient enough to challenge Wal-Mart's pricing power and its increasing reliance on private-label brands. But even this megamerger was not enough. As retail consultant Howard Davidowitz asserted when news of the merger was announced, "The power will stay with Wal-Mart."[33]

DEATH OF A SALESMAN

That power shift is evident up and down the supply chain. For decades several thousand "manufacturing representatives" made a decent middle-class living selling a line of products put out by small and middle-sized companies which found that a commissioned sales force was just the vehicle for getting their wares into thousands of stores all across the nation. The reps made sure that orders were delivered on time, sales staffs were knowledgeable, and buyers were aware of the latest model. And they often functioned as "category managers" who coordinated and advised the retailer on a set of closely related products. They epitomized the "entrepreneurial spirit which made this country great," as one of their spokesmen put it.[34]

But when Wal-Mart started buying 20 or 30 percent of a single manufacturer's production line, and when much of its buying took place on a computerized basis, the 5 percent commission paid to sales reps seemed like wasted cash charged to Wal-Mart's ticket. "I've seen Mr. Walton walk into the lobby and see the same faces week after week," a source told the *Wall Street Journal.* "He knows that isn't necessary."[35] Indeed, Walton was hostile to the hail-fellow-well-met culture that had long characterized the retail/wholesale buying relationship in New York, Chicago, and out in the hinterland. The friendships, lunches, and kickbacks were over. "All the normal mating rituals are verboten," a marketing vice president for a major Wal-Mart vendor told *Fortune* in 1988. "Their highest priority is making sure everybody at all times in all cases knows who's in charge, and it's Wal-Mart. They talk softly, but they have piranha hearts, and if you aren't totally prepared when you go in there, you'll have your ass handed to you."[36]

As early as 1972, Wal-Mart began phasing out the "automotive rack jobbers" who replenished the shock absorbers, windshield wipers, and sparkplugs that were so popular in rural America. After eliminating this wholesaling service, which cost the firm 10 or 15 percent on the base price of its automotive merchandise, Wal-Mart bought direct from the manufacturer.[37] It took a few years, but by 1986 Wal-Mart had eliminated all the reps who handled auto parts and accessories. Next came an across-the-board edict, promulgated by Wal-Mart in November 1991. In a letter to all its vendors, CEO David Glass declared that henceforth Wal-Mart would no longer negotiate purchasing contracts with anyone except those executives employed directly by the manufacturing firm in question. Glass explained that because of Wal-Mart's "growth and insatiable appetite for merchandise, we need to sit down with the manufacturers directly. That can't always be effectively done with an intermediary." The manufacturing reps were in no position to tell a supplier to ramp production upward by 50 or 100 percent; only Wal-Mart could negotiate such a vast transformation in the vendor relationship.[38]

The manufacturing reps responded with outrage. "We can't afford a future where a handful of customers dictate which manufacturers are allowed to come to market," complained Robert Schwarz, of the National Food Brokers Association.[39] The reps lobbied Congress, denounced "power buying as deleterious to the economy," and created an umbrella group, immodestly called Coalition of Americans to Save the Economy (CASE). They asserted that "our American system of marketing, which began before the turn of the century and has no peer group in the world, demands that someone make the sale—someone must do the job, and that function is part of the cost of the product . . . it cannot as these super buyers intimate be done with sophisticated computer inventory systems or other electronic means interfaced with a supplier."[40]

CASE was right in one sense: purchasing could not be entirely computerized. It required coordination, by a "category manager," a rep who had an overview of a particular product category and who determined which brands would complement the overall selection and which would compete with each other directly. This task required considerable knowledge of the industry and all its variegated products. "Category management cannot be a bar mitzvah," complained Schwarz of the Food Brokers. "Someone can't just come down one day and say, 'Today I am a category manager.'"[41] But that is precisely what Wal-Mart did, or rather it foisted upon its vendors this often time-consuming and complex task. In every major category of merchandise, from bath towels to body wash, Wal-Mart designates a "category captain," a company whose job is to analyze the performance of all the products in the category and recommend different mixes, displays, or arrangements that would increase sales, even if it meant increasing those of a competitor. As Charles Fishman writes in *The Wal-Mart Effect*, his insightful book exploring the travail of Wal-Mart supply firms, the Bentonville retailer "cascades data about its sales out to its vendors—giving companies a remarkable window on the preferences of their own customers—but it gives those vendors the responsibility of analyzing those waves of data and reporting the insights back to Wal-Mart."[42] This was the kind of knowledge power that was once the exclusive province of the brokers or the consumer product research firms. Now Wal-Mart collects, sorts, and owns it.

The commoditization of such information has shifted power to Wal-Mart at every point on the retail supply chain. In the late 1980s and early 1990s Paul Westerman was one of the chief designers of the Wal-Mart data warehouse system. Although a technically savvy computer wonk, he was immersed in the Wal-Mart retail culture, so the "warehouse" was designed with the ordinary Wal-Mart buyer in mind. With just a few keystrokes the buyer could "query" the warehouse and instantly retrieve a historical record of an item's sales, profitability, and inventory. "Before the data warehouse was created," notes Westerman, "the allocation of a new article [to various stores] was an educated guess." But afterward, "the buyers, with their newfound analysis . . . were much stronger during negotiations with suppliers." For example, after he left Wal-Mart, Westerman reports that he worked briefly for a large photo firm, probably Kodak, which routinely sold its overstocked film to the big retailer. A Kodak executive there told him that such periodic sales, amounting to $4 million each, took place several times a year. But this arrangement came to an abrupt halt as soon as Wal-Mart installed a data warehouse "workbench" right in one of its Bentonville negotiating rooms. At that point the Wal-Mart buyer could determine that on thousands of scattered discount store shelves the company had more than enough inventory to last for quite a while, so even if Wal-Mart bought at below cost from Kodak it would have to bear the inventory expense for the stock of unsold film. Kodak executives left Bentonville empty-handed.[43]

The vendors were unhappy; more important, Wal-Mart recognized that it was not in the company's interest to "surprise" its suppliers with sales information that made for futile negotiations and pointless air travel to northwest Arkansas. So Wal-Mart rolled out Retail Link, a data workbench for thousands of its supply firms. Retail Link contained many of Wal-Mart's own data warehouse applications but without competitive product cost information. Vendors could now exchange ideas with Wal-Mart for new products and new sales strategies, sometimes to their mutual benefit. But overall, the vendors merely internalized the enormous informational advantage that Bentonville now held over its supplier supplicants. In effect, Wal-Mart offered its vendors a Faustian bargain: use our Retail Link software program, play by our new rules, and we will be your gateway to sales beyond your dreams. Or refuse and be shut out of America's dominant retail chain. By sharing Retail Link, Wal-Mart penetrated the executive decision making at each of its suppliers and drew them into what then-CEO David Glass liked to call a "partnership."

Wal-Mart had the upper hand. By gaining access to much of the information on its suppliers' books, the company was in a position to virtually dictate the terms of its contracts on price, volume, delivery schedule, packaging, and quality. Each year, Wal-Mart hands its suppliers detailed "strategic business planning packets," and then a buyer meets with each supplier to establish sales goals for the coming year. A manufacturer that fails to meet its sales target—or has data-documented problems with orders, delivery, restock, or returns—can expect even tougher negotiations from Bentonville in the future. "It was a cultural change between retailers and manufacturers," concluded Bobby Martin Jr., the Wal-Mart executive who developed and then managed the Retail Link software system. "Part of the process people went through was fear that Wal-Mart would know their business better and run their business. Some of [the suppliers] were not even as computer literate or capable as Wal-Mart."[44] Bruce Hudson, a retail analyst at the Meta Group, an information technology consulting firm in Stamford, Connecticut, put it rather differently: instead of supply and demand, "Wal-Mart lives in a world of supply and command."[45]

CHAPTER THREE

THE CORPORATE CULTURE

By the end of the twentieth century, Wal-Mart's mastery of logistics and its command of the retail supply chain would be emulated by its competitors. But few could reproduce the rural, patriarchal, and Protestant culture that famously characterized Wal-Mart from its earliest days as an insular Ozark retailer. That managerial culture, "backward" by most of the criteria with which the business-school experts have evaluated the twentieth-century corporation, proved remarkably efficacious for Wal-Mart, and long after the company expanded beyond its Arkansas birthplace. Both friends and foes have observed that Wal-Mart's management conveys a political and cultural message that mirrors the conservatism of the Reagan-Bush ascendancy. Wal-Mart emerged out of a rural South that barely tolerated New Deal social regulation, the civil rights revolution, or the feminist movement. Instead, the corporation celebrates an ideology of family, faith, and small-town sentimentality that coexists in strange but compelling harmony with a world of transnational commerce, employment insecurity, and poverty-level wages.[1]

AFTER *THE GRAPES OF WRATH*

To understand the world that gave birth to Wal-Mart, recall one of the great scenes in American film. In the opening minutes of *The Grapes of Wrath*, John Ford's 1940 classic, a Depression-era farm family first resists and then stands aside as their Oklahoma homestead is seized by the financial capitalists of Tulsa and New York. Muley, a bankrupt tenant farmer who will soon join the Joads on their California pilgrimage, initially defends his ramshackle homestead by pointing a shotgun at the well-dressed land agent who has brought the tractor and the law to dispossess him. Of course, these agents of capitalist finance are not alone responsible for the plight of Muley and other Okie farmers. Dust storms and mechanization have put the squeeze on everyone, the smug businessman tells Muley. "The tenant system don't work no more. You don't even break even, much less show a profit. Why, one man and a tractor can handle twelve or fourteen of these places."[2]

Muley responds with a protest still fueled by all the emotive power generated through decades of populist outrage: "I'm right here to tell you, mister, there ain't nobody gonna push me off my land! My grandpaw took up this land seventy years ago. My paw was born here. We was all born on it. . . . An' some of us died on it. That's what makes it arn. Bein' born on it and workin' on it and dyin', dyin' on it."[3] But when the giant "cat" begins to lumber toward his shacklike home, Muley finds that the determined young operator is not an alien oppressor but the equally desperate son of a neighboring tenant, whose three-dollar daily pay is all that keeps his own family fed and sheltered. The forces of capitalist expropriation drive on, but with a friendly, familiar face at the helm.

Muley's anger resonated during the Depression decade and after. It sustained an expansive federal government that used new regulatory powers to raise the price of a bale of cotton and a bushel of wheat, insure family homesteads, and build an electoral alliance of farmers, workers, and other "forgotten men" that would make the Democratic Party dominant for two generations. But Sam Walton was also born and raised not far from where John Ford filmed the exodus scenes in *The Grapes of Wrath*. The culture and cohesion that made his retail empire so distinctive also grew out of the desperate defense of family and farmstead embodied in the film.

Bankers and their mortgage repossessors were not the only agents of metropolitan capital that farmers like Muley feared and disdained. In the years before World War II, upwards of 70 percent of the public had a negative impression of chain stores, emphatically so in the South and Midwest. The "chain store menace," marveled the *Nation*, was "the question most talked of below the Ohio." One Georgia Klansman linked "socialism, atheism, chain stores, and companionate marriage" as the four horsemen of the Apocalypse.[4] From the Midwest came a similar denunciation of the chains. "All the future holds" for chain store employees, wrote a Dakota proprietor, "is the chance of [becoming] an underpaid clerk, working in cog No. 689 in store 1237, without hope of advancement, gain, possible partnership or ownership of a store of their own; nothing but serfdom."[5]

For much of the twentieth century, Arkansas stood at the epicenter of the anti–chain store movement. Between 1931 and 1937, twenty-six states, including all those in the old Southwest, enacted tax and license laws that attempted to curb or stop the growth of chain stores. The Robinson-Patman Act of 1936, which made discount pricing illegal, was sponsored by senators from Arkansas and Texas who sought to defend small-town merchants and corner stores against a chain store encroachment that seemed the latest embodiment of aggressive northern capital, Jewish guile, and urban corruption.[6]

Antichain agitation lost the fight in the 1940s and 1950s when postwar expansion and legal challenges to "retail price maintenance" allowed a bewildering array of chains, franchises, and conglomerations to spread across America. But opposition to the chains nevertheless cast a long shadow, rooted in the idea of yeoman independence exemplified by Muley's fierce determination to preserve his way of life. Its deepest roots were sunk in the southern countryside, if only because the alternatives were so dreadful: a life of debt peonage as a tenant farmer or landless laborer, or serflike labor in one of the New South's textile factories or lumber mills. By the mid-twentieth century, this defense of the independent proprietor had metamorphosed into a celebration of the small-town merchant and the family-owned enterprise.

The landowning head of household or the proprietor of the village store was virtuous and independent because he called no man his master. The implicit corollary to this self-assertiveness was the dependence and subordination of other members of his household: women, children, and, at various times and places, servants and tenants. By extension, the mom-and-pop stores and small businesses of rural America were therefore not merely economic institutions but social, ethical constructions that sustained a patriarchal hierarchy ensuring at least a modicum of dignity and standing for the husband and breadwinner. As historian Bethany Moreton has pointed out, the inexorable spread of the chains threatened to transform these men, the white, Protestant heirs of the Jeffersonian homestead, into an effete "nation of clerks." Small-town youth who took routine jobs in the retail trade would never earn an income adequate to marry and have a wife and children.[7]

But if management posts in the retail trade were reserved for men, and if the women sales clerks were kept subordinate, then the moral order and male dignity found on the traditional family farm might well be reproduced in more promising economic circumstances. In other words, if Muley lost both his livelihood and his manhood when forced off the land, perhaps his heirs might regain them running a discount store. We don't know how conscious Walton and his associates were of all this, but in the decades of blistering expansion that began in the early 1970s, Wal-Mart management effectively capitalized upon these long-held rural values. Walton admitted that for years management jobs in his stores were considered "the exclusive province of men."[8] And not just men but family men. "There was no such thing as a single store manager," remembered Larry English of his experience in the 1960s and 1970s.[9] Indeed, when the courts forced the company to release once-confidential employment data in the famous *Dukes v. Wal-Mart* gender discrimination class-action lawsuit, it became clear, even in recent years, that store managers, assistant managers, and management trainees were far more likely to be male at Wal-Mart than at its competitors. Although women made up two-thirds of those in the hourly paid ranks, they received just one-third of all promotions to store management positions.[10]

The life story of Wal-Mart manager Chuck Webb embodied the company's successful effort to transmute rural values into a retail setting. "We were plain old farm people," Webb recalled of his small-town Arkansas youth. During the 1950s, poverty at home and opportunity in the big city brought his family to Kansas City, where his father was a mechanic and his mother clerked for Sears. With just a high school education Webb worked for Spartan Stores, a troubled chain, but he really came into his own at Wal-Mart. "Working for Mr. Sam, you personally felt like the store actually was yours and you were glad to get a piece of it." The pay was good, with a bonus much better than at Spartan or Kmart, and the prestige considerable. "The manager is the kingpin in a small town," he recalled of his early postings in places like Broken Arrow, Oklahoma. When Webb turned around a deficit-plagued Jefferson City store, he got a bonus of thirty-two thousand dollars for his efforts. He read the numbers on the check and cried; it was more money than he had ever seen at one time in his life.[11]

A Wal-Mart publicity photo from a store opening in the late 1970s offers visual confirmation of the opportunities that awaited young men in a world where patriarchal authority seemed entirely natural. Forming a semicircle around a suited, youthful store manager are some forty-five blue-vested saleswomen, wearing opening-day corsages and belting out the new Wal-Mart cheer:

Give me a W!
Give me an A!
Give me an L!
Give me a Squiggly! (shaking of the hips)
Give me an M!
Give me an A!
Give me an R!
Give me a T!

What's that spell?
Wal-Mart!

Whose Wal-Mart is it?
It's my Wal-Mart!

Who's number one?
The customer! Always!

Many of these women are clearly middle-aged, although a majority seem young. There are a few twenty-something men standing at the edges of this animated female circle, but they wear a shirt and tie without a blue vest, which signifies their status as managerial trainees or assistant managers.[12]

The employment experiences of Wal-Mart women and men diverged radically. In 1977 Laverne Jones began work at a store in Pontotoc, Mississippi, right out of high school. She was ambitious and told her manager she wanted to move up. And she did, but just once, eight months after she was hired. She was put in charge of a clothing department, an hourly post that was 80 percent female. And that was it. Dozens of young men trained at her store over the next quarter century and then moved on and up, but despite her exemplary record Jones was never allowed to participate in the management-training program with all those young men. She married and gave birth to a son in 1986 but quickly returned to work. When in the mid-1990s she asked her district manager why a certain young man had been promoted and not her, she got a reply that revealed much about how Jones's ambition violated the familial hierarchy that defined Wal-Mart's corporate culture. Jones was told that she "did not want to go into management because [she] had the best job in the store" and that she "did not want anything else." Of the young man who was promoted, the district manager said, "He's a man, he doesn't have a family."[13]

This brazen sexism did not come out of thin air. For twenty years such managers had functioned in an organization where many women, perhaps most, were content to play the nurturing, supportive service roles offered them by Wal-Mart and the community that sustained it. To these company men, family obligations made women ineligible for the formal supervisory jobs, especially when they entailed long hours, frequent moves, and unfailing dedication to the company.

The career of John Sherman is a case in point. In 1975, right out of high school, he was hired as a stock boy at his hometown Wal-Mart in Wynne, Arkansas. Like Laverne Jones, he was promoted to hourly departmental head within a few months, but his career did not end there. He was trained—often by veteran female clerks—to handle several departments in the store, and he began a dizzying set of annual transfers from one small-town Wal-Mart to another. His nomadic life usually won him a pro-

motion, a bigger store, and more money, but it must have taken
a toll: Paragould, Ash Flat, and Berryville, all in Arkansas, then
on to Livingston, Clarksville, Corpus Christi, Giddings, Alice,
and Gainesville in Texas, next to Ardmore, Oklahoma, and
Wichita Falls, Kansas. Along the way he married and divorced
a clerk in Paragould, had an affair with a cashier in Ardmore,
and saw several of his female relatives, including his second
wife, take hourly jobs with the company. The latter followed
him about. As Sherman recalled, "There might or might not be
an opening for her. . . . She couldn't work in the store I worked
in."[14] By 1990 Sherman was the manager of a large store and
making good money, about ten times more than a cashier. But
in his mid-thirties, he seems to have entered an early midlife
crisis. He separated from his second wife, got back together
with her, and then decided to quit Wal-Mart and try another
company. "I was just really burned out with Wal-Mart. I mean,
I had been with them a long time and I hadn't tried anything
different."[15]

But Sherman was unable to switch gears midcareer. Steeped
in the Wal-Mart family ethos, he found his new employer, the
owner of a Dallas craft store, insensitive and discriminatory—
he wanted only attractive, young females at the checkout stands—
so Sherman begged his way back into Wal-Mart, starting over
again as an assistant manager in Plano, Texas. Sherman realized he was a Wal-Mart loyalist, "a total company man," as one
personnel evaluation later put it. "I am very pro Wal-Mart,"
Sherman proudly asserted, "the basic beliefs and culture are
everything to me."[16] Once again he was on his way up, to store
manager in Murray, Utah, then district manager in Wyoming
and Montana, where he supervised half a dozen newly opened
stores, then on to the really big time as a district manager in
high-volume metropolitan America, first in Los Angeles in 1995
and then Seattle two years later. His career exemplified Wal-Mart's

promise to ambitious young men from rural America: work hard, devote yourself to the company, find a series of mentors, and you'll escape, if not forget, the poverty and limits of your small-town youth.[17]

WOMEN AND WAL-MART

Women and their labor have been essential to the Wal-Mart story. More than 70 percent of company employees have always been female, even more in the stores themselves. In securing this cheap and grateful workforce, Walton profited mightily from the agricultural revolution that belatedly swept through Arkansas, Missouri, and Oklahoma. Farm women, who had once had their hands full with the chickens, the cows, and the canning, now found that electrification and better roads made wage work attractive, available, indeed necessary. In one down-state Illinois county, not all that different from northwest Arkansas, a careful study found that wage work by farm women tripled in the thirty years after World War II, with most getting jobs in the new grocery stores, restaurants, and hospitals that had turned rural towns into small cities serving thousands of customers and clients. "It was either I work, or we sell the farm," remembered a farm wife of her 1954 decision to take a job in a state mental hospital.[18]

Likewise in the postwar Ozarks, most people wanted to stay rooted. For men, construction work on the dams and roads financed by the government tided them over until they found a job driving a truck for Tyson Foods or doing a bit of repair work in one of the retirement and resort communities to which many budget-conscious midwesterners flocked in the years after 1950. For women minimum-wage garment assembly proved a new source of cash. A northern observer at the 1962 opening of a Mountain Home shirt factory reported, "The money the women earn is needed so desperately by people in the hills and valleys that they are willing to do almost anything to accommodate the plant to their simple lives."[19] In Rogers, where Walton put his first discount store, the local chamber of commerce touted the region's "large reserve of unspoiled labor" as well as its cheap water, gas, and electrical power.[20] Munsingwear opened a couple of small nylon knitting mills in Rogers and Bentonville and Daisy Manufacturing fled unionized Michigan for Rogers, where a workforce of up to four hundred, largely women, produced toy rifles for nearly half a century.[21]

Sam Walton's stores were therefore godsends to the farm wives and daughters displaced by the agricultural revolution. Like the Lowell Mill girls of the early nineteenth century or the Piedmont farm families who staffed the New South textile mills, they measured the value of their labor by a standard forged in the hardscrabble effort to preserve family, farm, and personal dignity. Jackie Lancaster, who worked in Sam Walton's first Ben Franklin store in Newport, remembered that in 1945 she was thrilled to exit the cotton fields and take a fourteen-dollar-a-week job as a checkout clerk. Of Walton she remembered, "There were two things he told us that I have never forgotten. He would praise us for the good job we were doing but he told us never to think that we got so important that we couldn't be replaced."[22] Elvena Walter, who started her Wal-Mart career in Rogers, was also grateful for the work. Awarded a twenty-year pin in 1989, she "gave the credit for her work record to her family, her Father in Heaven, and a good company." After accepting an engraved plaque signed by Sam Walton, Mrs. Walter recalled the early days: "Everyone started part-time then, and no one knew how long this new store in town would remain open. No intercom system, no profit sharing, no stocks, just a good job, hard work and good people to share the load."[23]

Indeed, Wal-Mart's family atmosphere, rural informality, and cultural homogeneity proved of enormous usefulness to the company. "The enthusiasm of Wal-Mart associates toward their jobs is one of the Company's greatest assets," declared the 1973 *Annual Report*.[24] When the company dedicated a new general office and expanded distribution center in Bentonville, more than fifteen hundred employees, nearly half the total workforce, turned out by bus, car, and plane. Some drove over seven hundred miles to attend. "That's an indication of their loyalty, interest and pride in Wal-Mart," boasted Sam Walton in his chairman's letter.[25] One seemingly trivial indicator: hundreds of thousands of Wal-Mart workers, largely women, have been trading their store seniority pins for decades. The pins symbolize recognition and community, a link between employees and the company that assumes shared sentiments, values, and experiences. "They're thinking about you," said a West Virginia store manager. "You don't feel left alone out there."[26] Don Soderquist, Wal-Mart's chief operating officer in the 1990s, understood the importance of all this: "In my judgment, the single most important element in the continued, remarkable success of Wal-Mart is our culture."[27]

"THE PAST IS NOT DEAD"

That culture was also marked, to a large degree, by the geography of race. The Ozarks were not just rural and poor. They have long been uniquely homogeneous, among the most exclusively white regions in the nation. But it was not always so. During the Civil War the Ozarks of Missouri and Arkansas mostly sided with the North. Indeed, the Union army recruited heavily in northwest Arkansas, which helped make that Confederate state second only to Tennessee in the number of volunteers it sent to the Yankees. These Ozark farmers defected from Confederate Arkansas because they hated the plantation oligarchs of the Mississippi Delta, who had long controlled state politics. And for almost a generation after the war, an interracial, Republican coalition played a large and vigorous political role in northwest Arkansas and southern Missouri. African Americans lived in almost every Ozark county. They had churches, lodges, and numerous small farms. There was even a "colored" baseball league with teams in Bentonville, Joplin, and other towns.[28]

But this racial pluralism collapsed in the 1890s when the plantation oligarchy, backed by New South railroad and industrial barons, emerged as the near hegemonic ruling class of the states that had once composed the old Confederacy. The defeat of the Republican/populist challenge quickly transformed racial mores in the Ozark uplands. Historic hostility to the delta employers of cheap black labor was transferred into a bloody antagonism to local African Americans, in the process reviving, indeed inventing, a sense of regional loyalty to the Southern cause. Thus, the monument to the Confederate private that stands in the Bentonville town square, facing directly toward Sam Walton's first store in that community, is not so much a tribute to the heroism of the region's soldiery as it is a symbol of the massive shift in white racial sentiment that began in the 1890s.

Confederate nostalgia was hardly the most important fruit of this reconfiguration of upper South politics. In the plantation districts black residents lost their vote and their voice, but in the Ozarks and other parts of the border South, where African American labor competed with that of white, a wave of pogroms and lynchings forced thousands of black residents to flee. Between 1894 and 1909 what we would today call ethnic cleansing was rife in the Ozarks. White mobs lynched at least eight African Americans in small-town Missouri and expelled hundreds of others from Monett, Pierce City, Joplin, and Springfield. In Harrison, Arkansas, where Walton would put his second discount store, violent mobs attacked local blacks in

1905 and 1909 and expelled all of the three or four hundred African Americans who lived there. One historical account of the episode described how "from house to house in the colored section they went, sometimes threatening, sometimes using the lash, always issued with the order that hereafter, 'no Nigger had better let the sun go down on 'em.'"[29]

The black population of the entire Ozark region was cut in half, vanishing completely in many counties and small towns. Aside from some of the larger cities, like Springfield and Tulsa, where a 1921 race riot killed at least three hundred African Americans, the entire Ozarks went proudly "sundown." The merchants of Rogers, Arkansas, bragged that their city had "no Negroes or saloons," while nearby Siloam Springs crowed that it enjoyed "No Malaria, No Mosquitoes, and No Negroes." In 1960, when Walton was laying plans for his first discount stores, Benton County had but twenty-three blacks, most elderly servants.[30]

Sam Walton had nothing to do with this ugly history, but the corporate solidarity that distinguishes Wal-Mart's culture was in some measure a product of the region's racial legacy. "The past is not dead," William Faulkner wrote of the South. "In fact, it is not even past." Indeed, Walton's future career was mightily shaped by the racial dynamics of the population from which he drew his clerks and customers. Had he remained in Newport, the delta town where he lost his lease, his clientele would have become increasingly biracial, especially after his discount idea took off, targeting the bottom half of the population for both employees and customers. By the 1960s retail establishments from Greensboro to Baton Rouge were at the epicenter of the civil rights revolution, nowhere more so than in the small towns on both sides of the lower Mississippi, where pickets and protests demanded employment for African Americans and better treatment for people of color. At Woolworth, whose stores achieved fame as the sites for many of the first lunch counter sit-ins, dozens of white southern managers quit or were fired when the New York headquarters began to insist on integration of all facilities. Conversely, in Mississippi and other Deep South states, the homegrown merchants were often integration holdouts, and therefore the boycott target for African American picketers.[31] And, in the small towns of eastern Arkansas, high levels of racial tension over jobs, politics, and education continued well after passage of the 1964 Civil Rights Act.[32]

Ensconced in the nearly all-white Ozarks, Wal-Mart escaped all this. It is true that when in the early 1970s Walton opened stores in black areas of Arkansas and northern Louisiana, he adopted the sales code practiced by many southern white merchants following passage of the civil rights laws. He hired few African Americans and then sought to keep them out of direct contact with white customers, even if this meant violating Mr. Sam's famous "ten-foot rule," which mandated that all Wal-Mart employees must smile and ask any customer who came within ten feet of them if they needed assistance.[33] But as Wal-Mart opened stores in the Deep South, largely in the 1980s, the civil rights winds had ebbed. White customers were less reluctant to shop in an integrated store, and most African Americans saw the arrival of a local Wal-Mart as a sign of racial progress. Of Neshoba County, Mississippi, race relations, a young journalist observed in 1989, "While black or white is still an important label, everyone shops at Wal-Mart."[34] And Mr. Sam and his heirs were now hiring plenty of African Americans as well, so many that by 2001 Wal-Mart was the largest private employer of African Americans in the country. When Wal-Mart released once-confidential Equal Employment Opportunity data a few years later, the company proudly reported that, as a proportion of the national workforce, African Americans were overrepresented, not just among sales workers but in the managerial ranks as well.[35]

All this was in the future, however. In the turbulent years of the civil rights movement, the codification of a communal, homogeneous Wal-Mart culture would have been far more difficult, if not impossible, had the company expanded as a discount house headquartered in the tension-filled Mississippi Delta. Under such conditions it would have been impossible for a southern retailer to claim, as Sam Walton did in the 1973 *Annual Report*, "There is one factor that I must rate above all else that makes our total Wal-Mart program both unusual and successful—the 3,500 dedicated and enthusiastic associates who comprise our Wal-Mart family. . . . I have a strong feeling that our folks are behind our Company to an unusual degree."[36]

So Walton's eviction from Newport allowed him to avoid both the confrontations and the immediate consequences of the civil rights revolution. His retail chain would grow in a world of exclusively white, Protestant, small-town folk. The magic circle that hosted almost all of Wal-Mart's first hundred stores comprised an Ozark region that precisely coincided with the territory that had generated so many sundown towns seventy years before.[37] Wal-Mart's welcome and the cultural fit it enjoyed in the communities in which it built its stores faltered only when the company expanded beyond this homogeneous homeland.

THE CULT OF MR. SAM

Sam Walton symbolized this Wal-Mart Ozark culture, and he proved remarkably adept at reproducing it. He became a cult figure years before his death, famous for his country twang, muddy boots, and the aging pickup trucks he drove around Bentonville. His persona embodied Wal-Mart's reputation as an earthy and virtuous enterprise. When he visited a store, the clerks remembered the occasion for the rest of their lives. His

Arkansas bird dogs and their exploits on his frequent hunting trips were legendary. Old Roy dog food, named after Walton's favorite, is now the world's best-selling brand. Somewhat less was said about his more upscale daily tennis game, but it made little difference to his admirers, because even as the nation's richest man, an honor *Forbes* awarded him in 1985, Walton disdained conspicuous consumption and overt self-advertisement. He kept the same wife for forty-nine years, brought his eldest son into the business, and got to work at dawn. "Just your basic homespun billionaire," crowed *BusinessWeek* in an essay that made Walton's cultivated country virtues interchangeable with those of the company. "He seems to run Wal-Mart like a larger version of his original dime store. He doesn't bother with pricy industry consultants and marketing gurus."[38] Despite the technological sophistication of the Wal-Mart infrastructure, Walton derided computer-age expertise and instead celebrated hard work, steadfast loyalty, and the mythos of small-town America. "We are no tech, not high tech or low tech," Walton told thousands of admirers who attended his last shareholders' meeting in 1991.[39]

Wilma Rader, who worked in an Oklahoma Sam's Club, recalled the excitement generated by one of Walton's unexpected appearances: "Mr. Sam would come to the warehouse and visit us just like family. He never forgot a name! One morning he came to the Admiral (Tulsa) Store and immediately got on the intercom to say 'good morning' to all the folks. Our two managers shot to the front like a streak of lightning! Everybody looked forward to visiting with Sam."[40] These stories struck a deeply resonant chord. In a 1989 ditty a Monroe, Louisiana, sales clerk summed it up.

Who is this man? The man they call Sam.
I would love to meet him and shake his hand.

He started with an idea and made it an empire
Through work and dedication, a man to admire.

Enthusiasm, excitement, and a deep family we share.
No hostility, rudeness or smoke (for that matter) fill the air.
They plowed the fields where stood nothing but trees.
Companies know what's coming and are shaking at their
knees.[41]

Walton's image recalls that of Henry Ford, the only other twentieth-century entrepreneur whose innovations were as revolutionary in their economy-wide impact and closely identified with a single individual and a single firm. Like Walton, Ford advertised his small-town roots, rural values, hands-on management, and hostility to New York money and credentialed expertise. Like Walton, Ford became a household name that embodied not just a set of new business practices but an ethos. Ford's reputation, however, had nothing like the popular staying power of Mr. Sam, especially among those who actually worked under him. Ford was neither charming nor paternal: he ran his great factories, the River Rouge complex above all, like a military dictator. More important, the Detroit industrialist died twenty years too late, in 1947, after the Model T had become quaintly obsolete and after the travail and tumult of the Great Depression—including a bitter battle with the emergent trade unions—had permanently stained his reputation. In contrast, Walton succumbed to cancer in 1992, at the very moment when the world recognized that Wal-Mart had become a retail hegemon. Immediately, Wal-Mart executives practically deified the founder, treating him as the fount of all the business values and the retail techniques responsible for corporate and career success. In Aldous Huxley's *Brave New World* (1932) fictional characters deploy the phrase "In the Year of Our Ford." Today, thousands of warm-blooded

Wal-Mart employees still incorporate into their workaday vocabulary the invocation "So help me Sam."

WAL-MART LOYALTIES

Walton's cult proved to be long-lasting not just because of his own attractive persona. Wal-Mart management constructed and institutionalized an imaginary social landscape that depended upon an adroit manipulation of language and organizational mores. Beginning in the 1970s the company labeled all employees "associates," routinely used first names in conversation and on identification badges, and renamed the Personnel Department the Wal-Mart "People Division." Associates who perform below par are not disciplined but rather "coached" to achieve their potential.[42] Low-ranking employees who feel aggrieved can use the Wal-Mart "open door": that is, they can skip one or two levels of authority and take their complaint straight to a top executive in Bentonville. In daily practice this system is dysfunctional, because it undercuts the authority of those whose job it is to exercise routine supervision, but in times of crisis—a union organizing effort or an expansion program gone awry—top executives tell their underlings that they are sympathetic and understanding, and that the company can correct mistakes brought to their attention.

This policy is alluring. In one well-known instance, Walton opened his door to a truck driver who had been repeatedly disciplined and then fired for drunkenness. When the CEO gave him one more chance, other top Wal-Mart executives protested. Walton was undermining their authority; moreover the driver would almost certainly take to drink again. But Mr. Sam knew what he was doing: like a king dispensing alms, the tale of Walton's mercy and the seeming humiliation of the subordinate executives traveled far and wide, humanizing and personalizing the company for thousands of employees who might never make use of the open door themselves. And the next time the driver came in drunk, he was out on the street, no questions asked.[43]

Symbolic leveling of this sort can become carnivalesque. *Wal-Mart World*, the company's magazine for its workers, has long been full of stories and snapshots that advertise the ritualistic humiliation of store managers: they dress as babies who beg for donations in the annual United Way campaign, serve as Santa's slaves during the store Christmas party, or man the cash register, collect the carts, and greet customers during "Ladies Day."[44] A store manager with twenty-seven years at Wal-Mart recalled, "I have taken a pie in the face when I lost a contest. I've swapped jobs with people. I've dressed up in a clown costume and then stood at the door greeting customers. . . . I've seen management shave their heads when a goal is achieved." Sam Walton and the home office executives who succeeded him encouraged such games and bonding rituals because these shenanigans "had high impact and no cost."[45]

To the outside world, much of the Wal-Mart culture gets displayed at the company's annual meeting. Sam Walton forged its distinctive character in the early 1970s when he conjured into existence an event that would appeal to two very dissimilar audiences. First, he wanted to entice and entertain the New York retail analysts who were hardly enthusiastic about making the long trip to a remote Arkansas town. So Walton hosted a barbecue in his backyard, led canoe trips on the nearby Ozark rivers, and brought in some country singers. The New Yorkers were impressed, if not by the music and food, then by Wal-Mart's amazing 40 percent sales growth each year.

But Walton also wanted a meeting that would bring together thousands of Wal-Mart employees within a corporate culture that emphasized familial sociability and entrepreneurial achievement. Each year as the event grew larger and more scripted, it put suited executives and country singers on stage, delivered sentimental tributes to veteran Wal-Mart associates, while displaying sales and profit reports from the CEO and benedictions from Mr. Sam or his heirs. At recent meetings, now held at a basketball arena at the University of Arkansas, top executives have performed skits, songs, and vaudeville-like routines that embarrass them before thousands of raucous associates.[46]

Everyone, including the most loyal employees, knows that Wal-Mart's communal culture sits uneasily alongside a work regime emphasizing discipline and hierarchical authority. This tension was on display at the 2007 shareholders' meeting, where the comedian Sinbad, who served as the master of ceremonies for the four-hour event, played the jester to the king. Every joke and skit was a transgression, in which Sinbad, playing a Wal-Mart associate, defied company executives, ate potato chips on the job, insulted the customers, and ridiculed corporate rules and slogans. To waves of nervous laughter he told the crowd that he wanted a quick promotion, that the customers, not the associates, needed more training, and that he was looking for a one-aisle Wal-Mart store into which he could quickly duck in and out.

All this may seem hokey and self-serving, but such ritual inversions express the self-confidence of executive authority, attest to the authenticity of a shared culture, and admit to a carefully monitored degree of internal tension. Among other critics, organizers for the United Food and Commercial Workers have understood that it works. The corporate culture is hard to challenge. Thus when that union did succeed in forcing Wal-Mart to post in the break room National Labor Relations Board notices advising employees of their organizing rights, the UFCW soon realized that the associates took little notice of a poster with the heading "To All Employees." They had no idea who an "employee" might be, so the union asked the NLRB to adopt Wal-Mart's own nomenclature.[47]

For the committed, the Wal-Mart "culture" represents something akin to a religious fellowship, testimonies to which the company has recently posted on a bloglike Web site, "Life at Wal-Mart." Debra, who works in the legal department at the home office, found that the "Wal-Mart family culture" was as strong in a Florida distribution center as it was among her white-collar colleagues in Bentonville. "We cry together, laugh together, and share our lives with each other." Concluded Debra, "Wal-Mart is a dream for those who could not dream before, a goal for those who did not know how to achieve, and an extended family to those who are willing to give the same respect they receive."[48] Likewise, a manager in Power Springs, Georgia, testified that early in his work life he found a career at Wal-Mart so attractive that he traded a high-paying factory job for a far less remunerative sales position with the retailer. "I can never pay back this great company for what they did for me and my family," testified Charles R., who earned well above one hundred thousand dollars a year as the manager of a Supercenter. "I love Wal-Mart, and I am Wal-Mart. Thank you Sam. I can never repay you."[49]

WHERE THE HEART IS

Wal-Mart culture resonates with millions of Americans, including both those who work for the firm and those who merely shop there. Wal-Mart has long attracted an unusually loyal clientele, especially on its home turf in the South and the Midwest. In the early 1990s retail surveys found that in heartland cities like Atlanta, Dallas/Fort Worth, and Indianapolis, shoppers overwhelmingly preferred Wal-Mart to rivals like Kmart and Target. By margins of four and five to one they selected Wal-Mart, not just because of its low prices but because it seemed to be a store "concerned about and actively involved in the community at large." Wal-Mart shoppers were "sticky," reported the retail experts. No discounter did a better job keeping customers coming back than Walton's big-box chain.[50]

This loyalty, sometimes amounting to fanaticism, was confirmed by *Discount Store News* in the mid-1990s when it brought together twelve women from around the country to get their thoughts on the contemporary shopping experience. No business journal covered Wal-Mart with more energy or appreciation, but the focus group conversations still proved startling. "I hate to say their responses were scary—but they were scary. Think Stepford Wives and you begin to get the picture," observed executive editor Jennifer Negley, who listened in on the cross talk. "What was uncanny in each group was the way that Wal-Mart managed to spring up—unbidden—within moments after the moderator swung the conversation toward shopping." Women who didn't have a Wal-Mart in their community spoke wistfully of the day Wal-Mart would arrive. One woman in Tennessee—the only one who expressed an active and hearty dislike for the store—eventually broke down and admitted she shops there all the time.[51] Kitty, a Florida psychologist, offered a utilitarian calculation for her frequent trips to the local Wal-Mart: "They have what I want and will probably have a competitive price." But Anne, a born-again Christian homeschooling her children in Franklin, Massachusetts, saw Wal-Mart as part of her community: "It doesn't matter about the convenience. I like Wal-Mart because it's friendly. We've always found the people there very nice. They pretty much call us by name now. It's really nice. They are a different type of people."[52]

A novel by Billie Letts, *Where the Heart Is*, captures the aura. Published in 1995, the novel sold 2 million copies after Oprah Winfrey made it one of her book club selections. It was then made into a movie and translated into a dozen languages. It tells the story of Novalee Nation, a pregnant seventeen-year-old abandoned by her no-account boyfriend in a Wal-Mart store in Sequoyah, Oklahoma. Novalee may be penniless and surreptitiously living in the Wal-Mart itself, but it quickly becomes clear that she is not alone. The Wal-Mart parking lot is the de facto town square, so she quickly meets the "family of friends" who will sustain and nurture her until her child, named Americus Nation, finally arrives. Sam Walton makes a cameo appearance, visiting a briefly famous Novalee in her hospital bed to give her five hundred dollars and offer her a job at the local Wal-Mart. However, the novel is not so much a paean to Wal-Mart, the company, as it is an affirmation of the extended familial values that an institution like Wal-Mart claims to embody. The heartwarming essence of the book is Novalee's story of destitution and redemption, facilitated by Wal-Mart itself.

Letts modeled the Novalee character on the many poor, uneducated, unwed mothers, some recently divorced or never married, who passed through her Oklahoma community college classes. Many were "victims of alcoholic, redneck, small town he-men." They held marginal jobs, as waitresses, motel maids, nursing home workers, and retail clerks. They were the new generation of uprooted Okies, dispossessed not by the dust storms or tractors of the 1930s but by the economic upheaval that has destabilized and depopulated towns and cities on the high plains in more recent decades. Letts calls them "Ma Joad's children" who "keep coming, they keep trying. And Novalee Nation is among the best of them."[53]

But much has changed since John Steinbeck wrote *The Grapes of Wrath* at the climax of an era when poor farmers and underemployed workers looked to the government for security and sustenance. In Steinbeck's imagination, the Joad family found temporary shelter and a warm, democratically organized community in the government-run migrant camp presided over by a kindly New Deal administrator. But in the small-town Oklahoma world evoked by Billie Letts, there is neither government assistance nor organized charity. Even the library, where Novalee meets her love interest, is run out of a private home. In the local hospital, where she recovers after birthing Americus, the staff she encounters are cold and condescending, a talisman of the country's miserly and bureaucratic welfare state. As Letts describes it, "Novalee had seen that look before. On the faces of clerks as they watched welfare mothers count out their food stamps. In the eyes of some teachers when kids lined up for free school lunches. Behind the tight smiles of secretaries who patiently explained that the water couldn't be turned on again until the bill was paid."[54] And this is precisely the moment at which Sam Walton, displacing the New Dealers and social workers of a bygone era, lends his helping hand to Novalee.

Where the Heart Is reflects Wal-Mart's world in another respect as well, in terms of the dichotomy between the social aspirations and the economic reality of those who inhabit it. Although family and community are celebrated in the novel, there are no traditional family units and little by the way of actual community. Divorce, abandonment, poverty, violence, and death have left a trail of misshapen people, often related or connected in complex and temporary fashion, who are clustered in the same households for economic survival and emotional warmth. Even the local Wal-Mart, the key community institution, is closed after a devastating tornado, only to reopen in another, more sales-worthy town, fifty miles away. But despite all the economic devastation and social chaos around them, Novalee and the other characters keep dreaming of a neat little house, a fulfilling job, and a husband or wife with whom to share it all.

In much of contemporary America, such simple familial stability has become part of the package of private privileges available largely to the well-to-do. It takes a couple of good jobs to pay the mortgage and keep a family. So regardless of their religion or their cultural values, lower-income individuals live in a much more unstable society, with higher divorce rates, more single moms, more abortions, and more interpersonal and interfamily strife, than do the middle- and upper-middle-class people whose income and lifestyle they covet. The rural South remains the nation's poorest region, not long removed from the dispossessions that accompanied the agricultural revolution of the 1950s and 1960s or the wave of exurban plant closures that came a generation later. So it should come as no surprise—although it usually does—that the old Bible Belt has the highest divorce rate in the nation. There, in states that constitute the Wal-Mart heartland—Arkansas, Oklahoma, Tennessee, Alabama, Mississippi, Louisiana—divorce rates are 50 percent above the national average and twice as high as in more affluent New England. Rates for out-of-wedlock births and births to mothers under twenty years of age are also much higher than in the North and West. Southern Baptists actually have the highest divorce rate of any Christian denomination.[55]

So Wal-Mart's identification with family, community, and the supposedly traditional values of a bygone era attracts many customers and employees whose own lives are far removed from the stability they crave. In flyers and advertisements the company is never "Wal-Mart" but "Your Hometown Wal-Mart." The result is an imagined community where economic and moral lives are interconnected and virtuous. The fact that Wal-Mart itself contributes to the conditions that lead to so much social and familial instability may be of far less consequence, if not actual irrelevance, to those who shop and work there. Indeed, the low pay, high turnover, awkward shifts, and general precariousness that have become the norm for so many American workers create a longing for community and stability that the ethos of the company seeks to fulfill.

During recent years, as Wal-Mart has come under blistering attack from unions, journalists, academics, and the Democrats, the company has responded with an aggressive public relations campaign. One revealing aspect of the campaign has been the testimonials and minibiographies of Wal-Mart associates posted on the corporate Web site, telling of the rewards and pleasures they have gained from their work. Of course, this is not the first time that a corporation has solicited employee assertions of loyalty and satisfaction. In 1947, when General Motors was also under attack by liberals and unionists, company president Charles Wilson organized a hugely successful contest, in which employees were invited to write on the theme "My Job and Why I Like It." Like the Wal-Mart testimonials, the GM contest, for which winning workers took home Chevys, Cadillacs, and GM-made refrigerators, was controlled by the corporate PR department. However, there are some striking differences in tone and substance. GM employees, mainly family men, valued their work for its security, its career-building potential, and for the high pay.[56]

Many of the Wal-Mart responses evoke similar themes, especially those written by home office personnel in Bentonville. But a far larger sample spoke of the rewards of the "family" Wal-Mart evokes—a family experience that is either missing or damaged in their own personal lives. Wal-Mart redeems and makes whole; it generates a sense of community and obligation. Tammy, a home office financial analyst whose husband was deployed in Iraq, wrote, "Wal-Mart truly has become my second family."[57] Virdia, who works in a San Angelo, Texas, store, thanked her "Wal-Mart family at Store 601" for their help, financial and emotional, when her uninsured adult daughter was diagnosed with breast cancer.[58] Suzanne, another financial planner at the home office, recalled the "outpouring of love" that came from her "Wal-Mart family" when her thirty-four-year-old husband died of a heart attack.[59] A loss prevention associate in Union City, Georgia, asserted, "All of the negative feedback and criticism that I read in the news has no effect on me. . . . I am confident that we, as a family, will overcome the obstacles that stand in our way. . . . I do not think that I could have learned the life lessons that I have gathered anywhere else but here, and for that, I stand by my Wal-Mart."[60]

Often employee testimonials recall moments when an illness or accident generated a crisis, after which Wal-Mart's health insurance paid most of the bills. Although all employees with insurance paid a portion of the premium and a sometimes sizable deductible, none of the associate letters that Wal-Mart chose to post labeled the reimbursements they received as an entitlement or a routine insurance payout. Rather, the Wal-Mart workers saw the sometimes large health insurance payments as something close to an act of corporate benevolence. After incurring more than forty-five thousand dollars in medical bills, Laurie, who works in merchandising at the home office, wrote, "Thank you, Lee Scott!"[61]

AN EVANGELICAL COMPANY

Evangelical Protestantism has become embedded in Wal-Mart's corporate culture. Even the most casual observers of the company are aware of those well-publicized instances where Wal-Mart executives have jumped to bring their merchandising practices into accord with the wishes of vocal conservatives and influential evangelicals. This began in the 1980s, if not before. The company has banned everything from rap music to the best-selling diaries of rock star Kurt Cobain. In 1986, when the televangelist Jimmy Swaggart attacked Wal-Mart and Kmart for carrying magazines harmful to children, Wal-Mart banished some thirty-two titles including *Playboy* and *Rolling Stone*.[62] In the 1990s Wal-Mart reported that more than half its book sales were of Christian titles, which prompted a number of mainstream publishing houses to start their own religious/conservative imprints. Tyndale House, publisher of the *Left Behind* series, credits Wal-Mart with a pivotal role in turning the evangelical thriller *Armageddon* into the country's best-selling novel in 2003.[63] During that same year, Wal-Mart stopped selling the racy men's magazines *Maxim* and *Stuff* after years of pressure from groups like the Family Research Council and the Timothy Group, an organization of evangelical mutual fund investors based in Grand Rapids. Recently, Wal-Mart refused to sell the Plan B contraceptive until threatened with legal action.

Don Soderquist, for many years an executive close to Sam Walton, took it upon himself to be the foremost articulator of the Wal-Mart culture. In his 2005 memoir, *The Wal-Mart Way*, he wrote, "I'm not saying that Wal-Mart is a Christian company, but I can unequivocally say that Sam founded the company on the Judeo-Christian principles found in the Bible."[64] Actually, Walton took his Presbyterian identity rather lightly, and unlike Soderquist, who was a graduate of evangelical Wheaton College and who has contributed heavily to the Campus Crusade for Christ and like-minded Arkansas churches, the company founder thought that profit-sharing schemes and Ozark picnics were more central to the Wal-Mart ethos.[65] But even if corporate officers refrain from declaring Evangelicalism an explicit component of the Wal-Mart credo, Soderquist is right in emphasizing the extent to which Wal-Mart exists within a cultural universe that is Protestant.

Like the megachurches, the TV evangelists, and the Zig Ziglar motivational seminars, Wal-Mart links personal salvation to entrepreneurial success and social service to free enterprise.[66] At the Bentonville airport, the convenience store shelves books on Wal-Mart alongside the Christian self-help books of Ken Blanchard, Frank Warren, and Joel Osteen. The store manager grouped them all under the "motivational" rubric and noted that "They sell real well."

Indeed, Wal-Mart publications are full of stories of hard-pressed associates, once down on their luck, who find redemption, economic and spiritual, through dedication to the company. Conversely, much of the ethos of contemporary evangelical Protestantism has become thoroughly integrated into a world of capitalist markets and economic insecurities. For most evangelicals, indeed for most Americans, the market has been naturalized. The free market is seen as a well-designed instrument to reward Christian behavior and punish and humiliate the unrepentant. Class conflict and social disorder are the product of false ideas or opportunist leaders because God would not create a world at war with itself. Thus, ever since the nineteenth century, evangelicals have judged the business leader as a heroic figure, his wealth a triumph of righteous will.[67]

In *The Transformation of American Religion*, Alan Wolfe explains the extent to which both Wal-Mart and the new megachurches operate on some of the same sociological and ideological principles. They are huge centralized organizations, inspired by charismatic leaders, often located in the white suburbs and exurbs. Like Wal-Mart, they are concentrated in the Sun Belt and Midwest. Both are high-intensity experiences that value communality and informality but which are remarkably porous to those who move in and out of their organizational orbit. Wal-Mart has a huge turnover rate among new employees; the new churches put up few barriers to entrance or exit. They are nondenominational, they downplay theological orthodoxy, and they take a remarkably pluralistic approach to the lifestyle choices of most congregants. Both company and church deploy the latest telecommunications technology with great efficacy, but neither claims that expertise or education is of paramount importance. Wal-Mart, although highly dependent on the latest computer technologies, expresses indifference or outright disdain for formal education and technical expertise. "Just ordinary folks, doing extraordinary things" is a slogan often heard at home office meetings for the uninitiated.

And just as Wal-Mart's success is dependent upon its reflection of many of the cultural and social values of an exurban America that yearns for some mythic rural heritage, so too Evangelicalism's popularity is due as much to its populist and democratic urges—its determination to find out what believers want and offer it to them—as it is to certainties of the faith. As Wolfe puts it, the biggest challenge posed to American society by the popularity of the megachurches and other forms of growth-oriented Protestantism "is not bigotry but bathos. Television, publishing, political campaigning, education, self-help advice—all increasingly tell Americans what they already want to hear. Religion, it would seem, should now be added to that list." The church historian Randall Balmer sums it up: "Jesus will save your soul and your marriage, make you happy, heal your body, and even make you rich. Who wouldn't look twice at that offer?"[68]

SERVANT LEADERSHIP

Of course, Wal-Mart is not a church. It is a profitable business dependent upon the labor of almost 1.4 million Americans, the majority of whom are poorly paid and closely supervised. To make this system work, Wal-Mart can hardly rely solely on a rural sentimentality or a spirit of Evangelicalism. The company needs tens of thousands of store managers and their assistants, whose own careers depend upon keeping labor costs down, productivity up, and profits on target. These managers are motivated and constrained by an elaborate set of guidelines and metrics that flow from Bentonville to every one of the four-thousand-plus domestic Wal-Mart stores. But these managers also work within an ideological/theological framework that has been pioneered by Wal-Mart. It is called "servant leadership."

Wal-Mart celebrates selfless service, to the customer, the community, and the company. The 1991 *Sam's Associate Handbook* declared that Wal-Mart "believes management's responsibility is to provide leadership that serves the associate. Managers must support, encourage and provide opportunities for associates to be successful. Mr. Sam calls this 'Servant Leadership.'"[69] That phrase, with its subtle Christian connotation, is a staple part of the Wal-Mart culture, adopted in recent years by a growing number of vendors as well. Between 1990 and 1992, Wal-Mart annual reports listed company directors under the rubric "Board of Servant Leaders."[70] In 1999, when H. Lee Scott was being groomed to take over the company, Joe Hardin, a former Sam's Club executive, then CEO of Kinko's, told *Discount Store News*, "Lee is a great Wal-Mart person. He is someone who has grown up in the culture, and he openly communicates and listens to other people's ideas. He is a true servant leader who knows how to build a team and get them to work together."[71]

The "servant leader" idea did not in fact have an explicitly Protestant origin. Its author was Robert K. Greenleaf, a career personnel director at AT&T who rose to become head of that corporation's management research before he retired in 1964. Greenleaf was caught up in the intellectual ferment of the late 1960s, and in particular the need of large organizations like the telephone company to find new sources of institutional legitimacy to win the allegiance of both customers and employees. Older motivational ideas emphasizing personal security, organizational efficiency, and career enhancement seemed to be losing their appeal as the spirit of the times seeped even into the most traditional enterprises. So Greenleaf founded the Center for Applied Ethics in his native Indiana and in 1970 wrote *The Servant as Leader*. Servant leadership emphasized a holistic approach to work, a sense of community, teamwork, and a sharing of power in decision making. The Lilly Endowment funded the early work of Greenleaf and his followers, but the servant leader concept has been popularized by business writers, some with an explicitly evangelical orientation, like Ken Blanchard, Steven Covey, and Larry Spears.[72]

It is precisely this kind of Christian teamwork that has become the functional ideology for those millions of megachurch goers, from the Carolinas to Orange County, who constitute the vast reservoir from which labor-intensive companies like Wal-Mart draw their managerial cadre and loyal employees. In an economy increasingly devoted to sales, service, and commoditization of the self, the servant leader idea rationalizes self-exploitation and lends a sacerdotal air to the corporate hierarchy. "Thank you to Jesus Christ for he is the one that gives me the Servant Leadership," avowed a store manager to higher-ranking executives at a Wal-Mart meeting in the mid-1990s. "He is the ultimate example of Servant Leadership and then Mr. Sam closely follows."[73] Likewise, a Sam's Club executive hardly thought of himself as a cynic when he told a group of company managers, "Servant Leadership is our way of managing people. . . . It's the difference between one person trying to run a club, rather than a hundred and fifty people supporting one person to run a club."[74]

The concept has been valued and refined at Wal-Mart.[75] In the *Wal-Mart Associate Handbook* of 1993, when the company had just overtaken Sears as the largest retailer in the nation, several paragraphs are devoted to the meaning of servant leadership. An effort was made, since abandoned, to abolish the word "management" in favor of the phrase "coaching team." "Wal-Mart believes that we should provide leadership that serves each associate. Your Coach is there to guide, support, encourage and provide opportunities for every associate to be successful. These principles are known as Servant Leadership. . . . Sam taught his Coaching team to visualize an upside-down pyramid. The Coach is at the bottom of the pyramid supporting and maintaining a balance for the rest of the pyramid, our hourly associates."[76]

The servant leadership concept is a particularly important motivator at the lower reaches of the management hierarchy. Store managers and assistant managers have the toughest job in the company because they are responsible for meeting the sales targets and expense ratios that Bentonville's computers relentlessly put before them each week. Their work requires no prior expertise, no formal education other than the capacity to read, write, and understand arithmetic. The job is essentially one of labor management, conducted with more sticks than carrots, more actual sweat than inspirational speeches. These managers must accommodate the insistent demands that flow down from the district manager, at the same time keeping the shelves stocked, the cash registers staffed, and the store profits growing. Store managers constantly feel squeezed, and when workers quit, the managers have to fill in the gaps. The job is difficult, the hours long—the salaried workweek is often sixty hours—and the career prospects not always golden. Yet Wal-Mart needs dedicated people, enthusiasts and warriors who will throw themselves into the job. "Servant leadership" is an ideology that fits the requirements of this kind of work.

It is a plastic concept, however, and the meaning of the servant leadership idea has shifted over the years. After the company faced both a union organizing effort and multiple waves of public criticism targeting its low pay and high turnover, Wal-Mart announced in 2007 that some thirteen thousand four hundred hourly workers with more than twenty years of service would take home an extra week's pay, a "Servant Leadership Bonus," perhaps designed to compensate for the wage caps the company imposed on veteran employees just the year be-fore.[77] By this point Wal-Mart had reverted to the use of the word "management" or "supervisor" in place of the phrase "coach-ing team." But the company continued to emphasize the servant leadership concept, especially in tandem with an explanation of Wal-Mart's open-door grievance policy, seen as a key bul-wark against the trade union threat.[78] Indeed, in the employee handbooks published at the height of the union's campaign, an explanation of the servant leadership concept immediately pre-cedes and directly serves as a rationale for the company's aggres-sive anti-unionism, to wit, "It is our position that every Associate can speak for himself or herself without having to pay hard-earned money to a union in order to be listened to and have issues resolved."[79]

REPRODUCING THE WAL-MART CULTURE

It is one thing to formulate a distinctive corporate culture, but it proved quite another to preserve and reproduce that set of ideological beliefs and organizational structures beyond Wal-Mart's home territory. Wal-Mart has succeeded, however. Dur-ing its years of rapid expansion the company did not leapfrog into the rich but culturally alien suburban markets, but spread like molasses, building stores through tier after tier of rural and exurban counties. Although Wal-Mart was opening or acquir-ing hundreds of stores in the early 1980s, the average distance of a new store from Bentonville was still less than three hun-dred miles. Moreover, Wal-Mart recruited executive talent al-most exclusively from the south-central states: after the death of Sam Walton, the company's next two CEOs were David Glass, a graduate of Southwest Missouri State University, and Lee Scott of Pittsburg State University in Kansas.[80]

When Wal-Mart did place its stores farther than a hard drive from northwest Arkansas, the high degree of centralization ensured that the Bentonville message would not be diluted. Compared with its competitors, Wal-Mart has always concentrated a far higher proportion of all its managers at the home office. As late as 1999, after the company had already put stores in Maine, Alaska, and California, 15 percent of all Wal-Mart salaried managers, more than six thousand, still worked out of the company's Bentonville headquarters. This was almost twice the ratio that Sears had in Chicago or Target employed in Minneapolis.[81] By this time, Wal-Mart had replaced its ramshackle collection of small propeller planes with a modern fleet of corporate jets, enabling almost all its regional managers to live in Arkansas, even as they administered a far-flung retail territory. The company's yearly annual meeting extravaganza in Fayetteville and its weekly Saturday morning managerial show-and-tell put the top brass, scores of middle managers, and a selected group of lesser folk together in a ritualized setting that may be "quaint and hokey," but which to a visiting *Fortune* reporter "makes the world's largest enterprise continue to feel as small and folksy as Bentonville." And "whatever makes Wal-Mart feel smaller and folksier," he wrote, "only makes it stronger."[82]

STUDENTS IN FREE ENTERPRISE

The story of a Wal-Mart front group, Students in Free Enterprise, demonstrates the potency of such an ideology-cum-theology when coupled with a retail organization seeking to recruit and promote a workforce that shares its vision and values. In the early 1980s, Wal-Mart faced a recruitment crisis. With more than a hundred new stores opening each year, the company had to hire or promote upwards of a thousand managers or management trainees to staff them. Wal-Mart faltered. Recruitment from within meant the promotion of a lot of women, which ran headlong into those Wal-Mart family values that tilted toward small-town patriarchy. Of course, the company's sexism had its own logic. The feminist revolution had barely reached middle America, which meant that the kind of women who worked for Wal-Mart were still largely responsible for rearing the children, putting dinner on the table, and taking care of elderly family members. Most were not about to relocate to a distant town in order to move up Wal-Mart's unpredictable managerial ladder. But if Wal-Mart promoted them into management in their hometown store, they were likely to be poor disciplinarians. How were they to "coach" old friends and relatives who had once shared gossip in the break room?[83]

So Wal-Mart looked to the universities to recruit a new generation of managers. But here they faced another problem. Few freshly minted MBAs were going take an arduous assistant manager job, and even the undergraduate business majors at the big schools became frustrated when they found that Wal-Mart had little use for their accounting and marketing skills. The solution was to search for a fresh cohort of management trainees in the denominational colleges and the branch campuses of the state universities, where diligence, Christianity, and modest career expectations were already the norm. Wal-Mart wanted the B and C students, the organization men, the undergraduates who were the first in their family to take college courses.

Wal-Mart sent recruiters to small middle South colleges, worked with established organizations like the Distributive Education Clubs of America, and advertised on cable, at local military bases, and in area churches. However, Wal-Mart would soon recruit as many as a third of its management trainees from the ranks of a dynamic new group, Students in Free Enterprise (SIFE), which claimed a presence on more than seven hundred U.S. campuses by the end of the century.[84]

SIFE had its origins in Dallas early in the 1970s at the moment when the conservative Texas establishment began an aggressive and successful pushback against the cultural and political liberalism that threatened to inject "antibusiness attitudes in college and university classrooms," even in the Lone Star state. William Seay, chairman of the Southwestern Life Insurance Company, was a key figure in this effort. Well connected among the Dallas elite, Seay was an owner of the Texas Rangers, a board member of the Billy Graham Evangelistic Association, a founder of the modern Republican Party in Texas, and a patron of the political careers of both Texas Bushes.[85] He first funded the Youth Leadership Institute in 1970, designed to educate a generation of campus leaders and activists in winning elections for conservatives. It would metamorphose over the next few decades into a Washington-based training school for tens of thousands of Republican operatives and policy makers.[86]

In SIFE, founded in 1975, Seay sought to build a youth group specifically designed to defend and staff American business. At the first meeting, one hundred Texas undergraduates were brought to the Inn of the Six Flags at Arlington, just outside Dallas, "to discover and discuss what they might do to counteract the stultifying criticism of American business which was flowing from the campus, the press, and elsewhere, seeking to tear down the very system which gave the critics their jobs and their warm, comfortable homes." Thereafter, Seay and his aids established the basic structure of SIFE: campus chapters mentored by ideologically committed management or economics teachers, annual competitions where sympathetic business executives judged student presentations and skits, and the simultaneous recruitment by those same corporate sponsors of the bright young talent on display. Seay allocated the grant of $2,500 that went to the winning college. The event "provided an opportunity for me to strengthen my belief that our country will be left in good hands," wrote one participating executive to Seay.[87]

The Texas SIFE created by Seay and his corporate friends was naturally linked to the state's oil, gas, manufacturing, and real estate businesses. As they boomed, so did SIFE, acquiring up to one hundred corporate sponsors in just a few years. But then the oil bust of the early 1980s dried up both the spare change Texas corporations had showered on these young free enterprisers and the entry-level jobs they sought. Corporate sponsorship dropped off, leaving SIFE in the lurch. If an evangelical brand of modern pro-capitalist ideology were to find new champions, it would be unlikely to arise among those businessmen who were struggling to survive within the crisis prone industries of petro-America.

SIFE therefore shifted its base of operations from Texas to the heart of Wal-Mart country, to Southwest Baptist University in Bolivar, Missouri, not far from Springfield and Bentonville. There, a freshly minted attorney and SIFE faculty adviser, Alvin Rohrs, took over the organization in 1983. Southwest Baptist was a natural fit. Like so many other hard-pressed denominational colleges in the South, SBU, "an evangelical university with roots stemming from a longstanding Baptist heritage," had recently added vocational and business programs to its Christian educational mission. This combination fit Wal-Mart's needs as well, and within a year the company had taken SIFE under its wing. Thereafter, every chairperson of SIFE was either an executive from Wal-Mart or one of the retailer's key vendor collaborators. Sam Walton put up the money to fund twenty-five faculty "Free Enterprise Fellows," Jack Shewmaker, another top company executive, persuaded scores of Wal-Mart suppliers to support SIFE operations, and William Seay joined the Wal-Mart board, symbolizing the friendly character of this corporate acquisition. SIFE flourished.[88]

SIFE remains an ideological formation that propagandizes on behalf of free market capitalism within the conservative Christian world nurtured at places like College of the Ozarks, Harding University, and John Brown University, all in Arkansas; Southwest Baptist and Drury in southwest Missouri; East

Texas Baptist University; and Union College in Kentucky. SIFE rarely has a presence at the flagship state universities, but the second- and third-tier public colleges, like Chico State (California), Pittsburg State University (Kansas), Colorado State at Pueblo, and University of North Florida are more likely to sponsor SIFE "teams."[89]

Their activities during the school year are essentially ideological and propagandistic: the students develop skits, games, and exercises, often for use in elementary and middle schools, which explain and justify markets, entrepreneurship, deregulation, low taxes, and business ethics. Wal-Mart's Don Soderquist explained that the retailer supported SIFE because "young people today are being given an opportunity to understand really—not what capitalism is, because I cringe a little bit with the word 'capitalism,' but what free enterprise is and how it fits with the democracy that we enjoy in these United States."[90] Thus the development of actual business skills, like accounting or sales techniques, is largely ignored. Instead, reported one disillusioned Canadian student, "they were essentially doing missionary work and substituting free markets for religion."[91]

Like Wal-Mart, which always has a couple of its top executives on the SIFE board, the organization does not openly celebrate a neoliberal world of naked self-interest and Darwinian struggle. SIFE skits and presentations are not a remake of the Reagan-era film *Wall Street* in which Gordon Gekko, played by Michael Douglas, preached that "greed is good." Instead the organization prepares students for entry-level management posts by linking the collegiate quest for self-esteem and humanitarian good works to an opportunity for career advancement and an ideology of market capitalism. SIFE's slogan is "Changing the World," and its statement of principles declares, "We believe that the best way to improve the lives of others is through Free Enterprise practiced morally." Propagated successfully, this is just the kind of philosophy needed to generate the dedicated and youthful cadre Wal-Mart requires to staff its ever-expanding retail empire. The "student" group therefore has a coveted place on the official Wal-Mart Web site as well as in the company's internal "Pipeline," where job openings are posted.[92]

SIFE is highly centralized and hugely ambitious. During the early years of the twenty-first century it had a budget of nearly $5 million with over fifty people on the payroll. The SIFE board is largely comprised of executives from firms with the largest stake in the Wal-Mart supply network, plus a few specialty retailers, like Walgreens, Office Depot, and RadioShack, whose businesses mimic the methods of the Bentonville monarch. Wal-Mart puts only about two hundred thousand dollars a year directly into SIFE; the rest comes from the two hundred or so Wal-Mart vendors who are eager to curry favor with Bentonville. "Wal-Mart always finds the most economical way to do everything, and we're an economical way to get talent," says Alvin Rohrs of SIFE.[93] And as Wal-Mart expands abroad, so too does SIFE, which now claims campus "teams" at more than six hundred foreign schools, mentoring young people in free enterprise in the republics of the former Soviet Union, in South Africa, throughout Britain, and above all in East Asia, which is capitalism's most dynamic frontier. SIFE claims to be growing rapidly in the Philippines, Malaysia, and South Korea, and it has established itself at twenty-nine universities in China.[94]

Thus Wal-Mart's entrepreneurial success can hardly be divorced from the ideology and culture that has sustained it. Just as conservative America is defined by far more than its politics, so too is Wal-Mart a product of a great deal more than a clever business model turbocharged by the most sophisticated advances in telecommunications technology. Secular America once thought that the industrialization and urbanization of the countryside would extend to the South and Midwest a way of life linked to political liberalism, gender equality, and social mobility. But Wal-Mart has demonstrated that the technological and organizational avant-garde can coexist, even thrive, within a world in which patriarchy, evangelical religion, and a faux communalism reproduce themselves.

The social upheavals that transformed American agriculture at midcentury and the U.S. manufacturing economy a few decades later did not just provide Wal-Mart with a huge supply of eager workers. These psychic and social disasters left in their wake a set of values and visions that proved highly useful to the retail revolution Wal-Mart was about to launch. For many employees, as well as some customers, Wal-Mart has represented the community ethos and family values that have been so frequently distended and devalued by the social and economic churn that has characterized American life in recent decades. Many women found a new site of sociability and in return offered the company their heartfelt loyalty; and for a sizable number of young men displaced by agricultural consolidation or factory dislocation, the management of a store replaced the proprietorship of a farm or small business as a road to dignity and respect.

Wal-Mart therefore stands at the center of a service economy in which interpersonal relationships, between managers and workers, salespeople and customers, even buyers and vendors, are all important. Only their wholehearted dedication generates the kind of devoted, empathetic, psychologically humane engagement that defines quality work in the service economy. As the sociologist Nicole Biggart, the author of *Charismatic Capitalism*, puts it, "Physical labor can be extracted through supervision, but intellectual, emotional, and morally committed labor is more elusive. It requires commitment to ideals as well as routines and to people as well as positions."[95]

Sam Walton evoked this kind of fervent commitment. But

Walton died in 1992, nearly a decade after his creation had broken out of its southern homeland. How would his associates fare in a company that was now the largest and most competitive retailer in the world?

CHAPTER FOUR

BEAT YESTERDAY

By the 1990s Wal-Mart's distinctive sense of its own culture faced a powerful enemy of its own creation: the corporation's relentless emphasis upon a profit-driven workplace in which store managers have every incentive to squeeze the maximum amount of labor out of their associates. This has generated a schizophrenic tension within the company that periodically bursts into public view when Wal-Mart is found guilty of gross violations of U.S. labor, immigration, and safety laws. Top executives tell their store managers both to obey all these statutes and to adhere to a demanding set of workforce guidelines from the home office. But Sam Walton built his corporation upon an ingrained resistance to the Yankee-inspired laws that regulate the American workplace, and Wal-Mart provides plenty of tangible rewards—big bonuses for store managers and their district supervisors—for those who ignore the laws and hold labor costs in check. In fact, as dozens of successful wage and hour lawsuits brought against Wal-Mart in the past decade strongly suggest, company policies effectively pressured tens of thousands of managers and their assistants into becoming lawbreakers. This situation is exacerbated by the recruitment of a new generation of retail workers whose aspirations and expectations were formed in metropolitan America and are therefore quite different from those of the grateful midcentury

Wal-Mart employees who were just one generation off the farm.

Many of these tensions were apparent in the experience of Dale Stiles, who took a job with Wal-Mart in 1992. Stiles, a manager at BellSouth for more than twenty-five years, enjoyed his work in the sporting goods department of the local Wal-Mart in Hot Springs, Arkansas. With the phone company's managerial pension flowing into his bank account, Stiles's retail sojourn was a bit of a lark. He knew sports, liked to socialize, and was good at selling things. Stiles admired Wal-Mart's technological proficiency, and he marveled at the company's enormous growth. He wanted to figure out how it all worked, get a feel for what it was like to be a Wal-Mart associate.

Stiles described his political outlook as "very conservative." He got on well with his supervisors and enjoyed the work. Unlike at the phone company, there was no union—Stiles liked that—and the roles and tasks at Wal-Mart seemed far more flexible and changeable. But he noted a couple of things about how a Wal-Mart store operated that puzzled and appalled him. Most wages were just above the legal minimum. Moreover Stiles was "shock[ed]" by the rigid policy that limited almost all hourly associates to but thirty-four hours a week. Overtime was a "deadly sin in Wally World, as bad as being short of money in your cash register when the store closes at night." Stiles calculated that this combination kept the wages of an average associate with one year of service at about 40 percent of the median family income in Arkansas, hardly a high bar in itself.[1] But Wal-Mart was not sheepish about the low pay. A poster in the employee lounge explained it this way:

AN ASSOCIATE WITH ONE YEAR OF SERVICE EARNS AN AVERAGE OF $4.60 PER HOUR. BUT THEY ALSO GET:

FICA	$.3455
LIFE INSURANCE	.0060
STOCK PURCHASE	.0438
PROFIT SHARING	.3680
HOLIDAY PAY	.1239
SICK LEAVE	.1062
HEALTH INSURANCE	.1870
ASSOCIATE DISCOUNT	.0577
VACATION PAY	.1769

SO THE ASSOCIATE REALLY EARNS A TOTAL OF $6.015 PER HOUR

Stiles later wrote that most companies don't consider such "overhead" part of what a worker earns. It is undoubtedly a labor cost, but some of it is mandated by the government and a good deal of it will become part of the employee's income only many years hence, or under circumstances, such as an illness, when one is burdened by so many other expenses that few people think of it as income at all. The poster seemed a graphic representation of Wal-Mart's distaste for the entire New Deal system of social provision, which added to the base wage of most American workers, including those employed by the billion-dollar corporations at the core of the economy, a set of public-private entitlements that companies have generally accepted as the cost of doing business. Hence Wal-Mart's prohibition against overtime pay, which workers in so many other industries had come to count upon to fatten their paychecks, and the company's decision against establishment of a pension plan, even in the 1970s when pensions were still common in the corporate world. Instead, Wal-Mart opted for profit sharing as a substitute, but this plan hardly represented much of a social compact with its employees. When Stiles picked up a copy of the company's *Associate Handbook*, he found out why. The key passage read: "Although the Company expects to continue the Plan indefinitely, it may terminate the Plan at any time."[2]

The second remarkable thing that Stiles noticed about working in a Wal-Mart store was that there were hardly any managers, people on a salary who supervised and evaluated his work. The Hot Springs store employed 235 associates, of whom but five took down a salary, the store manager and his four assistants. At Stiles's old employer, the phone company, every twenty workers had a managerial supervisor, and in most manufacturing plants a foreman was responsible for no more than fifteen or eighteen employees. But at Wal-Mart the ratio was more like one to sixty, which meant that Stiles might see the store manager or the assistant manager for just a few minutes each day. We were "essentially unsupervised," he later remarked.[3]

However, the absence of a hectoring supervisor hardly meant that Wal-Mart workers escaped the pressure to "produce." Then again, what exactly was production in a discount retail store? In a factory, it is easy enough to count the output of cars or canned goods, and if someone slacks off on the job, production itself declines. At Ford in the early years, foremen knew how to shout "Hurry up!" in a dozen languages. Managers there could tally the precise number of cars built each hour and how many workers it required to do so. And should enough people fail to show up on an assembly line, it ground to a halt.

Not so in retail, where production, the sales of any given store on any given day, is relatively independent of the number of workers who are scheduled, or who actually show up, during each work shift. A Wal-Mart discount store is not like the Sears of old, where a clever salesman could persuade a customer to buy the more expensive dishwasher, or the contemporary high-fashion boutique, where a saleswoman's observation that a particular dress compliments the figure can make the sale and generate a substantial commission. Sales volume at Wal-Mart is more like a river whose course can be charted, measured, and forecast, but over which individual store managers have little day-to-day influence. However labor costs, the actual hourly pay and the total number of associate hours needed to staff the cash registers, straighten the shelves, and unpack the stock are very much theirs to control. This means that Wal-Mart managers are relentlessly and mercilessly graded on their capacity to hold labor costs below a fixed ratio of the sales generated by their store in any given week. And it is this hypersensitive ratio that defines and measures "production" in a discount store. Should it rise beyond the limits set by the home-office computers, the hours worked by associates are slashed, wages are frozen, and the regional vice president tells the store manager to relinquish his keys and find another job.

"WE MUST HAVE CHEAP HELP"

Because retail is such an enormously labor-intensive industry, keeping a lid on the price and volume of labor is the easiest way to boost the bottom line. Wal-Mart has sought to hold wages and benefits to a slim 10 percent of sales, compared with 11–13 percent at other discount store retailers. This doesn't sound like much, but when an individual Wal-Mart Supercenter generates $100 million per year, a competitive advantage of 1 or 2 percent represents $1 million or $2 million that can be used to keep prices low, boost profits, and fatten bonus checks for store managers.[4]

"We must have cheap help or we cannot sell cheap goods," wrote Frank W. Woolworth to his store managers in 1892, when his chain of five-and-dimes had but a handful of outlets. "When a clerk gets so good she can get better wages elsewhere, let her go. . . . It may look hard to some of you for us to pay such small wages but . . . one thing is certain: we cannot afford to pay good wages and sell goods as we do now, and our clerks ought to know it."[5] Sam Walton understood this as well. As he wrote in his memoir, "No matter how you slice it in the retail business, payroll is one of the most important parts of overhead, and overhead is one of the most crucial things you have to fight to maintain your profit margin. That was true then, and it is still true today." By his own admission, Walton was a "chintzy" employer in the early years. Since all retail clerks were exempt from the federal minimum wage law in the 1950s, Walton could pay as little as fifty cents an hour, which was a rock-bottom wage even for small-town Arkansas. When in 1955 Charlie Baum, the manager of Walton's Fayetteville Ben Franklin, gave his "girls" a twenty-five-cent an hour raise, Sam was immediately on the phone: "Charlie, we don't give raises of a quarter an hour. We give them a nickel an hour."[6]

But all this changed in the early 1960s. Like the domestics and farmworkers whom the southern political and economic elite had excluded from coverage under New Deal social legislation in the 1930s, the chain stores, backstopped by a Republican–southern Democratic alliance in Congress, waged a bitter rearguard battle to exempt some 4 million retail workers, mainly white women, from minimum wage guidelines.[7] John F. Kennedy made a raise and an extension of the minimum wage for retail workers one of the key issues in his quest for the presidency, while conservative Republicans, led by Senator Barry Goldwater, the Arizona department store heir, denounced the idea.[8]

Kennedy and the liberals won this round, although the new law faced tough going in the rural South, where the $1.15-an-hour minimum almost doubled the going rate for female clerks. Sam Walton, for one, hated the new minimum wage law, and he would simply not abide by it. Of course, Walton's attitude was not unusual for a white southerner of this era. If their seniority-rich representatives in Congress failed to stanch a law they thought unfair to the racial or labor arrangements characteristic of their region, many otherwise law-abiding southerners simply violated it. And Walton thought he saw a loophole that fit his business practices.

The new minimum wage law exempted all retail establishments whose annual sales were less than $1 million a year, a ceiling lowered to $250,000 in 1965 when Congress was briefly controlled by liberal Democrats. Taken as a whole, Walton's chain had sales well above this limit, but as he expanded into the discount sector in the 1960s, he created a series of single-store, family-dominated corporate shells, each with a slightly different ownership structure. Initially, these had been designed as a vehicle by which store managers, local investors, and members of the Robson family could contribute their capital to the cash-short Walton chain. By the 1960s this increasingly baroque ownership structure also had the decided benefit of allowing Walton to duck under the new minimum wage sales standard. This saved him a lot of money, because in 1968 the minimum wage had climbed to its twentieth-century apogee, but Walton could employ, at "pin money" wages, thousands of women who were pouring off Arkansas and Missouri farms during the years when the revolution in American agriculture belatedly reached the Ozark plateau.[9]

When the courts finally ruled that his decentralized ownership structure was but a scheme to avoid the new wage and hour law, Walton and most of his store managers were furious. They hated the assistant district attorney from Fort Smith who pressed the case, because, as one manager put it, now "dingbats in the store would be making $1.15 an hour." When a court order called for Walton to issue checks to the clerks at his stores in Harrison, Rogers, and Springdale for back pay, including a double-time penalty for what they had lost, he told a meeting of his employees, "I'll fire anyone who cashes the check." Cooler heads soon prevailed, but Walton's determination to hold the line on his labor costs had hardly softened.[10] Nor had his contempt for the regulatory state and its laws.

If in the 1960s Walton bowed to the minimum wage law ever so reluctantly, his successors have devoted enormous skill and energy to the avoidance or emasculation of almost every other governmental mandate, some originating in the Progressive era, that sought to regulate the price and quality of the labor that Wal-Mart workers offer their employer. Indeed, Wal-Mart's managerial ethos is fundamentally allergic to almost all the most taken-for-granted workplace reforms and regulations of the twentieth century: the Wagner Act, the 1935 statute designed to facilitate trade unionism in private-sector workplaces, as well as workmen's compensations laws, unemployment insurance, overtime pay, and the civil rights laws governing race, gender, age, marital status, and disability.

BEAT YESTERDAY

Store managers, over six thousand of them worldwide, are the key figures responsible for making the Wal-Mart system work.[11] Actually, the word "manager" is a bit of a misnomer for this job, because the hyperintegration of the Wal-Mart supply chain has stripped them of so much of the discretion that once came with the job. When Sam Walton ran his Ben Franklin franchise stores in the 1950s, he managed every aspect of the business and chafed mightily at the guidelines laid down by Butler Brothers in Chicago. Later, Walton kept a close watch on the managers who ran his early Wal-Mart discount stores, but since his own purchasing system was often chaotic and opportunistic, a store manager in Harrison, Fort Smith, or Jonesboro had authority to snap up a wholesaler's closeout deal or take delivery of large quantities of an item at a seasonally low price. Walton hired most of these early store managers from the competition, they were encouraged to buy into the business, and they were in almost daily contact with Mr. Sam himself.[12]

All this changed as Wal-Mart became an efficient selling machine. From the increasingly lofty perspective of the Bentonville home office, these hundreds, later thousands, of salaried store managers looked like a regiment of foot soldiers, there to take orders and "execute 100 percent." Walton created new layers of management during the years of frantic growth in the 1970s. A district manager came to supervise six to eight stores; above these district managers were the regional vice presidents in charge of seventy or eighty stores. And in Bentonville there emerged the powerful home-office complex responsible for worldwide purchasing, logistics, and strategic planning. Replenishment and supply—Wal-Mart calls it the "perpetual inventory" system—have long since been automated and centralized. Store managers have the authority to lower the price on some slow-moving items, but 98 percent of all sales, prices, quantities, and delivery dates are out of their hands. Bentonville issues "modulars" to every store, which detail the precise layout of the aisles and merchandise and specify the exact height of the shelves, the location of the pegs, and the number of items of each product on each shelf. Home-office computers monitor every purchase, reorder the basic commodities, and note high-volume items to keep them in stock. If an employee fails to close a freezer door in the grocery section, the home office registers it in real time.[13] Region, culture, and demography have some impact on the kind and quantity of goods sold by each store, but the Bentonville data-processing system can easily slice and dice these variations. Even the thermostats are controlled by the home office.

Wal-Mart is, however, in the mainstream of American management practice. Since the early-twentieth-century days of efficiency expert Frederick Taylor and GM president Alfred

Sloan, business firms have sought an organizational structure that combined a decision-making "general staff" with something close to a militarized organization in the field, structured to quickly and uniformly put into effect the instructions that flowed from the executive headquarters. In recent years, some U.S. companies have experimented with a degree of decentralization and outsourcing, but not Wal-Mart.

The same information technology that enables Wal-Mart to trace the global flow of sodas and soap can also cheaply and accurately control a million daily personnel decisions in thousands of dispersed workplaces. Firms like Wal-Mart, McDonald's, and Jiffy Lube succeed by endlessly reproducing, in an amoeba-like fashion, a thoroughly well-tested and standardized selling unit. Business school academics call such companies "replicator organizations" because of their single-minded focus on uniformity, growth, and interchangeability, of both product and personnel. For the store managers they have crafted an "electronic leash" that makes it feasible for executives at Bentonville and elsewhere to monitor hundreds of real-time activities at every store location: How many hours did the clerks work in hardware? Have the assistant managers filled out all of their performance reviews? What is the turnover rate for cashiers with less than one year on the job? All big firms record such data, but Wal-Mart is obsessive in its quest for knowledge and control.[14]

But the Wal-Mart electronic leash is not designed to turn the store manager into an automaton. "Some people might say the three most important things in retailing today are store manager, store manager and store manager," reported Wal-Mart vice president Don Shinkle in the mid-1990s.[15] Despite all the controls and restrictions, Wal-Mart managers must be creative and resourceful in the successful accomplishment of one essential task: the recruitment, scheduling, supervision, and disciplining of a labor force on a payroll budget that almost always seems inadequate to the task. The base pay of a Wal-Mart store manager is about sixty thousand dollars a year, but managers can triple that if they "hit their numbers," that is, the ratio between the sales generated each year by their store and the labor budget mandated by Bentonville. But this task is formidable. Sam Walton always carried a book in his back pocket that he called his "Beat Yesterday Book," a brief statistical reminder of sales and expenses designed as an ever-present prod, pushing his managers to improve on last year's figures. "We had numbers to hit," remembered Larry English, who became a store manager in 1970 at the age of twenty. "Mr. Walton was a numbers man. If he called you at eight a.m. on Saturday, you better know your sales for the week, by day. And you by damn better know what your payroll [cost] was, by percent of sales."[16] Store managers who allowed their labor budget to get out of hand might find themselves in deep trouble, "busted down" to an assistant manager and transferred out of town. Even in the booming 1980s, 10 to 15 percent of all store managers were demoted each year.[17]

The "beat yesterday" mentality has, of course, long since been computerized and institutionalized. Bill Thomas, a former Wal-Mart manager interviewed by the sociologist Ellen Rosen, remembered: "Every morning I would go in and evaluate my sales for the week. I would do what's called 'forecasting.' For example, last year I did $1.2 million in sales. This year I think I can do $1.5 million. So I forecast a conservative percent increase or decrease, whatever my trend is, and then I key that into the computer. The computer spits out a daily payroll figure that is scaled and based on how much volume we did a day last year. It has last year's sales by hour and by department." And that information can be very detailed, reported Thomas. "I could tell you last year on July the 13th during the hours of 7 and 8 p.m. how much sales a store did and how much of it was rung up by Sally Jo, the cashier with the operator number 347, [within] that hour."[18]

A manager like Thomas would then figure out the "labor budget" for his store for the next three weeks: how many workers he could schedule, at what rates of pay, based on when they were available for work. Wal-Mart provides store managers with a computer-generated "preferred budget" which would allow them to hire adequately. But no store is actually allowed to staff for it because such an expense would slash the bonus and the career prospects for the store manger and his immediate superiors. For example, if a store increased its sales by 7 percent last year compared to the previous year, the goal is to save 0.1 percent of that increase during the next year. Thus the wage bill for the next year could not be budgeted to rise more than 6.9 percent. Not unexpectedly, Wal-Mart stores are chronically understaffed, operating with a "skeleton crew" that struggles to unload the trucks, stack the merchandise, clean the floors, and zone (tidy up) each department.[19]

Should a store actually exceed Bentonville's "preferred labor budget," all the other store managers in the same district are expected to tighten their own belts to make up the shortfall. Thus Joseph Hawkins, who was a Wal-Mart store manager in western Washington State during the 1990s, bore the brunt of the corporation's "zero tolerance" policy when it came to overtime pay. "Wal-Mart doesn't need associates who can't get the job done in 40 hours," he was told by his regional vice president. The pressure to avoid overtime was ever present, but especially intense during the slow winter months, and then again during the frenetic Christmas rush, "in order to maximize profits." When Hawkins's regional vice president thought wages in his area were "out of control," all the store managers would start getting "chain" phone calls two or three times a week; when overtime itself exceeded the guidelines projected by Bentonville's computers, the phone calls came every day.[20]

Wal-Mart managers therefore occupy the role of the factory foreman of old, the "man in the middle," who was squeezed from above by top management's demand for production and cost savings, and harassed from below by a seemingly unreliable workforce. To keep them engaged in the enterprise demands a skillful combination of seduction, discipline, and artifice. Thus if store managers have little control over wages and none over the benefits offered Wal-Mart employees, they do have a small basket of carrots that, if skillfully deployed, can win the loyalty and dedication of a core of long-service associates. Most Wal-Mart stores have three shifts, a morning stint that begins around 7 a.m. and ends in the early afternoon, an evening shift that lasts till 10 or 11 p.m., and an overnight shift, in which the main business is restocking the shelves and cleaning the floors. Part-timers and low-tenure associates are often stuck with the most chaotic and unpredictable schedules, "closing" the store after working the afternoon shift on one day, then "opening" it early in the morning on the next, and perhaps getting "short" hours at midweek. The afternoon shift is always the most inconvenient and unpredictable. Workers may clock in at a well-established hour, but the end of the workday is frequently a ragged affair, full of last-minute tasks, on or off the clock, that may extend into the very late hours of the night.

Getting a regular day shift is a prize that all Wal-Mart workers seek. So too is "full-time" work at the store, defined by Wal-Mart as thirty-four hours per week, which makes associates eligible to purchase company health insurance and participate in various bonus and profit-sharing programs. Most part-timers, who constitute at least 30 percent of the workforce, want full-time work, and almost all the full-timers want to increase their hours beyond thirty-four. Managers can purchase loyalty and hard work if they satisfy these mundane but vital aspirations, all the while maintaining a workforce whose flexible deployment is essential to the efficient operation of the store.[21]

This task became much more difficult when Wal-Mart announced its deployment of a computerized scheduling system in early 2007. Instead of having individual store managers post associate work times—a sometimes vexing task that can consume a dozen hours each week—home office computers now fire out a detailed work schedule for every store and every worker, based on the press of business, the availability of the associate, and a determination, prompted by a raft of successful multimillion-dollar legal claims against the company, that all Wal-Mart employees take their lunch breaks and avoid unpaid overtime. The new system has reduced the length of many checkout lines and slashed the time store managers spend on staffing schedules. But, for tens of thousands of Wal-Mart associates, computerized work scheduling has generated, in the words of one frontline personnel manager, "grief and heartbreak for people" as they find themselves subject to fluctuating work schedules that seem both unpredictable and inconvenient. "The cashiers are suffering. They have to fight for their hours." This is because those associates whose "availability" is not constrained by school, child care, or another job are the kind of "flexible" employees the home office computer program privileges, while those whose lives are more constrained find themselves scheduled for an increasing measure of part-time work.[22]

SOCIAL MOBILITY: ILLUSION OR REALITY

For single moms and other caregivers, assignment to a desirable shift is far more crucial than money, and becoming more so as Wal-Mart and the rest of the service sector run on a 24/7 schedule. Until the early 1990s Wal-Mart operated most of its stores just twelve hours a day, sometimes even closing on Sunday. But the twenty-four-hour cycle has now become the norm, especially in the big Supercenters, which keep staff on the registers and stockers in the aisles throughout the wee hours of the morning. Wal-Mart wants as many workers as possible to indicate that their "availability" is 24/7 or something close to that. So a tolerable shift becomes an important inducement to long service at a store like Wal-Mart. And if two or three members of the same family can find work in the same Wal-Mart, or one nearby, then household income rises accordingly even if the wages and benefits remain paltry. This seems to be a strategy adopted by an increasingly large number of employees, even in metropolitan areas, a work life arrangement encouraged by Wal-Mart management itself. Indeed, such intergenerational work and income sharing represents a return to the survival strategies of the nineteenth- and early-twentieth-century family, when children joined their parents to labor in the textile mill villages of the New South or in the canneries, bonanza farms, and coal mines of that same era, thereby piecing together an income sufficient to pay the rent and stock the pantry.

All this seemed evident when the *Fortune* reporter Mark Gimein visited a family of Wal-Mart workers in Madisonville, Kentucky, in 2002. By then most of the coal mines and light manufacturing plants had long since closed; the biggest employers were all in retail, county government, or at the hospital. The intertwined employment of the Salmon and Haynes families began when Alison Salmon, age twenty-two, took an entry-level job at the new Madisonville Supercenter, after which she persuaded her father's girlfriend, Stephanie Haynes, who had been injured while working a warehouse job, to try employment at Wal-Mart as well. Stephanie then brought in her own daughter Lynn, nineteen, who became a cashier, and boyfriend Tony Salmon, forty-four, who got a job on the night shift as a stocker. Meanwhile, Alison met and married Shane Alexander, then age twenty-two, who had started pushing carts at Wal-Mart in high school. After his graduation Shane moved inside and became manager of the hardware department. His future now seemed promising; Wal-Mart has traditionally tapped young men, with small-town roots, for its management trainee program, so when this 2002 story opened, Shane was busily at work completing the retailer's seventeen-week management training course. He seemed destined for a Wal-Mart career.[23]

But upward mobility at the company is a highly problematic affair. Wal-Mart has long boasted that a large proportion of its store managers—76 percent by latest count—come from the ranks of the hourly associates. Neither Sam Walton nor his successors put much stock in a college degree or in specialized training. The first requirement for promotion at Wal-Mart has always been commitment and dedication to the company and the job. Skill and knowledge are far less important than "attitude" and identification with the Wal-Mart culture. As seen from Bentonville, the Wal-Mart managerial hierarchy looks wonderfully open, a democratic stairway that is always full of eager and successful associates thrilled to have become part of the Wal-Mart family. And in this corporate world it is easy to find example after example of a well-paid store manager or of a well-placed executive who started his or her work life, fresh out of high school, as a cashier or stocker in some out-of-the-way discount store.

Ramona Muzingo, for example, graduated from a Santa Ana, California, high school in 1976, got married, followed her husband to Texas, had a son, and then worked in an ice cream parlor, a dress shop, and at State Farm Insurance, before she took a job as a part-time phone operator in a Porter, Texas, Wal-Mart. Her first promotion came a few months later when she headed up the candy and tobacco department there, after which she held a variety of hourly-paid jobs, including a stint in charge of the toy department lasting all "through the Cabbage Patch and Transformer period" in the mid-1980s. But by now Muzingo was divorced and the sole support of her child, so she needed a better-paying job. Luckily, she was well liked by her manager, who got her into Wal-Mart's assistant manager training program in a Houston store. Thereafter, Muzingo flourished. Moving from store to store in Texas, she made it to the managerial rank in the fall of 1992, when she got her first "metro 88," an eighty-eight-thousand-square-foot Plano, Texas, store located in the highly competitive Dallas metropolitan region. Next came management of a big, high-volume "122" in Lewisville and then a promotion to regional personnel manager in charge of Texas and four other south-central states. From there it was but a short jump to an executive personnel post at the home office in Bentonville, salary $139,000 in 2002.[24]

But if you look at the Wal-Mart managerial job hierarchy from the perspective of a cashier or an overnight stocker, the opportunities for advancement are very different. A typical discount store has about 250 employees; some Supercenters have 700 associates on the payroll. But salaried managers are few and far between, and the selection of a lowly associate for the coveted assistant manager trainee program seems like a gift from the gods. There are dozens of department heads, the men and women who are in charge of jewelry, sporting goods, clothing, fresh produce, hardware, and other departments. They may supervise several people, but they are still hourly employees making just two or three dollars more than a fresh-faced teenager. Unlike most offices, where a high proportion of the white-collar employees are on salary, or even a modern factory, where up to 20 percent of the jobs involve a good deal of well-paid skilled work, Wal-Mart has a pay hierarchy that is shaped like a short stack of pancakes with a long thin strawberry perched in the middle. Thus a huge Supercenter will employ, on salary, one manager, a comanager or two, and nine or ten assistant managers. Some hourly department heads do make the leap to assistant manager, but for the overwhelming majority an hourly post is the end of the line. These jobs often come with regular daytime hours, a tolerable routine, and a bit of respect from the store manager. But Wal-Mart has neither the interest nor the capacity to put many of these long-service women on the road to management. "Hourly Jobs, Salaried Careers" is how Wal-Mart itself phrased this dichotomy in an institutional advertisement broadcast during a recent series of Tavis Smiley shows.

Return, therefore, to the story of Stephanie Haynes and her extended family. When I talked with her on the phone in early 2006, she no longer worked at Wal-Mart; indeed she vowed never to shop at the store again. "It sucks," she told me. Haynes considered herself a good worker, with successful experience as a manager at Burger King. But like so many other middle-aged women, she faced the runaround when she sought admittance into the assistant manager training program. Until recently, promotion into management at Wal-Mart has required a "tap on the shoulder." The Impact Fund's highly publicized gender bias suit, *Dukes v. Wal-Mart*, has forced the company to post promotional openings on its internal "Pipeline," but managers still exercise almost complete discretion, and women with household responsibilities find themselves at a disadvantage because management training invariably requires them to move a considerable distance from their home store.[25] Even more pressing, Haynes failed in her repeated efforts to get a reassignment from the ragged swing shift to a daytime routine that began in the morning. Indeed, Haynes's "decision day"—Wal-Mart jargon for firing—came right after she had changed her "availability" from evening to daytime. She switched to protest the late and unpredictable hours, 4 a.m. in one instance, that her store manager insisted she work. Haynes had no trouble getting another retail job, at the local Kmart, but the pay was only six dollars an hour, just ten cents more than Wal-Mart paid when she began working there two and a half years before. Kmart was a more relaxed and easygoing place to work, but except for the

Christmas season, it could not give Stephanie enough hours to make it worth her while, so she quit in January 2005.[26]

The experience of the rest of the Haynes family demonstrates how the term "employee turnover" covers a multitude of personal issues and choices. Stephanie's boyfriend Tony had diabetes, so his eyesight was poor and his medical expenses were high. The Wal-Mart health insurance plan is full of loopholes and high deductibles that take big, recurring chunks out of the income of people with chronic health problems. Tony quit Wal-Mart because he could not keep up with the work quota imposed by his third-shift manager: unloading sixteen merchandise pallets each evening, four more than he could handle. Due to Tony's impaired eyesight, he had to use a magnifying glass to read the bar codes, which slowed his work. Stephanie's daughter Lynn also left Wal-Mart when medical problems led to irregular attendance, after which an insensitive store manager threatened to terminate her outright. And Shane, who had put in the most years at Wal-Mart, quit the company as well. Sent to a store in Tennessee, he found the life of an assistant manager enormously stressful. The hours were long, the pace was frenetic, and the tension was constant. He told Stephanie, "I just didn't want to take it anymore." On the other hand, Shane's now estranged wife, Alison, "lived for Wal-Mart." She found work in the photo lab, on the day shift, in a job that required a certain skill and gave her a bit of autonomy. She is a "Wal-Mart freak," said Haynes. "She even likes the cheer."[27]

TURNOVER TROUBLES

The experience of the Haynes family mirrors that of hundreds of thousands of other associates. Although some employees find a comfortable niche, for many others an awkward shift, frustrated expectations, or conflict with their manager leads to dismissal or a huffy good-bye within two or three years. Hence

Wal-Mart's chronic turnover, which has averaged above 40 percent in recent years, and far higher for those newly hired.[28] This employment pattern, characteristic of the entire retail and service sector, now constitutes a new normality for millions, but it is actually a radical break from the managerial practice and state social policy that was the norm, or at least the ideal, during most of the twentieth century. When the great mass production factories and assembly lines were put into operation a century ago, turnover seemed the subversive handmaiden to inefficiency and social unrest. "Just as quicksand cannot be kneaded in the hands into a solid lump," wrote one personnel executive in 1916, "so also will it be difficult to take hold of an ever-changing mass of employees and transform it into a homogeneous, intelligent, contented body."[29] An entire profession, that of personnel management, and an entire corporate outlook, welfare capitalism, were designed to bind workers to the companies for which they worked. In the 1920s "progressive" firms like General Electric, Metropolitan Life, and National Cash Register all invested heavily in what would later be called corporate "human relations."

The Great Depression proved that this was beyond the capacity of any individual company. We remember the Social Security Act of 1935 for the pension system it put on the books. But that law was also designed to stabilize employment, and workers' income, by establishing a national system of unemployment insurance and by putting in place a corporate tax system designed to encourage managers to provide steady employment and avoid layoffs. The idea was twofold: The state governments that administer the unemployment pay system assign every firm an "experience rating" based on the extent to which its employees draw upon the pool of money each state has reserved for that purpose. Companies whose employees rarely use these state funds pay low taxes. Those whose ex-workers are always crowding the Employment Security Office get socked with a higher quarterly tax rate, based upon their employment "experience" during the previous several months. So the retail industry, with Wal-Mart in the vanguard, should be paying through the nose because of its chronically high turnover. Right?

Wrong. Over the last half century, turnover rates in the retail sector have advanced decade by decade, largely a product of the eclipse of the traditional department store and the rise of the discount chain. Today they are among the highest in the nation. Only those who work in construction, entertainment, and restaurants come and go with greater frequency. But virtually all of these employment separations in discount are defined as "voluntary."[30] When Wal-Mart and the other big firms want to reduce the size of their workforce, they avoid formal layoffs. They just slow their hiring for a while and wait for normal turnover to reduce the labor force. Or the big retailers, Wal-Mart first among them, slash hours, which immediately reduces their labor cost and soon generates a wave of pseudo-voluntary good-byes. If a manager seeks to get rid of a particular employee, but can't find an excuse to actually fire her "for cause," he just assigns the worker to an awkward shift, slots her into a lowly job, or, if she is in management, insists she take a post at a distant store. Of the half million workers who cycle through Wal-Mart each year, the proportion who actually end up with an unemployment check is minuscule. "Fight each and every unemployment claim" is the way Joseph Hawkins, who managed stores in Washington State during the late 1990s, remembered Wal-Mart corporate policy.[31]

As a consequence, Wal-Mart has a wonderful experience rating, hardly inferior to traditionally stable employment havens like the utilities and local government. Indeed, if one accepted as a reflection of employment reality the experience rating generated by the mass merchandisers in the state of

Texas, where I examined the figures, one would have to believe that retail clerks have a far more stable work life than those employed by virtually any manufacturer, transport company, investment firm, hospital, or even the postal service. Wal-Mart, which employs more than 152,000 in 459 stores and distribution centers throughout Texas, probably pockets, in that state alone, something on the order of $50 million a year as a result of this sham.[32] And, of course, those thousands of employees who have been induced to "voluntarily" quit are left out in the cold, with no unemployment pay.[33] All this amounts to a repeal of one of America's bedrock pieces of social legislation. The Progressives designed it, the New Dealers implemented it, and the administrators of the Great Society expanded unemployment coverage to far more women and people of color. But it's a dead letter at Wal-Mart.

Although Wal-Mart manages to escape the government's tax penalty, too much turnover is not healthy even for a company that has learned to live with it. In retail, it costs upwards of three thousand dollars to train even the lowest-level hourly worker.[34] Service suffers, and at Wal-Mart the famed corporate culture becomes harder to pass on to the next cohort of hourly clerks. By the late 1990s the problem had reached something of a crisis because Wal-Mart was putting stores in metropolitan regions well outside its traditional, small-town turf. Unemployment reached historic lows, which made it a lot easier for Wal-Mart clerks to tell an overbearing manager, "You can take this job and shove it." With the rapid opening of so many Supercenters, most stores now operated twenty-four hours a day, seven days a week. Sunday and night closings were a thing of the past, so shift schedules were necessarily inconvenient for an increasingly larger fraction of the Wal-Mart workforce. Turnover therefore reached an astounding 70 percent in 1999; among entry-level hourly employees 67 percent quit within their first ninety days on the job. Coleman Peterson, an African American hired to lead the Wal-Mart "People Division" in 1994, admitted that things were "spiraling in the wrong direction."[35]

According to Peterson, Wal-Mart's solution to the turnover problem was a renewed emphasis on the company's familial "culture," a demonstration that managers "care" about the associates. There may have been some unpublicized wage increases in the most labor-tight metropolitan markets, but Wal-Mart remained determined to hold the line on labor costs. And Wal-Mart got lucky once again. When the tech bubble burst in 2000, it did a lot more than deflate the trendy San Francisco housing market. Unemployment jumped upward all across Wal-Mart's America, even as pricy gasoline robbed exurban commuters of several hundred dollars in disposable income each year.[36] The kind of people Wal-Mart liked to hire were living right on the edge, so every time the company announced that it would open a new store, thousands of applicants mobbed the Wal-Mart hiring hall, usually set up in a nearby hotel or temporary set of offices. Turnover dropped to 44 percent as early as 2003, putting Wal-Mart on par with most other discount retailers, but still far above higher-wage firms like Costco (24%), IKEA (22%), and grocery stores like Publix (11%) and Wegman's (6%). All this was reflected in *Fortune* magazine, where in 2003 and 2004 an executive survey rated Wal-Mart "America's most admired company." But in a simultaneous and somewhat less well noted survey of ordinary employee views, Wal-Mart, for all its talk of cultural cohesion, failed to make a list of the "100 Best Companies to Work For."[37]

Employee turnover is a double-edged sword when it comes to the cost of labor. Given its rapidly revolving workforce, Wal-Mart probably spends above $2 billion a year on employee training. But how much is that really, in a company that has annual sales of over $400 billion? Raising wages by two dollars an hour for a million workers might well slash turnover in half, but that would cost the company twice as much a year in wages, and even more when all the implicit costs associated with giving people a longer work career are factored in. High turnover keeps the workforce green, which means that relatively few workers move up the hourly wage ladder or buy into the package of benefits, skimpy as they might be, offered by the company.

Like other retailers, Wal-Mart has been loath to acknowledge the bottom-line advantages of turnover, but Michael Bergdahl, who worked in the home office as head of the Wal-Mart People Division during the last years of Sam Walton's life, let the cat out of the bag in his 2004 memoir-advice book, *What I Learned from Sam Walton*. "It's hard to believe, but turnover drops millions of dollars to the bottom line in cost savings for the company. When an experienced associate leaves the company he or she is replaced by an entry-level associate at a lower wage. Turnover of associates, for this reason, actually appears, from an expense standpoint, to be a competitive advantage." The rule of thumb in retail, points out Bergdahl, is summed up by the "30/60/120/240" formula. Translated, that means that, on average, store managers turn over at the rate of 30 percent a year, assistant managers at the rate of 60 percent, full-time salespeople at 120 percent, and part-time or seasonal salespeople at 240 percent a year. So Wal-Mart looks good in comparison.[38]

Wal-Mart is constantly trying to figure out ways to automate the hiring (and even the firing) process. When prospective hires first walk into a store, they sit down at a computer terminal, plug in their address and work history, and take a "survey" that is designed to determine if they should be weeded out even before they meet their first Wal-Mart manager. Jill Seskin, a sociology grad student who took the exam in 1992, remembered that it was clearly designed to elicit answers that would demonstrate a loyal and thankful attitude toward the employer. Wal-Mart wanted "subservient" workers, she recalled, so "I lied on every answer of my psychological exam in order to be hired." Likewise, the writer Barbara Ehrenreich's wry view of how a big bureaucracy functions nearly caused her to fail the section of the test that asked if she agreed "rules have to be followed to the letter at all times." She had replied "strongly" rather than "totally."[39]

Except for management trainers, Wal-Mart has no formal mentorship program for the people who do get hired. But the company has invested heavily in Computer Based Learning models. There are scores of these ten- to twenty-five-minute programs, constantly being updated from the Bentonville home office. They first introduce the associate to Mr. Sam and his vision of the company, quickly move on to admonitions against unions, and theft, of both money and time, and then instruct the worker on a wide variety of tasks: how to run the cash registers, fold clothing, talk to customers, spot shoplifters, and avoid accidents to themselves and their customers. When Wal-Mart introduced its CBL program in 1993, it cut training times in half. Every store has about five CBL stations, and each new employee is expected to complete his or her set during the first ninety days of employment. Indeed, like everything Wal-Mart does, Bentonville computers keep track of the training, so store managers get penalized if their associates are not current on the latest CBL tutorials.[40]

THE SHOCK TROOPS

Wal-Mart deploys a legion of assistant managers to hold this system together. They are the ambitious and mobile cadre who discipline the troops and plug the gaps when the hourly workers are stretched too thin. There are upwards of thirty-five thousand assistant managers at Wal-Mart, each earning, in salary, about forty thousand dollars a year. They work long hours, a minimum of forty-eight a week, but more likely fifty-five and sixty, eating on the fly and never quite sure when they'll leave for the evening. In November and December their hours can easily rise to eighty per week. They are the "grunts of the business," complained one longtime assistant manager.[41] Assistant managers who want to advance are constantly on the move, taking new posts at Wal-Marts far from family and friends. When a new assignment is offered, the company gives them about two weeks to make the transfer, and as with so many other corporate functions, it in-sources the expense, normally providing a Wal-Mart semitruck, a driver, and three local stock boys to load and unload furniture and other effects. Management's game, complained a store comanager who had bought and sold three houses in five years, "is to move you as far from home as possible and make you work your way back." As a district manager told her, "You need to be hungry. You need to prove to the company how bad you want it."[42]

Julie Pierce was one of the hungry ones, and her story explains part of the allure Wal-Mart holds for ambitious, working-class families who are willing to dedicate their lives to the company if only for a few years. By the time that Pierce became an hourly associate at a Florida Wal-Mart in 1998, she had had twenty years of experience in retail. She'd once owned a deli catering business and had even worked at a unionized grocery store in New Jersey, where her pay, in actual purchasing power, was double the $6.50 an hour Wal-Mart first offered her. But Pierce thought the male meat cutters in New Jersey were disrespectful, and she claimed the "unions sold us out" after a disastrous strike in the 1980s. So she was "actually glad Wal-Mart was anti-union when she finally stumbled on it."[43]

Pierce took to heart Walton's injunction, "First God, then family, then Wal-Mart." She was not a particularly devout Christian, but she was fiercely loyal to her family and a dedicated and ambitious Wal-Mart worker. Within a couple of years every member of her family worked at a Wal-Mart: in addition to herself, all three of her children, her son-in-law, and her husband worked for the company. Indeed, throughout her eight-year career at Wal-Mart Pierce arranged for every member of her family to get at least some kind of hourly job there, even as they collectively moved to central Alabama, to New Hampshire, and then to Louisiana.

Pierce was a competent manager of the meat department in the Supercenters where she worked, and she fought to become an assistant manager, even if this meant moving her whole family hundreds of miles across a state or across the country. At first it all seemed worthwhile. Her wages doubled once she finished the seventeen-week training regime. She had access to more company information, policies, and procedures than at any other place she had ever worked. Equally important, Pierce felt as if she was finally and genuinely a part of the corporate team. "I was raised to the level of the chosen few who have someone behind them at Wal-Mart," she remembered when first informed of her promotion to the assistant manager rank. "You feel an inclusiveness hard to describe," as if you were "being accepted into a religious organization or sorority." For a time it was all very heady. "You feel what most typical retail employees seldom if ever feel. A sense of power that is almost indescribable."[44]

Pierce and her family seemed on the way up. In the first years of the new century they moved to Wal-Mart's New England frontier, where dozens of stores were opening up, all in need of managers. But the demands, both psychic and physical, were also extraordinary. She was putting in sixty- and seventy-hour weeks on a routine basis. "Assistant managers were dropping like flies," she recalled. Meanwhile, Pierce found herself at odds with the store and district managers under whom she worked. She pushed and prodded managers and higher-ups for the promotion she felt she deserved. But like so many other dedicated and "pushy" Wal-Mart women, she never made the leap to her own store, which would have tripled her wages and finally given her family an income that was not exhausted immediately after cashing each paycheck. Pierce therefore dragged her family back to the Deep South for another shot at the brass ring, but conflicts with higher-level management continued and she became increasingly disenchanted with the Wal-Mart ethos. She made frequent use of the "open door" but to little avail. When her district manager learned that she had been interviewed for Robert Greenwald's film, *Wal-Mart: The High Cost of Low Price*, her fate was sealed. She was fired in February 2005.[45]

THE END OF OVERTIME

Managerial culture at Wal-Mart stands in opposition to much of the labor legislation put in place during the twentieth century. Take the forty-hour workweek, for example. It took a hundred years for labor activists and social reformers to put it on the political and legislative agenda before it was finally made a part of the federal Wage and Hour Law in the late 1930s. Overtime pay, at time and a half the normal hourly wage, was designed not to reward workers for long hours but as an economic incentive to spread the work and maintain a livable pattern of work and leisure. Although designed for the blue-collar working class, white-collar office and service workers reaped much of the benefit. By the 1930s all the big department stores cut back drastically on evening hours. The traditional Saturday half day of office work came to an end. And the "weekend" finally came into its own after World War II, when the unions fought mandatory overtime.

But a reverse course has been charted during the last thirty years. A huge proportion of all American workers, perhaps 30 percent, are now defined as employees "exempt" from the U.S. Wage and Hour Law. Professionals, consultants, subcontractors, the self-employed, managers making as little as $23,000 a year, and all those whose wages amount to more than $100,000 are no longer covered by either the minimum wage or the overtime penalty. The eight-hour day and the forty-hour week have been virtually eliminated for tens of millions of working Americans.

Life at Wal-Mart's home office in Bentonville reflects these new stress-filled patterns of work. There a well-schooled technical staff and a cohort of savvy merchandise buyers occupy thousands of windowless cubicles in the sprawling collection of old warehouses and stores that have been converted into a starkly utilitarian workspace for the headquarters staff. When Michael Bergdahl took over the corporate People Division in 1990, he asked a more experienced executive how to budget for overtime. "I was told every department, every store, and every distribution center had the same budget for overtime, but unfortunately that budget had zero dollars in it." When he inquired how all the work was completed after the hourly associates left for the day, he was informed that salaried managers were free to work as many hours as they needed.[46]

Fifteen years later this regime remains entrenched. A programmer-analyst in Information Systems reported that fifty hours and more comprised the standard workweek. "Getting off on Sunday was a celebration," reported another from the same department. "There were several days I went in at 7:30 a.m. and did not get home for a nap till 8:00 a.m. the next morning; two years in a row vacations were cancelled." Top managers joked, "You have 24 hours in a day, use them!"[47] Long hours for computer geeks and ambitious executives are nothing new, but Wal-Mart has actually codified the long workweek for all its salaried employees, including those whose incomes and career prospects are not glamorous at all. At corporate headquarters the standard workweek is forty-five hours minimum. Moreover, managers and salaried professionals are expected to attend two of the corporation's famous Saturday morning meetings each month. While these are often celebratory affairs, with skits and guest performers, there is no denying the transformation in the work life, where despite casual Fridays and lots of bantering in the hallways, a sixty- or seventy-hour workweek is not unusual for midlevel managers.[48] Despite Wal-Mart's deference to a small-town pace of life and to family values, "they very much want you to sacrifice your life to Wal-Mart," reported another home-office manager.[49] As a consequence Wal-Mart executives, even those making hundreds of thousands of dollars a year, often retire or take a new job when they hit their early fifties.[50]

Meanwhile, Wal-Mart has tossed aside many of the nation's laws governing wages, hours, and conditions of employment, especially for the hourly employees those statutes were designed to protect. Because Wal-Mart's electronic leash is so tightly drawn, store managers use carrots, sticks, and outright theft to bring down their labor costs to assuage Bentonville and preserve their own end-of-the-year bonus. Not only managers and assistant managers but hundreds of thousands of hourly workers also put in more than forty hours per week, the legal maximum before time-and-a-half overtime pay kicks in. But Wal-Mart associates rarely see any of this extra cash. During the last decade more than three score class-action lawsuits against Wal-Mart have unearthed a mountain of evidence demonstrating that the Wal-Mart way simply ignores or subverts the pay standards long prescribed by federal and state law. In some instances, store management unilaterally fixed the time cards of those workers with more than forty hours a week; in others, unpaid lunch hours appeared on the records of associates who had taken none. Steven Quiriconi, an assistant manager in Omak, Washington, testified that he "regularly adjusted" the time records of "five or six associates per day to add rest breaks or increase meal periods."[51]

"I knew I had to do what I did with employee time records

to protect my job, so I did it without hesitation," admitted Quiriconi.[52] Sometimes managers would tell an entire department to clock out at 9 p.m. or 10 p.m. and then return to their station to "zone" the merchandise until all was tidy for the next day. "Employees were habitually caught between trying to finish all of the tasks assigned to them and struggling to keep below 40 hours," testified Quiriconi. "We Assistant Managers leaned on the Department Managers the most to get the work done."[53] Meanwhile, assistant mangers like Quiriconi practically lived in the store, keeping track of two shifts, which put them at work for eighty hours per week.[54]

Ironically, employees probably do more "off-the-clock" work for the managers that they respect than for the slave drivers. They know that overtime pay would get them and their manager in trouble, so a lot of self-policing takes place. Hawkins remembered that workers were well aware of the pressure under which he managed the store, so they often clocked out on their own, "as a means of keeping him from being reprimanded for having overtime and to help keep the store profitable." This was also the experience of Stan Fortune, a manager in Loss Prevention who became a union organizer after a long career at Wal-Mart. During a farewell dinner with his Las Vegas staff, he was surprised to learn how much unremunerated overtime they all put in as a way of making Fortune look good to higher-ranking managers.[55] And this was also the more general conclusion reached by Wal-Mart's personnel department in Southern California, which noted that a high proportion of all associates didn't want to "'let down' their management team" by admitting they couldn't complete all of their duties within 40 hours."[56]

Such off-the-clock work became another routine part of working in a big institution with its own set of rules. John Hiser, an hourly associate who testified against Wal-Mart in a Washington State wage-and-hour case, recalled working off the clock almost every week. "I worked a regular Monday through Friday schedule at the Bremerton store, and as Fridays approached, I would calculate how many hours I could work without exceeding 40 hours. When I reached the limit, I clocked out and returned to the floor to finish my work." Departmental managers, who were typically middle-aged women of long tenure, were undoubtedly the most frequent off-the-clock workers. Pride and fear motivated them, since a messy or poorly arranged department was both a shameful reflection on their own competence and a potential threat to their job security. For those who bought into the Wal-Mart culture, off-the-clock work seemed just another way of helping friends and workmates succeed in a difficult situation; for the more cynical, it was necessary just to keep store management off their backs.[57]

The attitude of most Wal-Mart managers, from the local store right up to the top of the People Division in Bentonville, was almost always "If you are working off the clock, I don't want to know about it." While everyone within the Wal-Mart organization knew of some manager who had been penalized for a violation of the no-overtime rule, the New York Times reporter Steven Greenhouse was greeted with a painful silence when he asked Coleman Peterson, who headed up the corporate People Division, if he knew of any case in which a manager had been disciplined for allowing off-the-clock work in his store.[58] Indeed, Wal-Mart is an outlaw. "We're going to quit breaking the law," Regional Vice President Larry Williams told a Tulsa meeting of store managers in 1994. "The OSHA laws we have, the wage and hour laws that we have, the federal firearms law, we're going to quit breaking the law."[59] But without a radical shift in the corporate work culture, such top-down admonitions were but futile wishes, ignored by Wal-Mart's army of hard-pressed managers. Although both Kmart and Target also proscribe overtime pay and squeeze their managers and workers to keep labor costs in line, neither has been the subject of a class-action "off-the-clock" suit. Wal-Mart, on the other hand, was defending itself against seventy-five such suits as of December 2008 when the company announced a settlement, perhaps costing as much as $640 million, in sixty-three of these wage and hour lawsuits covering hundreds of thousands of workers in some forty-two states.[60] Wal-Mart's effort to clean up its act almost certainly represented a concession to the more stringent regulatory climate that would characterize Obama administration enforcement of the labor laws. Whether it represented a fundamental shift in the managerial culture at Wal-Mart remains to be seen.

EMPLOYEE THEFT AND WHY IT IS CHRONIC

The Wal-Mart way, with its enormous turnover at the bottom, its stressed-out managers in the middle, and a corporate culture hostile to the main body of legally established work norms, leads directly to all sorts of employment pathologies. An egregious example made the headlines in October 2003 when U.S. immigration officials rounded up 250 illegal immigrants working as cleaning crews in sixty-one Wal-Mart stores across twenty-one states. The raids, dubbed Operation Rollback by Immigration and Customs Enforcement in a cheeky reference to the company's well-known price-cutting strategy, revealed the existence of a conspiracy that linked a cohort of Wal-Mart managers, some at the district or regional level, to a set of criminal entrepreneurs, often Russian or Czech, who imported hundreds of desperate eastern Europeans for illegal and underpaid subcontract work at stores throughout the East and South.[61] About half of all Wal-Mart stores used a cleaning subcontractor of some sort.

Wal-Mart managers saved a lot of money by using these contractors, since they never paid insurance or benefits to their countrymen and sometimes simply robbed them of whatever pay they had promised. Isolated in a strange town, most on these cleaning crews worked seven nights a week and slept together in a cramped apartment. Many were as honest and hardworking as possible under the circumstances, but a sizable minority had been recruited out of the post-Soviet underworld, so theft on the night shift became epidemic. And since contractors recruited illegal immigrants through overseas ads and charged them as much as ten thousand dollars to come to America, "stealing was one of the ways they labored to pay off the debts," reported federal agents investigating the scam.[62]

Wal-Mart managers countered this threat by locking all their employees inside the store, the cleaners and overnight stockers alike, after which the manager went home with the keys. This draconian policy was unique even among hard-nosed discounters like Kmart, Home Depot, Toys "R" Us, and Costco. If illness or injury struck a third-shift associate, he or she was stuck inside until the manager showed up, sometimes several hours later. "Locking in workers, that's more of a 19th-century practice than a 20th-century one," remarked the well-known retail consultant Burt Flickinger.[63] In this instance, pressure from the government and much bad publicity forced Wal-Mart to cut back on the use of maintenance subcontractors and institute a new policy: a night manager with a key had to be present to let workers out of the store in an emergency.

But the larger criminalities endemic to the Wal-Mart employment model could not be so easily ameliorated. Take the issue of discount store theft, for example. Most people think that shoplifting is the bigger problem; it is certainly the most obvious to the average shopper who notes the electronic tags, the prominent in-store cameras, and the ever-present Wal-Mart greeter, who doubles as a lookout for people speeding out of the door with unpackaged merchandise. But a far greater problem, at Wal-Mart and most of the other big retailers, is theft by employees themselves. The average impulse shoplifter is likely to grab a twenty-dollar toy, switch boxes on a video game, or hide a forty-dollar dress, but this is petty when compared to employees whose average take, when caught, approaches one thousand dollars and often in a fashion that is far more difficult for company management to detect. Third-shift theft by stockers and cleaners is chronic. At the checkout counter, cashiers sometimes practice "sweethearting" or "sliding." The former takes place when the employee charges the customer less than the actual price, often substituting a spare bar-coded tag in place of that on the merchandise. Sliding is when the employee covers the bar code at the point of sale. Or the cashier might fail to give the receipt to the customer, then cancel the transaction after the customer leaves, and pocket the money. Sweetheart theft also takes place at the service desk, where Mr. Sam's no-questions-asked return policy has been an open invitation to illicit collaboration between an employee staffing the post and his or her customer friends.

Theft, from employees, vendors, and customers, is called "shrinkage," and it amounts to about 1.5 percent in the discount sector. Wal-Mart's shrink is a bit lower, because the company is near obsessive about the problem, but this still amounts to over $30 billion a year in unexplained inventory losses for the retail sector. For discounters, employees are estimated to be responsible for some 46 percent, while customers steal but 29 percent. The rest comes from vendor fraud and paperwork errors.[64]

So why do employees steal? Well, some are dishonest and some are linked up with organized criminal gangs. But the overwhelming impulse that leads to employee theft is a sense of betrayal, of injustice, of taking what's due. Theft represents a kind of compensation for the marginalization and disrespect characteristic of retail employment. And when employees feel aggrieved and perhaps also know that their weeks behind the cash register are numbered, shrinkage, either willful or careless, becomes a chronic feature of the store's "counterculture."

Employee theft tracks turnover like two lovers on a stroll. Richard Hollinger, a University of Florida criminologist who conducts a "National Retail Security Survey," is often asked by retail executives for a solution. "I always say that the single most dependable variable in predicting shrinkage is turnover. Nothing else comes even close. . . . It seems so obvious that it's hard to believe the retail industry doesn't see this as their Achilles' heel and do something about it. Yes, it may mean paying people more money. It may mean promoting from within. It may mean giving better benefits. But there are a number of retail companies that do this and have very low levels of turnover and also very low levels of shrink and are very profitable companies."[65]

Wal-Mart is not among them. It is highly profitable, and it has a shrink that is probably lower than the rest of the discount industry. But the corporation has achieved this record only through the construction of a kind of internal police apparatus whose reach and power have steadily expanded. All big retailers have departments called "Loss Prevention" or in more recent years "Asset Protection." Wal-Mart founded its Loss Prevention Department in 1973 when the company had but eighty-eight stores, almost all still in the Ozarks. But something must have been amiss even then, because shrinkage stood at 3 percent of total sales, extraordinarily high by any standard. Apparently, all that small-town camaraderie could not forestall the pilferage. "We were bleeding badly," recalled Jack Shewmaker, one of Walton's most trusted executives.[66]

Shewmaker recruited Tom Coughlin to run the company's Loss Prevention Department. Coughlin was the son of an Irish cop from Cleveland, a defensive lineman in college whose three-hundred-pound, six-foot-four-inch bulk and imposing demeanor put him at home among the ex-policemen and detectives who staffed the Wal-Mart LP Department. Shrinkage was still "off the charts" when Coughlin took over in the late 1970s, so he and his successors deployed the carrot and the stick to stanch this drainage from the bottom line. In 1980 Wal-Mart instituted a "shrink incentive plan."[67] Store managers and ordinary associates were offered an incentive bonus if their store came in at the target set by Bentonville. For the store associate this could amount to as much as $250 in an exceptionally good year. Such "material" incentives were necessarily accompanied by relentless "ideological" hectoring, in the break room, in the Wal-Mart employee magazine, and at the daily store meetings attended by most associates. Thus a cheerleading squad of "Shrinkettes" from New Iberia, Louisiana, danced and sang at Wal-Mart's 1988 annual meeting. But two years later, when Wal-Mart fell short of its shrink reduction goal by some $36 million, a top executive hectored associates, "We must take ownership in our various job responsibilities and continually push ourselves and ask, 'What are we doing today to stop shrinkage and prepare for the inventory process? How can I do my job more effectively?' YOU and I are the key!"[68]

Throughout the 1980s and 1990s Loss Prevention exploded in size, power, and authority, transforming itself into a kind of internal police force that had the authority to intervene in store operations even, or perhaps especially, when store managers objected. By 2000 there were more than 550 salaried managers in Loss Prevention, scores of internal auditors, and thousands of in-store hourly employees to keep associates and managers both vigilant and fearful. In a rare collective protest, more than one hundred Sam's Club managers circulated a letter that complained, "Loss Prevention or Internal Audit can come in at any time and find something, anything, to get rid of a manager!! We admit it, we are terrified! We feel like ruling by 'intimidation' is the new standard."[69]

Take the case of Lamon Griggs. He had been a Mississippi state trooper for twelve years when in 1990 he tripled his pay by signing on with Wal-Mart as a truck driver working out of the company's new distribution center in Brookhaven, Mississippi. Griggs, who also investigated accidents for Wal-Mart, soon became highly respected among both fellow drivers and fleet managers. He was a straight shooter, a by-the-book kind of guy whose scrupulousness made some of the good ole boys uncomfortable. On the night of October 16, 1997, after Griggs had backed his truck up to the loading dock at Wal-Mart Store Number 489 in Hammond, Louisiana, he walked inside, picked up a $1.48 pouch of chewing tobacco, and then remembered that he had to call his dispatcher back in Brookhaven. Since the lines were long in front of the cash registers, he returned to the front door, said hello to the greeter and showed her the tobacco, and said he'd be right back after using the pay phone in the foyer. That phone was busy, so he stepped outside the store to find another. And that was when two Loss Prevention detectives apprehended him. It turned out that they had had their eye on Griggs, whose driver's uniform identified him as a Wal-Mart employee, because Loss Prevention awarded its employees with far more credit for nabbing an associate than an ordinary shoplifter.

Griggs spent a couple of uncomfortable hours in Loss Prevention's claustrophobic back-of-the store office in Hammond, until he was sprung by an outraged supervisor who had driven over from Brookhaven. "Forget about it," Griggs was told; it was just a "misunderstanding." So Griggs returned to work. But like the dogged Inspector Javert in Victor Hugo's novel *Les Misérables*, Loss Prevention executives in Bentonville would not let the case die. They complained to Griggs's supervisors, demanding his immediate termination, and faxed out new evidence to make their case. Logistics management, including people in Bentonville, suggested a compromise, a "performance coaching," but LP demanded the full pound of flesh. "Do you mean to tell me that Loss Prevention tells Wal-Mart what to do?" asked Griggs as he was being officially fired. "Well, it appears so," replied his manager, "they have a lot of clout, and this became somewhat of a political issue . . . it's kind of a push and shove issue, who can boss the other."[70]

As with the secret police in an authoritarian country—Griggs called them "the Gestapo"—Loss Prevention's influence has become pervasive. LP provides the security for top Wal-Mart executives at picnics, meetings, and when they are on the road. Since the LP Department installed the hidden store cameras designed to keep track of customers and cashiers, it was also called upon to track union organizers and anti-Wal-Mart protesters when they showed up in the parking lot. A whole squad flew into Las Vegas at the height of the UFCW unionizing attempt there in 2000. Wal-Mart Loss Prevention personnel also kept tabs on dissident shareholders, nosy journalists, and community groups seeking to keep Wal-Mart from putting another Supercenter in their town. When confidential memos embarrassing to Wal-Mart began to appear in the press, Loss Prevention turned its attention both to those who published the information and to the consultants and executives who might have leaked them.[71]

Surveillance of those Wal-Mart executives thought to be engaged in dishonesty, adultery, or sexual harassment turned into another LP duty, especially when the subjects were considered unreliable or disloyal employees. Indeed, gender transgressions were an all-purpose tool, which Wal-Mart used to force out troublesome managers. Thus when top Wal-Mart executives found James W. Lynn, a factory inspector for the company's Central American operations, a bit too fastidious in his reports, Loss Prevention was tasked to dig up some dirt on him. It sent a team to Costa Rica and Guatemala, where Lynn and a lower-level female colleague were subject to intense surveillance until alleged evidence of a romantic liaison surfaced, sufficient to end Lynn's heretofore unblemished career with the company.[72]

Wal-Mart formalized many of these new LP responsibilities in the years after 9/11. The company needed to marshal its resources for the political and public relations battles in which it was now continuously engaged. So Loss Prevention changed its name to "Asset Protection" in 2003, and a separate Office of Global Security was set up that same year under Kenneth Senser, a former CIA and FBI official. Wal-Mart also spun off an even more shadowy security organization two years later, the Threat Research and Analysis Group, a twenty-person unit whose key executives were often recruited from military intelligence and the most sophisticated firms within the telecommunications industry.[73] Bruce Gabbard, a security officer whom Wal-Mart fired when it became known that he had improperly intercepted the phone calls made by a *New York Times* reporter, said his spying activities had long been sanctioned by his superiors. "I used to joke that Wal-Mart paid me to be paranoid and they got their money's worth." Indeed, the intelligence unit used many of the data mining and Internet surveillance techniques developed by Homeland Security and the Pentagon to spy on Wal-Mart's own employees and consultants, investigate hostile bloggers and activists, and keep tabs on the weak links in Wal-Mart's international supply chain. Threat Research employees nicknamed their windowless work area in the David Glass Technology Center the "Bat Cave."[74]

THE FALL OF TOM COUGHLIN

The career of Tom Coughlin exemplified the growth in the power of Wal-Mart's internal police apparatus and the suspicious atmosphere that it nurtured. He took over Human Relations in the mid-1980s and then headed up the rapidly expanding Sam's Club division. By the mid-1990s he was CEO of Wal-Mart's U.S. operations and a rival to H. Lee Scott to fill the shoes of David Glass as the next CEO and chairman of the entire multinational corporation. Coughlin had become close to Sam Walton during the 1980s, shooting quail with him in Texas, visiting stores as part of the Walton entourage, spending endless hours on the phone with associates and managers who used the open door to tell Coughlin their troubles. Sam gave Coughlin access to his own personal funds so he could set up the Walton Institute at the University of Arkansas, where Wal-Mart managers were retrained by, or at least exposed to, top B-school academics. By this time the Cleveland-born Coughlin had transformed himself into an Ozark "cowboy," which is what a lot of his underlings came to call him: a tough-talking, self-described bubba with a temper that exploded if he found a store in poor shape or a vendor seeking a price hike. He started wearing a Stetson, listening to country music, and raising bulls on a twelve-hundred-acre ranch outside of Bentonville.[75]

Coughlin was not a grand strategist, but rather a man whose forte was execution, discipline, and motivation of the troops. He liked to quote George Patton, "A good plan violently executed today is better than a great plan tomorrow." And Norman Schwarzkopf, "When in charge, take command." After Walton's passing, Coughlin codified the founder's principles into a set of bulletlike directives: "Stock it. Price it right. Show the Value. Take the Money. Teach them." When in the mid-1990s Wal-Mart took a loss for the first time in one hundred quarters, Coughlin played the key role in refocusing store managers on their basic tasks: restocking the shelves, refurbishing the stores, and holding labor costs down. He once sent a directive to every manager demanding that they immediately shave one hundred hours from the payroll of every store, so Wal-Mart could hit its quarterly profit estimate. "Tom has an unusual capacity to sort out all of the chaff and get back to what's important, and he has the determination to stick with it," observed his original Wal-Mart mentor, Jack Shewmaker.[76]

Given Coughlin's cowboy persona, a lot of people were ready

to believe him when he claimed, early in 2005, to have laundered upward of half a million dollars in Wal-Mart corporate funds for a secret, and highly illegal, "union project" designed to bribe UFCW officials into fingering pro-union Wal-Mart workers in Las Vegas and elsewhere. Coughlin's sensational claim was not the product of a guilty conscience. Late in December 2004 his career at Wal-Mart imploded in spectacular fashion. Coughlin and several of his closest associates were summarily fired after what appeared to have been a wild drinking party, complete with strippers, to which executives of several vendor companies had been invited, the latter a violation of one of Mr. Sam's most celebrated corporate principles. Initially, the circumstances surrounding Coughlin's dismissal were concealed; Wal-Mart called his leaving a voluntary retirement for reasons of health. Both Chairman of the Board Rob Walton and H. Lee Scott gave Coughlin an effusive public send-off— "Coughlin believed fervently in the concept of servant leadership," asserted another executive—and he was to be allowed to complete his term on the board of directors.[77]

But by this time Wal-Mart had put almost a dozen Asset Protection investigators on the Coughlin case, and they turned up a long list of what appeared to be clear misappropriations of Wal-Mart funds: $1,359 for a pair of custom-made alligator boots, a $2,590 dog pen for Coughlin's Arkansas home, $6,500 for a hunting guide service, Wal-Mart gift cards used for his own purchases, as well as $3.54 for a Polish sausage—more than $250,000 in all, going back to the late 1990s. Wal-Mart threw Coughlin off its board in March 2005, went after a chunk of his pension, fired four more headquarters employees whom it accused of conspiring with him to defraud the company, and turned over thousands of pages of evidence to the U.S. Attorney's Office in Fort Smith. Wal-Mart vehemently denied that any "union project" existed, and so too, by implication, did the UFCW, which could find no evidence that any of its partisans had been bribed by Coughlin or his underlings. Coughlin himself finally gave up in February 2006, by pleading guilty to tax and fraud charges, admitting "serious personal mistakes in judgment."[78]

Is Coughlin's downfall just another example of a corporate highflier brought low? Not quite. At first glance Coughlin's petty misappropriation of company funds and his use of subordinates to reimburse him for personal expenses seem incomprehensible. After all, he was making more than $6 million a year, flew around the country in a corporate Citation, and was genuinely popular among a large slice of the Wal-Mart associates. But like so many other Wal-Mart workers, many nabbed by Coughlin's own Loss Prevention Department, his criminality sprang from a growing sense of personal affront, of wounded dignity and unrecognized effort. Coughlin, who saw himself as the natural heir to Sam Walton, had been edged out for the top corporate spot by the more adept Scott. Indeed, his first "union project" expenditures coincided with the bitter realization that he would not take over the company, that in the post-Walton years he was seen around Bentonville as something of a buffoon. And they continued as Scott consolidated his power and placed his people in all the top posts.

And what about that phantom "union project"? Would it have really made any difference had it actually existed? A large slice of Coughlin's entire work life was designed to keep the unions at bay and Wal-Mart's workers invested in the company's ideology. Coughlin's near-constant travel, his assiduous cultivation of associate goodwill—he had his signature attached to more than three thousand birthday greetings that poured out of the home office each day—the hours he spent on the phone with associates high and low, all this was part of an anti-union project that required no bribes or payoffs. In Coughlin's eyes and in those of Wal-Mart, undermining the edifice of the American labor law was one vast "union project," a war designed to thwart, derail, and corrupt the efforts of U.S. workers to achieve collective bargaining. The Wal-Mart People Division, and especially the anti-union Labor Relations subunit, has proven itself a remarkably effective weapon in this battle. To keep more than four thousand North American stores union-free, Wal-Mart does not have to revert to bribery or outright criminality to thwart worker self-organization. Like so many other companies, it has created a vast policing mechanism that uses, abuses, and manipulates the existing U.S. labor law in order to sustain the obedience and fear that are so central to its competitive success.

CHAPTER FIVE

UNIONS: KEEP OUT!

Like the federal minimum wage, American labor law is also designed to raise wages, albeit through a collective bargaining relationship between a group of employees and the firm for which they work. But companies like Wal-Mart have found trade unionism far more obnoxious than any federal mandate that boosted wages or ensured payment of overtime and lunch breaks. By its very nature a trade union challenges managerial authority, questioning the moral, paternal claim that executives and managers speak and act on behalf of an essentially harmonious enterprise. "We have never had a union in Wal-Mart and don't need one now to represent our associates," Sam Walton told readers of *Wal-Mart World* in October 1989. "We resent outsiders coming in and saying things which aren't true and trying to change the Company that has meant so much to all of us."[1] Larry English, one of Walton's best young managers, would not tolerate any challenge to his authority as a store manager. Of unions he said: "I hated them because they wanted to tell me how to take care of my people. I don't need someone to manage my store for me. I'll go to my grave believing that."[2]

Such sentiments flourished in Arkansas. In the United States a militant hostility to trade unionism arose not where union labor was strong and pervasive, but where it seemed a threat to a regional economy long structured around cheap labor, competitive enterprises, and a local elite that was anxious about the future. That was Arkansas in the second half of the twentieth century. Here the fear of union organization united the plantation owners of the Mississippi Delta, the Ozark branch plant managers whose only competitive advantage lay in cheap labor, and entrepreneurs of northwest Arkansas, like John Tyson, J. B. Hunt, and Sam Walton, who saw their booming firms as an expression of their paternalism and autonomy. Led by the delta planters, who remembered well the biracial uprising of the Southern Tenant Farmers' Union in the 1930s, Arkansas was the first state to pass a "right-to-work" law—in 1944—which made illegal the union shop contract. Such right-to-work laws weakened existing unions because they made dues collection so much more difficult. But their greatest impact was ideological, so that throughout the South and Mountain West they were taken as a sign of government hostility to the very existence of trade unionism.[3]

When Wal-Mart expanded beyond the small-town South, however, the situation changed. If the company were to take its paternalism, low wages, and hostility to organized labor beyond northwest Arkansas, it would have to develop a more sophisticated, systematic, and ostensibly legal modus operandi. And this would require a revolution in American labor law.

EMPLOYER FREE SPEECH

When in 1935 Senator Robert Wagner drafted the famous act that bears his name, he made sure that under its provisions employees in any given enterprise had the right to select "representatives of their own choosing" who could speak for them in the collective negotiations with the management of the firm. To make sure this happened, the Wagner Act included a section that defined a set of "unfair labor practices" for which employers, but not unions, might be held accountable. When conservative critics of the law complained that the Wagner Act was one-sided, the New York senator replied that this was a "false equation." The kind of "unfair labor practices" in which workers might engage—physical or verbal intimidation of their workmates, punched noses, and nasty threats—all that had been illegal for centuries, since the birth of the common law itself. But when it came to economic coercion, and economic coercion of the sort that declared "You're fired if you mess with the union," well, that was almost exclusively an employer weapon, which Wagner and other labor partisans sought to proscribe.[4] The New Dealers whom President Franklin Roosevelt first appointed to the National Labor Relations Board interpreted the Wagner Act so as to make the foreman and manager nonparticipants, mere bystanders, when the workers they supervised decided for or against forming a union. Indeed, the NLRB ruled that given the imbalance of power in an unorganized factory, mine, or mill, any kind of employer speech was inherently coercive and therefore an "unfair labor practice."[5]

When the Republicans won the 1946 elections, it was just a matter of time before resentful employers got the New Deal-era Wagner Act fixed to their liking. Executives running factories, warehouses, and offices wanted to call the workers together in a big meeting and lecture them on why joining a union would be a bad idea. Sure enough, "free speech for employers" was soon enshrined in a new law—the Taft-Hartley Act—which gave employers and their law firms the right to campaign against unions trying to organize in the workplace. Particularly affected by Taft-Hartley were the retail unions, which were making a major push in the late 1940s and early 1950s to organize chain supermarkets and department stores. At an educational conference held by the Retail Clerks in 1951, union organizers reported that "captive-audience speeches"—employer anti-union talks to work-

ers who had been ordered to attend—were "beginning to grow
by leaps and bounds" at larger stores, contributing to major
union losses in NLRB elections. Initially, the labor board insisted
that unions get equal time, on company property, if management held such compulsory meetings, but once the Republicans
gained control of the NLRB after Dwight D. Eisenhower's election, employers got almost everything they wanted. As one of
the conservative businessmen appointed to that board put it in
his confirmation hearing, referencing one of his successful campaigns against unionism, "We 'free-speeched' them. . . . Now,
you could say, if you like, in that instance I was a union buster."[6]

The labor law still held that employers could not retaliate
against workers who voted for a union by threatening them
with firing or plant closure. But this doctrine became in
creasingly formalistic. Thus in a case involving Chicopee Manufacturing, the NLRB enunciated a "prophecy doctrine" that
permitted employers to state that voting for a union might result in a plant being moved. This employer advantage was further refined in *Mt. Ida Footwear Company*, where executives
of an Arkansas-based shoemaker asserted that if employees
signed union cards, "this could be fatal to a business such as
Mt. Ida Footwear." The board ruled that such threats could be
rendered permissible if an executive "sanitized" this kind of
coercive and threatening speech by merely inserting a catch-
phrase like "we are here to stay," which was the stratagem of
Mt. Ida management. Meanwhile, in two rulings from the early
1950s the NLRB transformed employer free speech into a powerful managerial weapon. In *Livingston Shirt*, the board ruled
that an employer "does not commit an unfair labor practice if
he makes a pre-election speech on company time and premises
and then denies the union's request for an opportunity to reply"; and in *Esquire* employers won the right to threaten that
a pro-union vote would generate lengthy legal proceedings

instead of the collective bargaining mandated by the original Wagner Act.[7]

JOHN TATE AND HIS AMERICA

Enter John Tate, the man who would sharpen these legal weapons, stock them in Wal-Mart's arsenal, and deploy them in furious combat with the unions. A man of Sam Walton's generation, he was born in North Carolina, took a law degree from Wake Forest Law School, and became a bitter foe of trade unionism, all before he enlisted in the army. Tate acquired his hostility to unionism in the labor wars of the late 1930s, when he crossed a union picket line thrown up around the Reynolds Tobacco Company in Winston-Salem, his hometown. Aside from the catcalls, Tate took a blow on the head, which he would never forget. "I hate unions with a passion," he would later remark after he had established a pioneering law firm dedicated to what in the 1950s and 1960s was a newly aggressive "union avoidance" stratagem.[8]

Tate perfected his anti-union skills in Omaha, not North Carolina. He landed there right after World War II when Nebraska and the rest of the northern plains states were an industrial frontier on which factories, warehouses, and meatpacking sheds blossomed like prairie flowers in the spring. Nebraska was a battleground state in which big, vigorous unions such as the Teamsters and the Packinghouse Workers sought to organize the firms that had just begun to flee high-cost Chicago, Minneapolis, and St. Louis, and quite often succeeded. The ideological warfare became as intense as the bargaining sessions and the strikes that so often accompanied them. Tate was right in the middle of the fight.[9]

Throughout the rest of the decade and into the 1960s Tate traveled in right-wing political circles that linked a militant anti-unionism to a libertarian rejection of the welfare state, fair employment legislation, and regulatory oversight by the federal government. This put him in league with the John Birch Society and the Christian Anti-Communist Crusade, as well as those who organized seminars and summer schools where the ideas of the conservative intellectuals Friedrich Hayek and Ludwig von Mises were celebrated. When in the early years of JFK's New Frontier the Federal Communications Commission sought to encourage Omaha's TV stations to air more public interest programming, Tate denounced "faceless government bureaucrats," who thought of midwesterners "as congenital incompetents who must be fooled and ruled by a special elite with some unspecified claim to superior wisdom and a lust for power."[10]

In 1956 Tate organized the Midwest Employers Council as a vehicle through which he could offer legal counsel to smaller companies seeking to avoid unionization. Today, every major city has at least one big law firm that specializes in "union avoidance" law. When corporation executives get wind of a union effort at one of their facilities, they pick up the phone, sign a contract, and let the outside legal experts take over their labor relations until the threat is eliminated. Back in the 1950s, however, almost all "labor lawyers" were just that, pro-union advocates whose expertise and resources were often far greater than that commanded by Nebraska's entrepreneurial businessmen. Unions still won a majority of all the NLRB elections, after which they quickly negotiated a first contract. Although most of the three hundred firms that paid dues to Tate's Employers Council were family-owned manufacturing firms, some of the most bitter battles came in the bakeries, department stores, and grocery chains, including their attendant warehouses, that the Teamsters and the Retail Clerks sought to organize.

Tate saw himself as a crusader for "freedom" rallying the business class of Omaha and Lincoln in order to turn back this union invasion and stiffen the ideological backbone of his clients. He urged them to boycott unionized printing shops and buy as many meat products as possible from Wilson and Company during a long and divisive Packinghouse Workers strike. When a local chain of grocery stores sought to buck a strike early in 1963, Tate called for solidarity: "We do hope you care enough for freedom that if you are not buying some groceries from Shavers Stores—you might do so. Will free people like you and me help union coercion—or stop it—by good old honest methods of a free customer in a free market?"[11]

But Tate was not just a propagandist. He was a pioneer in the nascent union avoidance industry, realizing that the fight against unionism had to be fought simultaneously on multiple fronts: before the NLRB and the courts, in the political arena, and, most important, within the firm itself, where Tate developed a whole repertoire of programs and techniques designed to generate employee loyalty to management and hostility to "third-party" representation. "The issues that are most frequently the cause of company-union disputes today are philosophical, not economic," claimed Tate in 1960. "The battle is for the minds of employees."[12] Backstopped by a phalanx of expert antilabor law firms, this behavior has become commonplace for employers in recent years, but in the 1950s and early 1960s it was so audacious, innovative, and, in the hands of John Tate, so successful that Nebraska unionists labeled the Midwest Employers Council, along with the John Birch Society, a "fascist trend" in the United States.[13]

Tate codified for his clientele all the key anti-union tactics that Wal-Mart and so many other firms would later deploy. Among these are profit-sharing schemes designed to give employees a stake in the productivity of the enterprise, NLRB election delays that demoralized union advocates, a tough negotiating posture that leaves the workforce in limbo and without a contract, and aggressive efforts to decertify unions already representing the workforce.[14] Employer "free speech" was the key element that made this strategy work, enabling executives to conduct compulsory meetings of the workforce, hold one-on-one interviews with employees, and imply—the courts had ruled that an outright threat was illegal—that unionism would have disastrous consequences for the lives of all concerned.[15] As Tate told warehouse employees facing a Teamster organizing drive in 1959:

> Remember this—*no union can guarantee you anything!* The law says that if you force us to deal with some outside third party—some union strangers, we have to bargain, but the law does not say we have to agree to a single solitary thing! If these union salesmen call you off your jobs so you can't pay your bills—the law says we can go right out and hire someone else to take your place. If we never reach an agreement with the union, we never have to hire you back![16]

Tate's reputation as an effective union fighter spread throughout the Midwest, especially after he founded Omaha's largest labor relations law firm in 1967. Sam Walton called on him in 1972 when Wal-Mart faced union trouble at two stores in central Missouri. In truth, the St. Louis–based Retail Clerks local had not put together much of an organizing drive: it established informational picket lines at a couple of stores, but the union put few resources into organizing them, especially the small, thirty-four-employee store in Mexico, a farm town near Columbia, where Sam Walton had attended the state university. But Wal-Mart executives had made an embarrassing and illegal hash of their efforts to squash the union. As the National Labor Relations Board would later note, Jack Shewmaker, one of Walton's rising stars, had been overheard telling the store manager Robert Haines that "if he caught any employees with union cards, he should fire them even if he had to hire all new employees." Then, when Connie Kreyling, a young but highly competent office manager, began to talk up the union idea among her workmates, she had been summarily fired by Haines. The Retail Clerks took her firing to the NLRB. There Haines was shown to be a liar—he claimed that he had fired Kreyling for poor work habits rather than "protected" union activity—and Wal-Mart was ordered to rehire Kreyling and post "in conspicuous places" a Notice to Employees that asserted, "We will not discourage membership in or activities on behalf of Retail Store Employees' Union, Local No. 655 . . . by discharging, or in any other manner discriminating in regard to hire or tenure of employment of any of our employees because of their union activities."[17]

By this point Tate had visited the store, where his well-tested anti-union spiel, plus the judicious transfer of Haines to another store, ended once and for all the union buzz. However, the incident worried Walton, who asked Tate what could be done, especially now that his chain was rapidly opening stores outside the old "magic circle" where rural poverty and southern mores had made so many clerks grateful for a job with Mr. Sam. Tate told Walton: "You can hire me or someone like me to hold these people down, and fight them the rest of your life. Or you can decide to get them on your side."[18] This was a script Tate had long rehearsed, made urgent by the legal war he was then waging against the Amalgamated Clothing Workers, whose strike at the slacks maker Farah Manufacturing deployed one of the union movement's earliest and most effective "corporate campaigns." Tate later remembered, "I won every [NLRB] election with Willie Farah in El Paso, we won every court case including a Supreme Court case, but we lost the war." That was because the Catholic archbishop of El Paso and the mainstream Protestant denominations sided with the union, prompting big retailers like Marshall Field's, Wanamaker's, and Macy's to heed the union boycott and drop the Farah line, thus forcing Farah to recognize the union.[19]

The defeat stuck in Tate's craw, and he was determined to apply the lessons at Wal-Mart. It was not enough to denounce trade unionism and intimidate its partisans. In addition, Wal-Mart needed a high-profile corporate campaign of its own that would convince both employees and the public that the company took care of its workers. Tate therefore proposed that Wal-Mart expand its profit-sharing plan, codify an open-door policy, and give the employees access to much store-level information on sales, profits, and inventory "shrinkage." This was Wal-Mart's "We Care" program, which Tate explained to Wal-Mart executives early in 1973 at the lakeside Tan-Tar-A Resort in southern Missouri. "Saying 'we care' isn't enough," Tate told the assembled managers. "If we can prove we care, then our people will care," adding that employees who feel a vested interest in the company won't be as likely to steal or lie down on the job.[20]

Sam Walton and his publicists later attributed much of the impulse for this idea to his wife, Helen, who told her husband that unless the clerks and cashiers "were on board, the top people might not last long either."[21] Profit sharing seemed a generous, commonsense way to spread Sam's wealth among his hardworking and devoted employees. But in the early 1970s almost all policy makers, corporate benefit managers, and trade unionists considered the very idea of such a scheme economically problematic and ideologically retrograde. Instead, most companies, unionized or not, offered their employees defined-benefit pension plans, which paid out a fixed monthly stipend at retirement, based on their salary and years of service. Social Security was a fixed benefit plan that the Nixon administration had just strengthened by indexing it to inflation. In 1974 came the Employee Retirement Income Security Act, designed to regulate private pension plans in order to make them a secure counterpart to Social Security.[22]

Profit-sharing plans were not unknown in the early 1970s, but they carried a distinctly right-wing inflection, especially when they were substituted for traditional pensions. In an era when security—national, social, union—was much valued, profit-sharing schemes shifted risk to the employees and linked their fortunes directly and exclusively to those of the firms for which they labored. In the 1960s Tate put together a number of such schemes for undercapitalized Nebraska firms determined to keep out the union, but on the cheap.[23] Sears, Roebuck, then the country's greatest retailer, developed one of the most famous plans. With most of its assets invested in Sears stock, that plan paid out at least 10 percent of all profits, with long-service employees, largely male, enjoying the largest corporate contributions. Everyone watched the stock price, which Sears posted daily at every store and warehouse. The investment plan generated a sense of shared purpose and community; in the words of one executive, it was "the central unifying symbol around which the entire organization revolved." The plan and the ideology it embodied proved a bulwark against efforts by the Retail Clerks and the Teamsters to organize the big store in the 1950s and early 1960s.[24]

Wal-Mart's scheme was a discount version of the Sears plan. It was not actually a profit-sharing program per se. Rather the company contributed about 6 percent of an employee's earnings to the plan dependent upon the degree to which Wal-Mart hit certain predetermined earnings and profit targets. It required one year of service to kick in and seven years to fully vest. By the turn of the millennium the corporate contribution had dropped to about 4 percent as Wal-Mart's growth slowed. Thus only one Wal-Mart associate out of fifty ever accumulated fifty thousand dollars in stock.[25] Still, for those employees who remained with the company during the 1970s and 1980s, when the stock price soared, the profit-sharing plan reaped huge dividends. In 1990 *Wal-Mart World* bragged that ninety-three associates had retired in the past year with more than $100,000 in each of their accounts. Betty McCullough, who worked in Fabrics at Sikeston, Missouri, for twenty-one years, retired at age fifty-two with $167,000; Virginia Arnett, also in Fabrics, retired from a Newport, Arkansas, store with $175,800 after just nineteen years' employment; and Thomas Cole, who worked as an assistant manager in various Tulsa stores for fourteen years, left the company at age fifty-five with $149,000 in his profit sharing.[26]

But as Tate understood, the most important impact of the profit-sharing scheme was ideological, linking the employees to the fate of the company, but also justifying the self-exploitation that was integral to the Wal-Mart culture. "Store associates are willing to work long years for modest pay and slim wage hikes," marveled *Discount Store News*, "content on knowing they will hold small fortunes in Wal-Mart stock upon retirement."[27] A company profit-sharing executive put it even more pointedly in 1990: "Your profit sharing account balance will depend upon how well you and every associate in our company does his or her job. There is no place for coasters or people just halfway doing their jobs—just as there is no place for shrinkage or other needless expenses. People who don't do their jobs take dollars out of your profit sharing just as theft and other factors that cause shrinkage in our company reduce profits and profit sharing."[28]

Although Walton boasted that more than four out of five Wal-Mart workers owned company stock, massive turnover at the bottom of the organization made profit sharing a scheme that enriched only those with long tenure or high wages, especially after 2000 when Wal-Mart's stock price went nowhere. A store manager complained to H. Lee Scott in 2005: "My associates—especially the long-term ones—would really like a full explanation as to why we as the largest company on the planet cannot offer some type of medical retirement benefits. . . . All we really get aside from our hard-earned profit sharing and 401(k) is a discount card." Scott's uncharacteristically hostile response, offered on an ostensibly confidential corporate e-mail hookup, found the very question something close to treasonous. "This is a store manager who has a problem," Scott replied. "I worry about him representing all of us in management to his associates." Wal-Mart was not going to go the way of General Motors, argued Scott, and become "a benefit company that sells cars to fund those benefits." Sure, there is a health-care "mess" in this country, he admitted, but until the government gets involved, managers who want to take billions out of earnings and put this in retiree health benefits "should look for [another] company where you can do those kinds of things."[29]

CARROTS AND STICKS FOR THE LABOR ARISTOCRACY

Profit sharing was never going to be enough to keep Wal-Mart union-free, especially among those young, blue-collar men whose labor was absolutely vital to the company's efficiency and success. A unionization of the Wal-Mart logistics system seemed a real possibility in the late 1970s. That decade had been an Indian summer for labor in the south-central states. Arkansas unionists thought conditions ripe to repeal the state's anti-union "right-to-work" law in 1976; although they fell short, the campaign was well financed and well organized. Two years later an even larger and more vigorous labor effort in Missouri persuaded voters there to reject right-wing efforts to amend the state constitution with a similar prohibition against the union shop. The Teamsters, among the most powerful unions in this region, still had more than 2 million members nationwide. In Little Rock, St. Louis, and Kansas City aggressive locals were organizing the warehousemen and truckers who worked for the wholesalers and supermarkets of the region. Despite much well-publicized corruption at the top of their organization, these locals were vigilant enforcers of their contracts, which for over-the-road drivers were not much inferior to those negotiated by the militants of Chicago and Detroit. And this was an era of unprecedented prestige for the long-distance trucker, whose CB radio slang and working-class persona enjoyed a fleeting moment of high visibility in American popular culture.[30]

At Wal-Mart these blue-collar drivers and warehousemen felt themselves slighted, their dignity and manhood called into question. In the 1970s, when Walton and his CEO of the time, Ron Mayer, were setting up the company logistics system, confusion, speedup, and poor wages dogged the rapidly expanding system of distribution centers and the trucks that serviced them. "We were always behind with our distribution," remembered Thomas Jefferson, who was in charge of the first distribution centers. "We never opened a warehouse soon enough, and we always had too many stores to service before the warehouse would get opened."[31] As a consequence, sixty-hour workweeks were routine, trailers and trucks were backed up, and the drivers were expected to lend a hand with the loading and unloading, even after a hard day on the road. Warehouse wages were far lower than those blue-collar workers could command in nearby Missouri and Texas, while the wages of truck drivers were pegged to those who hauled product for Tyson Farms, the nonunion, hardscrabble, chicken-processing operation also headquartered in northwest Arkansas.[32]

Urged on by the resentful truck drivers, the Teamsters launched organizing efforts at company distribution centers in both Bentonville and Searcy during the late 1970s and early 1980s. Each of these DCs employed about eight hundred warehousemen in conditions that were more akin to a fast-paced factory than a pink-collar store. Accidents were frequent, and compulsory overtime was exhausting. In 1980 and 1981 some Searcy distribution center employees even slept in their cars in the parking lot between double shifts. They wanted more money, less pressure, and a measure of day-to-day respect that the company's open-door policy failed to provide. At Searcy, where the Teamsters were most active, the warehouseman Randy Powell told reporters: "All we're asking right now is the right to negotiate hours, wages, and working conditions. They claim we have that now on an individual basis, but when you're one of 38,000 they're not going to hear you."[33]

Walton responded to this organizing attempt with a combination of personal contrition and adroit institutional concessions, backstopped, of course, by an unrelenting, hard-nosed determination to rid the company of those workers whose union sentiment was not assuaged by company paternalism. "You'd think I'd learn, wouldn't you?" he asked the Searcy workers, shaking his head and apologizing for letting conditions get so bad. He asked for another chance; he'd straighten out the work shifts, cut down on the overtime, bring conditions at Searcy in line with those at Bentonville, where workers had just voted down the union. But Walton may have gone to the well one time too often with these blue-collar men. The Teamsters seemed close to having the critical mass they needed in order to win. Around 300 out of 415 workers at the distribution center had signed cards asking the union to represent them.[34]

Wal-Mart executives took off the gloves. An NLRB election was scheduled for February 1982. When Walton and his brother Bud flew down to Searcy just before the election, the company founder assembled the workers to tell them he'd strip them of their profit sharing if they voted for the union. Walton told them he had five hundred job applications on file, some from the evangelical, anti-union students at nearby Harding College. Warming to the subject, he made a threat that was then and now an explicit violation of labor law. "He told us that if the union got in, the warehouse would be closed," one of the workers recalled for Walton's biographer Bob Ortega. "He said people could vote any way they wanted, but he'd close her right up."[35]

Meanwhile, John Tate stirred the pot with a propaganda barrage that has since become a classic in the anti-union arsenal. Workers want justice, but not divisiveness. They seek harmony and cooperation, as well as dignity at work. They organize for a voice on the job, not a strike that puts them outside on the picket lines. Anti-union strategists like Tate had long been well aware of these social and psychological needs and how to turn them against the union impulse, promising violence, division, conflict, and an immediate strike if workers cast their lot with the union. Workers arriving at the Searcy distribution center one morning found Tate's rendition of this anti-union stratagem in the form of a ninety-foot-long bulletin board, covered with four decades' worth of newspaper clippings describing every Teamster strike, violent incident, and allegation of criminality that Tate's researchers had been able to piece together. It was headlined "Walk the 90-Foot Wall of Teamster Shame," recalled Ronald Heath, who ran the organizing campaign for the Teamsters' local in Little Rock.[36]

Not unexpectedly, the Teamsters lost the election, after which Walton gloated in the company magazine, Wal-Mart World: "Our good associates at our Searcy distribution center rejected the union by an overwhelming margin of over three to one. Bless them all. . . . We will never need a union in Wal-Mart if we work with and for one another and keep listening to each other."[37] It was a historic defeat. The Teamsters failed to contest the election, and the hard-core unionists were soon eased out of the Searcy DC. The Arkansas labor movement, the Teamsters included, never renewed the struggle. That in turn sent a signal to the AFL-CIO in Washington that, for the moment at least, Wal-Mart was too difficult to tackle and that company employees, in both the distribution centers and the stores, were too satisfied, complacent, or fearful to organize.[38]

Still, the truck drivers are an absolutely vital link in Wal-Mart's increasingly sophisticated supply chain. Each day they follow a carefully plotted itinerary that gets them from the distribution center to the store and back in the shortest time, burning the least amount of gas. The timely completion of their task is vital since these drivers—eventually there would be more than eight thousand of them working out of more than one hundred DCs—must arrive at their designated Wal-Mart store at an appointed moment each evening so that the overnight stocking staff can unload the truck. If they are off schedule, money is lost and confusion reigns.[39]

Wal-Mart management was therefore determined to consolidate their allegiance. Even as deregulation of the larger trucking industry turned many over-the-road trucks, especially those of the owner-operators, into "sweatshops on wheels," Wal-Mart drivers were elevated to something resembling a labor aristocracy.[40] By the early 1980s Wal-Mart paid them wages equivalent to union scale. In Mississippi and some of the other southern states this meant that they were earning triple the pay of a state highway patrolman, five times that of an hourly sales clerk. Equally important to many truckers, the word went out that drivers were no longer required to help load and unload their shipments. Their uniforms were now always clean; their equipment was the best in the business. "We drop, hook, and drive. We don't load and unload," bragged a self-satisfied driver when interviewed by *Discount Store News* late in the 1990s. "Wal-Mart is the Cadillac of trucking," asserted another.[41] To become a Wal-Mart trucker required three hundred thousand miles of accident-free driving, as well as approval from a committee of working Wal-Mart drivers.[42]

The drivers, an almost entirely white, male fraternity, developed a strong esprit de corps, even a certain arrogance toward rival truckers or other Wal-Mart employees, both managers and associates. H. Lee Scott learned this in an incident during the early 1980s, just a few years after he had been hired away from autocratic, nonunion Yellow Freight to run the company's logistics operations. Scott was a wiz at optimizing schedules and solving routing problems. Before the deployment of specialized computer software to figure all this out, he found the task mentally rewarding, like a "challenging crossword puzzle," he once recalled. But the truckers were not ciphers to be similarly slotted about. When Scott tried to regiment their behavior with a series of dictums, admonishing drivers for an uptick in accident rates or too many speeding tickets, a group of drivers reacted with righteous fury. Some complained directly to Wal ton, asking him to fire Scott. Mr. Sam, in turn, made young Scott listen to the drivers' complaints and thank each one individually for bringing their grievances to his attention. None were penalized. When Scott became CEO in 2000, this incident was told and retold as a tribute to the company's unique culture and the "open door" hosted by top executives.[43]

But only truck drivers ever received this kind of collective good treatment. And it paid off: turnover rates for long-haul drivers, which sometimes reached 100 percent in the nonunion cartage industry, never left the single digits at Wal-Mart. Accidents involving Wal-Mart trucks, frequently costly and litigious affairs, were rare. And even more vital, Wal-Mart achieved a 99.8 percent on-time delivery standard for its stores, a truly astounding figure.[44]

Not all who worked in logistics were admitted to this labor aristocracy, however. Wal-Mart's growing list of distribution centers required a lot of staffing, and unlike the truck drivers, who always enjoyed a degree of highway autonomy, the blue-collar men who ran the forklifts and threw boxes into the truck trailers did not get any special privileges. As the depth and precision of logistic computerization intensified, their work was increasingly Taylorized and closely supervised. They were paid more than the cashiers and clerks, enough to avoid a debilitating labor shortage at the DCs, but no more than necessary. When a Searcy warehouseman asked Walton why they were getting paid $1.50 less an hour than those in a newly opened Texas facility, Sam replied forthrightly, "I can hire you for less in Arkansas." In future years Wal-Mart often sited its DCs in rural areas with a high degree of underemployment, even if this put them at a considerable distance from the interstate. A study of retail distribution centers in New York State found a strong correlation between corporate culture and DC location. The Gap chose a sophisticated area north of New York City, Target selected a fast-growing, middle-class suburban location, Kmart settled on a community with a substantial Hispanic population, and Wal-Mart put its DC in a remote rural county in the midst of New York's dairy industry, some distance from the interstate highway.[45]

WAL-MART VERSUS THE UNIONS

Wal-Mart followed a similar strategy in its stores. Until the mid-1980s Wal-Mart avoided metropolitan America whenever possible. This was where trade unions had their greatest strength, in an archipelago of cities and suburbs that stretched from Boston to the District of Columbia, from New York to Minneapolis, and from Seattle to San Diego. In Missouri, for example, Wal-Mart built scores of stores, but all were in small towns or in the exurban ring that skirted such union strongholds as St. Louis and Kansas City.[46] And this was the Wal-Mart pattern in other border or midwestern states. At the same time trade unionism encountered an increasingly hostile political and social environment in these years, first sent reeling by the deindustrialization of the old union strongholds and then slapped hard by Ronald Reagan and a generation of increasingly aggressive Republicans who saw the unions as a bar to U.S. international competitiveness and a financial prop for the Democrats.

Thus John Tate could brag in 1990 that Wal-Mart had not faced a single union petition for an NLRB election in more than a decade. But the battle was about to be joined. Tate quit his Omaha law firm to become an executive vice president and a member of the Wal-Mart board of directors in 1987, an extraordinary status for an executive heading a corporate personnel department. He retired in the mid-1990s, but Wal-Mart would continue to make use of his services well into the new century, when many of the anti-union techniques and strategies he had developed decades before would form a rampart against a new wave of labor organizing.

Wal-Mart needed to be tough because the once-rural retailer was now putting its stores in states and regions that had long been friendly hosts to a vigorous trade union tradition. It was as if Lee's army was once again moving across the Potomac and into Yankee territory. By the early 1990s the company had stores in Wisconsin, Minnesota, Michigan, Ohio, Pennsylvania, and California. This was the context in which Orson Mason, who would later become a successful hospital-industry union fighter, wrote one of the most infamous documents in the history of Wal-Mart labor relations. "Labor Relations and You at the Wal-Mart Distribution Center #6022" is a step-by-step guide for supervisors at Wal-Mart's huge Greencastle, Indiana, facility, in a part of central Indiana where the Teamsters, the Auto Workers, and the Railroad Brotherhoods had deep roots and much support. "Any suggestion that this Company is neutral on the subject or that it encourages associates to join labor organizations is not true," asserted the guide, which was aimed at a readership of blue-collar foremen and supervisors. "The commitment to stay union free must exist at all levels of management—from the chairperson of the 'Board' down to the front-line manager. Therefore, no one in management is immune from carrying his or her 'own weight' in the union prevention effort."[47]

Wal-Mart's avoidance of metropolitan America was not the only reason it had escaped a serious encounter with American trade unionism. Both the Teamsters and the United Food and Commercial Workers Union were decentralized trade unions in which a militant organizing tradition was dying out. The Teamster effort to unionize the Searcy distribution center in the late 1970s had been organized out of Little Rock, not the union's national headquarters in Washington. More important, the Teamsters were a rudderless union in the 1970s and 1980s, presided over by a series of weak, corrupt national officers full of bluster on occasion, but who could do nothing to either stanch the membership losses that were the product of trucking deregulation or coordinate the organizing activities of the hundreds of fieflike local unions whose outlook was resolutely parochial. And of course the chief issue occupying Teamster officials in the late 1980s was not Wal-Mart or any other organizing effort, but the effort by a young New York district attorney, Rudy Giuliani, to purge the union of scores of corrupt officials. By the time the feds were finished, more than 150 tainted Teamsters were out of office and out of the union.

The UFCW was in better shape. Supermarkets were a big, successful business in the postwar United States. By the end of the twentieth century they employed 2.5 million workers, fully 2 percent of the U.S. workforce. With 1.3 million members, the UFCW had organized about eight hundred thousand of these workers in chains that represented just over half of all supermarket sales. Union wages in this industry never approached those once paid in the core of the old manufacturing economy, but they were enough to sustain a modest, recognizably middle-class standard of living. Most surveys put the cost of pay and benefits in the unionized grocery stores at about 30 percent above that found at Wal-Mart. Wages were indeed higher, but the big, qualitative difference between Wal-Mart and the union groceries lay elsewhere, in those aspects of the job that made a real career possible: forty-hour workweeks, defined benefit pension plans, adequate family health insurance, and a seniority system that facilitated a steady progression through a series of higher-paying and more responsible jobs.[48]

The UFCW itself was the product of a series of mergers in the 1960s and 1970s among unions representing packinghouse and food-processing workers, furriers, meat cutters, and retail clerks, most of whom worked in the nation's highly regionalized set of supermarket chains. The clerks, whose old union had once been called the Retail Clerks International Protective Associa tion, were now the dominant element in the UFCW, and this did not bode well for any attempt to stand up to Wal-Mart. The Retail Clerks had emerged in the Progressive era, when they championed early closing hours and rest breaks for the poorly paid women who staffed the big downtown department stores. By the 1940s and 1950s real unions existed in Macy's, Marshall Field's, and a few other flagship stores, but the Retail Clerks never succeeded in organizing chains like Woolworth, Penney's, Sears, or Kresge. The Retail Clerks were not a militant trade union, and they rarely struck a chain, certainly not on a national basis.[49]

This conciliatory strategy continued well into the postwar decades. In the mid-1980s, when a packinghouse local at Hormel conducted a long, militant strike that evoked memories of the great organizing battles waged by the industrial unions in the 1930s, UFCW leaders were chagrined, then actively hostile, and finally so enraged that they seized the Austin, Minnesota, local, squashed the strike, and allowed Hormel to impose a dramatic, multiyear wage cut.[50]

Nonetheless, the Retail Clerks had succeeded in quietly organizing much of the postwar era's booming supermarket industry, where many jobs, like those in produce and meat cutting, were of higher skill, and hence male, and where local supermarket chains, which had established a near monopoly within their own metropolitan region, were not averse to allowing the Retail Clerks to set a modest wage standard for themselves as well as any competitors who might seek to invade their sales territory. For more than half a century, locals of the Retail Clerks/UFCW bargained uneventfully with regional chains like Giant in the Washington area, Pathmark in New York and New Jersey, Stop and Shop in New England, Ralph's in Southern California, Fred Meyer in Seattle, and the Star Markets of Boston. They won excellent health insurance benefits and a good pension scheme. But this regional success had a downside. The UFCW remained highly decentralized. It did little to coordinate organizing among its jealously autonomous locals. In Canada it was a Steelworkers' local, not the UFCW, that made the biggest push to organize some of the Woolco stores taken over by Bentonville in 1993. Indeed, since Wal-Mart was not on the radar of most of the big regional locals, the UFCW barely noticed the rapidly growing discounter, at least until the early 1990s when the huge company began to build hundreds of grocery-selling Supercenters, now often located in the suburbs right down the street from a union supermarket.[51]

Wal-Mart's Supercenters were a sensation, something genuinely new in a supermarket business approaching middle age. By adding a full line of groceries to the discount store format, Wal-Mart not only burst onto the scene in a trillion-dollar industry but also ramped up its general merchandise sales by about 30 percent in each grocery-selling store. This was truly one-stop shopping. So Bentonville put Supercenters on the map at a furious clip: about 100 a year in the mid-1990s, and then 113 in 1998, 157 in 1999, and 167 in 2000. By the end of the next year, one thousand Supercenters had been built and Wal-Mart commanded the number one spot in the U.S. grocery market. "Wal-Mart Is Eating Everybody's Lunch," pronounced *BusinessWeek*.[52]

Wal-Mart's cost advantage over traditional supermarkets came on two fronts. First, the Bentonville selling machine rejected the traditional, Byzantine system of supermarket "vendor allowances," which determined how an item was promoted, the shelf space it required, and the price it commanded. Although profitable in the short run, these barely veiled kickbacks added enormous complexity and rigidity to the procurement process. Wal-Mart would have nothing to do with them.[53]

Even more important, Wal-Mart held a decisive competitive advantage over the supermarkets when it came to labor costs, which were often 70 percent of the operating budget. When Wal-Mart was competing against Kmart and Woolworth, its cost of labor was but marginally lower, but in the grocery business, the difference was substantial. The UFCW was caught in the squeeze, both by Wal-Mart, which put unionized firms out of business, and by the old-line grocery chains themselves, which were determined to hold the line on their wage and benefit costs to meet the challenge. In the Midwest Kroger was hurting; in the South Piggly Wiggly would soon be forced out of business; in California Safeway began to slash office staff and prepare for battle with its unions. In Las Vegas for example, Wal-Mart opened sixteen stores in the 1990s, which led to the demise of Raley's, a unionized, California-based grocery chain that operated eighteen supermarkets in southern Nevada. All were shuttered by the end of 2002, leading to the loss of fourteen hundred union jobs.[54] In all, Wal-Mart proved the catalyst for the closure of thirteen thousand traditional supermarkets and the bankruptcy of at least twenty-five regional grocery chains in the years between 1992 and 2003.[55]

The UFCW effort to organize Wal-Mart has therefore been

an essentially defensive one. And like any entrenched formation, the big grocery union had certain tactical advantages. It
was one of the few U.S. trade unions that could still organize;
the work of its members could not be outsourced to Mexico
or China, so the fear of job loss was not an immediate worry
when organizers approached potential recruits. UFCW membership actually grew by one hundred thousand during the
1980s and early 1990s.[56] At Wal-Mart, the union adopted an opportunistic organizing strategy, supporting workers wherever
a few union sparkplugs could be found: in Aiken, South Carolina; Greencastle, Pennsylvania; Loveland, Colorado; Kingston,
Arizona; but mainly in union-friendly Las Vegas, where Wal-
Mart's evangelical communalism had made few inroads. When
Stan Fortune, who had begun his Wal-Mart career in Arkadel-
phia, Arkansas, was assigned to the Loss Prevention Department in Las Vegas, he thought he had entered a Wild West drama,
where violent shoplifters, alienated associates, and sky-high
turnover made a mockery of the famous Wal-Mart cheer that
opened his Supercenter each morning. Surely union organization would not be impossible in this volatile situation. Fortune
was among the ten former Wal-Mart managers the UFCW
hired, most of whom were flown to Las Vegas to stir the union
waters.

On its face this strategy could never win, certainly not in
terms of traditional union-management conflict and compromise. With more than three thousand domestic Wal-Mart stores
at the time, UFCW organizing victories at a handful of scattered sites were unlikely to make much of an impression upon
Bentonville. But the union hoped that the publicity generated
by the campaign would force Wal-Mart to raise wages, improve its health insurance, and encourage the growth of union-
community collaborations against the giant retailer. Even more
important, the UFCW wanted to demonstrate that Wal-Mart's
violation of the labor law was so widespread and so systematic

that the NLRB should impose an "extraordinary nationwide remedy" against the company. In almost all unfair labor practice complaints issued by the board, the sanctions applied are narrowly local. But if an employer is caught using the same illegal tactics in various places, the NLRB can impose nationwide penalties, which if enforced in the federal courts can have a real impact on the way the company conducts its anti-union campaign. So the UFCW barraged the NLRB with allegations of unfair labor practices against Wal-Mart, and it seemed just possible that the labor board might slap Wal-Mart with a serious company-wide penalty, "an extraordinary remedy" that would have personally fined Wal-Mart store managers themselves ten thousand dollars for willful violations of the labor law. But Wal-Mart circumvented the entire process by appealing straight to the newly installed Bush administration. Just days before Wal-Mart was set to argue its case, Leonard Page, the union-friendly general counsel for the NLRB, took a phone call from the White House. He had thirty-six hours to clear out his office. Page's more conservative successor decided against bringing a national complaint against Wal-Mart.[57]

Indeed, the deck was stacked against the union. Although Wal-Mart could not move its stores overseas, it could transform the technology or organization of a job so as to eliminate the workers who were potential union recruits. This was an old management stratagem, which had eviscerated trade unionism in newspaper press rooms, tobacco processing factories, wireless telecommunications, and a large slice of the broadcast industry. Wal-Mart adopted the same kind of technological fix after nine meat cutters had the temerity to actually stick together long enough to win an NLRB election in 2000 in a Palestine, Texas, Supercenter. Their grievances were typical of the trade: they wanted wages equal to those enjoyed by the unionized butchers across town, and they insisted on regular hours and a certain deference from store management. For more than a century meat cutting had been at the core of unionism within the grocery industry. Consumers wanted their ribs, steaks, and roasts freshly cut at the grocery store itself, often to their exact specification, and this work required skill, speed, and judgment, applied to a product that was perishable and relatively expensive. So grocery-store butchers had always enjoyed a premium wage, not to mention the kind of craft autonomy that was anathema within the Wal-Mart organizational culture.

So when Bentonville got word of the unexpected union inroad at Palestine the company cauterized the wound in the most radical fashion. Henceforth, Wal-Mart announced that it would cease cutting meat in its stores altogether. This was almost certainly a form of illegal retaliation against its newly union-certified butchers. But for Wal-Mart that was an insignificant detail that could and would languish in the courts. Of far greater import was the company's decision to become the first big grocery chain to adopt a new system of buying "case-ready" beef and pork prepackaged by the meatpacker. For Wal-Mart shoppers, the switch meant no more custom orders; for the packers, it pushed even more of the responsibility for salability and quality onto their shoulders, along with the profit-enhancing capacity to "brand" their product. Earlier efforts to sell case-ready meat had failed because airtight packages didn't take on the red color, or "bloom," that consumers associate with freshness. But food scientists had learned how to flush the packages with a mixture of oxygen and carbon dioxide that let the meat bloom slowly. For Wal-Mart this process proved a clever technological fix that tightened the corporate supply chain even as it eliminated its vulnerability to the union. The *Cattle Buyers Weekly* called Wal-Mart's move "the single biggest change in the history of meat retailing."[58]

But Palestine was the exception. When it came to trade unionism, Wal-Mart rarely had to make such a structural readjustment to stanch the threat from organized labor. It de-

ployed multiple and overlapping lines of defense like the inter-
secting lines of cannon fire that protected a well-constructed
fortress. By the time the UFCW began its effort to organize Wal-
Mart in the late 1990s, "union avoidance" strategies, at Wal-
Mart and other corporations, had been well under way since
the days when John Tate and Sam Walton browbeat the Searcy
warehousemen. An entire anti-union industry had grown up
in the United States since the 1970s, when the lawyers and consultants who orchestrated such work were thought to be just
a step or two above ambulance chasers and bail bondsmen.
But Ronald Reagan's celebration of the free market during his
White House years legitimized an ideological and operational
hostility to organized labor at just the moment when sharper
competition at home and abroad had convinced many businessmen that the unionized workplace was both too expensive
and too inflexible. So a flourishing set of consultants, law firms,
personnel psychologists, and strike management firms peddled
their services during an era when it was finally possible, in the
North and West as well as the rural South, to promote what
one consultant called the "morality of a union-free environment."[59]

The work is outsourced. When corporate executives get
wind of a union organizing drive or some other indication of
discontent, they turn matters over to outside consultants and
lawyers. At a cost that often reaches several million dollars
for a few months' work, these union busters deploy a well-tested
set of stratagems to ensure that their new client is kept union-
free.[60] First, the lower-level supervisory staff is assembled and
told that they are hereby drafted into the anti-union effort; any
equivocation or desertion will result in instant dismissal, if only
because these "managers" have no protection under existing
interpretations of U.S. labor law. Then comes a barrage of leaflets,
videos, personnel shifts, and meetings with individual employees, often climaxed with an on-site visit by top corporate

executives. Captive audience assemblies become more frequent and more intimidating as the presumptive date of the NLRB election draws near. Should the union manage to eke out an election victory, another round of delay and resistance begins, often organized by the same law firm that orchestrated the anti-union campaign in the first place. It's expensive but highly effective: union organizing efforts using traditional labor law procedures have virtually ground to a halt in the United States. Only about one union campaign in twenty ends with a signed collective bargaining contract.[61]

HOW WAL-MART WINS

Wal-Mart does all this and more, in-house, with its own people taking on the key tasks, and thus making the techniques and stratagems developed by the union avoidance experts an integral, organic part of corporate practice. As Wal-Mart came under high levels of scrutiny in the 1990s, the company ritually announced, "We are not anti-union; we are pro-associate." But every store manager knew that his or her success depended on keeping trade unions at bay; certainly that was the message driven home in training manuals such as one titled "A Manager's Toolbox to Remaining Union Free."[62]

Wal-Mart's Tom Coughlin, who in 2000 was number two in the corporate hierarchy, presided over this effort, an approach that was truly one of the iron fist inside the velvet glove. In the 1980s Coughlin had been tutored by John Tate, and a decade later he led the company effort to defeat the UFCW. He was uncompromising. "These union issues are going to get worse," he told a Bentonville staff meeting in March 2000, so managers should quickly identify the most "fertile ground for unions" among the Wal-Mart associates and immediately report back to Bentonville. Then the regional vice presidents and district managers must ensure that all labor relations directives are "executed 100%! There is no room or tolerance for slippage."[63]

For Coughlin and all other Wal-Mart managers, unions were always referred to as "third-party representatives." This was a worldview driven home during a 'new employee's very first day on the payroll. A Wal-Mart training video, "You've Picked a Great Place to Work!," makes the point with great effectiveness. Through a conversation among a human resources manager; two newly hired workers, one of whom was a former union member; and two current workers, of whom one also previously belonged to a union, the video pounds home Wal-Mart's disdain for trade unionism and the terrible consequences that befall workers and businesses that succumb to union blandishments. In just twenty-seven minutes the video encapsulates a generation of right-wing imagery and propaganda designed to demonize and marginalize the trade union idea. Unions are portrayed as essentially corrupt and parasitical institutions, marginal businesses—not unlike pawnbrokers or payday lenders—which are primarily concerned with the dues income collected from naïve workers seduced by their promises.

Wal-Mart's video portrays the unions as "political," spending dues money on campaigns for candidates that workers "don't even vote for," and "to pay union bigwigs and their lawyers." And the "politics" extends to the internal life of the workplace itself: work rules base promotions on "seniority or union politics," rather than merit; union procedures prohibit members from communicating directly with management and require workers "to go to your union steward," who will relay the message to management only "if he likes what you say." And most important, the union is ineffective or worse. Strikes—frequent, violent, and divisive—are certain to be lost, likewise "every benefit . . . could go on the negotiating table" and "unions will negotiate just about anything to get the right to have dues deducted from your paychecks." The video concludes with the former unionist, now a newly minted Wal-Mart associate, seeing the light. Speaking directly into the camera, he asserts, "All of us every day, we see how our management listens and cares. . . . We see how many chances there are to move. There's no way we'd want a union to come in."[64]

There's a racial subtext to this propaganda as well. The two most forceful and self-confident anti-unionists in the video are African Americans. The human resource manager who occupies the central role in the video is an attractive black women in her forties, who embodies the mature and kindly spirit of Mr. Sam. One of the former unionists, now a Wal-Mart associate who tells tales of union mendacity, is an African American man. And one of the naïve new-hires, initially favorable to the union idea, is a young white man. All of this completely inverts the usual alignment, which finds African Americans most sympathetic to the union idea and young white males either indifferent or hostile. Wal-Mart understands this as well, which is why the company has populated the executive ranks in its "People Division" with numerous high-profile Latinos and African Americans.

Such indoctrination and training are hardly enough, so Wal-Mart keeps a close watch on what its workers think about their job, their boss, the company, and themselves. The "employee attitude survey" has long been a staple of the nonunion workplace. Sears perfected the system in the 1950s when it employed skilled social scientists to identify patterns of discontent and the employees who were most disloyal, before such sentiment could metastasize into a fatal union cancer. Anti-union consulting firms made heavy use of such surveys from the 1980s on.[65] Wal-Mart adopted a more down-home approach but a hardly less effective one. In the early 1970s Walton took the pulse of his workers by hosting an annual "grassroots" meeting for selected associates, in which top management heard complaints and exchanged ideas. Meetings were eventually held in every store. By 1994 they were replaced, in all but name, by a sixty-eight-question survey that sliced and diced employee morale according to job, gender, ethnicity, age, length of service, and hours of work. The top five problems uncovered by the survey were always inadequate pay, the cost of health insurance, management favoritism, poor training, and the company policy that forced employees to relocate if they wanted a promotion into management ranks.[66]

Bentonville's computers also manipulated the data to generate something Wal-Mart called a "UPI," which originally stood for Union Probability Index, later renamed Unaddressed People Issues. About 20 percent of all Wal-Mart stores, most located outside the South, generated a UPI high enough to signal low morale and therefore require the attention of company executives whose job it was to keep unionism at bay. "Maintaining high morale in a facility is crucial to remaining union free" was the way Wal-Mart's Pipeline, its intranet for store managers, put it in a confidential message in 2001. "If a union organizer approaches an associate in a facility with low morale, the associate may believe the organizer's 'sales pitch.'"[67] Store managers who presided over a facility with a high UPI were vulnerable to transfer or demotion.

Of course, actually raising morale was either far too expensive or far too disruptive. At the turn of the century, the top two worker grievances were all about money, and the rest challenged corporate authoritarianism. The Pipeline did identify "Wal-Mart's Open Door policy as our greatest defense to union influences trying to change our corporate culture and union-free status." But the open door was but another part of the paternalistic culture, "a morale tool to enhance the Wal-Mart family image," according to one disgruntled store manager who was advised to minimize the time she spent on the "typical Associate concern or complaint."[68]

Wal-Mart's own store managers and assistant managers are both the frontline troops and potential traitors in the battle against the unions. Like foremen in the factories and supervisors in the office, they are men and women in the middle, required to "execute 100 percent" the directives that come from above but also charged with the creation of a productive and harmonious workplace. Although they may be intensely hostile to "outside" union organizers, managers and assistant managers are enmeshed within a world of friendships and other relationships that makes them unreliable union fighters. Trained for their entire career to conceive of the store as a communal family, they may well be reluctant to institute the divisive tactics necessary to split the workforce, create internal tensions, and thereby defeat the union campaign. Thus Brent Rummage, a former youth minister with the Church of God, who had been admitted to the Wal-Mart management training program, was supposed to report any union talk to his store manager. But when his own mother, who worked in the same Hillview, Kentucky, store to which he was assigned, ventured that unions might not be so bad, Rummage balked. "I wasn't going to report my mother," Rummage told a reporter. Likewise Stan Fortune was managing a Wal-Mart in Weatherford, Texas, when his boss instructed him to fire an employee suspected of talking to the union. "I told him 'I'm not firing him,'" Fortune later recalled. "'That's illegal.' . . . He got in my face and said 'You fire him or I'm going to fire you.'" A week later Fortune was gone.[69] Both Rummage and Fortune were later hired by the UFCW as part of the union's organizing drive at Wal-Mart.

Almost as troublesome to the company were those managers who took their hostility to unionism too personally. At the turn of the century, Wal-Mart faced hundreds of unfair-labor-practice charges filed by the UFCW and other unions. They were expensive, time-consuming, and sometimes embarrassing to litigate, so Wal-Mart tried to teach lower-level managers to walk a fine line between militant but legal anti-unionism and those tactics that would generate an NLRB charge. This was the TIPS program, spelled out in Wal-Mart's "Managers Tool- box to Remaining Union Free." "Know your TIPS. As long as you do not Threaten, Interrogate, Promise, or Spy on your asso- ciates, Wal-Mart, through your efforts, will be able to share its views on unionization in an open, honest and legal manner."[70] Naturally, it proved impossible to adhere to such admonitions in practice. How could managers warn workers of the union dan- ger if they did not implicitly threaten them, on the one hand, and promise a better future, either individually or collectively, on the other? And how were managers to know when they should pick up the Wal-Mart "union hotline" to Bentonville, un- less they interrogated or spied on those who worked for them?

Trade unions lodged 288 unfair-labor-practice charges against Wal-Mart between 1998 and 2003. These included 41 charges claiming improper firings, 44 instances in which employees were threatened if they joined a union, 59 charges involving im- proper surveillance, and another 59 asserting that Wal-Mart illegally interrogated its associates to determine their views on sensitive labor-related issues. In all, 94 of these complaints were weighty enough to generate a formal NLRB complaint against the corporation.[71]

When the union hotline did ring in Bentonville, Wal-Mart immediately put key members of its "labor team" on a corpo- rate jet and dispatched them to the troubled store. At the height of the UFCW organizing campaign, there were about twenty midlevel Wal-Mart executives assigned to this corporate office. Although some had a law degree, their function was not litiga- tion before the NLRB or any other agency of the government. That was left to one of many law firms on retainer with the cor- poration. Instead, the labor team directed itself exclusively toward the "education" of store management and the associates who might have sparked the union drive or become subject to its siren song. Until the union campaign was defeated, the labor team's skilled operatives sidelined local management and effectively took over the store, orchestrating the anti-union effort so as to stay on legally justifiable terrain. As a manager in Colorado told Human Rights Watch, "We have a union activity hotline. If you hear associates, you don't confront them. You or the store manager calls the hotline. Then higher-up management takes care of it." Liz Boyd, a department manager at the Aiken, South Carolina, Wal-Mart, reported that during the union campaign there, "It was our duty . . . to report any union activity and call the Union Hotline. Even now, if I hear of a union rumor, I'm supposed to notify management or call the hotline."[72]

BLITZKRIEG AT KINGMAN

The labor team was extremely active during the first years of the twenty-first century when the UFCW organizing campaign was at its height. Thanks to the work of Human Rights Watch, which has made a thorough and devastating study of Wal-Mart's anti-unionism, we have an exceptionally well documented account of how this specialized unit operated to propagandize workers and thwart a union organizing effort at a typical Wal-Mart. The young men who work in the Tire and Lube Express (TLE) Department have always been among those most receptive to the union idea. They get their hands dirty, they have few prospects for promotion, and they are well aware that similar blue-collar jobs in garages and car dealerships pay a lot more. Such was the case in the Kingman, Arizona, store, where an otherwise humane manager, under corporate pressure to keep labor and maintenance costs down, refused to spend the two hundred dollars needed to repair an air-cooling system essential in the 110-degree summer heat. Throw in an arrogant young—and female—TLE department head, and all the ingredients were present for a unionization attempt. So TLE workers got in touch with the UFCW, which on August 28, 2000, filed a petition with the nearby Phoenix office of the NLRB to represent as many as eighteen automotive service technicians.[73]

The reaction from Wal-Mart was immediate and overwhelming. Within twenty-four hours a Bentonville-based labor team was in Kingman, along with district and regional managers from Arizona and Nevada. In all, more than twenty outside managers flooded the store, some to keep tabs on the mood of the associates via the Wal-Mart CBWA system, or "Coaching By Walking Around"; others to help out with the time-consuming annual inventory while the regular staff watched anti-union videos and attended near-daily captive meetings. At the TLE Wal-Mart replaced the manager there with a high-level personnel executive, untutored in changing oil or tires, but well versed in the corporation's union avoidance program. Loss Prevention got busy as well, training a new set of cameras on work areas in the tire and lube shop. "I had so many bosses around me, I couldn't believe it," remembered Larry Adams, a union supporter who worked in the TLE at that time. "They weren't there to help me. They were there to bug me. It was very intimidating."[74]

The key labor team figures were Vicky Dodson, a thirteen-year veteran in Wal-Mart's People Division, and Kirk Williams, a young law school graduate from Chicago whom Wal-Mart had hired just a few months before. Dodson was a pro, a forceful and controlling "pistol," remembered one of the assistant managers who came under her authority; "an intelligent, articulate, sophisticated individual," in the more judicious words of an NLRB administrative law judge.[75] Williams, who had worked his way through Kent State as a Wal-Mart assistant store manager, including a stint in Loss Prevention, was a coldly ambitious functionary who would soon spend enormous amounts of time on the corporate jet putting out union fires throughout the company's retail empire.[76] Most people in the store, management and worker alike, called the Bentonville labor team the "union busters" or the "Nazi SS." Not unexpectedly, Dodson and Williams were contemptuous of the existing store management, whose maladroit handing of layoffs and scheduling issues they blamed for precipitating the union uprising. "They took us out of the store for a couple of days," remembered Assistant Manager Tony Kuc, "took us to a hotel, telling us how to handle the union, how to stop them from coming in ... what to say, what not to say." Within a few weeks the store manager had been transferred and demoted, his two assistant managers marked for dismissal, and the TLE district manager fired outright.[77]

Within less than a week Dodson and her confederates met with 95 percent of all workers eligible to participate in the NLRB certification vote. Meanwhile, the labor team held daily meetings at 8 a.m. with all the salaried managers, as well as the hourly department heads, who they said were part of the store "management" and therefore ineligible to take part in an NLRB certification election. "We were basically spies, spies for the store, spies for the company," remembered a disenchanted department head. "We had to run our departments, do everything normally, and then be spies for them. The stress level was so high."[78] Unionists complained, at Kingman and elsewhere, that "Wal-Mart has tricked hourly department managers into thinking they were part of the management team and therefore obligated to report any signs of union activity," even though the NLRB ruled repeatedly against the company about the status of these hourly employees. Observed Michael Leonard, a UFCW official, "Wal-Mart's MO is to test the limits of the law, and to only change its prepackaged anti-union program when it is forced to."[79]

The labor team screened one of five different anti-union

videos every day. "Wal-Mart Under Attack" was a lurid depic-
tion of union thuggishness and disruption directed at a company that was portrayed as merely trying to provide inexpensive
goods for ordinary working people. "Sign Now, Pay Later" urged
Wal-Mart workers to resist the siren song of the union organizers, who would do and say anything to win another signature on a union card, all the while ensnaring the hapless retail
worker in a world of burdensome dues and serflike subservi-
ence to an alien, boss-ridden organization. These videos, always
followed by a Q and A with a member of the labor team, were
highly effective. A worker later interviewed by Human Rights
Watch remembered, "I actually had fears after seeing videos of
Molotov cocktails and rocks, pelting rocks, hurling bottles."
Another said, "After those meetings, minds started changing"
as onetime union supporters turned against the UFCW.[80]

On one alarmist charge Wal-Mart was at least partially correct. If the union got in, the "store would run with a steward. . . .
The union will run the store. They will dictate the store. The
store manager [will] respond to the steward, not the district
manager." Indeed, unionization of even part of a Wal-Mart store
would curb managerial authority; it might also reduce management bonuses and introduce the seniority principle into the
making of assignments and schedules.[81] John Lehman was a
successful Wal-Mart store manager in the 1990s, who never
made less than $140,000 a year during that decade. When he
briefly left Wal-Mart to manage a unionized Meijer store in
Louisville, he found that while his pay was not as high as at
Wal-Mart, the headaches were a lot less. Meijer's contract with
the UFCW circumscribed the store manager's power to assign
work hours and to offer raises, instead providing a well-defined
matrix of job descriptions, grade levels, and pay categories
that existed only in rudimentary and contingent form at Wal-
Mart. Likewise, unionized stores had a far higher proportion

of full-time workers on schedules pegged to their seniority, a system that Wal-Mart executives declared would "fundamentally change the store's business model."[82]

Dodson, Williams, and other top managers from the Southwest stayed in Kingman for two months. During this period the local NLRB held hearings to determine the size and composition of the TLE unit, and both the UFCW and the Wal-Mart labor team marshaled their forces for the certification election itself. In minutely detailed reports back to Bentonville, labor team members described every instance of possible union talk, every wavering worker, and every meeting. Dodson kept track of the workers who wore union pins and the ones who took them off, what comments were made at the captive meetings, and the degree of union sentiment in various departments of the store. The labor team authorized raises for 85 percent of all workers, fixed the TLE cooling system, and repaired other equipment in that same department.[83] On October 9 Tom Coughlin jetted into Kingman to tell a group of TLE workers that the Wal-Mart "open door," not the UFCW, was the solution to their problems. This was a clear violation of the spirit, if not the letter, of the existing labor law, which forbade management efforts to bribe, promise, or cajole employees in the midst of an organizing effort. "If you have any questions or problems," Coughlin told his grease-stained listeners, "don't hesitate to call me, and I will get you some results. I can override anybody." Then with a flourish Coughlin put his home telephone number on the white board and told store managers to leave it there.[84]

Given all this, it is hardly surprising that the UFCW organizing drive collapsed in inglorious defeat. Although the labor board ruled that the TLE was an appropriate bargaining unit, the union lost key supporters there within weeks of the labor team's arrival in town. Union partisans had virtually no opportunity to counter the propaganda barrage unleashed by the

Bentonville labor team. If they sought the telephone number of undecided associates, this violated Wal-Mart's "no solicitation" rule; if they distributed leaflets in the parking lot or break room in the store, managers immediately called Loss Prevention and then patrolled the facility to pick up any stray literature. And when UFCW organizers made evening house calls, Wal-Mart denounced this tactic as harassment and intimidation. So on October 24 UFCW lawyers filed a broad set of unfair-labor-practice complaints against Wal-Mart, thus postponing indefinitely the NLRB election scheduled for just a few days later. Working life for the remaining pro-union people in the Kingman store became increasingly intolerable. Within little more than a year virtually all would be fired, forced to quit, or simply leave in disgust.

As at Kingman, the UFCW organizing effort hit a brick wall wherever it mustered enough support to organize a few house meetings or file for an NLRB election. The labor board eventually ruled, at Kingman and elsewhere, that Wal-Mart had systematically harassed and spied upon numerous workers, that it had threatened employees with a loss of benefits and raises if they supported the union, and that the company had fired key labor partisans outright. But none of this had any real impact on Wal-Mart's anti-union operation, if only because the penalties were so trivial: a few thousand dollars in back pay for a few unjustly fired employees, plus a formal notice briefly posted in the break room pledging to obey the labor law. In its authoritative report on Wal-Mart, *Discounting Rights: Wal-Mart's Violation of U.S. Workers' Rights to Freedom of Association,* Human Rights Watch concluded that the company "has translated its hostility towards union formation into an unabashed, sophisticated, and aggressive strategy to derail worker organizing at its US stores that violates workers' internationally recognized right to freedom of association."[85]

True enough, but John Tate deserves the last word. When in September 2004 Tom Coughlin introduced the eighty-six-year-old union fighter to a large meeting of store managers and other Wal-Mart executives assembled in Dallas, Tate was in a valedictory and triumphant mood. The UFCW, decisively beaten in every store where it had managed to rear its head, had laid off its key organizers and abandoned any concerted effort to unionize Wal-Mart. "Most of you know that my chief interest has had to do with unions," Tate told the expectant crowd in a short speech captured on video. And then hoarsely and with great dramatic effect he declared, "Labor unions are nothing but blood-sucking parasites living off the productive labor of people who work for a living!" In a flash, hundreds of Wal-Mart managers jumped to their feet, cheering, shouting, and hooting. Fifty years ago union labor represented more than a third of the private sector workforce, Tate reminded his audience. "I am part of the reason that today they represent nine percent [another standing ovation]. Sam would have been proud of you for that [sustained cheering]! The battle isn't yet won. I want to conclude by challenging you to reduce that percentage. You can do it and at the same time insure your own future."[86]

CHAPTER SIX

WAL-MART'S
LONG MARCH TO CHINA

If a relentless squeeze on its labor costs represents one essential element of the Wal-Mart success story, another is cheap goods, a huge proportion of which now come from China. Indeed, Wal-Mart considers itself in a "joint venture" with the Chinese government. In part, this is because so many Chinese municipalities and businessmen have negotiated an ownership share in one of the Wal-Mart vendor factories. More fundamentally, however, Wal-Mart and other multinational companies doing business in China appreciate the country's stable currency, developed infrastructure, political reliability, and compliant workforce. A *YaleGlobal* study found that it took four days for exports to clear customs in Guangzhou, the old Canton at the head of the Pearl River, eight days in Calcutta, and more than two weeks in Karachi. Likewise, the proportion of total production lost to power outages totaled 2 percent in Guangzhou, but 6 percent in Calcutta and Karachi.[1] "There might be places in other parts of the world where you can buy cheaper, but can you get [the product] on the ship?" asked Andrew Tsuei, managing director of Wal-Mart's global procurement center in Shenzhen. "If we have to look at a country that's not politically stable, you might not get your order on time. If you deal in a country where the currency fluctuates, every day, there is a lot of risk. China happens to have the right mix."[2]

POWER AND PLACE IN THE
RETAIL SUPPLY CHAIN

To make this trans-Pacific supply chain work, the giant retailers of our day, Wal-Mart first among them, "pull" production out of their far-flung network of Asian vendors. The nearly continuous stream of container ships that move between Shenzhen, Singapore, and Shanghai and the Long Beach/Los Angeles port complex carry billions of dollars of goods that have been ordered by, and in many instances actually designed specifically for, Wal-Mart and other big retailers. They are therefore "pulled" across the Pacific, not "pushed" by the East Asian manufacturers that stuff their products into nearly 10 million forty-foot containers each year.[3] "Pull" production requires speed, predictability, and the subordination of the manufacturing vendor to the American or European retailer that stands at the apex of this trans-Pacific distribution system. While the very phrase "supply chain" hardly existed before the rise of Wal-Mart and the other big-box merchants, today it is universal. "Supply Chain Management"—now the business school buzz phrase—is the "science" of making sure the retailer's interests are satisfied in the most timely and cost-effective way.[4]

Elements of this system have existed for decades. Before the 1980s "logistics"—the task of scheduling production, storage, transportation, and delivery—was a purely military term, familiar to all those who studied why the Russians took so long to mobilize in 1914 and how Patton's army was resupplied during its dash across France in the summer of 1944. "Amateurs worry about tactics, but professionals worry about logistics," asserted old hands at the Army Quartermaster Corps.[5] The Vietnam War ended in a humiliating U.S. military defeat, but it delivered a triumph of supply chain logistics when civilian-run container ships proved enormously efficient on the trans-Pacific run between Oakland and Cam Ranh Bay. A decade later, Japanese "just-in-time" production methods, first in automobile and electronic production, demonstrated that inventory and labor costs could be slashed if subcontractors were kept on a tight leash by the firm that held the ultimate power within the manufacturing supply chain.[6]

These Pacific Rim logistical innovations were then assimilated into the retail supply chains when, in the 1970s and 1980s, Sears, Kmart, and numerous U.S. apparel makers began to take advantage of the cheap labor and growing sophistication of the export manufacturers that fueled the rapid growth of the Asian tiger economies, especially Hong Kong, Taiwan, and South Korea. At first this was largely through contract manufacturing. U.S. retailers directly sourced batches of specialty goods for sale in niche American markets. The bulk of the importing was done by the local manufacturers that sold goods to Wal-Mart and other mass merchandisers. Of key significance, economically and in the realm of culture, was the rise of the "branded" firms. They took an idea native to the fashion industry and extended it from upscale women's clothing to shoes, blue jeans, swimwear, toys, athletic equipment, and electronics. Once a brand becomes well established, or the store that sells the brand achieves cachet, it is no longer necessary for the Gap or Nike or Eileen Fisher to manufacture anything. These firms design and advertise their product, contract for its manufacture and transshipment, and promote its sales either through other retailers or through their own outlets. Production has been reduced to but one subordinate link in their tightly coordinated supply chain.[7]

MR. SAM'S "BUY PLAN"

The history of Wal-Mart's overseas procurement activities exemplify this transmutation, but with a distinctive Arkansas twist. Sam Walton hated jobbers and salesmen. He resented the expense, the overhead, the time, the meeting and greeting that had long been part of the American merchandise-buying system. Out-of-town apparel, toy, and housewares buyers visiting New York City on their annual or semi-annual sojourn had always mixed business with pleasure. It was an exciting and rewarding ritual, especially for those who liked the bright lights, more often than not Southerners who hailed from Dallas or Durham, Memphis or Montgomery. After a day on Seventh Avenue buying blouses and underwear, stockings and bras, there would be plenty of time for a good meal, a play or concert, and then a restful night in a nice hotel. But not for Sam Walton's crew. Gary Reinboth, an early store manager who doubled as a buyer, remembered: "Sam was always trying to instill in us that you just didn't go to New York and roll with the flow. We always walked everywhere. We never took cabs. And Sam had an equation for the trips: our expenses should never exceed 1 percent of our purchases, so we would all crowd in these little hotel rooms somewhere down around Madison Square Garden. . . . We never finished up until about twelve-thirty at night, and we'd all go out for a beer except Mr. Walton. He'd say, 'I'll meet you at six o'clock.' "[8]

Walton's aggressive, no-nonsense approach extended to every aspect of the procurement process. When shipping merchandise back from New York, he saved a bundle by using local Arkansas truckers who took processed chicken to the metropolitan area and on their return trip backhauled skirts and T-shirts for Wal-Mart.[9] His home-office buyers were equally tough bargainers. Although the retail purchasing platoon in many other firms had often been led by style-conscious women with few prospects for advancement, virtually all Wal-Mart buyers in the 1970s were young men, alpha males who would rise high in the corporate hierarchy. Brent Berry, a roommate of Walton's eldest son, Rob, while both were attending the University of Arkansas, went to work for Wal-Mart in a job that put him in charge of buying lingerie and foundations. He went on to become head of World Wide Procurement in the 1990s, while Joe Hatfield, a toy buyer in 1976, eventually took charge of all Wal-Mart stores in China.[10]

These Wal-Mart buyers noticed that the salesmen who flocked to the Bentonville office often got their goods from Jewish importers based in New York: children's apparel from Puerto Rico and Japan, shoes from Korea and Taiwan. Walton was determined to make a direct purchasing connection to those factories. He actually got the idea for his company's famous cheer—Give me a "W," give me an "A": W A L M A R T!!!, shouted out at early morning store meetings—from an exploratory trip Walton made to a South Korean shoe factory in 1975.[11]

Thereafter, Wal-Mart moved quickly to cut out as many middlemen as possible in its overseas purchasing operations. In 1976 Wal-Mart sent its first buyers to East Asia in order "to get merchandise in bulk directly," as one executive put it.[12] An office was set up in Hong Kong in 1981 and Taipei in 1983, then five regional offices on Taiwan during the next five years. By 1989 there were ninety staffers in what Wal-Mart called "the Orient." These operations were kept on a tight leash because all purchasing decisions were made at the Arkansas home office. There buyers would take a look at sample goods brought by salesmen and then ask Hong Kong or Taipei to find a direct supplier. Sam Walton described the procedure in his autobiography: "We would just take our best-selling U.S.-made items, send them to the Orient, and say, 'See if you can make something like this. We could use 100,000 units of this, or more, if the quality holds up.'"[13]

Buyers at the home office had a detailed list of items, a "buy plan" tilted toward cheap, high-volume products, which they periodically telexed to the company's Asian offices. Staffers there searched out manufacturers, negotiated prices and production schedules, and monitored quality. As early as 1981 they were visiting mainland China to attend the Canton Trade Fair and inspect factories owned by Wal-Mart's Hong Kong–based vendors.[14] Goods were shipped directly to Wal-Mart storage warehouses located in Edmond, Oklahoma, and Macon, Georgia. Boasted *Wal-Mart World*, "By Wal-Mart acting as its own importer, the profits from the importer, or middleman, are eliminated."[15]

At that point, direct imports by Wal-Mart and other discounters made up only a small share of all the foreign goods they sold in the United States. In the mid-1980s Sam Walton estimated that his company's direct imports accounted for but 5.8 percent of its total sales. But a lot more stuff was bought abroad and sold on Wal-Mart shelves because many of the American vendors with which Bentonville did business were themselves importers of a growing stream of foreign-made goods. Thus even in the 1980s 40 percent of all the products sold at Wal-Mart may well have been produced abroad.

Until about 1985 the supply chains that led from East Asia to the United States were loosely linked and relatively unstable. But around that time two developments took place that decisively shifted production to mainland China, and in the process tightened up the retail supply chains and gave the big-box stores even more leverage against their vendors, both foreign and domestic. The first was the 40 percent revaluation of most East Asian currencies negotiated in September 1985 at New York City's Plaza Hotel. Combined with rapidly rising real wages in South Korea and Hong Kong, the Plaza Accords set off a scramble for a new set of export platforms, chiefly in Guangdong and other sites in coastal China. This production shift was rapid. A set of Taiwanese and Hong Kong contractors, already supplying American retailers, set up new factories in southern China and naturally maintained their existing links with the United States.[16] But Wal-Mart buyers also became directly involved in this production shift, educating mainland Chinese on how to make goods that would sell in the North American market. "You'd go into a factory in Taiwan that's making men's shirts. You see what works," a Wal-Mart buyer told a researcher for the PBS *Frontline* series. "And then you go into China and tell a factory in China 'This is why we're not buying from you.' Chinese people are not dumb. They're tenacious. They know they need to learn very quickly."[17]

THE "BUY AMERICAN" ROAD TO CHINA

Wal-Mart led the way in squeezing labor costs out of its vendors both at home and abroad. Ironically, the company's famed "Buy American" campaign of the late 1980s proved most useful in this endeavor. Beginning in the late 1970s international competition had hit U.S. workers hard. Japanese cars, German cameras, and quality machine tools were the most high-profile imports, but international competition also appeared precisely among those items that discount stores like Wal-Mart sold in such abundance: children's and women's clothing, underwear, footwear, hardware, small kitchen appliances, radios, television sets, and the first generation of electronic calculators, watches, and toys. In the apparel industry imports accounted for 31 percent of U.S. sales in 1976, shooting up to 57.5 percent in 1987. More than 250 domestic garment factories closed between 1980 and 1985. No region was hit harder than the rural South, where the chief resource had been cheap labor in the first place. Now Central America, East Asia, and Bangladesh had the corner on that advantage.[18]

The unions, which still had a good deal of clout in Washington, complained loudly. The AFL-CIO had been free trade militants all during the Cold War, agreeing with the architects of American foreign policy who saw a prosperous and export-oriented western Europe, Japan, Taiwan, and Latin America as bulwarks against the advance of Communist ideology and arms.

But the unions shifted course in the 1970s: they were unwilling to continue subsidizing U.S. foreign policy at the expense of the jobs and income of their members. Their opponents called the union strategy protectionism. Labor partisans said it merely leveled the playing field by eliminating tax incentives for U.S. corporations operating abroad; prohibiting the low-wage "dumping" of surplus products on the American market; and raising tariff and quota barriers against some foreign goods. The unions played the nationalist card: the International Ladies' Garment Workers' Union spent millions on a campaign designed to fuse the ancient call to "Buy Union" with a new and forthright "Buy American" imperative. Famously, a union chorus sang out:

> *Look for the union label, when you are buying a coat, dress*
> *or blouse.*
> *We work hard, but who's complaining*
> *But through the I.L.G. we're paying our way.*
> *So always look for the union label.*
> *It says we're able to make it in the U.S.A.*[19]

Sam Walton was aware of all this. The company was now big enough, and so involved in Central American and Far Eastern sourcing, that any successful legislative effort designed to curb imports would have an immediate impact on its competitiveness. In 1983, in an early Washington foray, Wal-Mart had made clear its opposition to import quotas on foreign-made apparel. But Walton could not ignore the clamor, especially when it came from like-minded industrialists of the South, such as the anti-union billionaire Roger Milliken, who helped bankroll a textile industry effort called "Crafted with Pride" that sought to wring costs out of the apparel industry supply chain while protecting his Carolina mills from foreign textile imports.[20]

Something had to be done. The closure of several Arkansas

firms led to an outcry against the import practices of big retailers like Wal-Mart. Governor Bill Clinton was among many state officials who appealed to Walton to reconfigure his purchasing program in order to keep more production at home. After Wal-Mart worked out its first deal with Farris Fashions, a Brinkley, Arkansas, shirt manufacturer in 1984, Walton realized that he could turn a potential liability into an enhancement of the corporation's image. "What can we do with this?" Walton asked Bob Bernstein, who ran Wal-Mart's advertising agency in Kansas City. "I want to make it big."[21]

Wal-Mart's "Buy American" program proved "a public relations coup historic in its dimensions," rued Discount Store News, which reflected the chagrin of the Bentonville retailer's competitors.[22] By 1986 Wal-Mart stores were festooned with red-white-and-blue BUY AMERICAN banners and signs on the counters that proclaimed, THIS ITEM, FORMERLY IMPORTED, IS NOW BEING PURCHASED BY WAL-MART IN THE U.S.A. AND IS CREATING OR RETAINING—JOBS FOR AMERICANS![23] Wal-Mart buyers called them "conversions," in which products once purchased abroad were "converted" for manufacture in the United States. Since the company asked state economic development agencies to help find U.S. manufacturers for these conversions, Wal-Mart won extravagant praise from governors and other political officials around the country.[24] Bill Clinton was effusive at a 1986 meeting of Wal-Mart store managers: "I never dreamed when Sam Walton and David Glass and the others told me they were going to start a Buy America Program . . . and it could sweep the country that they would be able to do that. And I just want to thank you for what you have done for America, Mr. Walton."[25]

Even today, long after its formal abandonment, Wal-Mart is thought of as a more "American" firm than some of its competitors that actually import fewer goods. It is possible that the

Buy American program did briefly slow the import tide, but Wal-Mart never released any firm figures on the proportion of its product costs that came from overseas. However, Asian procurement rose steadily all during the heyday of the Buy American program as the corporate buying staff resident in East Asia more than doubled in size. "Buy American is a two-edged sword," reported *Wal-Mart World*, the company's official publication for associates. "First of all, it creates jobs in the USA, which is good for Wal-Mart and America. Secondly, it gives us a lot of leverage overseas for new items. If the Orient knows we are shopping hard in the United States, it makes them that much sharper. It also means our Import Program is working twice as hard for Wal-Mart. We're not seeing the same old vendors and getting the same old quotes anymore."[26]

Sam Walton did not deny that Asian imports were rising, but he sought to distance the company from this uncomfortable fact, especially following the brutal suppression of the Chinese democracy movement in Tiananmen Square in 1989. Walton was also disturbed by charges of human rights abuses in supplier factories, both in Central America and along the Pacific Rim. At the very least this could be a huge public relations problem. "Keep this under the radar," Walton told Brent Berry, who had become increasingly active in Asian procurement during the 1980s.[27]

One way to do that was to create a buffer—a middleman or a buying agency that would purchase Asian products without showing Wal-Mart's hand. That Wal-Mart was thereby retreating from its relentless effort to strip costs and bureaucracy out of its procurement system may well demonstrate the sensitivity with which Walton viewed the issue. "The decision was to go to an exclusive buying agency," remembered a Wal-Mart buyer closely involved with the decision. "The main reason for going into [the deal] was not to be exposed as going into Communist China."[28]

Walton turned to a close friend and tennis partner, George Billingsley, to serve as titular head of the operation. Billingsley, who had sold real estate at nearby Bella Vista and ran a travel agency there, knew little about retail or procurement, but he held Walton's absolute confidence, which was the key ingredient in a multibillion-dollar business that might well come under a barrage of media scrutiny. To actually run this import business, Bill Fields, Wal Mart's head of merchandising at the time, brought in Charles Wong, a seasoned Wal-Mart vendor who would run the day-to-day operation out of Hong Kong. Within two years, Billingsley and Wong had set up Pacific Resources Export Limited (PREL) as Wal-Mart's exclusive buying agent, a shadow organization really, which shifted onto its payroll virtually the entire Wal-Mart buying staff in Asia. PREL soon had twenty-nine offices from Dhaka to Seoul. With a staff of over seven hundred, it was the largest commissioned buying agent in the world.[29]

Billingsley served Wal-Mart well, although he proved unable to actually shield the big retailer from the criticism that it confronted in the 1990s, when instances of abominable and illegal working conditions came to light in vendor factories. He grew rich but kept PREL's overhead so low that it satisfied Bentonville's relentless cost squeezers. Equally important, Billingsley presided over Wal-Mart's first factory inspection regime. Because they knew English and were prepared to travel widely, Filipino inspectors were favored by PREL rather than Chinese or U.S. nationals, and they annually visited some of the five thousand factories from which Wal-Mart sourced its products. They had a checklist, covering both product quality and factory working conditions. On occasion, PREL pulled a contract from a vendor whose hazardous conditions posed a threat, either to the workers themselves or to Wal-Mart's reputation. For example, PREL dropped a factory in Shenzhen two years before a fire there killed thirty-nine people. An inspector had noted that four exits were blocked. If the factory had still been a Wal-Mart vendor, Billingsley told a reporter in 2001, the story on the front page of the *New York Times* would have read "39 Dead at Wal-Mart factory in China." "When you're No. 1, everybody's shooting at you," Billingsley said.[30]

Wal-Mart's Buy American campaign and its increasing reliance on Asian imports were inexorably linked. Wal-Mart would increase domestic purchasing, but the company used the prospect of such procurement as a hammer to drive down supplier costs, including their wages and profits, and transform these vendors into Bentonville pawns. "One of our big objectives" in the Buy American program, a Wal-Mart board member told Walton's biographer Bob Ortega, "was to put the heat on American manufacturers to lower their prices."[31] The company knew that U.S. labor costs were much higher than those in Central America or East Asia, but it sought to make up the difference by freezing wages and forcing logistic and production efficiencies on its suppliers. "Our American suppliers," said Sam Walton, "must commit to improving their facilities and machinery, remain financially conservative and work to fill our requirements, and most importantly, strive to improve employee productivity."[32]

Ed Clifford, a hardware buyer for Sam's Club, explained just how imperious Wal-Mart could be in all this: "Making conversions takes patience. It's very difficult to get an American manufacturer to respond to the request. They may in fact look at it and decide they can be 40 percent over the Orient price and think that is acceptable. The first thing you have to do is sit down and explain exactly where that product has to be in the market place, exactly what the cost is coming out of the Orient, exactly how much we buy of the product, and how far out front we can forecast our order quantities. Then, let them go back and kick it around—it's a strange idea for a lot of them."[33]

An embittered spokesman for the National Knitwear and

Sportswear Association complained that Wal-Mart used its "flag-waving" Buy American campaign "as a negotiating club that forces domestic manufacturers to compete, often unrealistically, with foreign suppliers who pay their help pennies an hour. As a result vendors see their gross sales sky rocket and their net profits plunge." Indeed, a packaged goods vendor told *Discount Store News* that "Wal-Mart's highly proactive approach to product development may, unintentionally, be making American business less competitive." Because Wal-Mart set the parameters of product development, companies like his were "no longer manufacturers." Instead they are becoming sources who "produce only the products that Wal-Mart has decided it wants to sell, which in turn makes R&D and introduction of new products redundant and unprofitable."[34]

Such was the case with Farris Fashions, the Arkansas producer of plaid work shirts (later made famous when Lamar Alexander ran for the presidency in 1996), which became the poster boy for the Buy American campaign. Arkansas had been hit hard by the recession of the early 1980s, which wiped out more than 1.6 million blue-collar jobs nationwide. In 1984 Phillips-Van Heusen decided to move its production of shirts offshore to meet demands from Sears and Penney for lower prices. In Brinkley, a small manufacturing and cotton-processing town deep in the heart of the Mississippi Delta, ninety jobs, held by a workforce largely composed of African American women, were at stake. So Governor Clinton got on the phone to David Glass, then head of Wal-Mart stores, and asked for help. The governor wanted to know if the Bentonville merchant could send some business to Farris Fashions, the locally owned firm.

Sam Walton immediately called up Farris Burroughs and invited him to Bentonville to see if his plant could be converted to produce a shirt that Wal-Mart had heretofore imported from abroad. Burroughs, whose career as a mechanic and plant engineer had hardly been spectacular, could scarcely believe that Mr. Sam himself was on the line. "It was like talking to President Reagan," he remembered. But the stars were now in alignment, so in early 1985 Farris Fashions signed a contract for production of nearly a quarter of a million cotton flannel shirts. Clinton helped get the company a three-hundred-thousand-dollar economic development loan, and Walton touted Farris Fashions as a prime example of a product "conversion" that could "Bring It Home to the USA." At a press conference announcing the Farris Fashions deal, Clinton pronounced Wal-Mart's Buy American program "an act of patriotism and it makes good economic sense in the long run."[35]

But Farris Fashions was now Wal-Mart's creature. "The problem is I have no access to markets other than Wal-Mart," admitted Burroughs. The big retailer designed the shirts, sold them under its "American Edition" label, found a Taiwanese supplier from which it purchased the flannel in huge bulk, and bought the entire factory output.[36] Employment soon rose to 350, but the jobs were poorly paid, without health insurance, and often subject to chaotic and inequitable piece-rate variations. Wal-Mart's pressure for lower production costs never slackened. Pointedly, the company continued to import from Turkey, Pakistan, and Kenya a nearly identical shirt sporting Wal-Mart's "Ozark Trail" label. When Farris Fashions workers signed up with the Amalgamated Clothing and Textile Workers Union in 1990, company president Farris Burroughs told them "to stop messing around with the union" because Sam Walton "wouldn't buy union goods"; otherwise he would turn the plant into "a chicken coop." Brinkley's mayor agreed: "You guys don't want to lose your jobs," he told the workers at a plant meeting arranged by Burroughs. "You need your job more than you need anything else." Farris kept making Wal-Mart shirts, but neither unionism, nor higher wages, nor stable jobs ever made their appearance in Brinkley. Since the company was entirely dependent on Wal-Mart for the vast majority of its sales, it had neither the money nor the freedom to develop new products or diversify its customers. Thus when consumer demand for its distinctive plaid product declined, the company's fortunes plunged. Employment dropped to about one hundred by the time Farris Burroughs, who had grown more interested in raising cattle than exploring new entrepreneurial frontiers, shuttered the plant in October 2005. The factory quickly became derelict, a companion to the abandoned stores and gas stations that lined Brinkley's desolate main street.[37]

THE SWEATSHOP UNIVERSE

By this point, Wal-Mart had long since abandoned its Buy American program. Imports from Asia had begun to soar in the mid-1990s after China devalued the yuan almost 40 percent against the dollar. In 2006 the company bought about $27 billion worth of Chinese-made goods, up from $22 billion the previous year and $9.5 billion in 2001, which was when China became a full-fledged member of the World Trade Organization. Wal-Mart, no longer fearing an import backlash in the United States, then abandoned PREL and brought its vast buying and inspection apparatus under direct company control. In 2002 Wal-Mart moved several hundred staffers to Shenzhen, where they occupied three floors of a nondescript glass office tower. Like the home office in Bentonville, the downscale accommodations masked a dynamo of power and influence. Within a year of the move, Wal-Mart made the Shenzhen office its global purchasing headquarters, an emphatic declaration of China's central importance to the company's fortunes. By 2006 about 80 percent of the six thousand foreign factories in Wal-Mart's supplier database were located in China.[38]

Inside the Shenzhen procurement center, representatives for Chinese manufacturers hoping to pitch their products wait long hours in a room full of dirty beige plastic seats. It is not unlike the way things work in Bentonville; the same posters of Mr. Sam adorn the walls, likewise some of the identical corporate aphorisms, including OUR PEOPLE MAKE THE DIFFERENCE. Each day hundreds of entrepreneurs from all over China take a number and, as they've learned in Wal-Mart training sessions, skip the chitchat and get to the point. In the Shenzhen "negotiations center" there is none of the palm greasing and favoritism endemic to traditional Chinese business.[39]

The experience can be brutal. Those whose goods are not selling are shown the door, unless they have used Wal-Mart's Retail Link software to come up with a quick solution. Supply deals can be made, or terminated, in a matter of minutes. When the *Newsweek* reporter Sarah Schafer interviewed the apparel salesman Wang Jianpang late in 2004, he told her he had "understood immediately that the Wal-Mart style was different." The Wal-Mart people demanded he upgrade his company's green terry-cloth jackets, were annoying sticklers for quality, deadlines, and price, and did not want to be entertained in expensive restaurants, much less bordellos. In effect Wal-Mart has sought to replace a Chinese business culture, noted in personal relationships—*gwache* it is called in both northern and southern China—with its own modern supply network, built on information technology and rigid price and production standards. "When we started with Wal-Mart, I thought their way was too much of a hassle, too complicated," Wang told Schafer. "But later I understood their way was better." His employer, Huada Manufacturing, expanded dramatically on the strength of its Wal-Mart contracts, from twenty sewing machines to four hundred.[40]

Wal-Mart also boosted the fortunes and transformed the culture of another small manufacturing enterprise, Weishi Brothers Industrial and Trade Company, which sold paper cups in its home province, Yunnan. When the firm became a Wal-Mart vendor in 1999, it quickly increased its workforce from 10 to 150 and began selling cups throughout China. Weishi general manager Ding Weigang reported that he felt more "safe" with Wal-Mart than with some Chinese customers. "Wal-Mart's practice is clear. Work is work, quality is quality, and all business is conducted without regard to personal relationships or feelings," Ding asserted. "If the products meet the requirements, Wal-Mart will pay you according to your contract."[41]

Wal-Mart drives a hard bargain. Indeed, because Wal-Mart orders are so large, the company can demand a lower overall cost per unit than any of its competitors. This generates an excruciating squeeze on all of its suppliers, resulting in a cascade of social pathologies that corrupt and distort every supply chain relationship: between the prime Wal-Mart vendor and its subcontractors, between factory inspectors and factory management, and between the production supervisors and the young women workers who compose the overwhelming bulk of the factory workforce. Xue Hong, a diminutive, thirty-year-old graduate student in sociology at the Chinese University of Hong Kong, has been among the few researchers to really get inside this dysfunctional universe. Depending upon what clothes and hairstyle she adopts, Xue easily traverses the class hierarchy of southern China. She is often mistaken for one of the millions of migrant factory workers who have flocked to Guangdong Province, but when she interviewed manufacturing reps at the Canton Trade Fair, many assumed she was a buyer for a big retail house. She has toured the factories of Chenghai—"City of Toys and Gifts"—as an academic studying the supply chain in plastic export toys, and she has interviewed scores of migrant girls and women, some of whom were told to lie about their age and status so as to offer the "correct" answers to the inspectors periodically sent by the corporate social responsibility departments of Wal-Mart and other big buyers.

When Xue interviewed a Mr. Hua at the Canton Trade Fair,

he told her that Wal-Mart orders were simply gigantic; from his garment factory in Nantong, Jiangsu Province, Wal-Mart usually ordered more than ten thousand dozen T-shirts in just one size and style, while Japanese buyers would order but several hundred pieces. Hua made a profit of 40 or 50 percent on the Japanese order but could earn little more than 10 percent gross profit from the big American retailer. Likewise, a craftworks company in Guangzhou reported that it earned about 10 percent less profit per unit on an order from Wal-Mart than from Target, but to refuse a Wal-Mart order was unthinkable, since it was five times as large. Given Wal-Mart's intense price consciousness, along with the avid desire of undercapitalized Chinese entrepreneurs to break into the huge Wal-Mart market, Chinese supplier firms often make no profit, or actually lose money, on their first production run for Wal-Mart; it is on the next few orders, as they wring inefficiencies out of the manufacturing process, that the Chinese capitalists hope to make some real money.[42]

But that is difficult as well, because Wal-Mart insists that its suppliers toe the line on a tight production schedule as well as on rock-bottom prices. As a supplier for a garment factory in Fujian Province explained to Xue, "Wal-Mart usually requests to deliver in 45 days. We should spend about 15 days in buying raw materials. We dare not prepare them in advance because the volume of the order is very large and we cannot guarantee to obtain the order until the last minute. If there is an emergency, Wal-Mart cannot accept any explanation and you have to face the paying of fines and even the cancellation of the order suddenly."[43] The manager of a Dongguan toy factory concurred: "We are under enormous stress. Customers place late orders, they change their orders partway through manufacturing, and they pay their bills late. At the same time they ask us to provide better training for our staff, better health and safety, and better accommodation. We just cannot do it all."[44] Wal-

Mart's relationship to its suppliers was sometimes referred to as *zamindari,* akin to that of landlord and tenants.[45]

Such production pressure generates a twofold response: Wal-Mart's first-tier vendors, who are at least subject to a degree of supervision from the big retailer, immediately subcontract a large proportion of their orders to a series of illegal, hyperexploitative subcontractors whose operations are untouched by even the most pro forma factory inspections. As a Mr. Wang explained to Xue at the Canton Trade Fair, "Our factory only has around 100 workers and we have no ability to get big orders. Usually we get subcontracting orders from several larger companies invested by Hongkongese and Taiwanese. . . . There are hundreds of toy factories here and most of them are small factories like us. . . . Wal-Mart is the biggest buyer in our industry zone. Along a street near us, maybe all the toy factories are working for Wal-Mart toys in peak season."[46]

Naturally these subcontractors ratchet up production by pushing the workweek to eighty, ninety, and one hundred hours per week, far in excess of both Chinese law and industry codes of conduct. In the rush season for toys, apparel, shoes, and household goods, which often extends from April through November, seven-day workweeks and eighteen-hour workdays are not uncommon. "These subcontractors," says Xue Hong, "squeezed the most among all Wal-Mart supplier factories, are really hell in the retailer's supply chain."[47] Workers are subject to fines for absence, lateness, and material spoilage, while complicated and ever-changing incentive pay schemes often leave workers bewildered as to their actual rate of pay. Indeed, some subcontractors are so undercapitalized that they frequently fail to meet their payroll. Signs and advertisements asserting "Wages Paid on Time" have now been posted by many of the more substantial companies in Guangdong Province, seemingly as a particularly attractive benefit designed to recruit a better-than-average workforce.[48]

Wal-Mart's influence is everywhere in southern China, but it is dominant in the Chinese toy industry, which now supplies more than three-quarters of all the playthings purchased in the world. At their peak more than eight thousand companies manufactured toys in China, employing at least 3.5 million workers. On the north side of the Pearl River, where many toy firms are concentrated, sprawling factory compounds stretch mile after dusty, smog-filled mile along the congested roads cut like scars across the landscape. Guarded gates control entry and exit, through which pour hundreds, and sometimes thousands, of young women recruited from the interior, rural provinces. Adjoining many of the factories are their multistory dormitories, where twelve or more women share a room crammed with bunks stacked on either side of a narrow aisle. At lunch breaks, thousands of them pour onto the streets or take a simple meal in the company canteen. Most are so young they look like schoolgirls, but pale and weary faces betray their long hours at the workbench.[49]

Wal-Mart is the number one U.S. toy-importing source, surpassing Toys "R" Us in 2000 as the largest toy seller in the United States. Wal-Mart uses toys as a "traffic booster": it markets hot-selling items at cost in order to get moms and dads into the store for their own purchases. This puts a premium on really cheap toys, produced in huge volumes for the more than six thousand stores Wal-Mart operates around the globe. Says the Guangdong Toy Association: "U.S. Buyers demand prices that are not reasonable. . . . Wal-Mart in particular puts a lot of pressure on prices and as they order so much from China, it has large influence."[50] Knowledgeable observers estimate that the bulk of all Wal-Mart toys are produced by scores, perhaps hundreds, of unlicensed subcontractors. Certainly, the company has a reputation for cheap products. On the first day of the Canton Trade Fair in April 2005, Xue asked a manufacturing manager if his company made toys for Wal-Mart. Thinking her a buyer for another retailer, he responded angrily: his company only made products that were well designed and of high quality, so he had no relations with Wal-Mart, whose merchandise was a byword for shoddy manufacture and cheap materials. "Anyone could make toys for Wal-Mart," he spat out.[51]

This subcontracting system stands at the heart of the vast new universe of sweatshops that fill the production end of the Wal-Mart supply chain. The word "sweatshop" itself derives its meaning from the "sweater," the Victorian-era middleman, who took advantage of the poverty and unemployment endemic in London's East End to subcontract garment manufacture to a burgeoning urban workforce, many of whom were migrants to the British metropolis from a countryside where tenants and farmhands had been dispossessed by the new international trade in wheat and wool. A technological innovation stood at the heart of the sweating system as well: the newly invented Singer sewing machine, which enabled relatively unskilled men, women, and children to replace the custom tailors who had long dominated the trade. Working in isolation in small shops or tenements, these garment workers were paid by the piece, unsure of their supply of work, and unable to organize against, or even know the name of, their true employer. Store-bought dresses and pants now came within the reach of millions of new consumers, but on both sides of the Atlantic, the proliferating sweatshops became a byword for exploitation and misery. As the American reformer Jane Addams described the Chicago scene in 1910, "An unscrupulous contractor regards no basement as too dark, no stable loft as too foul, no rear shanty too provisional, no tenement room too small for his workroom as these conditions imply low rental. Hence these shops abound in the worst of the foreign districts."[52]

That southern China has come to replicate these conditions should come as no surprise; rather, it is the logical outcome of a production system that divides legal ownership from operating control and overall power so as to actually generate incentives for the most exploitative and hazardous practices. As it was at the turn of the twentieth century, so it was again at the turn of the twenty-first century: sweatshop production is prone not just to work-a-day exploitation but to catastrophic fire and other disasters. The ultimate beneficiary is legally exempt from all responsibility. This was true in the most famous sweatshop disaster of all time, the 1911 Triangle Shirtwaist Fire, in which 146 young women, most Jewish and Italian garment workers, died when a raging inferno engulfed the ninth-floor loft in which they labored and from which locked exits and a flimsy outside ladder offered no escape. Most died of smoke, fire, or their panicked leap to the street one hundred feet below. The fire commanded sensational headlines and outraged an increasingly active coalition of social reformers and needle-trades unionists. But when city authorities began a search for those criminally responsible, no one was ever convicted. This included Max Blanck and Isaac Harris, the two owners of the Shirtwaist Company. As in all sweatshop systems, legal responsibility for the conditions of employment and the safety of the factory was muddy and multilayered. Since the owners had subcontracted actual production, they were unaware that the exit doors had been locked shut.[53]

All this has been replicated in the Far East. In 1993 the worst industrial fire in the history of capitalism killed 188 workers and injured 469 at a mammoth toy factory outside Bangkok. Forty percent owned by a Hong Kong firm, Kader Industrial Thailand supplied Wal-Mart and Toys "R" Us with millions of cuddly soft toys sold under the Fisher-Price, Hasbro, Tyco, and Kenner brand labels. As in the Triangle Shirtwaist tragedy, fire exits were blocked, doors locked to prevent pilfering, and flammable materials stacked randomly on the upper floors of the factory. And as in lower Manhattan eighty-two years before, scores of desperate young women plunged to their deaths in a vain effort to escape the worksite inferno.

But the Bangkok fire hardly proved unique. In 1991 a fire in a Dongguan raincoat factory killed 72 people. Two years later 87 women died in a toy factory in Shenzhen, and the next year 93 were killed and 160 injured in a textile factory located in Zhuhai on the other side of China's Pearl River. In 2000 another Shenzhen fire, this in an electronics plant, left 24 dead and 40 injured. The *China Labor Bulletin* described it as "a copycat of at least six similar fires in South China." One obvious cause of the fires and the large number of fatalities arises from the so-called three-in-one factory design adopted by the most undercapitalized entrepreneurs: migrant workers sleep in a dormitory on the top floor, with the factory and warehouse beneath them. When a fire starts, the women are trapped, often suffocated by noxious fumes. The arrangement is illegal in China but widely used. China's *Economic Daily,* an enthusiast for the nation's entrepreneurial growth, nevertheless lashed out at "the way some of these foreign investors ignore international practice, ignore our own national rules, act completely lawlessly and immorally and lust after wealth."[54]

TAMING THE SYSTEM?

Like other U.S. retailers and the high-profile brands they sell, Wal-Mart has been keenly aware that it cannot simply ignore the production responsibilities or the public relations fallout that threatens all retailers should the consuming public see them as callous or indifferent to the workers whose labor they command. This too is reminiscent of the early days of the sweatshop system when upper-class department store customers became alarmed that the clothing they purchased was sewn by exploited and tuberculosis-infected women and children. Josephine Shaw

Lowell, whose pedigree stretched back to the colonial-era New England aristocracy, thought consumers had the duty "to find out under what conditions the articles they purchased are produced and distributed, and to insist that these conditions shall be wholesome and consistent with a respectable existence on the part of the workers." Seeking to tap the moral righteousness of these prosperous and well-connected women, the National Consumers League, founded in 1899, lent moral support to the nascent union movement and sought to pressure the big retailers of the day to regulate their own supply chains. As the energetic NCL secretary Florence Kelley explained, "If the people would notify Marshall Field . . . and others that they would buy from them no clothing made in sweatshops, the evil would be stopped."[55]

Like the corporate codes of social responsibility that have become so widespread in the last decade, the National Consumers League created a "white label" that, when affixed to a piece of merchandise, certified that it was made by companies that obeyed state labor laws, banned child labor, and emphasized production "under clean and healthful conditions." Department store magnates like Field and John Wanamaker soon recognized the merchandising power of such a label. But the Progressive-era reformers knew that corporate self-reform was hardly enough. Despite their upper-class backgrounds, they supported the great garment strikes that built needle-trades unionism into a powerful force in New York, Chicago, and Baltimore. And they wanted their "white label" standards enforced not just by consumer sentiment or corporate policy but by the government. To this end, they pushed the army to ban sweatshop production of military uniforms in World War I, and in the early days of the New Deal they saw the government's "Blue Eagle" codes, which mandated minimum wages and maximum hours in hundreds of industries, as a kind of consumer labeling initiative now enforced by the power and authority of the federal government.[56]

Wal-Mart remains intensely hostile to governmental regulation of its vendors, both in China as well as in the United States. But like Nike, Reebok, and other branded distributors, Wal-Mart has established an elaborate factory certification program. The company put it together in 1993 immediately following a devastating NBC exposé that documented both the false advertising inherent in the company's Buy American campaign and the abusive child labor practices that were rife in Wal-Mart's overseas supply chain. NBC investigators had found rack after rack of clothing made in China, Malaysia, and Bangladesh on display under Wal-Mart MADE IN THE USA signs. And they had filmed three floors' worth of nine-, ten-, and eleven-year-old children cutting and sewing shirts for Wal-Mart. They worked twelve and fourteen hours a day at Bangladesh's Saraka factory, notorious for a fire just two years before that had killed twenty-five workers, most underage, who had been trapped behind blocked exits and locked gates. With tape rolling, NBC correspondent Brian Ross confronted Wal-Mart CEO David Glass with photos of the fire victims and recent film of children still working there. "Yeah, there are tragic things that happen all over the world," stuttered Glass. To which Ross replied, "That's all you want to say about it?"

By this point in the interview, Wal-Mart's top PR man, Don Shinkle, knew that Glass's encounter with the well-prepared NBC team, which was taking place in the TV studio that Mr. Sam had used to broadcast his cheery bromides, was turning into a fiasco. Shinkle broke in, cut the lights, and helped Glass flee the studio.[57] Wal-Mart executives, who until then expected TV coverage to conform to the upbeat puff pieces that had normally accompanied Mr. Sam's Buy American campaign, thought they had been sandbagged by NBC.

Glass was particularly outraged. Although he commanded none of the charisma of Wal-Mart's founder, Glass, then age fifty-six, was cut from much the same mid-South cloth as Walton. He was a product of small-town Missouri, where he had learned the retailing business at some of Wal-Mart's best competitors. Walton had tried to hire him as early as 1964, but Glass thought the Wal-Mart operation just a bit too hokey for his taste, especially after he had attended a chaotic store opening in Harrison, Arkansas, where, in the heat of a summer afternoon, the watermelons exploded and the mules—on-site for kiddy rides—dropped their smelly loads on the baking asphalt of the store parking lot. Walton finally hired Glass in 1976, and for the next decade he made his reputation as the company's key logistics and technology strategist. Glass had been the executive primarily responsible for persuading Walton to pour real money into the company's data management network and its satellite hookup. Some thought Glass had ice water in his veins, but that hardly seemed to matter, for it was during his presidency, which began in 1988, that Wal-Mart rocketed past Kmart and Sears to become the largest retailer in the world. The value of Wal-Mart stock quadrupled as well, making Glass and a lot of other executives very wealthy indeed.[58]

But now Glass faced public humiliation; more important, the company's entire sourcing operation seemed disreputable. Wal-Mart quickly moved into crisis management mode. An order went out to all Wal-Mart stores to rip down the Buy American signs. And a Wal-Mart executive was sent out to the Saraka factory in Dhaka to see if there really were children working there. As expected, he reported back to Bentonville that there were no underage workers employed. But this "investigation," conducted by a merchandising vice president with no knowledge of local conditions, was entirely self-serving. A few workers were interrogated, probably in the presence of factory officials, and of course no one admitted to being less than fourteen, the minimum official working age in Bangladesh. To do so would court instant dismissal. Indeed most workers knew that if too many violations of the labor and fire codes were found, Wal-Mart would simply pull the factory's contract, consigning hundreds to unemployment in a glutted job market. This was and is the catch-22 to which any regime of outside factory inspections is prone.[59]

Back in Bentonville, Wal-Mart decided that it had no choice but to invite Ross and the rest of the NBC crew back to finish the interview, although Glass swung a bit of corporate weight by extending the invitation through a complaining phone call to Jack Welch, the chairman of General Electric, which owned NBC. Glass told Welch he had been "ambushed," so Welch called NBC president Robert Wright, who in turn told Ross to go back and interview Glass again.[60]

But the second half of the shoot hardly went any better. Glass and Ross sparred over the definition of a child worker in Bangladesh, over the credibility of NBC's factory photographs, and over the effectiveness and authenticity of Wal-Mart's Buy American program. Once again Glass was on the defensive. When Ross persisted in confronting the Wal-Mart CEO with film and photographic evidence that plainly showed children working in the Saraka factory, Glass replied: "The—the picture—the-the-the pictures you showed me mean nothing to me. I'm—I'm not sure where they were or who they were, you know. Could have been of anything. I'm not sure."

"I'm telling you," Ross said directly, "they're not 'of anything': they're of the Saraka factory, of children making Wal-Mart clothing."

"Well" said Glass, "I'm—I'm comfortable with what we've done."[61]

But comfort was the last thing Wal-Mart executives felt in the weeks leading up to the *Dateline NBC* airing date on December 22, 1992. The show reached 14 million households, one of *Dateline*'s most-watched programs. Wal-Mart issued a press release in which Glass did apologize for mislabeling some clothing racks under the MADE IN THE USA banner. That mistake would be easily and quickly corrected. But when it came to corporate exploitation of child workers, Glass remained adamant, calling the rest of the show "inaccurate" and "misleading." For the Wal-Mart faithful, Glass was much tougher. He called the NBC allegations "sleazy," denounced the union role in supplying Ross with damaging information, and claimed that the network correspondents "distorted the facts in a very dishonest way."[62]

Wal-Mart's PR department mobilized the company's vast web of compliant and dependent vendors, who were encouraged to purchase large newspaper advertisements that reproduced a set of talking points worked up in Bentonville to defend Wal-Mart and its Buy American program. *USA Today* sold ten big display ads worth more than three hundred thousand dollars in all,[63] but many ads appeared in the small-town press. Typical was that of Southwest Cupid, an underwear maker, which ran a full-page ad in the *Hominy News-Progress*, a Blackwell, Oklahoma, weekly. "The recent 'NBC Dateline' program against Wal-Mart's Made in the USA program was untrue and we are an actual case study to prove otherwise," the advertisement asserted. Many companies like Koss Stereophones of Milwaukee took out a full-page ad in both the *Arkansas Democrat-Gazette* and their hometown paper, in this case the *Milwaukee Journal*. "They really work hard to work with us," said Michael Koss, the company president. "They are one of our top five customers."[64] A talk-radio show in Arkansas stoked the fire by asking its listeners, "Who's more American: NBC or Wal-Mart?"[65]

Still on the defensive, Wal-Mart assembled a factory inspection regime. As with PREL, the company needed an institution that would put some distance between its top executives and what might or might not be going on in the field. By Mother's

Day of 1993 Wal-Mart had announced a code of conduct, tacked on to the tail end of a press release devoted to charity fundraisers in the United States. It committed the company to few hard guidelines. There would be no use of prison or child labor, but the company pledged merely to "favor" vendors who kept the workweek under sixty hours and that workers "should" get at least one day off a week. More important than the provisions of the code was its enforcement mechanism: it was entirely self-policing. Wal-Mart would hire its own inspectors; it would not allow outside monitors to visit or even know of the existence of its suppliers. But by promulgating even such a weak set of guidelines, Wal-Mart was admitting that it bore some responsibility for the workers who labored at the far end of its supply chain. Indeed, Wal-Mart's Ethical Standards Department has replicated many of the features found in the factory inspection and certification programs that have been supported by branded companies like Nike and Liz Claiborne. By the early years of the twenty-first century, the ES Department employed more than two hundred, half in China. At least once each year Wal-Mart audits the factories from which it directly sources apparel, shoes, sporting goods, toys, and other foreign-made goods; and Wal-Mart has established an elaborate green-yellow-red "traffic light" system that categorizes factories according to their adherence to Wal-Mart's labor and environmental code. One percent of all factories fail inspection outright and are dropped from the Wal-Mart supply network.[66]

THE "DIRTY KING OF SOUTH CHINA"

None of this has enabled Wal-Mart to escape a drumbeat of criticism, however. Even before the NBC exposé, the AFL-CIO had been a persistent and resourceful critic, focusing on the use of prison labor by Wal-Mart suppliers in China. Then in

1995, when Kathie Lee Gifford was confronted with evidence that the factories producing her clothing line, marketed at Wal-Mart, employed children in Honduras sweatshops, she broke into tears on national television, a gratifying victory for anti-Wal-Mart campaigners. And criticism of the company continued. In 2001 KLD & Co., the largest mutual fund that uses "social responsibility" as one of its investment criteria, sold its shares of Wal-Mart and removed it from the Domini 400 Social Index because Wal-Mart wasn't doing enough to prevent sweatshop abuses. Five years later, the Norwegian government also divested its shares. Wal-Mart has refused to join the Fair Labor Association, a monitoring group endorsed by many companies in the apparel and shoe industry, and it contracts with commercial firms like Price Waterhouse Coopers, rather than local NGOs, to do its factory safety and labor audits. And in 2005 the International Labor Rights Fund inaugurated a lawsuit against Wal-Mart on the grounds that it systematically failed to enforce labor standards in its corporate code of conduct and then lied about it to the American public.[67]

So Wal-Mart remains the "dirty king of South China," as one NGO informant told me when I joined a group of California academics touring Guangdong factories and ports. It was the "the lowest of the low," observed a Reebok executive during a meeting on the same trip.[68] Managers at three Wal-Mart supply factories told the Shenzhen-based Institute for Contemporary Observation, whose scruffy, bustling offices we visited, that Wal-Mart staff from the company's Shenzhen purchasing department both sought and accepted bribes.[69] Moreover, workers are often coached by their foremen to lie about conditions to inspectors; otherwise, they are told, the factory might lose its orders and they will be out on the street. And the ICO found that many of Wal-Mart's social responsibility inspection teams "only spent about three hours at the factories, during which they verified wages, working hours and personnel records, made a brief inspection tour of the factory and met three or four workers in the factory office's reception room. Wal-Mart inspections were quite easy to bluff."[70] Indeed, even H. Lee Scott admitted that the company needs to become more "committed" and "transparent" in order to "provide additional credibility to [its] factory certification program."[71]

So why Wal-Mart's poor record? There are three reasons. First, there is an absolute conflict between Wal-Mart's drive for low prices and its effort to enforce a code of conduct. When Wal-Mart's Shenzhen buying headquarters advertises a contract for a big production run, Chinese entrepreneurs jump at the chance to fill it. "If Wal-Mart dangles a contract in front of you and you become its supplier, you might quickly become one of the largest shoe manufacturers in Guangdong," said Pao Kang-wen, an official at Bain & Company.[72] Given Wal-Mart's enormous appetite, and its bias toward large suppliers, the Chinese vendors must themselves subcontract, and the subcontractors also find their own sources of labor. No one can effectively police the complex network of contractors, subcontractors, and family workshops, especially when it is a private company, not the state, that is trying to do the police work. "The factory owners don't think they violate the law because they do not know the law," said Liu Kai-Ming of the ICO. "Ninety percent of Wal-Mart sub-contractors and suppliers cannot meet Wal-Mart's own code of conduct."[73]

Contributing to this price and production pressure is the telecommunications infrastructure that has integrated the trans-Pacific supply chain. Instantaneous links between Bentonville and Shenzhen are a mechanism that puts relentless pressure on the Chinese vendors to meet production and shipping deadlines. A quarter of a century ago, before Wal-Mart could make intelligent use of the river of point-of-service data that poured out of its bar code scanners, the time frame for inaugurating or increasing an overseas order was close to a year. Goods shipped from Hong Kong moved to warehouses in Oklahoma or Georgia, after which they were shipped on to the Wal-Mart stores when managers noted that stocks had begun to run low. But such "out of stocks" represented a huge loss of sales, especially when demand for a hot item really spiked.[74]

By the 1990s, however, the perfection of Wal-Mart's inventory control system meant that Bentonville can accurately forecast its inventory needs and change procurement orders almost instantly. It now expects the same kind of flexibility from its manufacturers as well. A spike in the sale of a particular item in the United States, usually in apparel or electronics, is now instantly translated into a production spike at a factory in China or Bangladesh.[75] Hence the stop-and-start nature of work in so many Chinese factories, the heavy overtime required to meet unexpected demand for product, punctuated by short workweeks and unpaid vacations. As a manager at a Dongguan company asserted, "We are forced to apply the labor codes . . . but we can judge from our intuition that when production and codes clash, which side we can cling to. Once I phoned their production department and asked, 'Do you still want your products on time?' The monitor then left our company alone."[76]

Third, although Wal-Mart itself is a "brand," few of the products it sells depend on the kind of brand reputation so carefully nurtured by Nike, Levi Strauss, or some of the fashion apparel makers. This is actually a relatively recent innovation. Walton and his key executives had built their Every Day Low Price strategy not on selling off-brand merchandise but on making well-known national brands available at highly competitive prices. But in the early 1990s, as Wal-Mart accelerated sourcing from China, the Goldman Sachs analyst George Strachan released a study concluding that Wal-Mart was in the midst of "a major strategic merchandising revolution . . . breaking from a history of almost exclusive commitment to national-brand products, expanding and improving its private-label offerings . . . and marketing them more aggressively than ever before." This surge in the sale of Wal-Mart house brands proved a watershed. Consumer surveys as well as shopping behavior had established that for most Americans low price trumped brand loyalty. The company was now free to ramp up the production from unbranded suppliers in China who had privileged access to Wal-Mart's four thousand stores across the United States and Canada. By the early years of the new millennium, Wal-Mart received about a quarter of its goods from branded manufacturers and the rest directly out of Chinese factories.[77]

The relationship between a brand—which is really just a disembodied reputation—and the tangible factory that turns out such branded commodities became graphically apparent when I visited the Nike headquarters, located right inside the Yue Yuen factory in Dongguan.[78] Yue Yuen/Pou Chen[79] Industrial Holdings Ltd., based in Hong Kong, is the world's largest maker of branded athletic and casual footwear, with $3.2 billion in revenues during 2005.[80] Its global workforce of 365,000 turn out some forty footwear brands on 342 production lines, producing nearly 160 million pairs of branded athletic shoes for export in 2005, one-sixth of the world total. The company is Nike's biggest supplier, providing about 15 percent of its shoes; other major footwear clients include Reebok, Adidas, Asics, New Balance, Puma, Timberland, Rockport (owned by Reebok), and Starter, which is featured at Wal-Mart. While most of its shoes are made in factories throughout southern China (four out of six are in Guangdong Province), the company also has plants in Vietnam and Indonesia.[81]

Yue Yuen was not our host when we visited that company's Dongguan factory complex, where upwards of 110,000 workers, 80 percent women, produced just under a million pairs of shoes each month. Rather it was Nike, which had offices in the same place. Its executives were happy to give us a royal welcome because Nike saw any group of visiting U.S. academics as another chance to advertise what they considered the exemplary working conditions under which their shoes were manufactured. We were told the Chinese labor codes were strictly enforced; the dining rooms did look clean, and the dormitories were safe, if crowded. And Nike had even built a disco and a reading room, full of the Chinese equivalents of *People* and *Cosmopolitan.* Their social responsibility staff numbered about twenty-five. All this cost money—we were told at another Yue Yuen factory that such social amenities and adherence to legal wage and safety standards had pushed the wholesale cost of Reebok shoes from seven to eleven dollars a pair. This seems excessive, but whatever the cost, Nike, Reebok, and other branded distributors felt it essential to sustain the reputation of their brand and the goodwill of the nongovernmental organizations that have begun to monitor production facilities in southern China. They don't want to turn CNN on one afternoon and watch an exposé of the poor labor or environmental conditions fostered by a footwear brand whose goodwill is measured in the billions.[82]

But the commodities Wal-Mart sells are interchangeable, making the company far less vulnerable to consumer pressures targeted at a well-known product. The advantages of this were driven home when Tiger Wu, a production manager at Nike, drove us over to the local Wal-Mart to inspect the shoe department. Nike does not sell its shoes to Wal-Mart, in either China or the United States. The company would not be able to command one hundred dollars a pair if its sneakers were found on the same shelf with plastic flip-flops. But Nike recently purchased the Starter line, which Yue Yuen now produces in increasingly large quantities.[83] At the Dongguan Wal-Mart the shelves were full of cheap Starter athletic shoes, also plentiful on the shelves of U.S. Wal-Marts. Mr. Wu was contemptuous of the workmanship, but even more so of their invisibility as a brand.[84] But from Wal-Mart's perspective, this is highly advantageous because it has no investment in the brand reputation, so it can easily and rapidly shift production from one Chinese source to another. As a consequence, the ICO found that "the level of enthusiasm in implementing codes of social responsibility among brand name companies far exceeded that of retailers."[85]

Indeed, Nike has famously posted the addresses of all its manufacturing suppliers on its Web page and permitted independent third-party inspections. Mattel, an even more brand-protective manufacturer, actually owns outright the Chinese toy factories that generate 50 percent of its revenue. This is most unusual. But in the 1980s and 1990s, when the company faced a set of well-publicized lawsuits over unsafe products, as well as a fear that outsourcing production merely enabled counterfeiters to flood the market with imitation Barbie Dolls and Hot Wheels, Mattel executives decided that a tightly monitored "command and control" of their supply chain was far more important than any cost savings they might reap from reliance upon a cutthroat subcontracting system. This was confirmed in the summer of 2007, when Mattel was forced to recall more than a million toys contaminated by lead paint, purchased and applied at Lee Der Industrial, in one of its contract factories not under direct company control.[86]

Although issues of worker safety and exploitation were not in the forefront of Mattel's effort to ensure brand reputation, they did play a key role in the decision by pants maker Levi Strauss to protect the integrity of its brand. When PREL or Wal-Mart found a factory in flagrant violation of its code of conduct, it simply pulled the contract, thereby penalizing and frightening the very workers who might have pointed out the substandard conditions in the first place. Levi Strauss, instead, strove to correct the problem without disrupting production. In Bangladesh, where a contractor was found using child labor in 1994, the jeans maker agreed to create a school at the factory, pay the underage employees what they would have earned if working, and then offer them jobs at the factory when they turned fourteen. This was not simple compassion, of course. Pete Jacobi, Levi Strauss's president of global sourcing, said that protecting Levi's brand name was crucial. "If that means we have to pay a little more to be sure that our company's reputation and brand image aren't sullied, then so be it."[87]

CHINA'S PROLETARIAN FUTURE

The real value of corporate codes of conduct, even for the best companies, lies in the realm of ideology. They legitimize the idea of a worldwide social standard, even as their chronic failures demonstrate that any real transformation of the global supply chains must come from other sources. For example, the Chinese government now endorses these codes of conduct, if only because of their value as a vehicle for international trade promotion. Before 2005 China saw Western agitation to improve labor standards as either a covert effort at protectionism or a violation of China's own labor codes and sovereignty. But official China's growing sensitivity to the ballooning trade imbalance with the United States, along with its effort to move production to higher quality and higher skilled work—to "sustained" rather than mere "rapid" development—has generated an about-face on the issue of corporate social responsibility. Key ministries, like that of the National Textile and Apparel Council, assert that corporate social responsibility is "no longer an individual problem of a region or an industry." Its implementation "will help protect brand image, improve productive efficiency, safeguard the interests of shareholders, satisfy the need of consumers, enhance legal sense of enterprise, avoid risks and evade trade sanctions."[88]

Meanwhile, in Guangdong, as in so many other parts of China, resentment, anger, and social conflict lie just beneath the surface. The workforce in Guangdong, like that of the other coastal provinces, is overwhelmingly composed of migrants from inland villages. The men work in construction and the women in export manufacture and commerce. Factory wages are low—about one hundred dollars a month—but far higher than in agriculture, and they are rising fairly quickly because of the labor shortage generated by the export boom in toys, garments, shoes, and electronic devices. But as in apartheid South Africa or along the employment pathways followed by so many Mexican workers in the United States, these millions of migrants are near stateless. Because their official residence remains the home village, migrant workers in coastal China do not have access to social services or adequate housing so long as they are without residence permits. Under Chinese law the *hukou*, or population registration system, links citizenship to birthplace, so local governments in the crowded coastal provinces have turned their backs on the needs of most migrant workers. Instead, they work and reside on the sufferance of their employer, who often holds their identity papers until they complete their labor "contract." This is why so many factories throw up huge dormitories, some housing eight or twelve workers to a room, where residence is dependent upon employment at the enterprise next door. Moreover, because workers lack classification as *gongren*, or proletariat, both state and factory ignore the labor laws. Women workers who are fired or get pregnant are practically compelled to return to their home villages. Marriage is difficult because there is so little affordable housing for couples who work in the contract manufacturing sector.[89]

China's Ministry of Public Security reports that the number of "mass incidents" rose eightfold in the decade after 1993. Labor Ministry statistics on industrial disputes have recorded an even more rapid increase, and hardly a week goes by without a report of a demonstration or police crackdown in the coastal industrial districts. During the last few years, rising wages and high employment in coastal China did little to ameliorate social discontent. Guangzhou City reported nearly nine hundred protests involving more than fifty thousand workers in 2004. One protest in seven involved more than one hundred people.[90] That same year, after the annual weeklong Spring Festival holiday, more than 2 million migrant workers, almost 10 percent of Guangdong's workforce, failed to return to the Pearl River Delta's export-processing factories. Turnover has always been high after the holiday, when many young workers visit their home villages, but this abandonment of the factory was unprecedented, one of the most massive unorganized withdrawals of Chinese labor in recent times.[91]

Although the 2009 economic slowdown has shuttered many factories, China may well face a labor shortage in the future. The combination of demographics (China's family planning programs have significantly lowered birthrates and hence slowed the increase in numbers of new workers) and exploding demand have given workers considerable bargaining power. Some are leaving Guangdong Province for better-paid work in factories in the Yangtze River Delta near Shanghai, or elsewhere in large interior cities. Via cell phones and instant messaging, workers have been able to communicate easily with friends and relatives who are working elsewhere in China, comparing wages and working conditions, moving elsewhere if they are dissatisfied with their current job.[92]

All this turmoil provided the context for the Chinese government's implementation of a new "labor contract law" in early 2008. It formalizes workers' rights on a series of tension-generating issues, including the requirement that employers sign written contracts with every employee, limit overtime hours, and offer a greater role for the trade unions. "The government is concerned because social turmoil can happen at any moment," argued Liu

Cheng, a legal adviser to the authorities on the labor law. "The government stresses social stability, so it needs to solve existing problems in the society." Most controversially, the law gives long-service employees protection against dismissal. After two contract renewals—about six years—workers automatically earn the right to work for the employer indefinitely, barring dismissal for clear cause.[93]

China has promulgated fine-sounding labor laws before, but this one seems to have some bite. Before passage by the national legislature in 2007, a vigorous public debate erupted among those most affected by the new law. "I've never seen a law attract so much public attention," said one well-placed Western observer. "At the factory level people are talking about it everywhere."[94] The All-China Federation of Trade Unions thought the new law would enable it to make some long-delayed inroads among workers in the export industries. However, the Shanghai-based American Chamber of Commerce lobbied hard against the employment security provisions in the proposed law and won some last-minute concessions.[95] But these were not enough, claimed some employers, to prevent a wave of factory closures and threats of more among the most labor-intensive manufacturers of Guangdong Province. By one account a thousand footwear and accessory producers had reduced output or closed up shop. Some moved to the Chinese hinterland, others to Vietnam and Myanmar, where labor was cheaper and legally defenseless.[96]

Not unexpectedly, Wal-Mart also sought to evade the impact of the law. No layoffs took place in its Chinese retail stores, but more than a hundred employees who worked in the company's procurement offices were dismissed during the fall of 2007, about forty in Shanghai and sixty in Shenzhen. Although relatively small in number, these white-collar layoffs by such a high-profile company created an uproar among advocates of the law. The company claimed that shifts in the nature of Wal-Mart's global sourcing mandated the layoffs, but it seems almost certain that top management in China wanted to get rid of those long-service employees who would soon be covered by the employment guarantees legalized in the new regulations.[97] Wal-Mart's allergy to the social regulation of its affairs crosses even the widest ocean.

Corporate resistance of this sort has already generated a wave of work stoppages, demonstrations, and legal challenges. Like so many other protests in the Chinese industrial provinces, they are most often directed toward local authorities, specific employers, and corrupt officials. They have not achieved, and seem unlikely to achieve, the national character of the Solidarity movement that challenged the Communist regime in Poland a quarter century ago. They have a more local thrust, seeking to pressure factory managers to live up to Chinese labor and environmental laws and to honor the specific employment contracts and working-condition promises that brought so many to the export factory districts in the first place. The protesters are fighting for the kind of democratic citizenship that will liberate them from a workplace regime that has left them in a kind of purgatory, half-stateless and half-free. As they push back against this system, they begin to break the chains, supply chain as well as others, that have given Wal-Mart and its retail competitors such overwhelming power in the global economy.[98]

CHAPTER SEVEN

DISCOUNT STORES
IN EVERY CLIME?

Among the sixteen thousand enthusiastic Wal-Mart shareholders and visitors attending the company's 2007 annual meeting
in a basketball arena on the campus of the University of Arkansas, few were there from the vast manufacturing archipelago
that constitutes the most weighty links in the Wal-Mart supply
chain. These Wal-Mart millions were rendered mute and invis-
ible among the stakeholders whose cheers and laughter reverberated throughout the Bud Walton Fieldhouse. There were,
however, plenty of overseas associates in attendance, including
large and boisterous contingents from Canada, the United
Kingdom, Mexico, Brazil, Argentina, and the People's Republic
of China. They dressed in matching T-shirts, waved their national flags, and erupted in chants at the slightest opportunity.
Most had been flown in to tour the sights of northwest Arkansas, attend workshops and concerts, and then turn out at 6:30
a.m. for a shareholders' meeting. That gathering meshed a set
of sales and profit reports offered by dark-suited executives with
a sound-and-light extravaganza that included vaudeville com-
edy, Hollywood dance numbers, acrobatic performances, and
a Jennifer Lopez finale that brought down the house.

Wal-Mart's International Division operates more than three
thousand stores in thirteen countries, employs 620,000 people,
and accounts for about one fifth of the company's total revenue.[1]

With sales growth slowing at home and the placement of new stores facing chronic resistance in coastal America, Wal-Mart saw the globalization of its retail business as a key to the vitality of the entire enterprise. Company executives had long been convinced that Wal-Mart's culture was exportable. In his *The Wal-Mart Way*, Don Soderquist wrote, "While we may do many things differently country by country, we will not sacrifice our beliefs or values. Customers and associates all across the world want to be treated with respect and dignity, to be part of something bigger than themselves."[2]

In a "third world" of economic upheaval, chaotic urbanization, and Protestant evangelizing, Wal-Mart's culture travels exceedingly well. At a time and place where both nationalism and family ties have begun to abrade, and where American commercial culture is everywhere, Wal-Mart's service ethic and its promise of personal mobility within a well-defined organizational community are powerfully attractive for millions of individuals otherwise left adrift by swift-flowing currents of global trade and social transformation. The combination does not work particularly well in Europe or Japan, but in parts of Latin America and East Asia, the Wal-Mart credo is almost a theology. "I met Sam Walton twice in person and quickly came to learn that financial success and Christianity were perfectly compatible," asserted a Nicaraguan student whose college education in the Ozarks had been supported by a Walton scholarship program. "Being successful and humble, being loving and demanding, being competitive and caring for others—all these were compatible," he affirmed in a 1992 interview.[3]

THE IMPERIAL IMPULSE

"Simply put, our long-term strategy is to be where we're not," announced H. Lee Scott in 2003.[4] And Wal-Mart still has a lot of room to grow. Compared to other transnational retailers,

Wal-Mart remains very much a North American company. Wal-Mart sales are about three times that of its closest international rival, Paris-based Carrefour, but the French company, which expanded abroad in the 1970s, has outlets in thirty-two countries and gets about half its revenue from its international operations. Other retailers are even more transnational. Ahold, based in the Netherlands, derives 80 percent of its revenue from outside its national base. Likewise, Metro, the giant German chain, operates stores in twenty-eight nations from which it extracts 53 percent of all its sales. IKEA, the Swedish furniture emporium, is the most international of all the big retailers, with more than 92 percent of its revenue deriving from stores located in forty-three countries. Even U.S.-based Toys "R" Us has outlets in thirty-two nations from which it derives nearly a quarter of its sales.[5]

Wal-Mart's march to global retail dominance has been a halting one. In the early 1990s Wal-Mart executives thought that within another decade a third of all revenue would be earned abroad, but they have missed that target. The company has come to thoroughly dominate the retail market in Canada and Mexico, and it has done quite well in the United Kingdom, but there have been some notable setbacks as well. Wal-Mart tried and failed to sustain retail operations in Hong Kong and Indonesia in the 1990s, while in 2006 it announced that it was pulling out of booming South Korea and affluent Germany. And in China, where Bentonville has staked so much of its future, the path toward retail gigantism is strewn with obstacles.

These failures are instructive because they shed light on which elements of the Wal-Mart model are truly exportable, and which part of the Bentonville success story is a product of U.S. politics, culture, and markets. Or to put it another way: is Wal-Mart just another manifestation of "American exceptionalism," or is it part of a more universal, neoliberal transformation of business practice and culture that will truly Wal-Martize the world given enough sales, profit, and time?

A few conclusions seem warranted after nearly a generation of experience in twenty countries. Wal-Mart is most successful where and when it simply purchases a large, existing chain and then puts it on steroids by linking the new stores to the company's hyperefficient distribution and communications infrastructure. This has clearly been the case in North America, where Wal-Mart's trucking fleet passes effortlessly through borders rendered porous by the North American Free Trade Agreement. And the Wal-Mart culture has traveled, although not quite so easily, to the United Kingdom. But Sam's world is quite at home in many "third world" countries where an ambitious, expanding lower middle class has linked its fortunes to the exuberant entrepreneurialism and the religious evangelism characteristic of the American megaretailer. However, Wal-Mart has been stymied in nations where either politics or a tough regulatory environment robs the company of the capacity to slash labor costs or build a new generation of suburban stores. China and Germany are very different societies, but in both instances an entrenched political resistance, combined with tough retail competition, has thus far thwarted Wal-Mart's expansive ambitions.

THE CANADIAN ANNEXATION

Although Wal-Mart purchased a stake in Mexico's leading grocery chain as early as 1991, Canada was the first foreign country in which Bentonville sought to replicate its business model. Americans often think of Canada as little more than another tier of states, the population of which all seems to press closely upon and pass easily through the international border that divides the two predominately English-speaking nations. The passage and implementation of the North American Free Trade Agreement in the mid-1990s turned this imagery into something of a reality. "There'll be no country distinctions," David Glass told a meeting of Wal-Mart managers in 1994. "We need to dominate North America. We need to be the absolute dominant retail-wholesale club, the operator in all of North America whatever it takes."[6] Indeed, Wal-Mart's move into Canada was an organic outgrowth of the company's expansion into the upper Midwest, New York State, and the Pacific Northwest. Wal-Mart supplies many of its Canadian stores from U.S. distribution centers, rotates hundreds of middle managers through its Canadian affiliate, and aggressively pushes its corporate culture, including the famous cheer, in French as well as English.

Wal-Mart has been a huge success in Canada. When it bought 122 Woolco stores in 1994, that chain, the discount remnant of defunct Woolworth, was a poorly performing also-ran in a retail market that was already well populated by groceries and discounters, of both Canadian and U.S. origin. But within just a few months, Wal-Mart restocked, remodeled, and relabeled most of the old stores. Woolco held but a 15 percent market share among general merchandise stores, but by 2007 the new Wal-Mart, then with 305 outlets, had grabbed half of the market, sending a jolt through such old-line Canadian merchants as Hudson's Bay and Zellers, which were losing thousands of customers to the American invader. Most impressively, Wal-Mart's low price strategy, combined with its distribution and stock management efficiencies, quadrupled annual sales per square foot in the old Woolco stores, making Wal-Mart far and away the most productive retailer in Canada.[7] Wal-Mart took a decade to introduce the Supercenter idea in Canada, but when it did the shock waves were immediately felt throughout the entire grocery industry, especially in 2006 when Loblaw, the largest supermarket chain, negotiated a new contract with the UFCW that lowered the pay structure at nearly a third of its existing stores, those slated to compete head-to-head with Wal-Mart.[8]

Wal-Mart's one problem in Canada has been that nation's somewhat more intrusive labor law. But despite a decadelong union organizing effort, much negative media coverage, and a string of adverse rulings from some of Canada's union-friendly courts and labor boards, Wal-Mart forged ahead, successfully imposing a Bentonville-model labor relations regime on all of its 140,000 Canadian associates. Because Canadian labor law is enacted and administered by each province, the unionization process is often far quicker and easier than in the United States. Union density is twice as great, and it extends well into the private sector, including retail. Quebec, Saskatchewan, and British Columbia will certify a designated bargaining unit as soon as a majority of workers have signed union cards—even without a vote. Quebec and Manitoba also have so-called first-contract laws that impose arbitration if workers can't reach a contract with an employer. Not unexpectedly, a militant union culture continues to thrive in many parts of Canada, especially in Quebec and throughout the isolated mining and timber towns of the Far West.[9]

But Wal-Mart has made no accommodation to any of this. Canadian unions have always had a close linkage to their confederates south of the border; the UFCW is an "international" union, which, since the early 1990s, has seen the fight to organize at least a few Canadian Wal-Marts as the kind of breakthrough initiative that would reverberate among the American associates. Wal-Mart understands this as well; in 1994 it excluded all ten unionized Woolco stores from among those it acquired, and in subsequent years the company has maintained a large and active Toronto-based legal and labor relations task force that deploys all the legal, administrative, and psychological weapons in the anti-union armory to forestall even the slightest labor foothold in any Canadian Wal-Mart store. In the late 1990s Wal-Mart stifled a Steelworker effort to unionize a Windsor store even after an Ontario labor board certified the union there as a quid pro quo for Wal-Mart's intimidation of union activists. In the negotiations for a contract, however, Wal-Mart offered moral, and almost certainly financial, support to a group of employees hostile to the union, a pattern that would reappear in a number of subsequent organizing efforts. Delay, divisiveness, and rapid employee turnover soon robbed the Steelworkers of whatever support they had once enjoyed in the store. The union defeat was compounded by the election of an unfriendly Ontario government, which soon passed legislation, known as the "Wal-Mart Amendment," stripping the provincial labor board of its power to certify unions victimized by illegal employer activity.[10]

Beginning in 2002, the UFCW renewed the union effort with a vigorous, nationwide organizing campaign, targeting stores in those provinces where the labor law has been most favorable. Union volunteers and staffers contacted Wal-Mart workers at scores of stores; more than a dozen elections were held, and provincial labor boards certified the UFCW at six bargaining units. But nowhere in Canada does a collective bargaining agreement exist between Wal-Mart and a union representing its employees. Wal-Mart lawyers have challenged the UFCW at almost every organizational and legal step, appealing routine labor board decisions to the courts, challenging the unbiased character of the Saskatchewan Labour Relations Board, and lobbying the government of Quebec to eliminate the "card check" certification system in the province and replace it with a mandatory representation election during which store management could have the time and opportunity to persuade employees to vote against the union. And when all this failed, when in early 2005 the Quebec minister of labor agreed to binding first contract arbitration at a Wal-Mart in Jonquière, Bentonville pulled out its weapon of last resort. Jonquière was one of those gritty mining towns where Quebecois nationalism combined with a steadfast sense of working-class identity to make the associates immune to the well-tested array of blandishments and enticements that Wal-Mart put before them. So Bentonville solved this particular labor problem by simply shuttering the store, ostensibly on the grounds that it was "not meeting profit targets." No one believed this obfuscation. The closure chilled union organizing drives throughout North America. Within just a few months the Canadian branch of the UFCW badly lost representation elections at Windsor and at Brossard, Quebec. In the United States, the Jonquière neutron bomb put a definitive end to the faltering UFCW organizing drive, which had encountered even more legal difficulties and company resistance than in Canada.[11]

IN EUROPE AND JAPAN: NOT EASY SAILING

Just a few years after its successful jump into Canada, Wal-Mart announced that it wanted "stores in every country in Europe." To this end, it has either acquired or opened negotiations with existing retail and grocery firms in France, Germany, Holland, Ireland, Russia, and the United Kingdom. With at least 300 million reasonably affluent consumers, Europe has even more purchasing power than North America. But all has not gone well.

Wal-Mart purchased ASDA, then the United Kingdom's third-biggest supermarket chain, in 1999. Like Wal-Mart, ASDA, which operated 229 stores, had gotten its start in the nation's agricultural hinterland. Metropolitan London and the whole populous Southeast were largely unexplored territory. ASDA flourished during the long years of Margaret Thatcher and her conservative successor, in part because it mimicked many of Wal-Mart's low-wage labor policies and automobile-friendly store-placement policies. It called all of its employees "colleagues" but provided even fewer full-time jobs than Wal-Mart offered in the United States. "When we were acquired," asserted Tony DeNunzio, ASDA's CEO at the time, "it was like acquiring a clone."[12]

As in the United States, Wal-Mart in-sourced much of its warehouse and distribution work, a break from the UK pattern. ASDA stores were already bigger than those of most rivals, but by streamlining the replenishment process according to the model perfected in the United States, the UK stores were able to shrink their backroom storage area and greatly expand the size of the selling floor. When a mezzanine was added, many of the new ASDA stores came to resemble U.S. Supercenters, with half the floor area devoted to nonfood items. As in the United States, ASDA's Every Day Low Price strategy attracted millions of new customers and put downward price pressure on key competitors. For example, ASDA's brand of men's jeans cost twenty-four dollars a pair before the buyout, but once Bentonville linked the UK retailer to its worldwide network of denim vendors, ASDA got its fabric at one-third the old cost. As a result Wal-Mart's British acquisition slashed its retail price in half and multiplied its annual sale of jeans almost sixfold. Within five years ASDA increased overall sales and profits by well over 50 percent, making it the largest subsidiary in Wal-Mart's International Division. ASDA also became the second-largest UK retailer, having overtaken Sainsbury in 2003.[13]

But ASDA never achieved in the United Kingdom the dominance Wal-Mart enjoyed in North America. Because of tough zoning and green belt laws, and the antitrust regulations enforced by the British government, ASDA could not expand its market share. The company thought it had the ear of Tony Blair's New Labour government: just before the ASDA purchase, the prime minister held a confidential and highly controversial meeting with Wal-Mart's vice president for international operations. Afterward Blair asserted that UK citizens liked to shop at edge-of-the-city big boxes, much to the annoyance of his government's own planners, who see such sprawl as the death knell of an efficient urban/suburban rail transport plan.[14] The planners seem to have won this bureaucratic tussle. In the first five years following its purchase, ASDA added fewer than fifty new stores, much to the annoyance of H. Lee Scott, who complained on the BBC that UK land-planning rules were stifling competition. Nor was ASDA able to grow through a merger with the Safeway chain, which was blocked by Great Britain's Competition Commission. Thus Tesco, itself a pioneer in the world of big-box superstores, has grown even more rapidly than ASDA and now serves about a third of the UK grocery market, almost twice that of Wal-Mart's subsidiary.[15]

ASDA's effort to further Wal-Martize its labor force encountered more resistance than in Canada. ASDA had long recognized a trade union, the old-line GMB (Gas, Maintenance and Boilermakers), but retail unionism in the United Kingdom was spotty and inside ASDA stores it existed in only the most attenuated form, much like the situation in Mexico or parts of Latin America. This was convenient for ASDA's new American owners, who could now defuse criticism with the claim "We are not anti-union. We have an agreement with the GMB." In 2000 ASDA put forward a new bargaining program, titled "Fit for the Future," which sought to institutionalize union weakness and Bentonville ideology. Hereafter, workers would need permission from a store manager to file a grievance, the work rules would be "modernized" to give the company more scheduling flexibility, and most stores would no longer support a functioning shop steward. ASDA would find out about worker concerns through its own internal canvas; the UK subsidiary called it a "We're Listening Survey," not unlike a similar scheme in stateside Wal-Mart stores.[16]

But retail unionists had one weapon not available to their counterparts in Canada or in the United States. At nine of ASDA's twenty-four distribution centers—known as "depots" in the United Kingdom—the GMB represented the warehouse workers. These were big, factory-sized workplaces with upwards of nine hundred workers. And at two or three "battleground depots" the workers were itching for a fight, especially after management sought to boost quotas, extend work time, and marginalize the union. Since the smooth operation of the supply chain is crucial, the GMB, led by a new generation of militants who assumed office in 2004, could leverage the power of just a few hundred activists to pressure ASDA's top management to open up the entire workforce to an unimpeded union organization effort. Over the next two years this industrial militancy "on the ground" was backstopped by a savvy "air game," a media offensive inspired by the high-profile, anti-Wal-Mart campaigns that have become such a staple of political debate in the United States. Some Labour MPs came to see a defense of the GMB as a repudiation of Tony Blair's neoliberalism, if only because one of Blair's former press secretaries had become an ASDA public relations consultant working to undermine the union effort.[17]

Labor's initiative reached a climax in the spring of 2006. Negotiating with the GMB in a Parliament meeting room, ASDA CEO Andy Bond actually arrived at a handshake agreement that gave the GMB a higher level of recognition and more organizing rights, but when Bond flew to Bentonville, presumably to explain his concession, H. Lee Scott repudiated the accord as a "misunderstanding."[18] The GMB prepared for a strike, cleverly set for the World Cup weekend in June, during which ASDA was expected to sell 10 million bottles of beer to stay-at-home fans watching England take on Portugal. The fragility of a just-in-time supply chain became abundantly clear when Bond and other managers realized that if even a handful of depots were shut, not only would the beer go out of stock, but millions of pounds of vegetables would perish in the summer heat. So ASDA caved, granting GMB stewards the right to distribute literature, hold meetings and elections, and recruit members in almost all stores and depots. According to the *Financial Times*, "[The deal] marks the most significant concession the global retailer has made to organized labor."[19]

If Wal-Mart's encounter with land use planning and union power limited ASDA's capacity to transform British retailing, Bentonville's effort to import American-style discount retailing to Germany was an outright failure—"a fiasco," reports Andreas Knorr, a leading German analyst of the retail industry. Wal-Mart acquired Wertkauf, a twenty-one-store German supermarket chain, in 1997 and then bought seventy-four more German stores from Interspar the next year. But the American giant could not grow to achieve the economies of scale necessary for profitability. A remarkably large proportion of German retail chains are closely held, family-owned firms, almost all of which have resisted Wal-Mart's efforts to buy them out. So even though it sold $3 billion in goods each year, Bentonville's German subsidiary remained but the eleventh-largest retailer in the huge German market. Wal-Mart remained too small to make its vaunted logistics savvy work, which meant that its Everyday Low Price strategy just spread red ink from Berlin to Bonn. The company lost an astonishing amount of money, upwards of $250 million in some years, before it pulled the plug in 2006. The reasons were both political and cultural.

Despite neoliberal efforts to erode German economic and social regulation, the political environment in that country is radically different from the United States and much more stringent than in the United Kingdom. As in Great Britain, rigorous planning and zoning regulations have prevented firms like Wal-Mart from developing edge-of-the-city, auto-friendly sites upon which to build big-box stores. And because Germany's power-ful trade unions have sought to limit shift work, nighttime restocking was proscribed, along with Sunday openings and late evening closing times. At eighty hours per week, Germa-ny's store hours are the shortest in Europe. Add to this a set of "fair trading" regulations that have restricted price competi-tion and eviscerated Wal-Mart efforts to squeeze German suppliers, and one can see why Knorr pronounced the Ameri-can company "the prey rather than the hunter" in the German market.[20]

Wal-Mart also proved culturally toxic to the Germans. The first four CEOs appointed by the Bentonville-based multi-national were unfamiliar with German retailing; they often appeared as arrogant and inept. Some did not even speak the language. And when Wal-Mart did hire native executives, many found the company's rural, southern managerial culture quite alien. Indeed, German customers seemed allergic to the faux cheerfulness that Wal-Mart projects throughout its stores. They did not like the greeters present at the entrance, nor did they feel comfortable with Mr. Sam's famous "ten-foot rule" that generated the frequent incantation "How may I help you?" For their part, most workers hated the morning cheer; some women workers were reported to have hid in the toilets during the group exercise. "We are workers, not clowns," asserted a trade unionist who helped pressure the company into abandoning the morning ritual.[21]

As in Britain, Wal-Mart faced a union culture that it in-stinctively rejected. The company failed to join the employers association that bargained with all unions in the retail sector, it refused to recognize the legally mandated works council pres-ent in every large retail chain, and Wal-Mart sought to impose its own labor relations regime without regard for German sen-sibilities. In one infamous incident, Wal-Mart announced a code of ethics that banned dating among workmates. This was subject to much ridicule, but of even greater disdain was another provision that urged employees to make use of a hotline to management that allowed them to offer confidential information on the transgressions of their workmates. In the United States this idea arose out of the anti-union open-door culture, which enabled disgruntled associates to bring to the attention of high management problems they found at any level of store operations. But in central Europe such an "informer hotline" had a far more sinister resonance, evoking memories of both Cold War anticommunism and the elaborate police apparatus constructed by the East German Stasi.[22]

Failure in Germany was not just a product of stolid Teutonic resistance to a company that embodied American ruralism. Wal-Mart encountered many of the same problems in Japan, the world's second-largest economy, despite that country's weak union tradition and more amenable set of economic regulations. Between 2002 and 2005 Wal-Mart bought a controlling interest in Seiyu, a 392-store chain, which soon underwent a rapid process of Wal-Martization. Hundreds of Japanese managers were fired, after which a team of executives from Canada and the United States, few of whom knew Japanese, were put in charge. To the grocery fare Seiyu normally offered, Wal-Mart added clothing, electronics, books, and other hard goods. And with Wal-Mart's worldwide procurement system pouring a river of cheap commodities through its own Japanese distribution center, Seiyu became a low-cost seller in the islands' huge retail market.[23]

But none of this made the food-finicky Japanese love Wal-Mart. In 2007 *Fortune* reported that with stagnant sales and large annual losses, Wal-Mart was "battling to survive" in an overcrowded market. The Japanese did not seem to like the sell-everything big-box stores, and when high-quality merchandise disappeared from the shelves, thousands of affluent, older customers left.[24]

Thus Wal-Mart's difficulties in Japan and Germany, the world's second- and third-richest markets, tell us something fundamental about the company and its business model. First, Wal-Mart's technological and organizational innovations have been substantially copied by its competitors, especially in economies with a mature set of sophisticated retailers. Second, in places where a high disposable income is shared relatively equally throughout the population, Wal-Mart's EDLP policy is not so much of a trump card. And finally, Wal-Mart's hypercentralization, its capacity to project a distinctive work culture throughout its far-flung network of stores, which has served it so well in the United States and Canada, seemed to generate a backlash among those whose own cultural sensibilities are reinforced by a resistant political culture and a powerful regulatory state.

THE LATIN AMERICAN CONUNDRUM

Resistance to the Wal-Mart model in these high-income, highly regulated economies made corporate expansion into Latin America and Asia all the more pressing. Indeed, Wal-Mart enjoyed huge success in Mexico, it controls the largest grocery chain in Central America, and it is a big player in Brazil, where the company is fighting an epic battle with Carrefour. But the Wal-Mart of Mexico, Guatemala, and China looks very different from that of the United Kingdom or even the United States. The clientele are relatively well-off, the wages of its workers are no worse than those paid by its competitors, and the company recognizes a trade union, if only because such state-controlled organizations are largely protection rackets, as in Mexico, or governmental institutions, as in China, that make few demands on the employer.

In Argentina, where Wal-Mart also has a few dozen stores, retail union leaders align themselves with the quiescent *gordo* (fat cat) faction tied to the ruling Peronist Party.[25]

Even more significant, the famous Wal-Mart culture generates few oppositional ripples; in fact, in both Latin America and China, the company's paternalism and its entrepreneurial ideology appeal to millions of individuals whose lives and livelihoods have been disrupted by the chaos of an increasingly globalized capitalism. In Mexico and especially in Central America, where evangelical Protestantism has made a huge recent advance, often with the aid of Wal-Mart-funded scholarships to Arkansas Christian colleges, the company has recruited thousands of managers and clerks from the ranks of these market-friendly denominations. And in China, the edicts of Mr. Sam and the culture of Maoist self-sacrifice bear striking similarities.

Wal-Mart vaulted to the top in Mexico when in 1991 it took a large stake in CIFRA, that nation's largest retailer. Passage of the North American Free Trade Agreement proved crucial to the success of the acquisition because Wal-Mart was determined to junk CIFRA's antiquated and insular procurement system and replace it with an integrated network of distribution centers built or expanded on both sides of the U.S. border. Soon, trucks were dispatched from Wal-Mart distribution centers in Laredo and Tucson directly to CIFRA stores in northern and central Mexico. By 2007 another twelve distribution centers served more than nine hundred stores, about 40 percent located in or near Mexico City. The renamed Wal-Mart de México proved so powerful and efficient that its three top rivals revamped their stores, introduced new products, and spent heavily on computer systems and new warehouses. In 2004 Mexican regulators allowed them to create a joint purchasing company that would enable the nation's homegrown merchants to compete with Wal-Mart on prices and profitability.[26]

But the Wal-Martization of the Mexican retail economy has definite limits. Although Wal-Mart controls nearly half of all Mexican supermarket sales, the company still accounts for but 7 percent of total retail sales in Mexico. That's because income polarization in Mexico is stark, real wages remain stagnant, and the informal economy continues to grow. For example, Wal-Mart sells a kilogram of rice for two-thirds what it would cost in the United States. That's a good deal, but a Mexican worker earning her country's minimum wage would have to labor for an hour and a half to be able to purchase that bag of rice, more than seven times longer than a minimum-wage worker in the United States. Corn oil is another staple. It takes a Mexican minimum-wage worker three hours to earn enough money to purchase a liter of corn oil at a Wal-Mart, nearly eight times longer than in the United States. Wal-Mart and its Mexican competitors have undoubtedly pushed down staple prices in Mexico, but the free trade regime upon which those low prices depend has devastated peasant farming and slashed real wages across many sectors of the economy. So most poor and working-class Mexicans do not find Wal-Mart the cheapest or most convenient place to shop. Instead, they frequent the street vendors, itinerant markets, and barrio stores, the untaxed, unregulated half of the economy that Wal-Mart and its competitors have barely touched. Indeed, Mexico's chronically high unemployment—the once booming maquiladoras along the U.S. border laid off thousands of workers as garment and TV production switched to East Asia—means that retail sales productivity (as measured by sales per employee) has actually declined in the new century. So Wal-Mart dominates the big-box retail economy in Mexico, but that sector remains merely an island of U.S.-style consumerism in a much larger sea of those who are just treading water.[27] It's a conundrum that limits Wal-Mart's growth throughout much of the rest of Latin America as well.

"WAL-MAOISM" IN THE MIDDLE KINGDOM

When Wal-Mart holds its annual shareholders' meeting in Arkansas, scores of associates are flown in from China. For many it is their first trip out of their home province, not to mention China itself. The verdant, rolling Ozark landscape is a pleasant relief for many of these Chinese city dwellers, who are equally impressed with the huge parking lots—filled with SUVs and big pickup trucks—that surround the exurban Wal-Marts they visit. They wave the Red Chinese flag with the same excitement as do flag-wavers from the larger Canadian, Mexican, and British delegations. Should Bentonville have its way, it will not be too many years before these Chinese associates occupy thousands of seats in the Bud Walton arena, dominating the space reserved for the international attendees.

For two centuries Western merchants have sought to tap the great Chinese market, composed of 400 million souls in the mid-nineteenth century and more than 1.3 billion today. If every Chinaman bought just one pair of shoes, dreamed the cobblers and jobbers of Lynn and Manchester, their shops and factories would hum for a hundred years. Wal-Mart executives cultivate this dream as well, even if the factories that make the goods Chinese consumers might one day buy are themselves mainly located in China. Of course, like Mexico and other developing nations, China has poor people in greater numbers than rich, but the country is so enormous that there are still more potential Wal-Mart consumers there than anywhere else on the globe. With upwards of a hundred cities of a million or more people, demographers estimate that 150 million urban families have an annual income of at least ten thousand dollars. And as China continues its breakneck pace of industrialization, those numbers are bound to grow. During the past decade overall retail spending has increased 15 percent each year. David Glass, Wal-Mart's CEO when the company first made the leap to Asia, told *Fortune* that China was "the one place in the world where you could replicate Wal-Mart's success in the U.S."[28]

Glass had a point. As in Arkansas half a century ago, the Chinese retail sector is inefficient, decentralized, and ripe for a radical transformation. Together, the top ten retailers hold but 2 percent of the market. Most are regionally based, and none have the kind of computerized distribution and warehousing system Wal-Mart has now made standard, even in Latin America. Meanwhile, overstaffing is endemic. From the corner market to the old-line department store, this legacy of China's Communist-era "iron rice bowl" is hard to miss. Buying a two-dollar umbrella in a downtown Beijing department store requires the services of three saleswomen, one of whom retrieves the product, another who writes up the bill, and a third who takes the money. In every department there are more clerks than customers.

Every time Wal-Mart opens a new store, consumers are wildly enthusiastic. Although most Chinese do not have cars, they flock to these clean, well-lighted, comparatively spacious selling emporiums. The shelves are well stocked and the groceries fresh. They can touch the merchandise, they can get in and out quickly, and they find the prices on par with traditional markets and neighborhood stores. Many shop there four or five times a week. Joe Hatfield, Wal-Mart's first head of Chinese operations, became something close to a business celebrity. An old Wal-Mart hand who had first bought toys for Mr. Sam in Bentonville, Hatfield thought he knew the secret for the company's Asian success. "The culture of Wal-Mart," which "is stronger in China than anywhere else in the world," he told

Time magazine early in 2005.[29] There's a good deal of truth in this, but perhaps not in quite the way Hatfield imagined it.

David Davies is a young American anthropologist, fluent in Chinese, who has studied that country's entrepreneurial culture for almost a decade. But even he was surprised when he interviewed a twenty-seven-year-old Wal-Mart store manager one afternoon in the summer of 2005. "Steve"—it is common practice for Wal-Mart's China employees to adopt English names for their store badges, suggesting American-style cosmopolitanism—extolled Wal-Mart's corporate culture as a comprehensive system that fosters positively motivated employees and creates a unique work environment essential to the corporation's global success. And the origins of that successful set of ideas, in the United States as well as China? Steve had the answer: "Sam Walton had studied Mao Zedong thought for five years before he opened Wal-Mart."

Like Mao, Steve explained to Davies, Walton had been born in a poor rural area; with a core group of committed comrades he had adopted the revolutionary strategy of "the countryside encircling the city." In contemporary China, Steve asserted, Wal-Mart practices an egalitarian management style based on the principles of "servant leadership," not all that different in tone from the Maoist "serving the people." The visual representation of all this may be found on the wall of each Wal-Mart store, where an organizational chart in the form of an inverted pyramid puts the manager at the bottom, his assistant managers above, overtopped by all the lower-ranking associates.[30]

The accuracy of Steve's historical revisionism is far less important than his effort to link a still-resonant form of Maoism with the Wal-Mart organizational culture upon which his career now depends. In China the entranceway to every Wal-Mart store offers a large poster panel portraying the history of the company, from humble Arkansas roots to worldwide preeminence. At the center is a picture of Sam Walton, in suit and tie, but also sporting a Wal-Mart badge and his signature base-ball cap, a symbol of his common touch. Yet the most striking thing about the Walton portrait is the hand gesture, palm-up, offering a benediction to all those who follow and venerate his cult. Beneath, in handwritten calligraphy as if penned by the founder himself, is written in Chinese: "pride comes from out standing performance." Such imagery is not found on U.S. Wal-Mart materials, but it is strikingly reminiscent of official Mao Zedong portraiture.[31]

According to Davies, the Chinese translation of Mr. Sam's "ten rules for business," prominently displayed on the break-room walls of every Chinese Wal-Mart, evokes a set of Maoist maxims familiar to even young Chinese. Instead of business rules for employees, the Chinese have translated Walton's apho-risms as a set of "ten great laws for success with the cause." Law number one, for example, which in English is "commit to your business," in Chinese says "be loyal to your cause." Law number three is "motivate your partners." Here, the Chinese employ the verb *jili*, "to impel" or "to inspire," a word used often in military affairs or in revolutionary-era party propaganda inspiring the struggle toward communism. And as for law number nine, "control your expenses better than your competition," the Chi-nese equivalent entreats employees to *jieyue*, "economize" or "be thrifty"—a term familiar during the Maoist lean years in the 1950s and 1960s when citizens were asked to accept an austere life for the greater good.[32]

Such conflation—"Wal-Maoism," Davies calls it—is not de-signed to revive Chinese communism. Rather, it offers a point of identification for a generation of strivers who want careers and wealth, but who find chaotic, corrupt, and contradictory the raw capitalist culture that has so pervaded contemporary China. With its insular business culture, Wal-Mart in China, even more so than in the United States, becomes a totalizing experience. In sharp contrast to traditional Chinese business practice, Wal-Mart managers are frequently moved from city to city, which means that they rarely have much of a life outside the company. Steve moved three times in three years; another Wal-Mart store manager in Beijing had moved six times in seven years. In return for such rootlessness, Wal-Mart offers a highly structured moral order and the prospect of social mobility. The teachings of Mr. Sam, not unlike those of other revolutionaries, have put honesty, dedication, hard work, and vision at the heart of an organization that promises to transform the world.[33]

POTHOLES ON THE CAPITALIST ROAD

Whether or not Wal-Mart's ideological success portends a profitable Chinese future for the company is not clear. This is because the politics of contemporary China have played a decisive role in determining Wal-Mart's success. And here the Maoist legacy remains a potent one as well. When the Communists assumed power in 1949, their rigid control of ideas, politics, and culture was accompanied by a large degree of economic decentralization. In part, this was a product of Maoist determination to make each Chinese region economically self-sufficient, lest foreign invasion or nuclear attack cripple the entire nation; in part it simply reflected a woeful deficit in good transport, communications, and finance. And retail was an economic sector to which the state gave a low priority, given the Maoist emphasis on heavy industry in the 1950s and 1960s.

Such economic decentralization, along with a measure of political autonomy, was advanced by Deng Xiaoping's market reforms that took hold in the 1980s. As long as the provincial authorities gave their ideological and political loyalty to Beijing, they would be allowed to reap the benefits of the capitalist transformation. Thus practically all foreign investment—factories, stores, hotels, office buildings—take the form of a "joint venture" in which a local municipality or business partners with the non-Chinese firm. As one might expect, bribery, kickbacks, nepotism, patronage, collusion, and political influence play their parts in establishing such ventures.[34]

Wal-Mart has not been particularly good at playing this game. Always more centralized and rule-bound than its competitors, the company, while hardly a stickler for legal niceties, has nevertheless pursued a policy that proscribes the gratuities and gift exchanges that have long accompanied Chinese politico-business relations. In contrast Carrefour, which began to establish a presence in China a few years after Wal-Mart, has proven more successful in placing its stores in the best locations. The French company allows its managers more autonomy, and it has been quite willing to simply ignore the law when necessary. Thus, for example, when in the 1990s Beijing decreed that foreign retailers would be limited to three stores per city, Wal-Mart largely adhered to the rule, even though it wreaked havoc with its logistics planning. But Carrefour carved out a series of local deals that enabled it to concentrate stores in northern China, especially in booming Shanghai.[35] And the fact that Carrefour made little effort to thwart the Communist All-China Federation of Trade Unions, while Wal-Mart strenuously resisted, probably contributed to the welcome the French retailer won from some Chinese officials.

So Wal-Mart's Chinese incursion has proceeded with much caution and delay. An early alliance with a Thai supermarket chain collapsed in the mid-1990s, forcing Wal-Mart to surrender planned developments in Shanghai and Shenyang. The purchase of another already established chain, the Taiwanese-owned Trust-Mart with some ninety rather scruffy, downscale stores, did not take place for more than ten years. This meant that in the world's most populous nation, the world's largest company had only 66 stores during its first decade of operations; as of 2008, it still has but 203, and these stores are certainly not located where the company would have liked had the choice been entirely its own. For all the publicity Wal-Mart's opening to China won in the international press, the company operates just a few more stores in that huge nation than it opens each year in the United States.[36]

Wal-Mart's politically determined pattern of store operations negated entirely the corporate distribution strategy, which mandated a cluster of stores, up to one hundred in the United States, serviced by a huge, highly automated distribution center. This would have been difficult enough, given China's still-underdeveloped transport and supply services. At present the country has no national freight carrier, like Yellow Truck; instead about 4 million businesses operate 5 million trucks. Almost all are local cartage. There is no uniform system for tracking goods, issuing invoices, or collecting payments by credit.[37] Wal-Mart has established warehouses at Shenzhen in the South and Tianjin near Shanghai, but these are modest in size, not the hyperefficient distribution centers for which Wal-Mart logistics are famous.[38] Wal-Mart insists that store managers order as much as 70 percent of their hard goods and apparel from these depots. But this system works poorly. Tastes vary radically among Chinese provinces and regions: Beijing and Shenzhen consumers are about as different as those found in Stockholm and Rome. A store manager in Beijing complained that if he were allowed more authority to order local clothing and packaged foods, his sales would do much better, perhaps not unlike the more stylish Carrefour across town, where local management has the authority to purchase up to 85 percent of stock on the local market.[39]

Wal-Mart has compensated for this organizational dysfunction by turning a substantial part of each store over to local peddlers, grocers, and fishmongers, resulting in a Wal-Mart store sans Wal-Martism. In remote Kunming, near the Chinese border with Myanmar, the American sociologist Eileen Otis found the local store "festival-like, even chaotic."

Crowds push and pry their way through the aisles as hawkers call out their wares, plying customers with free samples of chocolate, coffee, jello, dumplings, peanut paste candy, dried fish, shampoos, toothpastes and creams. One saleswoman pounds on a drum as she announces the day's discount on instant noodles. Others yell through loudspeakers. The effect is sheer cacophony. Customers gather around a small tub, fishing out pears floating in soup of licorice root, salt, and sugar, a specialty of Gezhou, south of Kunming. . . . At this store one can find Tibetan Stubby Barley wine, Yunnan coffee, tobacco bongs filled with local rice wine, full-belly clay pots brimming with condiments like eggplant paste, soy bean paste, ginger paste, and dried green bean paste and ten different kinds of dumplings, ready to eat.[40]

Most workers on the Kunming selling floor were not Wal-Mart employees. Instead, they were supplied by multiple vendors, willing to pay Wal-Mart about $1.20 per day, per salesperson, for the privilege of opening a stall or stand inside the store itself. In effect, Wal-Mart had created inside each store a milieu reminiscent of the traditional Chinese market. In a Beijing branch the atmosphere appeared more orderly, but the reliance on outside vendors proved just as great. Here they wore their own neat uniforms, kept their counters tidy and hygienic, and were subject to the disciplinary authority of the store manager. But most of the workers were not Wal-Mart employees. They mingled with the Wal-Mart associates in the break room, but they did not receive the free hot meal, nor did they share in the company cheer or the various bonuses and prizes the local manager offered as rewards to his most faithful and dedicated employees.[41]

A UNIONIZED WAL-MART?

Wal-Mart's logistical difficulty in China was not matched by any erosion of the retailer's infamous labor management system. As in the United States, workers are expected to memorize Sam Walton's rules and aphorisms, to meet work quotas, and to avoid romantic liaisons not only with fellow associates but with the vendors as well. For the cashiers, work pressures are probably even more intense than in the States because the Chinese shop so frequently and purchase supplies in relatively small quantities. Thus stores are always crowded and the checkout lines never-ending. Regular Wal-Mart clerks tend to be urbanites, not migrants, and their pay is somewhat higher than that of the women who toil in the export factories. But the job is not good enough to banish employee turnover, at least not among lower-level stockers and cashiers. In Kunming it seems to have been sky-high, above 100 percent a year, while in Beijing and Nanjing about a fifth of the workforce leave each year. Shrinkage, which is often a proxy for employee morale, is about twice as high as in the United States.[42]

Are Wal-Mart's China stores going to be unionized? The stakes are high because Wal-Mart has the most clout of any corporation that either derives or sells its merchandise in the world's largest nation. If unionization takes place among the employees of this corporation, surely labor organizing will spread to the rest of the foreign business community, and—who knows?—perhaps to the employees of Wal-Mart in the United States as well. All this would seem pretty important, but it pales alongside the even larger political and social issues raised by the prospect of a genuine trade union presence in China. Since the Chinese revolution, the All-China Federation of Trade Unions has been a classic Communist Party–dominated organization, designed, at best, as another rivet in the iron rice bowl that kept the lid on proletarian dissent. Should the unionization of Wal-Mart presage the appearance of a real transformation in the character of the Chinese unions, something close to radical social change will certainly be in the offing. In Poland, South Korea, South Africa, Indonesia, Ukraine, Brazil, and Spain, militant unionism and mass strikes were key ingredients in the overthrow or democratization of well-entrenched authoritarian regimes. Who is to say that in China the tinder for such an upheaval is not also present?

The ACFTU claims to represent more than 100 million workers, but few in the West consider it a genuine trade union federation. Controlled by the ruling Communist Party, it allows no competing labor unions, rejects free elections of its leaders, and often goes to bat on the side of management against the interests of its own members in order to advance the party-state's promise of economic growth in a "harmonious" society. It has thousands of functionaries and a huge income pegged at 2 percent of payroll of all those firms and institutions at which it is present. But the explosive privatization of the Chinese economy has put the ACFTU in a fix. Mass layoffs within the bloated and inefficient state enterprise sector have stripped the big union federation of millions of members at the same time that managers, both native and foreign, in the booming export sector have been notably cool to the presence of even a highly bureaucratic and cooperative union in their factories. Wal-Mart has not been the only entity that wanted nothing to do with the official union. Many provincial officials were unsympathetic as well, since unionism of any sort might discourage new foreign investments. And, of course, workers themselves were hardly clamoring for representation by an institution that seemed remote, ineffectual, and parasitic.[43]

Although the unions that composed the ACFTU had official backing from the government, their own efforts to "organize" companies like Wal-Mart were close to farcical. Never having been exposed to the idea of grassroots mobilization,

ACFTU officials normally extended the reach of their union by first meeting with factory owners and managers to convince them of the virtues and patriotic necessity of a workplace organization. If all went as expected, the unionists typically identified a couple of middle managers and asked them to serve as the new union chair and deputy. Under such conditions top executives had little reason to resist, if only because the ACFTU assured them of its cooperation. But Wal-Mart would not play ball, even after the Chinese union federation selected the company as a special, high-profile target. Wal-Mart remained ideologically hostile to unionism, saw the 2 percent payroll contribution as but another tax, and resented the presence in its stores of any institution, no matter how ineffectual, that might dilute the paternal communalism the company worked so hard to build among its employees. So when ACFTU officials called Wal-Mart headquarters in Shenzhen, the relevant managers were always out of town.[44]

This ACFTU failure was not just embarrassing; it was dangerous to the Communist Party and the Chinese state. It graphically demonstrated the tenuous hold exercised by Beijing in the industrial provinces, threatening to return the nation to the old treaty port system in which Western interests cut their deals with local warlords in exchange for a de facto fragmentation of the country. And the marginalization of the ACFTU made it harder to monitor the mounting social explosiveness at every sweatshop, warehouse, store, and construction site. Each year, the Chinese Ministry of Security reported a rising wave of strikes, demonstrations, and protests. Most were suppressed or accommodated with but minor concessions; still, the absence of even titular leadership from a government-allied institution like the ACFTU was asking for trouble.

Thus on October 24, 2004, the People's National Congress, China's highest state body, passed a resolution denouncing foreign companies, naming Wal-Mart, Kodak, and Samsung, among others, that refused to set up trade unions in their China-based operations. Within hours the ACFTU announced that it would sue Wal-Mart in accordance with the long-neglected Chinese trade union law. The official press headlined all this; in the *People's Daily* a high-level source in the Ministry of Commerce made clear that "the trade union crisis [was] likely to become a huge obstacle in the way of Wal-Mart's development in China."[45]

This got Bentonville's attention. Within four days H. Lee Scott and a high-level Wal-Mart delegation were on a plane to Beijing. There they endowed the Retail Research Center at Tsinghua University, met with a series of Chinese officials, and announced that the company intended to "honor" all of China's laws. As for unionization of its stores, which by now employed almost forty thousand, Wal-Mart asserted, "Should associates request formation of a union, Wal-Mart China would respect their wishes."[46]

The *New York Times* ran a story titled, WAL-MART BOWS TO TRADE UNIONS AT STORES IN CHINA. But little actually changed. In Nanjing, provincial representatives of the ACFTU visited their local Wal-Mart store twenty-six times over a two year period, but they never secured a meeting with the manager. Something truly radical would be necessary, perhaps even organizing on the QT, which required union officials to actually meet with the workers who were to be enrolled in the prospective labor organization. This probably took place in the first half of 2006, after which the district union in Fujian Province declared that a branch had been built at the local Wal-Mart store on July 29, complete with a rank-and-file organizing committee. At a founding ceremony, held after midnight to accommodate shift workers, they sang "The Internationale" beneath a banner reading, DETERMINED TO TAKE THE ROAD TO DEVELOP TRADE UNIONISM WITH CHINESE CHARACTERISTICS! Another five union branches, all with such rank-and-file organizing committees, appeared within the next week.[47]

Wal-Mart first responded with the tactics it had honed so well in the United States: captive-audience meetings for all employees, attacks on the union as a self-interested bureaucracy, threats of firings and layoffs. But company officials must have realized, or been told, that this hard-line approach would merely ensure the demise of Wal-Mart's plan to expand its retail footprint in China. So Wal-Mart signed an agreement with the ACFTU establishing union branches at all its stores. With store management in attendance, founding ceremonies were held during the day inside each store, rather than at night in the local trade union office. Despite the invocation of party-mandated "harmony" with Wal-Mart managers, Chinese unionists at all levels thought the Wal-Mart union branches a "major breakthrough." Instead of "persuading management to give support," announced one union activist, "we turn to propagating, inspiring, cultivating and reinforcing employees' trade union consciousness, instigating and mobilizing their aspirations to join the union."[48]

A year later the results seemed decidedly mixed. At one Beijing Wal-Mart, the only evidence of a trade union consisted of a plaque on the training room wall. "Chinese unions are different from those in America," the manager said with a sly grin. The union organizer assigned to that Wal-Mart store claimed that his only contact with the workers consisted of a forty-five-minute talk repeated four times a day for the benefit of the different shifts. But this was militant unionism compared to the "organizing" at a Nanjing store. After thirty workers signed up with the union there, the regional ACFTU leader Chen Siming presented them with a TV set, a DVD player, books, and 20,000 yuan in cash. He told a Western reporter, "I also treated all Wal-Mart employees to an American blockbuster movie, 'Mission Impossible III.' You know, with Tom Cruise." Chen added, "We trade union leaders will never organize the employees in launching a strike or asking for unreasonable benefits."[49]

CHAPTER EIGHT

HOW WAL-MART MAKES
THE RULES

It was never one of Wal-Mart's authorized cheers, but some managers and associates belted it out anyway: "Stack it deep, sell it cheap, stack it high and watch it fly! Hear those downtown merchants cry!"[1] In the 1980s, as Wal-Mart spread its stores through the small-town heartland—Oklahoma, Illinois, Iowa, Kansas, Wisconsin, Texas, and Colorado—Main Street proprietors indeed cried out in pain. But the merchants and their friends failed to stop the Bentonville steamroller. When it came to the zoning and development issues convulsing so many American towns, Wal-Mart was playing by a new set of rules that ensured it would win almost every contest. As the years passed, the same turned out to be true of virtually everything else the company touched, from its controversial health insurance offerings to its extensively politicized philanthropy. Wal-Mart has used its size and sophistication to leverage its political influence in almost every state and local government. The company has managed to circumvent those laws and regulations once designed to make corporations pay their fair share.

⸜ MAIN STREET VERSUS WAL-MART

For more than forty years Fannie and Leo Berkenbile were independent pharmacists in Pawhuska, Oklahoma. But when Wal-Mart opened a big store on the edge of town in 1983, the

Berkenbiles found longtime customers turning nasty. "People come in and say we're robbing them," Fannie Berkenbile told a *Wall Street Journal* reporter in 1987. The prices at the Berkenbiles' pharmacy were indeed higher than those at Wal-Mart. All the personal attention and friendly banter with the old familiar clientele could not make up the difference. So the Berkenbiles' pharmacy went out of business within a couple of years, along with a whole block of downtown stores, including the local five-and-dime, a J.C. Penney, and the Western Auto store. Like so many other small towns, Pawhuska, population 4,200, stagnated. "Wal-Mart didn't cause the trouble," reported Bonnie Peters of Peters Hardware, "but they haven't helped any." Indeed, the editor of the local *Daily Journal-Capital* called the store "a billion dollar parasite" and a "national retail ogre" for its miserly community contributions. Editor Dave Story denounced Sam Walton's company after a chamber of commerce banquet drew more than one hundred businesspeople intent on doing something to shore up the town's economy. No one from Wal-Mart showed up.[2]

Story might have been especially irked at the way Wal-Mart handled small-town newspapers. Local Wal-Mart stores were happy to send out a stream of press releases and announcements touting store openings, sports events, employee awards, and scholarships to local students, but the company starved the local press of paid advertising. "When Wal-Mart first came, there were four shops in town that sold men's dress shirts, and they all advertised," reported the publisher of the twice-weekly *Nashville* (Arkansas) *News*. "Now there's only one store that sells them—Wal-Mart—and it doesn't advertise." Where necessary, Wal-Mart used direct-mail circulars, but it normally relied on its "Every Day Low Price" policy as a kind of brand that customers knew about and valued. Indeed, Wal-Mart even forbade its suppliers to take out their own ads for sales and special promotions as an unnecessary expense that would raise the vendor's cost structure and dilute Wal-Mart's effort to project an unwavering EDLP. Although already far larger than rival Kmart in the early 1990s, the Bentonville company spent far less on print advertising.[3]

And then there were the horror stories, like the one about the town that Wal-Mart killed, not once, but twice. In 1980 Wal-Mart opened a discount store on the edge of Hearne, Texas, a once bustling railroad town that supported a set of whitewashed concrete stores along a two-block square. Bill's Dollar Store, K. Wollens, J. B. White, Western Auto—all were owned or managed by longtime residents, and they all quickly closed up shop. The town, which had already lost its movie theater and hospital and never had a McDonald's, was now left with a "business district" where the storefronts housed a pawnshop, a beauty parlor, and a couple of county welfare offices. All was not lost, however; the Wal-Mart had a payroll of about ninety, making it one of the three largest employers in town. For Hearne's 5,400 residents, the new Wal-Mart quickly became the town's de facto social center, and it paid tax and utility bills that came to almost 10 percent of the city budget.[4]

But then the ax fell once again. Late in 1990 Wal-Mart announced that it would close its Hearne discount store right after Christmas. It had never turned a profit, asserted a Wal-Mart spokesman, despite a wholesale replacement of the store's management just three years before. Hearne civic leaders were stunned. "Once Wal-Mart's gone, we won't have any place in Hearne to buy shoes or underwear," admitted the manager of the forlorn chamber of commerce. Steve Bishop, who had grown up in Hearne before heading off to divinity school, thought Hearne's travail was not just the product of Wal-Mart callousness but represented a kind of moral failure on the part of the town's citizenry. "Loyalty, friendship, history and civic pride could not keep us from spending our money at Wal-Mart," Bishop complained. "Wal-Mart promised us that our lives would be better if we saved money and shopped with them; our townspeople warned us that if they went out of business they would never be replaced. Well, the townspeople were right. . . . The soul of downtown was and is irreplaceable. We lost more than our businesses. We lost our friends."[5]

One reason for Hearne's shock was that the citizenry there had never heard of Wal-Mart closing a store; indeed only half a dozen had been shut down in the company's entire twenty-eight-year history. But all that would change. As Wal-Mart saturated its sales territory, the company presided over a fierce Darwinian struggle among store managers in every district and region. They even called it "cannibalization" when one store ate into the sales of another. Since the stores themselves were relatively cheap to construct—land and construction costs came in at about $10 million for a twenty-first-century, two-hundred-thousand-square-foot Supercenter whose annual sales could easily top $100 million—the company had no hesitancy in abandoning stores that were not pulling their weight. And a new store took less than a year to construct, from contract signing to the stocking of the shelves.[6] In the 1990s scores, even hundreds, of older, smaller discount stores were shuttered each year. Some found new tenants, though rarely a direct Wal-Mart competitor, but hundreds remained vacant, listed by Wal-Mart's own realty company as "dark" stores. Opponents call them "dead."[7]

Wal-Mart's impact on small-town America was more dramatic than that of Kmart or any of the other big-box stores for two reasons. First, Wal-Mart preferred to put its stores in communities as small as five thousand people, which meant that no one could ignore its outsized impact on the local community and the surrounding towns. By the 1980s, when the company was opening one hundred stores a year, it had site location down to a science. Interstates and cheap gas—the price dropped throughout that decade—made it possible for Wal-Mart to attract shoppers from forty or fifty miles in each direction, an area that even in the rural Midwest might well encompass fifty thousand potential shoppers. And second, Wal-Mart did not just come one store at a time; rather, the big boxes sprouted up like a patch of daisies, clustered around a regional distribution center. The Wal-Marts came to Iowa and Kansas in the early 1980s, to Colorado and Wisconsin later in the decade, to New England and the central valley of California in the early 1990s. Pennsylvania had no Wal-Mart stores in 1990; it had fifty-seven just five years later.[8]

Kenneth Stone, who achieved a certain minor celebrity as the first economist to study the impact of Wal-Mart discount stores on small-town America, found that business failures by local merchants accelerate after Wal-Mart has been in town for three to five years. In a study of Iowa retailing, he noted a short-term benefit to local businesses immediately after a Wal-Mart opened, but in the long term the local competition had to close its doors. Thus in the first decade after Wal-Mart arrived in small-town Iowa, the state lost 555 groceries, 298 hardware stores, 293 building supply stores, 158 women's apparel shops, 116 drugstores, and 153 shoe stores.[9] Stone found that 60 percent of the sales of a Wal-Mart store came from the revenue stream that had once gone to existing retail outlets.[10]

Most Americans, even those who live in sprawling metropolises, believe that small towns embody a social ideal, a site of political and cultural harmony. Anti-Wal-Mart activists naturally wrapped themselves in this mantle of civic virtue. Thus Al Norman, who drew attention in the early 1990s as the leader of a Greenfield, Massachusetts, movement that successfully forestalled a Wal-Mart in the Berkshires—and then went on to a second career as the founder of Sprawl-Busters—summed up the ethos of the merchant-citizen for CBS's *60 Minutes*: "If Main Street USA is dead as a dodo, then we are too. If Main Street goes, we're losing something very valuable. The ability to walk downtown and be able to greet people by their first name and know the guy who owns the camera shop and know his wife and know that she's on the school committee—these webs and these interconnections—we can't—we can't just afford to lose them to these large windowless boxes."[11]

Wal-Mart faced an increasingly hostile reception in small-town America. Thus guile and stealth often accompanied its expansion. Once Bentonville's real estate division had identified a new market, Wal-Mart contacted a local developer to assemble the land for a site, secure the building permits, and win approval from the city or county. Wal-Mart itself tried to remain hidden while this politically sensitive process was under way; otherwise, once local opposition did get started, the building process, even if successful, might well be delayed by as much as three years, during which a Supercenter could easily rake in upwards of $300 million. So Wal-Mart became increasingly sophisticated, wielding all the tools of public and political persuasion that have become so common in corporate affairs. The company hired dozens of regional operatives whose only task is to secure approval of its stores. It has learned to mimic the work of local opposition groups by setting up its own "astroturf" organizations, company-controlled civic groups. And Wal-Mart has been persistent, returning to the same town two and three times, often fighting over the same plot of land, or sometimes selecting another just a couple miles down the road.[12]

Al Norman's animus was therefore genuine and compelling, but it also embodied a certain romanticism. Despite his vigorous efforts and those of hundreds of like-minded citizens, Wal-Mart won far more site fights than it lost—two or three to one seems the best estimate[13]—because the company's opponents had been badly weakened and divided by the enormous changes that had transformed American society during the last half century. The traditional vision of harmonious small-town civic life had become an anachronism. It was not that

Americans were seduced by the lust for cheap consumer goods or that they had lost the capacity to use the tools of democratic life to plan their communities. Rather, the terrain had tilted sharply in favor of Wal-Mart and other big-box invaders. Thus when Wal-Mart came calling, every small town was instantly divided; a sizable slice of the population would either directly benefit from the presence of the big retailer or suffer in its absence.

SALES TAX SORROWS

Throughout this controversy, Wal-Mart had a powerful ally in the tax code. The nationwide revolt against taxes, especially against property taxes, which culminated in the passage of a 1978 California referendum limiting property tax increases, left public officials desperate for some new source of revenue. The sales tax seemed a godsend. One big-box store, a Home Depot or a Wal-Mart, whose sales might well top $150 million a year, could generate more revenue for a city than a thousand older homes.[14] When Paul Lewis of the Public Policy Institute of California surveyed the chief administrators in over 330 California cities, he found that retail development was the most favored type of land use for both vacant lots and redevelopment sites. Although most sales tax money went into state coffers, 1 percent was kicked back into the municipal budget. Thus California mayors and other top city officials rated new retail developments as far more valuable than new office buildings, light manufacturing facilities, or residential property, either single or multifamily. Lewis and other students of this phenomenon call these local rezoning efforts designed to increase the municipal revenue stream "the fiscalization of land use." Others use the term "cash box zoning." The "auto sales mall," now common throughout the country, was invented in California, not by the auto dealers but by local governments desperate to capture the gusher of sales taxes generated by eight or ten big dealerships in the same place.[15]

The lure of such new revenues could be compelling, and not only among green-eyeshade conservatives. Carl Morehouse was a pro-labor Democrat disdainful of Wal-Mart's "treatment of women ... associates treated as second class citizens ... their use of sweatshops and how they buy from China." But as mayor of cash-strapped Ventura, California, he worried that if a local coalition of labor and community groups succeeded in keeping Wal-Mart out of town, Ventura residents would continue to "sneak off" to the big-box stores across the river in Oxnard. "Right now we are hemorrhaging as a city, losing sales tax as it moves to Oxnard. ... We're not going to stop Wal-Mart. As an elected official, I have the obligation to protect the budget."[16] The immediate fruits of such additional sales tax revenue could be bountiful indeed. When both a Wal-Mart and a Sam's Club opened in a refurbished shopping center inside the city limits of working-class Maplewood, Missouri, $2 million in new money poured into the city budget, ending years of belt tightening and budget cuts for the old St. Louis suburb. The city hired two police officers and two firefighters, bought six new police cars, and raised employee pay by nearly five thousand dollars a year. "We've been tight for so long and reduced and reduced, all we did was kind of spread the [Wal-Mart] money out throughout the budget," reported City Manager Martin J. Corcoran. "We're starting to do [repair] streets again."[17]

The old merchant class might scream, but almost all city officials thought it essential to say yes when Wal-Mart came knocking. Indeed, the failure to land a big retailer left most towns with the worst of all fiscal worlds. They lost not only the new revenue generated by a big-box store but also a portion of the sales taxes generated by businesses in the old shopping district as customers flocked to the Wal-Mart or Target located in the next town over. "Sometimes you have to spend a nickel to make a quarter," explained Gary Klaphake, city administrator for Lafayette, Colorado, which in 2005 agreed to $2.3 million in subsidies for a Wal-Mart Supercenter that was expected to produce $18 million in sales tax revenue for the city over the next decade.[18]

"Cities are addicted to sales tax," remarked Larry Kosmont, a Los Angeles–based real estate consultant. "We have such a convoluted tax system that it is rational for a city official to say, 'Let's get this into our community, because if we don't, we lose out,' as opposed to asking what is the highest and best use for a site." When Wal-Mart first moved into inland California during the early 1990s, local officials scrambled to offer Wal-Mart the most attractive deal. In Riverside County alone, at least six subsidized stores opened between 1992 and 1994. Rialto provided a $2.6 million land write-down through a sales tax rebate to the developer, and Duarte offered $1.8 million for land in a similar arrangement. Corona, Redlands, and Riverside generated subsidies by signing long-term leases for Wal-Mart parking lots, making payments through a sales tax rebate to Wal-Mart or the developer.[19]

Wal-Mart moved aggressively to take advantage of this favorable terrain as cities, counties, and states competed in ever more lucrative and inventive ways to secure a big-box outlet or a distribution center for their community. Whether it was the state or the municipality, Wal-Mart was offered a tempting array of inducements, including free or reduced-price land, new roads and sewer hookups, property tax breaks, and the increasingly popular "tax increment financing," in which the tax increase expected from a commercial development is used to fund "TIF" bonds that pay for the land and improvements needed by the big-box retailer. Although originally intended to help revitalize blighted areas, many states now have rules that are so loose that TIFs end up being used for exurban projects near a healthy supply of well-heeled shoppers.

Researchers for Good Jobs First, an antisprawl research organization in Washington, D.C., compiled a list of all the various development incentives cities and states gave Wal-Mart during the decade ending in 2004 and found that the chain had received at least $1 billion. This was almost certainly an undercount because no level of government keeps tabs on the baroque and ever-changing set of financial incentives that the big-box stores can command. Good Jobs First found 244 instances in which Wal-Mart won tax concessions for its stores and distribution centers, but a Wal-Mart official said that "it is common" for the company to request subsidies for about one-third of its stores, suggesting that as many as sixteen hundred U.S. outlets have been taxpayer subsidized. According to the same survey by Good Jobs First, eighty-four of Wal-Mart's ninety-one big distribution centers were subsidized to some extent by county or state taxpayers. Although the subsidies granted individual stores were on the order of $1 million or $2 million each—not huge when compared to the hundreds of millions that some states offer in competition for a new auto plant or microchip facility—Wal-Mart enjoys scores of these bequests each year. As in retail sales, Wal-Mart makes its money through volume.[20]

SELF-INTERESTED PHILANTHROPY

Wal-Mart's financial whipsaw tactics were often manipulative and abrasive, but the company also offered its sometimes reluctant hosts a palliative that won a genuine measure of appreciation among customers and citizenry. "We have big hearts and strong hands," ran a 1990 story in *Wal-Mart World* praising the company's charitable giving program. "Wherever you go, we're always there: raising money for local children's hospitals; banding together to send relief aid to areas stricken by natural disasters; setting a leadership example in local town and civic organizations."[21]

Such corporate giving was nothing new for American business. Part genuine charity, part sophisticated public relations, foundations have been a part of the American landscape for more than a century, ever since the Gilded Age barons—Carnegie, Rockefeller, and Mellon—established tax-exempt foundations to advertise their Christian beneficence, legitimize their entrepreneurial success, and define the very meaning of social reform. In the 1970s and 1980s, however, a new sort of corporate philanthropy became a notable feature of American business: annual giving by foundations that derive almost all their income exclusively from the corporation that sponsors them. Among the biggest are those of the U.S. car companies, AT&T, General Electric, the Bank of America, and Exxon Mobil. They are an explicit part of the public relations apparatus of American business: oil companies give to environmental causes; Detroit automakers provide grants for the education of inner-city youth; the big pharmaceutical makers give to hospitals and medical research. "Somewhere between altruism and greed," writes the watchdog National Committee for Effective Philanthropy, "corporate philanthropy has become an integral part of a corporation's business plan."[22]

The Wal-Mart Foundation is by far the biggest and most active such corporate philanthropy in America.[23] The foundation began its work in the early 1980s, when controversy over the Wal-Mart invasion first became apparent in small-town America. Aside from the sometimes deleterious impact of the store on local businesses, Wal-Mart faced two additional challenges. First, Wal-Mart managers, who were frequently moved from one store to another, developed few connections with the local civic elite, even though the stores they managed were often among the largest employers in town. There was a danger that Wal-Mart would remain a permanently alien presence, with all the unpredictable consequences this might entail. And second, if Wal-Mart was to begin a philanthropic program, the company wanted to get its money's worth. Sam Walton himself was hostile to what he called the "standard guidelines" for corporate giving. As an efficient business that lowered the cost of living, Wal-Mart was a "powerful force" for good, argued the founder. "We feel very strongly," he wrote in his autobiography, "that Wal-Mart really is not, and should not be, in the charity business." Philanthropic money, he reasoned, would only come out of the pockets of "either shareholders or our customers."[24]

Wal-Mart therefore gave away an exceedingly small proportion of its net earnings before taxes, about one-half of one percent. In the late 1980s that was less than a third the level of then archrival Kmart, and between one-fifth and one-eighth the proportion donated by Sears and Dayton Hudson (Target). Based on its earnings, the average large corporation gave away more than twice as much per dollar as did Wal-Mart.[25] Today the Wal-Mart Foundation still has little endowment but receives all of its money—almost $300 million per year—directly from Wal-Mart Stores, Inc. Disbursed annually, a portion of the money goes to the usual kinds of charities: the Red Cross, the Salvation Army, and some Wal-Mart initiatives, most famously the Children's Miracle Network, a national organization that aids children's hospitals across the United States. In the 1990s Wal-Mart sponsored the "American Hometown Leadership Awards," which gave small economic development grants to 250 elected officials in towns where Wal-Mart had a store.

But more than 90 percent of all Wal-Mart funds are distributed through its four-thousand-plus stores. Although all grants require formal approval from the home office in Bentonville, the local store manager has the de facto authority to disburse about twenty-five thousand dollars each year, always within the local trade area of each store and almost always to local institutions that are popular among both store employees and customers. "We rely on our associates to know which organizations are the most important to their hometowns," asserts the foundation, "and we empower them to determine how Wal-Mart Foundation dollars will be spent." Thousands of small grants are made to local churches and sectarian organizations, a marked contrast to the policy of the more established corporate foundations, such as those sponsored by AT&T, General Motors, IBM, and Citigroup, which ban such giving. "We visually show the community our involvement and commitment," asserted a 1990 puff piece in *Wal-Mart World*. "This, in turn, creates benefits for our stores like increased customer spending (market share) and associate team spirit."[26] A decade later Wal-Mart Foundation executive Betsy Reithemeyer offered a more pointed message. "Not everybody loves us. So, how do we turn that around?" she asked more than one thousand store managers at a 2004 meeting in Dallas. "Meet with your community leaders. Meet with elected officials. . . . Utilize those [foundation] budgets. Develop a plan. . . . All of us have a commitment that we need to take once more to put a face on Wal-Mart."[27]

The sheer number of grants given away is unparalleled. The Target Foundation, which still distributes a larger proportion of the parent company's profits each year, offers fewer than two hundred annual grants, mainly in the $10,000 to $50,000 range and limited to civic and cultural institutions in the Minneapolis metropolitan area.[28] In contrast, the Wal-Mart program is hyperlocalized, with more than 150,000 tiny grants in recent years, usually no more than $1,000 each. Local churches, PTAs, schools, Boy Scouts, youth groups, museums, clinics, libraries, fire departments, civic clubs, and local sports teams reap the benefit. Thus on page 142 of the Wal-Mart Foundation's 2005 IRS filing, a massive document of more than three thousand pages, we find, among other disbursements, a $250 grant to Kecoughtan High School, $1,000 to Youth for Christ, $150 to City of Royalton Police Department, $500 to the Railroad Flat Elementary School, and two gifts totaling $1,500 to Young Life, a Christian mission for adolescents.[29] In some instances even these small disbursements are matching grants, linked to in-store bake sales and contests that involve hours of volunteer effort by Wal-Mart associates and customers.[30] "It's a hell of a plan, and it works," admitted a union leader in Arkansas, bemoaning the hegemonic influence of the company throughout the region.[31]

With so many Wal-Marts located in the Southeast and Midwest, the company has been particularly good at responding to the hurricanes, tornadoes, and floods that plague the region. The company's just-in-time distribution network makes it a fast responder in a situation where emergency aid and good business practice are necessarily intermixed. For nearly two decades the Bentonville home office has run the Emergency Operations Center, which tracks severe weather and alerts the Wal-Mart supply chain to the kind of goods that would be needed once the storm has passed: tools, building materials, bottled water, chain saws, and snack foods. Trucks and extra personnel have often been on the road even before the rain or winds reached their greatest intensity.[32] The company has often donated several hundred thousand dollars in cash and relief supplies and then conscripted its vendors to donate even more. Thus when Hurricane Hugo ravished the Carolinas in 1989 or when floods swamped Alabama two years later, Wal-Mart got the credit for the food, clothing, and tools ponied up by its vendors, because all the stuff arrived in a fleet of trucks emblazoned with the company logo.[33]

Hurricane Katrina proved Wal-Mart's finest hour, and one for which it earned a huge boost to a reputation recently tattered by chronic site fights, dozens of high-profile lawsuits over stolen lunch breaks and forced overtime, and a drumbeat of attacks on its wage levels and health-care benefits. Wal-Mart's tracking center knew a storm was brewing off the Florida coast as early as August 23, 2005, six days before Katrina made its disastrous landfall just east of New Orleans. At its height, more than 126 Wal-Mart stores were closed or damaged by a storm that destroyed much of the infrastructure in a huge swath of the Gulf Coast. Even as New Orleans filled with water on August 31, H. Lee Scott called an emergency meeting of his top lieutenants. He did not want a "measured response" to the hurricane, the usual donation of a few million dollars and three days' pay for every associate temporarily deprived of employment.[34]

Wal-Mart pledged $20 million in cash donations and the promise of a job for every one of its displaced workers. But even more important, the company put into overdrive its remarkable logistics system. Wal-Mart distribution centers at Opelousas and Robert, Louisiana, were both less than 150 miles from New Orleans, while the twenty-year-old DC in Brookhaven, Mississippi, was just a couple hours north of the ravaged Gulf Coast. During the next two weeks, Wal-Mart dispatched 2,500 truckloads of merchandise—for both donation and sale—food for one hundred thousand meals, and teams of workers to get its stores up and running again. Dozens of stores with water damage or without electricity turned their parking lots into de facto relief centers from which emergency workers distributed tons of perishable food and cases of soft drinks and water. In Waveland, Mississippi, comanager Jessica Lewis got her stepbrother to plow a bulldozer through her water-logged store to clear a path so that salvageable shoes, clothing, food, and drugs could be brought out into the parking lot and given away to area residents who had lost almost everything.[35]

To an admiring nation, Wal-Mart's logistics system demonstrated resilience and efficiency. The company was often in full-bore rescue mode even before local police and firemen had recovered from the storm's onslaught, and it was a tangible presence in the lives of tens of thousands days before either the National Guard or the Federal Emergency Management Agency made their tardy way to the disaster area. During a tearful September 4 interview on *Meet the Press*, Aaron Broussard, the president of Jefferson Parish, told host Tim Russert that if "the American government would have responded like Wal-Mart has responded, we wouldn't be in this crisis."[36] Likewise, Philip Capitano, the mayor of Kenner, Louisiana, told reporters, "Wal-Mart showed up with food and water so our people could survive. . . . The Red Cross and FEMA need to take a master class in logistics and mobilization from Wal-Mart." These themes were soon echoed in the national press. The *Wall Street Journal* declared, "The Federal Emergency Management Agency could learn some things from Wal-Mart Stores, Inc.," and the *Washington Post* editorialized that Wal-Mart was being held up as "a model for logistical efficiency and nimble disaster planning."[37] David Vitter, the Republican senator from Louisiana, promised to introduce a bill abolishing FEMA and contracting its job out to the private sector. John Tierney, a conservative columnist for the *New York Times*, nominated H. Lee Scott as the man the government should put in charge of rebuilding the Gulf Coast. His new organization: WEMA, the Wal-Mart Emergency Management Agency.[38]

This was the kind of glowing publicity money could not buy. In a piece headlined WAL-MART'S RELIEF EFFORTS PROVE PRICELESS, *PR Week* said that "a decade of media summits and press kits couldn't earn this kind of goodwill from the media." *Advertising Age* added, "Millions in corporate-image advertising in the past year failed to do much to help Wal-Mart's reputation. . . . But now, in the wake of Hurricane Katrina, Wal-Mart is getting the kind of advertising no marketer can buy." Even the harshest critics of the company recognized that Wal-Mart had scored a coup. Philip Mattera, who published detailed studies of the company's billion-dollar manipulation of state and local taxes, concluded, "The relatively ordinary accomplishments of the company looked extraordinary only because of the spectacular failures of government officials. Just because political hacks such as Michael Brown could not get the job done does not mean that big business is the solution to all our problems."[39]

The Walton family's own foundation pursues this same strategy: philanthropy that enhances the ideology and political appeal of a pro-business, free market solution to the nation's problems. As of 2008, the Walton Family Foundation has only about $1 billion in assets, but that will soon balloon to something close to $20 billion when the estate of Helen Walton, who died in 2007, is finally settled.[40] It's hard to say whether the other Walton offspring—Alice, Rob, Jim, and the widow of John, who died in a 2005 flying accident—will ever contribute a like amount to their family's foundation, because the clan has been a powerful, if behind-the-scenes, player in the Bush administration's effort to kill the estate tax, thereby allowing them to continue in de facto control of Wal-Mart Stores, Inc.[41] Still, $20 billion is a lot of money, and if recent history serves as any guide, it is likely to make the Walton Family Foundation by far the most powerful of the right-wing philanthropies that have proliferated during the last couple of decades.

Like other foundations identified with a particular area, the Walton Family Foundation gives a great deal of money to regional institutions such as the University of Arkansas, the Clinton Presidential Library, evangelical colleges on or near the Ozark plateau, and pet projects such as Alice Walton's effort to build a first-class art museum in Bentonville. But the family foundation's most consistent interest has been in the "reform" of K-12 schools. In his autobiography, Sam Walton said, "I'd like to see an all-out revolution in education."[42] Thus, under the leadership of John Walton and those who have followed him, the WFF has become the single largest source of funding for the "school choice" movement and a powerful advocate of charter schools and voucher initiatives.[43] To this end, John Walton personally bankrolled voucher referenda in California, Michigan, and Minnesota and proved highly influential in shaping the WFF approach, which favors tough, back-to-basics instruction such as that practiced by the private KIPP (Knowledge Is Power Program) academies. The foundation's goal is "to maximize private school choice options" for those opting out of the public system. "What Andrew Carnegie was to libraries, John Walton was to school choice," said Bill Oberndorf, a Bay Area banker who worked with Walton to fund the American Education Reform Foundation in 1991.[44]

Money therefore goes to scores of individual charter schools, to market-oriented educational research institutes and advocacy groups, and to right-wing think tanks like Cato, Heritage, and Manhattan Institute, some of which reciprocate by publishing reports and opinion pieces highly favorable to Wal-Mart.[45] The Children's Scholarship Fund, which John Walton cofounded in 1998 with Ted Forstmann, the Wall Street buyout artist, is almost certainly the foundation's single largest disbursement. As of 2005, more than sixty-seven thousand children had received scholarships to attend private schools from the CSF.[46] The Walton Family has donated more than $700 million to various educational initiatives since 1998.[47]

In reality, Walton funding allows some charter schools to spend more per pupil than competing public schools, observes Liza Featherstone, an investigative journalist who writes frequently about Wal-Mart. "The ironic result is that while these projects are supposed to demonstrate to the public the wonders of a marketized approach to education," the WFF's money actually gives its grantees an unfair advantage.[48] Because so much Walton and Wal-Mart philanthropy is crudely self-interested, critics are tempted to find a pecuniary motive for the Walton family's interest in education. But their support for competition and privatization is an entirely ideological project, based on a desire to enhance the social and cultural value of a free market in which government is weak while public goods like hurricane relief, education, and health care are the fodder for entrepreneurial transformation. Since the public schools are by far the most pervasive of public institutions, and highly unionized to boot, this "$700-plus-billion-a-year industry"—John Walton's phrase—has been a good place to start.[49]

DEDUCTIBLE HEALTH INSURANCE

The provision of health care has become the nation's most contentious policy issue. Wal-Mart's failure to provide health insurance for a majority of its 1.4 million domestic retail workers has therefore made the company a lightning rod for critics, subjecting Wal-Mart to even more debate and analysis than the company's store location policies, its hostility to trade unionism, or even its low pay. That just 50 percent of all Wal-Mart associates sign up for one of the company's medical insurance plans is shameful. But of equal cause for concern is the real cost of that medical insurance deficit, so often borne by the larger public whose taxes pay for one of the several state and federal insurance plans for which low-wage Wal-Mart workers are eligible.

Indeed, in some twenty-four states the offspring of those employed at Wal-Mart compose the largest group participating in the federal-state Children's Health Insurance Program, designed for families whose incomes are so low that they qualify for subsidized medical insurance. In Georgia 10,261 Wal-Mart children enrolled in "PeachCare," the state's health insurance program for poor children. This was a huge number, representing one in four children of all Wal-Mart associates. The runner-up was the Publix Super Market chain, whose employees enrolled 734 kids in the program, or just one child for every twenty-two employees in the state. H. Lee Scott added to the cor-

porate embarrassment when he tried to explain away these find-
ings. "There are government assistance programs out there that
are so lucrative," he told reporters in April 2005, "it's hard to be
competitive, and it's expensive to be competitive."[50]

In California researchers at UC Berkeley found that Wal-
Mart wages—about 31 percent below those in large retail establishments as a whole—made it necessary for tens of thousands
of company employees to rely on public "safety net" programs,
such as food stamps, Medicare, CHIPs, and subsidized housing,
to make ends meet. Some store managers and personnel clerks
even pointed struggling associates to the appropriate government agency where they could apply for Earned Income Tax
Credits, food stamps, and the like. The Berkeley study estimated that reliance by Wal-Mart workers on public assistance
programs in California cost state taxpayers about $86 million
annually, in part because the families of Wal-Mart employees
utilized an estimated 40 percent more in taxpayer-funded
health care than the average for families of breadwinners who
worked at most other large retail firms.[51]

But beyond even this corporate embarrassment, Wal-Mart's
health insurance policies are politically and socially controversial because they stand in the vanguard of a right-wing effort to
shift moral and economic responsibility for health-care insurance from the employer and the state to the individual and
family. Stung by a barrage of outside criticism, Wal-Mart has
struggled to bring its own employer-provided health care to
fully half of its workforce. But the cost of doing so has entailed
a transformation in the very meaning of what constitutes medical provision and health insurance, for both its own associates
and all Americans.

Employer-provided health insurance became the American
norm after World War II, when the big, stable corporations of
that era saw this "fringe benefit" as a good way to build employee
loyalty and thwart more far-reaching demands for a high-tax,

highly regulated European-style system of government-provided health care. Although most unionists had been advocates of national health insurance, they acquiesced in this firm-centered system and in each negotiating round sought to improve and extend company health insurance. The upshot was that workplace coverage soared. By 1980 essentially "free" health care was available to 74 percent of employees at companies with one hundred or more workers. And 54 percent of the workers at these companies had their family coverage fully financed as well.[52] The unionized grocery industry followed along, with the UFCW winning health-care benefits of the sort common in the older industrial companies and among the employees of most state and local governments.

Wal-Mart never adopted this model. By the time the company had expanded into metropolitan America in the 1980s, the older system of company-provided health insurance was already in crisis. Health-care inflation was often double that of the rest of the economy, and in the United States many firms competing with foreign rivals were at a disadvantage because employee health insurance costs in Canada, Germany, Taiwan, and Japan were subsumed within the tax and benefit structure that sustained the larger welfare state in those nations. By 1993 only 37 percent of big companies' employees in the United States had free coverage, and only 21 percent of them had fully-paid coverage for their dependents.

Wal-Mart kept its medical insurance costs low by sharply limiting the proportion of workers eligible to participate in the company health insurance plan and then by imposing a variety of other costs, including high deductibles, co-pays, and coverage restrictions that shifted a large proportion of routine medical costs onto those employees who signed up with Wal-Mart's self-insured medical plan. In the early 1990s the National Retail Federation, in which Wal-Mart was a major player, lobbied strenuously against the Clinton health-care plan, which would have mandated and regulated employer health insurance offerings. Thereafter, the company, along with the rest of the nation, enjoyed a brief period of relatively stable health-care expenses, but when medical inflation took off at the end of the 1990s Wal-Mart responded by making it even more difficult for associates to sign up for the company plan. In 2002 Wal-Mart raised its definition of "full-time" work from twenty-nine to thirty-four hours, thereby increasing the number of part-time workers to nearly four hundred thousand, or about a third of its total workforce. Since part-time workers had to wait two years before they could purchase the company health insurance plan, and since the turnover rate among part-timers was well above 50 percent per year, virtually all of them were barred from health-care coverage. At the same time Wal-Mart doubled to six months the health insurance waiting period for full-time workers, which was about twice as long as in the rest of the retail industry and far longer than that required by other large U.S. firms, institutions, and state agencies. (But note: at Wal-Mart full-time management employees become eligible to buy into the corporate health insurance plan from their date of hire.)[53]

Although eligibility requirements excluded many workers from participation in the Wal-Mart health-care plan, the real obstacle to their enrollment was the high deductibles they were forced to pay before the actual insurance kicked in, at which time they were still burdened with a 20 percent copay for most medical expenditures. When it comes to the kind of medical issues that families are sure to face on an annual basis—well-baby care, vaccinations, immunizations, adult checkups, ear infections, dental and eye care, muscle strains, and the like—Wal-Mart's medical plan is very expensive. In a confidential 2005 "benefits strategy" internal memo leaked to the *New York Times*, Executive Vice President Susan Chambers of Wal-Mart's People Division admitted, "Our coverage is expensive for low-income families. . . . On average Associates spend 8 percent of their income on healthcare (premiums plus deductibles plus out-of-pocket expenses) for themselves and their families, nearly twice the national average." For a family with kids, the cost shoots up even higher: most would have to pay health-care costs equal to 30 percent of their income before receiving most benefits.[54]

For example, in 2007 Wal-Mart's standard plan offered family coverage with a health insurance premium of between $2,320 and $4,093 per year. The cheaper plan seems almost affordable, but no benefits kick in until Mom or Dad pays a $3,000 deductible. For the more expensive plan the deductible is only $1,050. But regardless of its size, once that expense has been met, the out-of-pocket expenses don't stop, because the Wal-Mart plan only pays 80 percent of all covered medical costs. So a Wal-Mart family with just a few ordinary medical problems could easily find themselves paying $5,000 above and beyond their insurance premium.[55]

When Human Rights Watch talked to Wal-Mart workers about why they had not enrolled in the company plan, the answers were predictable. Joshua Streckeisen, who had once worked at a Pennsylvania store, said, "I couldn't afford it with the money I was making. I couldn't have paid the bills." Similarly, Alicia Sylvia, a full-time worker at the Loveland, Colorado, Wal-Mart, told HRW, "I don't have their health insurance because I can't afford it.... My kids are on CHP+Colorado.... It's like Medicaid, but for children only." And from Las Vegas, Valerie Gonzalez likewise explained, "I was not on their health insurance plan. It was too expensive.... We can't with five kids. We just didn't have insurance. The kids didn't have insurance."[56]

Wal-Mart argues that employees and the public should measure its health plan not in terms of comprehensiveness, but rather as a form of life insurance designed to cover essentially catastrophic health emergencies. For really serious illnesses, like cancer or a heart attack, the plan has no expense limit, a real plus compared to the offerings of many other employers. Wal-Mart institutional advertisements often feature employees who have run up huge expenses for life-threatening diseases, all paid for by their Wal-Mart health-care plan. For example, in 2001 John and Tina Millwood's son, Simuel, was born with biliary artesi, a liver disease that required a transplant. Mr. Millwood, whose annual salary as a store assistant manager was then $32,500, ended up paying about $5,000 a year on health care since his son's birth. But the child required $1.5 million in hospital and other medical services during the first two years of his life. At one point Wal-Mart even arranged for a private jet to fly the family from their East Texas home to the Mayo Clinic in Minnesota.[57]

The medical crisis faced and overcome by the Millwoods was just the kind of emergency to which the *Wal-Mart Benefits Handbook* pointed when it declared that the company health plan focuses on "protecting employees and their families from catastrophic loss," rather than on routine or preventive coverage. During a 2005 health insurance presentation at his store, reported Jared West, a Greeley, Colorado, associate, the Wal-Mart benefits manager compared "health insurance and car insurance. . . . Car insurance is there to take care of catastrophic situations. It doesn't pay for oil changes, new tires, or wiper blades because that would cost way too much." In the eyes of Wal-Mart management, "Your health insurance is the same way."[58] Indeed, Wal-Mart argues that if employees must pay a substantial amount of their health-care expenses out of pocket, they will be more careful in their health-care spending (fewer visits to the emergency room), and in return the company can provide health plans with smaller premiums. "The greatest incentive for health and wellness is high deductibles," Wal-Mart vice president Tom Emerick told a friendly Dallas business audience in the spring of 2007. "We'll tell anybody in America how we did it and how it works."[59]

Conservatives applaud this Wal-Mart strategy for keeping health-care costs down. "Wal-Mart is now pushing to limit soaring health-care costs," wrote Steven Malanga in the *City Journal*, organ of the right-wing Manhattan Institute, "by embracing a fundamental redefinition of health insurance as protection from catastrophic illnesses that can financially ruin employees, rather than a benefit meant to pay for every health-care bill. . . . As a result of its policies, Wal-Mart spends about 37 percent less per covered employee on health insurance than do similar companies."[60] Indeed, the high-deductible, limited-coverage, low-premium program does save money for those companies that adopt it. "They're moving the risk from their balance sheet to the employees," concluded Richard T. Evans, a health-care analyst with Sanford C. Bernstein & Co. "The risk is being transferred without the consumer really realizing it."[61]

To make this more palatable, ideologically minded conservatives have long advocated widespread adoption of the tax-deductible Health Savings Account, into which employers and workers would deposit money sufficient to cover their high deductible, as well as all the other routine expenses not covered by catastrophic insurance. The support for such individually controlled accounts accelerated during the 1980s and 1990s. Newt Gingrich, then Speaker of the House, proved a particularly vigorous advocate. Soon right-wing think tanks like Cato, Heritage, and the American Enterprise Institute championed Health Savings Accounts as an alternative to Clinton-style national health insurance schemes. Congress enacted an HSA law in 1996, limited to small business and the self-insured, but it was not until 2003 that President George W. Bush and his party attached a little-debated HSA amendment to the big Medicare prescription-drug bill of that year, thus making a renamed "Health Security Account" available to employees of even the largest corporations.[62] To qualify, the HSA must be paired to an insurance scheme with a deductible of at least one thousand dollars. "Health savings accounts all aim at empowering people to make decisions for themselves, owning their own health-care plan," the president proclaimed. He argued that consumer-driven decision making is more likely to control costs.[63]

Wal-Mart jumped to align its health-care offerings with the Bush HSA initiative. In her infamous strategy memo of 2005, Wal-Mart's Susan Chambers laid out a troubling scenario for the retailer's board. During the previous three years benefit costs were growing faster than sales. Health insurance expenses were the chief culprit, rising by 19 percent due to the disproportionate growth in the number of older, less healthy associates who utilized the company's health insurance program. The solution: "bold steps" to cut the growth of future costs and improve the corporate "reputation." Among the key proposals put forth by Chambers: "Move all Associates to 'progressively-designed' consumer-driven health plans to help control cost trends while allowing Associates to build up savings in Health Savings Accounts." Although Chambers recognized that such plans were probably less popular with workers than traditional health insurance, they were more "attractive to the healthy, productive Associate segment, because this segment now 'gets something' for enrolling in health insurance and staying healthy—they can save money in the HSA." Critics might well see such a Wal-Mart program as a "Republican answer" to the crisis, averred Chambers, but the savings to the company were considerable, between $400 million to $700 million per year after about five years.[64]

So Wal-Mart was among the first, and still among the relatively few, large companies to embrace the Bush health-care solution: high insurance deductibles combined with a Health Security Account to which the employer contributes a few hundred dollars per year that the worker can then use for two or three "free" annual doctor visits. To implement the new program, H. Lee Scott replaced Chambers, whose benefits memo had proved an embarrassment to the company, with Linda M. Dillman, a fifty-one-year-old dynamo who had heretofore supervised Wal-Mart's world-famous information technology division. Dillman's 2006 switch from tech to health insurance administration might well symbolize the company's belated recognition that its future now relied far more on politics and public policy than on any innovations coming out of its once-pioneering data warehouse.[65]

Dillman's job was to mollify Wal-Mart's critics. She deployed Wal-Mart's vaunted technological prowess to manage health-care record keeping, experimented with in-store health clinics staffed by licensed practical nurses, spoke at dozens of health policy conferences, and made a strenuous public effort to boost the proportion of all Wal-Mart employees enrolled in the company health plan. In Wal-Mart's 2008 iteration of its insurance offering, just over 50 percent of Wal-Mart's 1.4 million domestic staff had signed up, about seventy thousand more than the year before. The company achieved this increase by relaxing some of its eligibility requirements (part-time workers could now enroll themselves and their children after but one year of service), by putting forth a cafeteria-like menu of benefits and deductions, and by offering extraordinarily low premiums, as little as five dollars a month in some instances, targeted at the sort of young, single employees unlikely to think that they would ever actually make use of a high-deductible health insurance plan.[66]

But there was a sinister side to this expansion of health insurance coverage. It normalized an inequitable system that underinsured the vast majority of all wage earners and penalized outright that 20 percent of the population with chronic maladies who consumed 80 percent of the health-care dollar. The problem of overweight employees was particularly expensive and troublesome for the company. These middle-aged people, mostly women, are among the company's most loyal workers but also among those who make the most use of traditional health insurance offerings. Indeed, the prevalence of diabetes in the Wal-Mart workforce grew by 10 percent in the early years of the twenty-first century, three times faster than in the national population.[67]

So Wal-Mart has tried to get rid of these long-service employees, increasing the proportion of part-time workers and announcing— on the same August day in 2006 that it increased starting pay at a third of its stores—that wage caps would henceforth be placed on the hourly earnings of long-term workers who had not quickly moved up the managerial ladder.[68] "The cost of an associate with 7 years of tenure is almost 55% more than the cost of an associate with 1 year of tenure," reported the shameful Susan Chambers memo, "yet there is no difference in his or her productivity." Thus at several stores in Florida, Wal-Mart employees told the *New York Times*, managers barred older workers with back or leg problems from sitting on stools after using them for years while working as cashiers, store greeters, or fitting-room attendants.[69] Another solution, which Chambers had suggested, involved a redesign of all jobs to include some physical activity, such as cart gathering in the parking lot. While this might trim a few pounds off the weight of some cashiers, it was more likely to induce them to quit, voluntarily or otherwise.[70]

THE WORKERS' COMP SCAM

While Wal-Mart devised an array of stratagems by which to contain its health insurance costs, the company was obliged by law to offer yet another health-care "benefit," namely workers' compensation. The company found this quite burdensome, but it could not entirely avoid its legal responsibilities. Contemporary liberals bemoan the failure of the United States to establish a universal program of mandatory health insurance, but such a system has actually existed for nearly a century. Under the workers' compensation law adopted by most states during the Progressive era of the early twentieth century, employers were required to cover the medical bills of people hurt on the job. If injured workers needed time off, they were entitled to a portion of their lost wages. Those who suffered some kind of permanent damage could receive payments in perpetuity, depending on their loss of earning power. It was and is a no-fault system: the employee got paid regardless of who or what caused the accident. The employer, in turn, was happy to pay the taxes needed to fund the system because managers could now avoid defending themselves against unpredictable and costly lawsuits filed by hundreds of increasingly skillful lawyers for the thousands of workingmen maimed at work each year.

The system had its ghoulish side. Designed to compensate men in the steel mills, lumberyards, and construction sites of an earlier time, workers' compensation put a price on every limb and life, toted up by the injury tables of that industrial era: a lost finger, $50; severed hand, $1,000; loss of sight in one eye, $500; total blindness, $5,000.

Few workers lose an eye or a leg working for Wal-Mart, but they are subject to the kind of soft tissue injuries and maladies that have become commonplace in the retail trade: carpal tunnel syndrome, muscle strains, hernias, back injuries, and the kind of problems that are exacerbated by standing on your feet all day. Wal-Mart has an aggressive set of health and safety rules, drilled into its associates at meetings, through videos, and by bonus payments calibrated to each store's accident-free record. But a distribution center or a big-box store still taxes the body. "Everything's moved by hand," remembered Chuck Gibbons, an assistant manager injured while working at a Washington State Wal-Mart store. "You're up and down all night long. First, you unload the trucks, then you unload the pallets. You're carrying 30-pound boxes of hair spray or whatever and putting them in various positions. You take down product from the risers and fill holes on the display shelves. I hadn't done that kind of physical labor in a long time."[71]

So, like every other discounter, Wal-Mart has had its growing share of workers' compensation claims, which cost the company as much as 3 percent of total payroll, almost as much as medical insurance. Unlike so much health insurance coverage today, workers' compensation is designed to protect employees from the first day on the job. It requires no employee-paid premiums, no copayments or deductibles, and it puts no limit on the cost of treatment. By law that expense falls entirely on the company, which is why Sam Walton and his successors were determined to minimize it, even if that required a subversion of the whole workers' comp idea. Like many large companies, Wal-Mart has "self-insured," promising to pay workers' comp claims out of its own reserves rather than through an insurance company or a state workers' compensation fund. This saved overhead expenses, but it also gave the company a clear incentive to delay, reject, and litigate the claims that Wal-Mart's ever-growing workforce forwarded on to the home office each year.

The company got into trouble as early as 1982, just after the Wal-Mart payroll passed the forty-thousand mark. It hired an insurance company called Transit Casualty to handle, for a remarkably low flat fee, all of Wal-Mart's workers' compensation claims. The contract was "a knowingly illegal venture," declared a federal appellate court some years later, because both parties lowballed by more than 50 percent the number of workers who were covered, made no provision for an increase in the Wal-Mart payroll, and then tried to off-load the excess costs onto

Arkansas and other states. By 1985 Transit Casualty was bankrupt and Wal-Mart found itself responsible for millions of dollars in unfunded claims.[72]

After that, the home office kept a tighter lid on workers' compensation costs by in-sourcing the entire operation. Wal-Mart set up Claims Management Incorporated, a wholly-owned subsidiary, which employed scores of overworked and underpaid analysts to process and pay all claims from the company's own funds. Wal-Mart and CMI had two ways of keeping workers' compensation expenses down. First, the company discouraged workers from reporting an accident or filing a claim in the first place, encouraging them to get any required medical treatment through the company's health insurance plan, which cost Wal-Mart at least 30 percent less if a worker was signed up, and nothing at all for the hundreds of thousands who got their health insurance through a spouse, parent, or the government. But if an associate actually did make a formal workers' compensation claim, he or she was in for a rough, litigious ride because Wal-Mart's CMI delayed, denied, and shortchanged payment in an extraordinarily high proportion of all claims.[73]

Because their bonus is linked to the level of workers' compensation claims filed at each store, Wal-Mart managers have a big incentive to report that their store is "accident free." Safety is therefore taken seriously, but so too is the artificial maintenance of a good accident-free record, which can be ensured simply by keeping workers who do suffer injuries off the workers' comp rolls. All associates are reminded that a long string of accident-free weeks is essential to the store's bonus pool, from which every employee receives a small cut at the end of each year. Workers who file comp claims are therefore often seen as pariahs by their colleagues. Even more important, the word soon spreads that the fastest way to get on the wrong side of a manager is to actually file a formal claim. "After you get injured they harass you to quit voluntarily," reported Billie Sue, a distribution center associate who hurt her back shifting hundreds of cartons each hour. "They give you humiliating jobs to do in full view of all the other workers." In the discount stores, injured workers are made to work as "greeters," they are assigned to clean up broken bottles and busted cartons, and their hours of work are often shifted and reduced.[74] In many states, Wal-Mart requires a "voluntary resignation" from the injured employee in order to settle an employee's claim. Wal-Mart sees these injured workers as "troublemakers," reported Edward White, an Oklahoma attorney who has spearheaded a class-action suit against the company on behalf of scores of former associates victimized by the company. "[Wal-Mart] want[s] to get rid of them."[75]

But if workers do persist in filing a compensation claim, they face months and sometimes years of frustration and disappointment in getting it resolved. Although Wal-Mart has the world's most sophisticated and reliable system for tracking merchandise on its way from vendor to distribution center to store, none of this applies to the company's in-house CMI claims-processing department. Whether by design or accident, claimants, doctors, and attorneys report that the Wal-Mart subsidiary loses reports, misfiles information, delays paperwork, and fails to cut the necessary checks until threatened by an attorney retained by the injured worker. And CMI routinely challenges an extraordinarily high percentage of all claims. In Maine, which has one of the best state auditing systems, the Workers' Compensation Board reported that in 2004 Wal-Mart challenged the validity of more than 90 percent of all the compensation claims filed by workers in its Maine stores and warehouse facilities. This was "off the charts," said John Rohde, the state agency's general counsel. By way of contrast, Maine's largest employer, the Hannaford Brothers grocery chain, contested only 17 percent of its workers' claims.[76]

The situation was not dissimilar in Washington State, where

in 2001 the Department of Industry and Labor revoked Wal-Mart's right to manage its own workers' compensation program. "For the past seven years, our audits continue to show Wal-Mart has fallen far short in meeting self-insurance requirements under Washington law," reported the agency's director, Gary Moore. "We've provided training here and at Wal-Mart operations in Arkansas. We've taken corrective action and issued penalties. We've met with Wal-Mart staff many times. We've told them what they need to do. Despite our efforts, despite their promises, they've missed the mark."[77] Revocation of its self-insured status would cost the company at least $3 million in Washington alone, so the company settled with the state in 2002. In return for an agreement to build one of its huge distribution centers there, the state agreed that Wal-Mart could remain self-insured, but for another eight years Washington required Wal-Mart to hire an independent, state-certified third-party administrator to handle all its local claims. To sweeten the deal, and perhaps atone for a few past sins, Wal-Mart agreed to donate $175,000 to Kids' Chance, a charity that provides scholarships to the children of workers catastrophically injured or killed on the job in Washington State.[78]

Tough state regulatory action also forced Wal-Mart to toe the line in Maine. In September 2005 the state Workers' Compensation Board flew two auditors to Rogers, Arkansas, where CMI processes its paperwork under the expansive roof of what had once been an early Wal-Mart store. The Maine officials spent a week poring over CMI claim records, detailing scores of misfilings, late filings, and unfair denials. Faced with fines and a potentially expensive loss of license, Wal-Mart turned its "competitive zest"—the phrase is that of Steve Minkowsky, an official with the Maine Workers' Compensation Board in Portland—toward compliance with the letter, and even the spirit, of the state workers' comp law. Within a couple of years Wal-Mart had completely reversed its operating practice, now approving rather than denying the overwhelming majority of workers' compensation claims.[79]

Chalk up a couple of victories for the Progressive tradition and the New Deal state, but before the champagne flows, Minkowsky reminds us that Maine and Washington are but two states. In the rest, Wal-Mart still "pushes the envelope" where and when it can. Indeed, the company and the rest of the retail industry remain militantly hostile to any effort to federalize and thereby standardize workers' compensation law or to integrate these payments into a regulated system of national health insurance. So the fight to enforce the social bargain exemplified by the century-old workers' comp laws will still be left in the hands of entrepreneurial lawyers like Edward White or vigilant but isolated state regulators such as Steve Minkowsky.[80]

CHAPTER NINE

WAL-MART VERSUS
THE WORLD IT HAS CREATED

In the United States, unlike Europe or Latin America, harsh denunciation or extravagant praise for a particular privately owned corporation has often been a substitute for a more general debate about the business system itself. This is because American corporations, like the Pennsylvania Railroad, Carnegie Steel, and American Tobacco, were huge entities by the end of the nineteenth century, long before the federal government had developed the will or capacity to tame them. Reforms like antitrust laws or workers' compensation, or the right to unionize, usually arose out of public revulsion at a particularly obnoxious business practice. Thus it was the Southern Pacific Railroad that the Gilded Age novelist Frank Norris defamed as "the galloping monster, the terror of steel and steam, . . . the leviathan, with tentacles of steel clutching into the soil, the soulless Force, the iron-hearted Power, the monster, the Colossus, the Octopus."[1] Likewise, muckraking journalist Ida Tarbell observed how the rise of John D. Rockefeller's Standard Oil "kept town and country in a constant state of excitement, of suspicion, of hope, and of despair." She was contemptuous of Rockefeller and his ilk because their tactics caused misery to the merchants and small producers she had known in her youth: "Here was a product meant to be a blessing to men—so I believed; and it was proving a curse to the very ones who had discovered it, developed it."[2]

Conversely, when corporations seemed to do the right thing, American reformers looked to them as a model that might spread throughout the economy. Just a dozen years after she published her muckraking history of Standard Oil, Tarbell had a very different view of another of America's industrial-era business icons. After touring the Ford Motor Company and observing the beneficent impact of the "five dollar day" paid to its workmen, she enthused, "I don't care what you call it—philanthropy, paternalism, autocracy—the results which are being obtained are worth all you can set against them, and the errors in the plan will provoke their own remedies."[3] Likewise, IBM was once touted as an exemplary corporate citizen because of its technological sophistication, its mid-twentieth-century decision to put all employees on salary, and its no-layoff policy. And in more recent years, every turn of the entrepreneurial wheel has generated a new set of firms that seem to combine an exciting new technology with an equally innovative set of social mores and organizational structures. Xerox, Microsoft, and Google have not just been successful companies making a lot of money. Rather, their success has generated an aura that makes them model enterprises upon which every business might well take inspiration.

Wal-Mart stands firmly in this tradition. During the long campaign for the 2008 Democratic Party presidential election, one domestic policy question proved almost as fraught with emotion as issues like terrorism, Iraq, and immigration: "Is Wal-Mart a good thing or bad thing for America?" Hillary Clinton, who had served six years on the Wal-Mart board, answered cautiously. "Well, it's a mixed blessing," she said, noting both the inexpensive goods the company brought to rural America as well as the controversy over the company's health insurance program and its failure to promote women to management ranks. John Edwards weighed in with a more explicit denunciation of the "tax dollars [that] are helping provide health care for

Wal-Mart employees, because Wal-Mart's not doing it."[4] And Barack Obama asserted, "The battle to engage Wal-Mart and force them to examine their corporate values and policies is absolutely vital to America today."[5] To these politician critics H. Lee Scott had a ready answer when he spoke to a 2006 meeting of the National Governors Association. "Twice as many Americans shop at Wal-Mart over the course of a year than voted in the last presidential election," boasted the embattled president of the world's largest employer. Wal-Mart was neither good nor bad for the country. It was America.[6]

CONFLICT IN CALIFORNIA

The question would be fought out in California, the home of more than one in eight Americans. It is the lucrative epicenter of the national supermarket industry. Wal-Mart began to put its discount stores in the state in the early 1990s, often in Central Valley towns like Fresno, Bakersfield, Sacramento, and Redding that had a midwestern feel about them. By 2007 there were 140, served by six big distribution centers.[7] .

But Wal-Mart has been stymied in its effort to convert them into the giant grocery-selling Supercenters, the $150-million-per-year megastores that have become the company's key to continued growth and profitability. In 2002 the company announced that it wanted to build forty Supercenters in the state during the next few years and dozens more before the end of the first decade of the twenty-first century. But only thirty-one have been built. Texas boasts almost ten times as many; in Ohio, a state one-third the size of California, there are three times as many Supercenters.[8]

These numbers are suprising, especially since Wal-Mart's California competitors had felt greatly threatened by the Bentonville juggernaut moving, it seemed, with inexorable force into the state. In October 2003, fifty-nine thousand supermarket workers began a protracted strike at 850 Southern California grocery stores. They were on strike, or locked out, because executives at the unionized supermarket chains felt it essential to chop wages and reduce retirement and health-care benefits if they were to compete with Wal-Mart. By 2000 Wal-Mart sold more groceries than any other chain, including such nationwide competitors as Kroger, Safeway, and Albertson's. To fight back, executives like Safeway's CEO Steven Burd were determined to seek labor cost reductions, the one area in which Wal-Mart had always enjoyed an immense advantage.

The UFCW had been blind to this threat. For decades powerful locals, led by complacent officers-for-life, had negotiated regional agreements that were predicated upon cartel-like market-sharing arrangements between two or three leading chains. Rick Icaza, the seventy-eight-year-old president of Local 770, the largest of the Southern California UFCW locals, had made his career cutting deals with Ralphs and Vons, grocers that were now mere subsidiaries owned by the national chains. "I felt that by having that relationship . . . we had passed the era of a need for strikes. I thought those days were over."[9] Although the strike, which dragged on for 145 days, from October 2003 to the end of February 2004, had a remarkable degree of public support, Icaza and other strike leaders made a hash of the epic confrontation. They pulled union pickets from Ralphs, in the hopes that this once accommodating firm would reopen talks; but executives there rewarded the union's goodwill gesture by continuing the "lockout" of their UFCW employees, illegally putting hundreds of workers back on the payroll under phony social security numbers, and pledging to share profits and losses with the other chains struck by the UFCW.[10] Nor could Icaza and other UFCW leaders decide who was the real enemy: Safeway's "greedy" Steven Burd, a multimillionaire Democrat, or the looming Wal-Mart threat, which promised to bankrupt the old-line supermarkets.

The strike ended in a decisive defeat for the UFCW. Safeway, Kroger, and the other chains forced the union to accept a new contract that slashed pensions, capped health insurance payouts, and instituted a two-tier wage structure that made it almost impossible for new hires to earn a decent wage.[11] Turnover soared, health-care coverage declined, and employee morale plummeted. Health-care coverage for new hires in the supermarkets now tracked that of Wal-Mart, with yearlong waiting periods, employee-paid premiums, and high deductibles and co-pays. As a consequence, the proportion of Southern California grocery workers with health insurance through their job dropped from 94 percent in 2003 to 54 percent in early 2007. Among those hired since the end of the strike, just 7 percent signed up for job-based insurance![12] Combined with the failure of the five-year UFCW effort to organize even a single Wal-Mart store, the strike defeat in Southern California seemed yet another indication that the traditional tools wielded by the labor movement—union organizing and collective bargaining—were ineffective, if not obsolete, in that huge sector of the economy where Wal-Mart cast such a large shadow.

But this setback was not the end of the story. If Wal-Mart's low-wage, anti-union business model seemed impervious to trade union attack, perhaps it might yet be transformed, or at least contained, through political action. Indeed, the decline of American trade unionism—the proportion of all workers covered by a collective bargaining contract now stands at just above 11 percent—has reawakened interest in what Progressives and New Dealers used to call "the labor question."[13] Politicians today call it the squeeze on the middle class.

A century ago, when workers themselves proved incapable of ending child labor in the textile industry, transforming unsanitary and dangerous working conditions on the packinghouse "kill floor," or ending the twelve-hour day in the steel industry, reformers like Jane Addams and Florence Kelley

looked to the government for new remedies and new regulations. They lobbied city fathers for prohibitions against tenement
sweatshops and unsafe factories in then-booming industrial
cities like Cleveland, Toledo, and Chicago, or they campaigned
to regulate working conditions and raise wages for women and
children in Massachusetts, New York, and Wisconsin, where reformers and unionists exercised some influence. Today, the same
pattern is repeating itself. When an expansion of health-care
insurance and a substantial rise in the minimum wage was stymied at the federal level, reformers turned to the municipalities
and states where the wages and health-care policies of Wal-
Mart, the standard-setting employer, had become the object of
intense political struggle.

The obstacle to Wal-Mart's California expansion had its
origin in a particularly imaginative and successful reform coalition that emerged in Los Angeles. Although the unions lost
the grocery strike there, they remained politically influential,
especially with the rise of a progressive Latino leadership within
the Los Angeles Federation of Labor, a coalition of unions that
represented eight hundred thousand workers. Equally important, a new generation of liberals, in municipal government
and out, had scored a considerable success in California's affluent
coastal communities, where property taxes, rather than sales
taxes, filled municipal coffers. Businesses seeking to build and
operate new commercial developments—stadiums, shopping
centers, and hotels—were compelled or cajoled into signing a
Community Benefit Agreement. First, these CBAs committed
cities like Los Angeles to subsidize or rezone large and expensive real estate parcels for the kind of big urban projects that
employed thousands of low-wage workers. Second, developers
had to provide plenty of parking and meet environmental standards and aesthetic design requirements. In addition, project
proprietors agreed to employ local people at a living wage,
sometimes with good health-care benefits. Some CBAs helped

facilitate unionization by mandating employer neutrality during any organizing drive.[14]

In effect, these California cities were leveraging their zoning authority to re-create a set of mini–New Deals that ensured a more progressive distribution of the wealth generated by private interests who sought access to the millions of affluent consumers residing in the area. If developers were willing to deal, city fathers and mothers were ready to cooperate with zoning variances, tax concessions, and other forms of assistance. In the 2001 agreement that led to a $1 billion expansion of the Staples Center in Los Angeles, owners got public subsidies of more than $70 million, plus assurances that trade unions and neighborhood groups would end agitation and litigation against the project. In return, the developers agreed to hire a substantial proportion of the permanent employees from nearby neighborhoods, pay at least 70 percent of them the Los Angeles living wage, and remain neutral should a trade union attempt to organize the workers.

But Wal-Mart would not play ball. This became graphically apparent in Inglewood, an African American and Latino industrial city enfolded within Los Angeles, where Wal-Mart sought to build a Sam's Club and a Supercenter as the anchor stores on a sixty-acre redevelopment site near an abandoned racetrack. Wal-Mart negotiated with the municipality over the tax and infrastructure subsidies it might garner. But the company would provide no quid pro quo. Thus in September 2002 the Inglewood city council approved an emergency ordinance effectively banning stores of the size the company sought to build from selling groceries. When one city councilwoman, an investment banker, reversed herself near the end of her term, the UFCW ran its own candidate, a union business agent, in the next election and handily defeated her.

All this made Wal-Mart furious. The company had already breached the L.A. city limits by putting what it called "one of its first truly urban stores" on Crenshaw Boulevard in heavily African American Baldwin Hills, where it rehabilitated a long-vacant department store and turned it into one of the company's few multistory Supercenters. Soon TV commercials featuring effusive shoppers began to tout the revitalization Wal-Mart had brought to that inner-city community. Clearly, Wal-Mart exec-utives believed their own advertising. From H. Lee Scott on down, Wal-Mart officials seemed to regard just about any con-sumer purchase at one of their stores as an implicit endorse-ment of the company's expansionary aims, not to mention its distinctive labor and employment practices. "Wal-Mart and our customers are tired of being bullied by the unions," declared Peter Kanelos, the Wal-Mart community affairs manager re-sponsible for Southern California. After the UFCW demon-strated its capacity to influence Inglewood politics, he threw down a challenge: "If the union and the local politicians they put in office want to attack Wal-Mart, they can rest assured that we'll fight back."[15]

Wal-Mart organized and funded a local group called the Citizens Committee to Welcome Wal-Mart to Inglewood, which quickly gathered signatures requiring the city to put the Wal-Mart redevelopment plan to a popular vote. The group touted the twelve hundred new jobs the shopping center would bring, including three hundred at Wal-Mart, and the boost to sales-tax revenues of as much as $5 million a year. Wal-Mart had long experience with such astroturf campaigns, but in this in-stance the company went way overboard, putting on the ballot a seventy-one-page planning document that approved the stores as designed, without possibility of a public hearing or city re-view. "Under the guise of 'direct democracy,' Wal-Mart would shut out government and public oversight," the Los Angeles Times noted in an editorial, "A Big-Box Bully."[16]

The UFCW teamed up with the Los Angeles Alliance for a New Economy, a public interest policy group that had pioneered the CBA concept, to wage a campaign against the Wal-Mart development proposition. It was not an easy fight: the city needed the sales-tax revenue; the mayor, an African American, came out in favor of Wal-Mart's scheme; and Peter Kanelos supervised the expenditure of hundreds of thousands of dollars on an advertising and organizing blitz. But most of the African American community sided with the union. Just before the vote, Inglewood's fiery congresswoman, Maxine Waters, held a press conference with Jesse Jackson, who denounced the Bentonville corporation as "a Confederate economic Trojan Horse." LAANE, the unions, and the Los Angeles left saw the Inglewood fight as a chance to recoup some of the leverage and self-respect they had lost in the debilitating supermarket strike and lockout.

In an unexpectedly large turnout on April 6, 2004, Wal-Mart and its ballot measure lost badly, with less than 40 percent of the total vote. Robert McAdam, Wal-Mart's vice president for state and local government relations, blamed "outside special interests," that is, the unions, for leading Inglewood voters astray. But a few months later H. Lee Scott admitted that Wal-Mart's heavy-handed effort to circumvent normal democratic procedures in the city had been counterproductive. It "came across as arrogance," he told a business audience.[17]

BATTLE OVER A BUSINESS MODEL

From this point on, Wal-Mart's effort to expand into metropolitan America proved much more difficult. The UFCW had wanted an outright ban on all grocery-selling stores of more than one hundred thousand square feet. This was almost certainly unconstitutional, and besides, the Los Angeles progressives who had pioneered the CBA concept had a better idea. They successfully urged the Los Angeles City Council to pass a new ordinance that required all big-box retailers to fund a cost-benefit analysis, on a store-by-store basis, designed to demonstrate that any new retail outlet would not have an adverse economic impact on the surrounding community. Such an analysis would tally not only the jobs and sales-tax revenues generated by a new store, but the hidden costs as well: traffic, policing, downward wage pressure, and the cost of taxpayer-financed safety-net programs for the children of low-income Wal-Mart employees. Within just a few years, Inglewood, San Diego, Turlock, Santa Ana, and Long Beach had passed similar economic impact laws.[18]

Even more ambitiously, states and cities dominated by the Democratic Party sought to directly legislate a minimum level of wages and health benefits for big-box employers. In January 2006 Maryland passed the Fair Share Health Care Act—commonly known as the "Wal-Mart Bill"—mandating that corporations with over ten thousand employees spend at least 8 percent of their payroll on health care, either directly or through a state fund. Pushed forward by labor, it was also endorsed by unionized Giant Stores, the state's largest grocery chain, which already paid health-care benefits that met the new Maryland standard.[19]

The Chicago City Council passed a somewhat similar ordinance requiring big-box retailers, defined as corporations with over $1 billion in annual sales and ninety thousand square feet of retail space, to pay their employees at least ten dollars an hour and provide an additional three dollars an hour in benefits, mainly health care. In Chicago, as in Los Angeles, Wal-Mart's push into the inner city touched off a bitter debate within the African American community. Wal-Mart hired a public relations firm, assigned three full-time lobbyists to the city, put construction in the hands of a firm headed by a well-respected African American woman, and scattered contributions through the black Chicago wards on the south and west sides of the city. Wal-Mart supporters, which included the local NAACP and numerous ministers, argued that any job was better than no job in their impoverished neighborhoods, a perspective reinforced by Wal-Mart's announcement that its new generation of inner-city stores would be designated "Wal-Mart Jobs and Opportunity Zones." Within them the company would distribute five hundred thousand dollars to provide counseling and advertising help for neighborhood businesses. Opponents thought this Wal-Mart initiative was something close to a bribe. They argued that a big city like Chicago had the political leverage and the potential consumer market to force Wal-Mart to raise substantially its pay and health benefit standards.[20]

The fate of these high-profile attempts to alter the way Wal-Mart did business is instructive, demonstrating the limitations inherent in any regional effort to reform a corporation's core business practice. In Chicago, where an ugly brand of racial politics infected the big-box debate, the story paralleled that of hundreds of smaller towns and cities whose mayors and managers thought an outright ban on big-box stores would be too costly. Although the Chicago City Council had voted 35 to 14 in favor of the measure in the summer of 2006, Mayor Richard Daley vetoed the bill that September on the grounds that "it would drive jobs and businesses from our city, penalizing neighborhoods that need additional economic activity the most." Two days later, when the vote to override took place, three black aldermen and women switched sides, which was enough to sustain the Daley veto, the first he had issued during his seventeen years in city hall. "I have changed my mind," said alderwoman Shirley Coleman of the heavily African American sixteenth ward. "People need a job and I'm not denying them an opportunity if Wal-Mart expresses an interest, and they have, in my ward." Crowed an official of the National Retail Federation, which had lobbied extensively against what it labeled an effort to "handcuff" retailers into providing health-care coverage, "Hopefully the Daley veto is another nail in the coffin in this movement.[21] A statute reforming the Wal-Mart business model was stymied in Maryland as well, where a federal court declared the law unconstitutional on the grounds that it would "preempt" the 1974 Employee Retirement Income Security Act.

"Preemption" is key to the difficulties that face progressives at the state and local levels when they try to rein in a company like Wal-Mart. Both the federal labor law and that governing pensions and health insurance trump—that is, "preempt"—similar laws passed by every other level of government. Liberals and laborites once favored the preemption doctrine because they rightly feared that unless federal law was absolutely supreme, conservative state legislatures in the South and Mountain West would try to sabotage the progressive federal laws that were passed during the New Deal and subsequent moments of social reform.

But today, when states like Massachusetts and Maryland have become laboratories for progressive experimentation, the preemption doctrine has become a weapon in the hands of those who favor the status quo. Efforts to make union organizing easier or health insurance mandatory are unconstitutional, "preempted" by a suffocating burden of federal statutes subject to conservative interpretation by unsympathetic courts and administrators.[22] As the Wal-Mart-dominated Retail Industry Leaders Association put it when a federal judge struck down the Maryland statute, the decision sends a "clear message to other States considering similar Bills that such laws violate federal law."[23]

Of course, not every local law or city ordnance is blocked by federal preemption, which is why zoning and land use regulations have so often become a back-channel mechanism by which cities like New York, Los Angeles, and Boston have sought to block the big-box invasion. Small towns too: Al Norman, the veteran Wal-Mart opponent from New England, estimates that citizen groups challenge more than 60 percent of all Wal-Mart stores, arguing that the big boxes degrade local wetlands, require an egregious rezoning of local neighborhoods, and increase traffic flow beyond what roads and streets can carry. Perhaps 330 communities have blocked a big-box store, sometimes more than once.[24] But the laws and regulations used to stop a new store often have a Rube Goldberg quality that only by indirection pressure Wal-Mart, Target, and other discounters to raise their wages and improve their health benefits. The real battle will have to be fought in the national political arena.

POLITICS AND PUBLIC RELATIONS

"Corporate reputation" is the PR phrase for the image, credibility, and attractiveness of a business. Wal-Mart's has become the object of a fierce battle, defended by skilled operatives who deploy the kind of money, technology, and personnel usually seen in a presidential political campaign. "Unions have declared us enemy No. 1," said Ray Bracy, Wal-Mart's vice president for public affairs, in early 2005 when inaugurating the corporation's beefed-up lobby operation in the nation's capital. "We have to be reputation warriors and have got to set the record straight."[25] Another executive, Robert McAdam, a former political strategist at the Tobacco Institute, dubbed the company's public relations operation "Candidate Wal-Mart," which sought out "swing votes" among those consumers who were but infrequent shoppers in the company's stores. "They've got their base," said McAdam of his union opponents. "We've got ours. But there is a group in the middle that really we all need to be talking to."[26]

Nor was this just a clever metaphor for good salesmanship. By 2006 it was becoming commonplace for Democratic Party politicians, some potential presidential candidates, to cite Wal-Mart for its low wages, anti-unionism, and outsourcing of American manufacturing jobs. At an anti-Wal-Mart rally in

Iowa, Vice President Joseph Biden, then senator for Delaware, asked how the company could expect people to live on ten dollars an hour. "My problem with Wal-Mart," he said, "is that I don't see any indication that they care about the fate of middle-class people." John Kerry, the former Democratic standard-bearer, thought it "unconscionable" that five of the ten richest people in the country were from the Walton family, "but they can't find the money to secure health coverage for their own workers and families." And Hillary Clinton returned a five-thousand-dollar campaign contribution to protest the company's labor policies.[27]

Wal-Mart responded by mailing out "voter education" letters to its 17,271 employees in Iowa, where the first caucuses in the presidential campaign are always held. We "would never suggest to you how to vote," said the missive, "but we have an obligation to tell you when politicians are saying something about your company that isn't true. After all, you are Wal-Mart."[28]

Once Barack Obama secured the Democratic presidential nomination in June 2008, the company made its preferences clear. Regional executives organized hundreds of meetings for low-level supervisors and store managers, urging them to spread the word that if the Democrats won the company would face a disruptive and costly unionization campaign.[29] In the fall Wal-Mart began a voter registration effort on its in-store television network. "Pollsters have found that our core shoppers, Wal-Mart women, are an influential demographic in the upcoming presidential election," bragged a political operative for the company. Indeed, a postelection Zogby Poll found that consumers who most prefer to shop at Wal-Mart favored John McCain by 17 points over Obama, a Republican tilt far greater than that of shoppers at competitors Target, Macy's, Costco, or J.C. Penney.[30] Predominantly white counties in the Wal-Mart heartland—in Arkansas, Oklahoma, East Texas, and much of

Appalachia—actually voted for McCain by even heavier margins than for George Bush in 2004.[31]

To counter this corporate offensive, unionists and their allies mobilized in what the *Northwest Arkansas News* called "the hottest, highest-stakes political contest in America."[32] This was not the 2008 presidential election, but the ramped-up battle waged by the unions and their allies against the corporation's reputation. Immediately following the end of the California grocery strike, the UFCW had dismantled its Wal-Mart organizing campaign and put its resources into an activist Web site, "Wake Up Wal-Mart," under the direction of Paul Blank, the former political director of Howard Dean's Internet-savvy 2004 primary campaign. The Service Employees International Union put together another Web-based organization, Wal-Mart Watch, also staffed by former Democratic Party operatives. Neither campaign tried to do any outright organizing, but both sought to expose, embarrass, and mobilize public sentiment against Wal-Mart's expansion. When most active, between 2005 and 2007, Wal-Mart Watch employed forty activists, Wake-Up Wal-Mart another dozen.[33]

Such "corporate campaigns" were nothing new for the U.S. labor movement, but they were typically linked to a particular organizing drive or contract renewal. Once the dispute was resolved, the campaign would end. Wal-Mart, by contrast, now faced two well-funded national organizations seeking a wholesale shift in the way the company did business.[34] The UFCW effort was an extension of the war the union had long waged against Wal-Mart's low pay and low benefits, as well as its antiunionism. Former Wal-Mart workers told their story on the Web site, and viewers were urged to participate in pickets and demonstrations at local stores. Wal-Mart Watch reflected the politics of SEIU's ambitious president, Andrew Stern, who sometimes looked for ways to reach an accommodation with the big retailer. "We have no intention of trying to organize Wal-Mart workers," said Stern. "The purpose is to change Wal-Mart's business model—a business model that rewards shareholders and executives and doesn't reward workers."[35]

"Wal-Mart is the General Motors of our era," said Stern in explanation of why a union that chiefly organized health-care and municipal workers would put so much effort into challenging the big retailer. "Whatever business practices they adopt have a huge influence across other American businesses," he stated. Indeed, labor's defeat in the California grocery strike made SEIU efforts to win higher wages and better benefits for the janitors it represented in Los Angeles much more difficult. When the supermarkets cut their health-care plans, area cleaning companies complained to the SEIU that they, too, needed cost relief. According to Stern, "They came to us and said, 'We're not as big as the supermarket chains, and if they can't afford to pay for health care, how can we be expected to?'"[36]

If critics wanted to take the company on, H. Lee Scott told an audience of five hundred business leaders in Los Angeles, "they need to bring their lunch, because we're not going to lay down. We've got nothing to apologize for."[37] So Wal-Mart launched a huge PR offensive in 2004, purchasing several million dollars in full-page newspaper ads and television spots that touted not the low prices on the shelves but the good jobs available at the door and the good corporate citizenship practiced in the community. The company put up a Web site titled "Wal-Mart Facts" and paid for a research conference at which a number of orthodox economists substantiated Wal-Mart claims to job creation, equitable wages, and a generally beneficial impact on those businesses that did not compete directly with the retail giant. Wal-Mart even paid for two pages of advertising in the highbrow *New York Review of Books*, where it published an "open letter" over Scott's signature, "Wal-Mart's

Impact on Society: A Key Moment in Time for American Capitalism."[38]

Wal-Mart's counteroffensive proceeded on two fronts: a hard-nosed lobbying operation that extended from every city and state capital to Washington, D.C.; and a softer public relations gambit designed to make a set of strategic accommodations to its critics, especially those who found Wal-Mart retrograde on environmental, racial, and cultural issues. It had long been a point of Wal-Mart pride that the corporation had had little presence in the nation's capital. This was often attributed either to Sam Walton's stinginess or to his naïveté, but an arrogance, verging on contempt for the government's regulatory reach, was an even greater motivation. "Mr. Sam's reputation was that he really didn't care what the government did as long as it left him alone," remembered Representative Marion Berry, an Arkansas Democrat.[39] Beginning in the 1990s, however, Wal-Mart became far more politically conscious. It played an active role in the International Mass Retailers Association, which did its own heavy lobbying against the Clinton administration's effort to strengthen the Family and Medical Leave Act, raise the minimum wage, and enforce occupational health and safety regulations. "Each new regulation holds the potential to drastically change the way we do business and add unnecessary bureaucracy and costs," asserted Wal-Mart's Don Soderquist early in 1994. The company was particularly hostile to Labor Department efforts to "federalize the medical administration of workers' compensation."[40]

As one might expect, campaign contributions from top Wal-Mart executives flowed heavily toward the company's political friends. Bill Clinton had actually won much backing from Wal-Mart and the Walton family when he ran for president in 1992; as governor he had never thwarted the company, and from 1986 to 1991 spouse Hillary had served cooperatively on the Wal-Mart board, largely playing a symbolic role as the sole woman in that all-male institution. A company loyalist at that time, she pushed for more women in executive posts and greater attention to environmentally friendly stores, but kept silent when it came to union issues or wage standards. However, once the Democrats captured the White House in 1992, Wal-Mart's fear that the new Congress might investigate the retail industry or that employer mandates might be imposed to fund a national system of health insurance sent Wal-Mart money sloshing toward the Republicans. So Wal-Mart established a political action committee, from which Republican candidates received the lion's share of all the contributions. Less than 2 percent went to the Democrats in 1996, less than 15 percent in 2000. As the company sought to put stores in metropolitan America, the proportion of Wal-Mart donations to urban Democrats increased—to 32 percent in 2006—but the company was still far more of a GOP-linked enterprise than competitors like Target, Costco, or the rest of the retail industry.[41]

Indeed, congressional Republicans, most notably former Texas congressman Tom DeLay and Mississippi senator Trent Lott, who sought to advance the symbiotic connection between GOP power and K Street lobbyist money, were crucial to Wal-Mart's belated decision to build a lobby shop in the nation's capital. In 1998 Wal-Mart hired its first lobbyist, retired air force lieutenant general Norm Lezy, and began to coordinate its activities more closely with Republicans on the Hill.[42] During the last years of the Clinton administration Wal-Mart staved off a congressional investigation of its employment practices. And once George W. Bush occupied the White House, Wal-Mart used its own lobbyists or one of the many firms it hired to legalize the company's increase in the number of hours its truck drivers could work without a break; help kill Clinton-era ergonomics reforms; and advance free trade compacts in Latin America and Asia. In 2003 it overtook United Parcel Service as the biggest corporate giver to Congress. "We don't have any problems getting to see whomever we want," said Lezy. With stores in 406 of the nation's 435 congressional districts, "a lot of members have figured out that we create a lot of jobs."[43] In May 2004 Vice President Dick Cheney flew to Bentonville to kick off the GOP campaign, declaring, "The story of Wal-Mart exemplifies some of the very best qualities in our country—hard work, the spirit of enterprise, fair dealing, and integrity."[44]

Wal-Mart's D.C. lobby operation took a quantum leap forward in early 2005 when the company made Lee Culpepper director of its Washington office. Culpepper was the quintessential GOP/business operative. Active in conservative politics since his days at the University of Georgia, he had worked for business-friendly southern Democrats during the 1980s until he landed a job at the National Restaurant Association in 1993. The NRA was hair-trigger sensitive to every nuance and shift in federal labor, environmental, health-care, and trade policies. It was a militant opponent of both a rise in the minimum wage and an employer mandate designed to universalize health insurance. With sixty thousand members in every political jurisdiction, the association under Culpepper, who became director in 1999, mastered effective astroturf campaigns hostile to federal regulatory mandates.[45]

For much of this work, Wal-Mart worked through the Retail Industry Leaders Association, in which its influence was considerable. The RILA represented the low-wage, nonunion big-box wing of the retail trade, with Safeway, Kroger, and other unionized supermarket chains conspicuously absent. Wal-Mart used the RILA to do the kind of legislative and legal work that might have been embarrassing had the company acted alone. So RILA sued or lobbied states and localities when they sought to impose health insurance mandates or living wage pay standards on the big-box discounters. It fought new port security regulations and clean air standards that might have imposed extra costs on the big retail shippers, and RILA proved a militant opponent of Democratic Party legislative efforts to facilitate trade union organizing.[46]

Conservative political operatives moved easily between Wal-Mart and the Bush administration. In 2006 President Bush appointed Paul DeCamp, who had represented the company in the long-running *Dukes v. Wal-Mart* gender discrimination lawsuit, to head the Labor Department's wage and hour division.[47] In turn, Terry Nelson, a political director of the 2004 Bush campaign, organized "Working Families for Wal-Mart," a company-funded advocacy group that enlisted a range of public figures, including Andrew Young, the former civil rights leader and Carter-era ambassador to the United Nations, the entertainer Pat Boone, and a number of executives from supplier firms. The group recruited members at some of the meetings Wal-Mart organized for its vendors, from among shoppers entering and exiting Wal-Mart stores (for any other organization this would have constituted an egregious violation of the company's iron-clad no-solicitation policy) and among home-office consultants and employees.[48] It sought an "open and honest dialogue with elected officials, opinion makers and community leaders that conveys the positive contribution of Wal-Mart to working families."[49]

But what little credibility Working Families built soon collapsed after Young told a black Los Angeles newspaper that it would be a good thing if Wal-Mart ran the city's immigrant-owned grocery stores out of business, because they "have been overcharging us—selling us stale bread, and bad meat and wilted vegetables. . . . First it was the Jews, then it was Koreans and now it's Arabs, very few black people own these stores." And if that was not enough, GOP consultant Nelson was soon embroiled in an embarrassing controversy over a racist campaign advertisement—featuring an enticing white woman and a black senatorial candidate—in the hotly contested 2006 Tennessee race.[50] Both Young and Nelson severed their ties to Wal-Mart, after which their Working Families front group evaporated.

Wal-Mart needed a "reputational" strategy of more substance than this if it were to survive the skepticism and disdain generated by both its critics and its own maladroit efforts to counter them. So the company has invested at least $10 million in an outreach operation largely staffed by executives from Edelman Public Relations, the sophisticated, bipartisan firm whose clients have included other big companies, including oil and tobacco, that find themselves with public relations problems. The Edelman folks staffed a windowless "war room" at the home office, where they have tried to soften the Wal-Mart image by reaching out to environmental and minority groups and by advising the company on policies that will make it more acceptable to blue-state residents. The leader of this effort is one Leslie Dach, a former Edelman exec hired away by Wal-Mart at more than $2 million a year. His pedigree is decidedly not that of the usual Wal-Mart executive: Jewish, born in Queens, New York, a veteran Democratic Party operative who has worked for Edward Kennedy, Michael Dukakis, and Al Gore.[51]

Dach got into politics in the early 1970s as an environmental activist, so it was not unexpected that he urged Wal-Mart to deepen and advertise its commitment to "green" stores, products, and transport. The campaign got off to a high-profile start when Al Gore screened his Oscar-winning film *An Inconvenient Truth* at the home-office auditorium. Gore won a standing ovation from the managerial associates, followed by dinner with H. Lee Scott and Rob Walton. Thereafter the company has won its own round of applause for its $500 million investment in a "sustainability" initiative designed to make much of its supply chain and product mix environmentally friendly. To advance its program, experts from the World Wildlife Federation, the Natural Resources Defense Council, and even Greenpeace have made the pilgrimage to Bentonville.[52] Wal-Mart's goals are therefore ambitious: double the efficiency of its vehicle fleet within the decade, eliminate 30 percent of the energy used in its stores, and bring to market a variety of products, including fluorescent lightbulbs and organic cotton T-shirts, that save energy, save the soil, and can be easily recycled. Although an outspoken critic of Wal-Mart's low wages, Sierra Club executive director Carl Pope applauds the company's environmental initiative: "None of this is 'greenstanding.' Their metrics are impressive."[53]

Edelman reworked Wal-Mart's image in other ways. Remembered lobbyist Culpepper, "One of the things we decided to do at the beginning of 2005 was to try to do a better job building relationships and political support on both sides of the aisle, but in particular with Democrats."[54] Thus Wal-Mart, the nation's largest private-sector employer of African Americans, was the first high-profile company to back the renewal of the Voting Rights Act, which was of particular interest to the Congressional Black Caucus, an overwhelmingly Democratic group. The gambit paid off: despite the opposition of conservative southern Republicans, who objected to provisions in the bill requiring bilingual ballots and federal "pre-clearing" of state election-law changes, the act passed in 2006 and the president signed it into law. In return, many members of the CBC saw the big corporation as at least a sometime ally, which made it easier for eight minority congressmen and -women to vote with Wal-Mart on labor law enforcement issues.[55]

That same year, Wal-Mart hired a gay-marketing firm, joined the National Gay & Lesbian Chamber of Commerce, and extended limited benefits to same-sex partners of those on the company payroll.[56] Not unexpectedly, some groups on the right denounced Wal-Mart executives for "trying to appease" environmentalists, homosexuals, and advocates of multiculturalism. Tim Kane, a Heritage Foundation economist, thought Wal-Mart's success as a low-price, free enterprise marketer spoke for itself. "Now they are muddying the waters by trying to offer a softer image. It leaves them vulnerable to charges that they are insincere."[57]

On the liberal left there were also charges of Wal-Mart hypocrisy, and these undoubtedly had more bite. After years of critical coverage in the nation's major newspapers, on the nightly news, and in a series of investigative specials, Wal-Mart's reputation had taken a measurable hit. A confidential "Wal-Mart Positioning Report" prepared by GSD&M, the company's former advertising agency, asserted that Wal-Mart was "a highly politicized brand"; indeed, its politicization was the greatest challenge facing the company. Tens of millions still shopped at the megaretailer each week, but a slice of the consuming public—as high as 8 percent according to GSD&M—simply refused to shop at the store, either because they disdained the downscale merchandise or because they were participants in a de facto political boycott. A Pew Research report in early 2007 confirmed much of this negativity: for millions of Americans Wal-Mart was bracketed with Exxon and Halliburton in terms of its public image. It is not surprising therefore that Wal-Mart has no stores in New York City or Boston, just one in Chicago, and only a relative handful in metropolitan Los Angeles. Al Norman's Sprawl-Busters organization counted forty-seven Wal-Mart projects defeated or withdrawn in 2006. Bernstein Research, a marketing firm, pronounced Wal-Mart's growth "under siege in several regions of the country."[58]

All this was red meat for cultural warriors like the *Washington Post* columnist George Will, who argued, "Liberals think their campaign against Wal-Mart is a way of introducing the subject of class into America's political argument, and they are more correct than they understand. Their campaign is lib-

eralism as condescension. It is a philosophic repugnance toward markets, because consumer sovereignty results in the
masses making messes."[59] Steven Malanga of the neoconserva-
tive *City Journal* concurred. He blamed "elite opinion" for all
the anti-Wal-Mart bashing, pointing out that the Walton Family
Foundation was a major supporter of market-based solutions
to contemporary social problems, including school vouchers
and charter schools.[60] Wal-Mart's Scott also entered the culture war shoving match, complaining after New York had rejected a Wal-Mart effort to build a store in Queens, "You have
people who are just better than us and don't want a Wal-Mart
in their community."[61]

But these ideological fireworks should not obscure the bed-
rock economic interests that motivated the clash between Wal-
Mart and its opponents. Wal-Mart was actually quite willing
to accommodate its cultural critics where and when it could.
The company's détente with environmentalists and multicul-
turalists was predicated upon a larger strategic determination
to divide the anti-Wal-Mart forces; for when it came to trade
unionism, or those who sought a substantial boost to Wal-Mart
wages and benefits, there would be no compromise. Company
executives and publicists correctly understood that the unions
were the key institutions that linked, occasionally subsidized,
and often animated virtually all of the company's most important detractors.[62] As a memo distributed to store managers in
late 2005, just before release of Robert Greenwald's caustic
documentary, *Wal-Mart: The High Cost of Low Prices,* put it:
"Our critics will take everything they can and use it against us.
Remember, most of the anti-Wal-Mart activities come from
union sponsored groups."[63] Mona Williams, the Wal-Mart
spokeswoman, said, "We listen to all of our critics, because a
lot of times they have legitimate concerns. But the unions are
not in that category." The company will compromise with environmentalists, feminists, even gays, reported the *Wall Street*

Journal, "but here is what Wal-Mart won't do: let unions into the workplace. The company is convinced that would compromise its extraordinarily successful business model, based on an unrelenting push to cut costs."[64]

PRICES AND PURCHASING POWER

The relationship between retail prices and the purchasing power of the hard-pressed American consumer stood at the center of the Wal-Mart controversy. The company sometimes argued that its wages were not so low, especially when compared to the rest of the retail industry. Sure, admitted Scott and other Wal-Mart defenders, unionized grocery-store wages were higher, but they were confined to a handful of metropolitan regions on the coasts and a few cities in the Upper Midwest. Otherwise, Americans were pleased with, even desperate for, the kinds of jobs that Wal-Mart offered. If not, why would twenty-five thousand Chicago-area residents send in an application for one of the 325 new job slots opening up on the west side of that city? Why indeed did Wal-Mart have so little difficulty recruiting something close to half a million new workers each year?

The reason might lie in the vast sea of unemployment and underemployment that America's official jobless statistics fail to capture. Wal-Mart itself admitted, or rather boasted, that only 7 percent of the company's hourly associates try to support a family with children on a single Wal-Mart income. This was the argument H. Lee Scott put forward to the upper-middle-class readers of the *New York Review of Books*, where the company devoted two full pages to a defense of the corporation and its wage policy. To staff its stores, the company purposely seeks school-age youth, retirees, people who want a second job, and those willing or forced to work part-time.[65] It is a remarkable apologia; not since the rise of the textile industry early in the nineteenth century, when women and children composed a majority of the labor force, has the leadership of an industry central to American economic development consciously sought to staff itself with a workforce that it defined as marginal to the family economy.[66]

Far more important, however, than the PR effort to defend its wage standard has been Wal-Mart's argument that the company's downward squeeze on prices more than compensates for the wage-depressing impact of its overall labor policies, thereby raising the standard of living of the entire U.S. population. By one estimate this saves consumers upwards of $263 billion a year.[67] Another study concluded that retail productivity growth, as measured by real value added per hour, tripled in the dozen years after 1987, in part due to Wal-Mart's competitive leadership. As a consequence inflation moderated, even in the high employment years of the late 1990s. "These savings are a lifeline for millions of middle- and lower-income families who live from payday to payday," argued Scott. "In effect, it gives them a raise every time they shop with us."[68] Many commentators concurred, including the Obama economic adviser Jason Furman, who calculated that the company's low prices saved the average household $2,329 a year. In an economic brief, he called Wal-Mart "a progressive success story."[69] Extending Furman's argument, the conservative New York Times writer John Tierney concluded that any improvement in Wal-Mart's labor and health-care practices would lead to higher prices. "Why would anyone who claims to be fighting for social justice be so determined to take money out of the pockets of the poor?" he asked in a Times op-ed.[70]

"Wal-Mart's profit per associate is six thousand four hundred dollars," Wal-Mart spokeswomen Mona Williams told a reporter in the early spring of 2007. "If we were to pay two dollars more an hour to associates, that would cut four thousand dollars out of our per-employee profit. If anybody ever stopped to do the math, they'd see this. It would take two-thirds of the profit if we gave everyone two dollars more." She added, "You could raise prices, but what about the woman who is shopping for Easter shoes for her kids? We can't raise prices on her."[71]

In fact, Wal-Mart is almost certain to raise those prices. As the Chinese yuan is revalued upward, and as the pay of East Asian workers continues to rise, so too will the cost of imported shoes and other consumer goods inch higher.[72] And if Wal-Mart did raise wages and provide better health care, how much would its prices actually rise? Wal-Mart guards its real labor costs and product markups closely, but researchers for the Economic Policy Institute estimate that the company could maintain its current level of profitability and bring its wages and benefits to the same level as other large retailers for about $3 billion a year, which would indeed increase prices, but by only 1 percent, a penny per dollar in sales. Even larger increases, about four dollars an hour, that would bring Wal-Mart labor costs to the level of those of Costco or the unionized grocery stores would boost prices twice as much, to about 2.2 percent of sales.[73]

So prices might well rise in the future. Fortunately, the stuff that can be purchased at the nearest Wal-Mart actually constitutes an ever-shrinking share of family expenditures in the United States. People can buy their food, clothes, household goods, consumer electronics, toys, and some furniture at reduced prices. Bibles, rifles, and baseball bats as well. But most people don't spend as much on all this as they used to. In 1947 these kinds of consumer goods represented about 44 percent of the family budget, in 1974 about 30 percent, but today they have shrunk to little more than 18 percent. All this is a great tribute to the big-box revolution and the supply chain wizardry that stands behind it. However, this productivity miracle has had little impact on the rest of the family budget. The cost of housing, medical care, transportation, and education has risen steadily over the same time span, increasing from about 17 percent of household expenditures right after World War II to more than double that in the early twenty-first century. So the real pressures on family income are coming from those goods and services that can't be bought at a big-box store, even mighty Wal-Mart. They can, however, be bought with higher wages.[74]

In the final analysis, this is a reality that Wal-Mart itself cannot escape. Shortly after Lee Culpepper took over the corporation's Washington lobbying operation, H. Lee Scott gave a speech to home office executives in which he hinted that Wal-Mart might favor an increase in the minimum wage. By the fall of 2005, that federal minimum, then but $5.15 an hour, had not budged in nearly a decade. It had fallen so far behind the cost of living that Wal-Mart labor costs would be little impacted by a modest increase. But the price of gasoline had spiked to well over two dollars a gallon, and the cost of health care was once again advancing at a double-digit clip. Asserted Scott, "We can see first-hand at Wal-Mart how many of our customers are struggling to get by . . . our customers simply don't have the money to buy basic necessities between pay checks." And it was true: tracking sales, Wal-Mart's data warehouse found evidence of buying spikes on the first and fifteenth of each month, after which disposable money from paychecks and social security ran low.[75]

On Capitol Hill, reporters asked Culpepper if Scott's speech meant that the nation's largest company would now throw its weight behind a Democratic proposal to raise the minimum wage. But Wal-Mart's chief lobbyist, who had coordinated more than one successful GOP/business effort to thwart a minimum wage boost, choked on that one. His boss had been "misinterpreted," said Culpepper. Congress should merely study the issue. And there it rested: Wal-Mart's CEO remained on the record in favor of a minimum wage hike, but the company did nothing about it. When the Democrats proposed a minimum wage bill in June 2006, forty-two of the forty-six Republicans who voted to kill it had received campaign contributions from Wal-Mart. And the Retail Industry Leaders Association, the discount industry group of which Wal-Mart was the most powerful member, aggressively lobbied to defeat the minimum wage increase.[76] A minimum wage bill finally passed in 2007, but only after the Democrats had taken control of Congress and reached a deal with President Bush.

Scott and Culpepper were caught in a conundrum. Culpepper feared that if Wal-Mart broke ranks with other low-wage employers on the minimum wage, his old friends in the Restaurant Association and the U.S. Chamber of Commerce would prove unreliable allies the next time their immediate interests diverged from those of the home office in Bentonville. Indeed, there were retailers, including downscale Dollar General with more than eight thousand strip-mall stores, as well as the big fast-food chains, that actually paid less than Wal-Mart. For Scott, on the other hand, the politics of the minimum wage were intimately linked to the transformation of Wal-Mart from an opportunistic growth machine into a mature business whose future success seemed increasingly hobbled by the income stagnation that had become so chronic for the bottom two-thirds of the American consuming public. But with a raise in the wages of its own employees dismissed out of hand, Scott wanted the feds to rescue Wal-Mart from the consequences of the low-wage, low-consumption economy that the corporation had done so much to advance.

It was not a zero-sum game, however. Henry Ford used the enormous efficiencies generated by the deployment of the first automotive assembly line to double wages, slash turnover, and sell his Model T at prices affordable even for a tenant farmer. The quest for both high wages and low prices has been at the heart of America's domestic politics throughout much of the twentieth century. Indeed, during the Progressive era, the

New Deal, and in the first decades after World War II, workers and consumers found their interests closely aligned. They saw the relationship between wages and prices as a fundamentally public, political issue and not merely a dictate of corporate management or the interplay of market forces.[77] Thus, as late as 1960 retail wages stood at more than half those paid to auto workers, in large part because the new unions and the New Dealers had sought to equalize wages within and across firms and industries. But by 1983, after a decade of inflationary pressures had eroded so many working-class paychecks, overall retail wages had plunged to but one-third of that earned by union workers in manufacturing, and to about 60 percent of the income enjoyed by unionized grocery clerks in the big cities of the North and West. And this is just about where retail wages remain today, despite the considerable rise in overall productivity in the discount sector.[78]

Wal-Mart's hostility to a better-paid and healthier workforce is as much an issue of power as it is a question of prices and profits. High wages reduce turnover and awaken employee expectations, transforming the internal culture of the workplace. Decent wages lead to real careers and the expectation of fair treatment over a lifetime of employment. That in turn might well lead to demands for a steady work shift, an equitable chance at promotion, retirement pay, and even the opportunity to make one's voice heard in a collective fashion.

WAL-MARTIZATION WITHOUT WAL-MART

Wal-Mart has entered an era of midlife maturity that it heartily regrets but cannot escape. Growth has slowed. The stock price has gone nowhere for eight years; same-store sales inch up just a few percent a year, usually less than rivals like Target, Costco, Best Buy, and Walgreen's. The company has lost merchandising self-confidence: Should it move upscale with "cheap-chic" apparel, backed by a multipage advertising spread in *Vogue*? Or should the company fire its fashion buyers and get back to basics, an approach captured by the banner figuratively hoisted at a recent shareholders' meeting in Fayetteville: SAVING PEOPLE MONEY SO THEY CAN LIVE BETTER. Wal-Mart has done both, but neither has quite worked. "There are a lot of issues here, but what they add up to is the end of the age of Wal-Mart," contends Richard Hastings, a retail analyst. "The glory days are over."[79]

Wal-Mart's impasse is not a question of one growth strategy versus another, a different product mix, or even a new executive team. Rather, the company's maturity is a natural product of its very success. When Sam Walton died in 1992, his company operated almost all of its stores in just thirty states; it could still grow rapidly by simply building ever more stores and distribution centers in virgin territory while converting scores of old discount stores into the much larger and more profitable Supercenters.[80] But today, when growth of even a relatively modest 10 percent per year requires upwards of $35 billion in new sales, equal to the total revenue of Staples, Barnes & Noble, Starbucks, and Nordstrom, the task is far more difficult. Wal-Mart has begun to saturate its natural domestic market, controlling 20 percent of dry grocery, 29 percent of nonfood grocery, 30 percent of health and beauty aids, and 45 percent of general merchandise sales.

Add to this the outright opposition faced by the company, and stagnation is almost inevitable. In 2007 Wal-Mart abruptly slashed the number of U.S. stores it plans to open each year, from about 270 to 190.[81] That still comes to about 30 million square feet of new selling space per annum, but from the perspective of an institution the size of Wal-Mart that is tepid growth, ensuring that it has become at best a mature company, subject to all the vicissitudes of the U.S. business cycle.

Meanwhile, virtually every innovation and sales stratagem pioneered by Wal-Mart has been adopted, perfected, and deployed by its competitors. Every rival has learned how to manipulate the river of POS data pouring out of each cash register, organize an efficient supply chain, and take advantage of America's tattered labor laws and welfare system. Even Wal-Mart's John Fleming, the company's newly appointed chief merchandising officer, understands the situation: "We're now up against world-class competitors that are each taking a slice of our business."[82] Wal-Martization has triumphed, to Wal-Mart's consternation.

Take fast-rising Target Corporation, for example, the firm from which Wal-Mart recruited Fleming. This Minneapolis-headquartered company employs over 350,000 in the United States and abroad, and it operates more than 1,600 stores, supplied by thirty-one big distribution centers.[83] With $60 billion in 2007 sales, it stood at number 33 on the Fortune 500 list of large corporations. It gives more than 5 percent of pretax profits to philanthropic good causes, far higher than Bentonville. Target's stores are spaciously laid out and full of attractive displays, less messy than the typical Wal-Mart. Its style-conscious housewares and apparel have won for the company a customer base that is both more female than Wal-Mart and of a slightly higher income. Some loyal customers give to the company name a mock French pronunciation, "Tar-zhay."[84] Given this favorable aura, its stores have spread throughout metropolitan America, rarely subject to the kind of criticism and opposition that Wal-Mart routinely encounters.

But Target is in all other important respects a near clone of Wal-Mart. Its supply chain mimics that of its bigger rival, with a systematic squeeze on its vendors,[85] a procurement office in South China, and thousands of factories in low-wage countries like India, Indonesia, Guatemala, Bangladesh, Kenya, Vietnam, and Mexico. The wages and health-care benefits Target offers its "team members" are either identical to those of Wal-Mart or actually inferior. Target employs even more part-timers than Wal-Mart, and they don't get health insurance, so its turnover rate tracks that of other discount retailers. And as with its huge competitor, Target's hostility to unionism is uncompromising and its opposition to municipally mandated increases in wages and benefits just as adamant. "People ask what the difference between Wal-Mart and Target is," remarked a UFCW organizer. "Nothing, except that Wal-Mart is six times bigger."[86]

Over the past decade, other top competitors in most retailing specialties have adopted all or part of the same business model. They have squeezed their labor costs, remodeled stores, replaced warehouses with distribution centers, imported container ships full of goods from East Asia, and invested heavily in new technology to tie it all together. In California's Inland Empire every major retailer has erected a giant distribution center that feeds containerized imports from the Los Angeles/ Long Beach port complex to hundreds of smaller DCs and thousands of stores all across North America. Wal-Mart is there, of course, with a campus of four huge buildings—2.7 million square feet under roof—in Riverside County. In the city of Ontario, just a few miles to the east, is found the 1.7-million-square-foot DC put up by Kmart, now part of Sears Holdings. Pic 'N' Save in Rancho Cucamonga and Target in Fontana have distribution centers almost as large, likewise Costco, Pier 1 Imports, Staples, Home Depot, Mattel, and Skechers, the shoe chain.[87] When it comes to logistics, Wal-Mart's rivals have pretty much closed the enormous cost gap that once put them at such a competitive disadvantage with the Arkansas original.

One rival has followed a different road. The *New York Times* has labeled Costco "the anti-Wal-Mart." Costco is the Seattle-based warehouse/retailer whose FedMart and Price Club predecessors Sam Walton frequently acknowledged as the businesses that provided many of the ideas he later incorporated into his own retail operations.[88] But there was one big exception: Wal-Mart would have no truck with Costco's labor policies. The company pays veteran employees about five dollars an hour more than equally experienced workers at Wal-Mart, and it offers a generous health insurance plan that covers 85 percent of all employees. Naturally, its turnover is a third that of Wal-Mart and Target.

The company owes its character to Sol Price, the Jewish, New Deal Democrat whose social and cultural values were those of Depression-era New York. Price became a multimillionaire, but even in the era of Ronald Reagan, he favored increased taxes on high incomes, enhanced social welfare spending, and a confiscatory tax on wealth. He once remarked that in his entrepreneurial youth he still read the *Daily Worker* more than the *Wall Street Journal*.[89] Price wanted a world of customers and employees far different from that of Sam Walton. They were neither small-town ex-farmers nor struggling suburbanites. Instead Price's people belonged to that secure middle strata who had been given a leg up by the institutions and programs of the New Deal and the Keynesian welfare state. In his early years in Southern California Price sold only to those with steady jobs and good credit: aside from licensed businessmen, he sold club "memberships" exclusively to unionists, federal employees, schoolteachers, hospital and utility workers, and people who had joined credit unions. The company soon generated a bicoastal reputation for low-cost, high-volume quality, so customers spent about 50 percent more on each shopping visit than the clientele of other big-box retailers.[90]

So is Costco the "high road" alternative to Wal-Mart and all the other retailers that ape the Bentonville giant? Despite some Wall Street grumbling that the company's high wages and exceptionally low prices mean that "shareholders get the short end of the stick," Costco is booming. It is the fourth-largest retailer in America, earns a $1 billion profit each year, and has a stock price that has quadrupled during the last decade. It operates about five hundred warehouse stores, and each sells far more than the typical Sam's Club. Indeed, with few stores in the Midwest and none in the Deep South, Costco is definitely a blue-state phenomenon. Its executives donate to the Democrats and bargain with the Teamsters, whose contracts set the wage-and-benefit standard for most Costco workers, organized or not. Following a recent contract ratification, CEO Jim Sinegal, a Price protégé from the warehouse club's earliest days, remarked with satisfaction that his company's workers are "entitled to buy homes and live in reasonably nice neighborhoods and send their children to school." At the time, Sinegal was one of the lowest-paid executives in retail, making but a tenth of the income garnered by the CEOs at Wal-Mart, Target, and Home Depot.[91]

"We pay much better than Wal-Mart," says CEO Sinegal. "That's not altruism. It is good business." The company saves a lot of money on turnover costs: at least three thousand dollars a year to recruit, interview, test, and train a new hire. More important, Costco's well-compensated employees "fit" the upscale clientele—average family income more than one hundred thousand dollars a year—upon which the company is dependent. Customers spend a lot of money every time they shop, which means that as a percentage of sales Costco's labor and overhead costs are much lower than those at Wal-Mart's Sam's Club.

Why can't other retailers follow in Costco's footsteps? Sam's Club executives claim that the West Coast discount pioneer is really a niche player, whose limited selection of quality food, appliances, and clothing make it possible and necessary for Costco to offer better pay and benefits. But that does not mean that Costco is some boutique immune from the cost-cutting revolution that has transformed big-box retailing. Costco is just as manipulative and arrogant when it comes to winning tax subsidies and zoning variances for its big stores, building "the redevelopment game into the basic economics of its business," according to California planning experts. Likewise, it is just as tough as Wal-Mart when it comes to wringing every last advantage out of its supply chain. When Starbucks once failed to pass on a drop in the price of its beans, Sinegal threatened to banish the longtime coffee vendor from his stores. "Who do you think you are? The price police?" asked Starbucks CEO Howard Schultz, before conceding the point.[92] And Costco personnel policies are not always the opposite of those at Wal-Mart. It is being sued for failure to promote women into managerial ranks in a class-action lawsuit that parallels that of *Dukes v. Wal-Mart*. Moreover, Costco wants to shave its workers' comp expenses just as much as Bentonville, which is why it pressured its own employees to help California governor Arnold Schwarzenegger secure the signatures necessary to put an initiative slashing workers' compensation payouts on the 2004 California ballot.[93]

But Sinegal and the rest of his management team retain an otherwise liberal outlook because they have no alternative. Sol Price saddled Costco with fifty-six unionized warehouses, which now employ about 15 percent of all employees, mainly in California and the Northeast. Virtually no other Costco "warehouses" are unionized, a situation that suits Sinegal just fine. But this union minority has had a dramatic impact on the rest of the company. They are represented by a group of aggressive Teamster locals whose contracts with the company set the wage-and-benefit standards for everyone.[94] Costco management mimics the key provisions in its "Employee Agreement," which delineates benefits, compensation, wages, disciplinary procedures, paid holidays, bonuses, and seniority. It's as if the ghost of the New Deal has reached forward and put its impress upon a company that otherwise might well succumb to the same labor-cost-slashing pressures as Target or Sam's Club.

THE FUTURE

Many an analysis of the big-box phenomenon ends with a sort of mea culpa. If Americans were not so devoted to their cheap imports, their convenient shopping, if they were not so cavalier about purchasing things at stores that exploited workers and ruined the neighborhood, then we would be willing to pay the price or change our lifestyle to reform the system. In other words, consumers, middle-class shoppers especially, are just plain selfish.

Not so. There is nothing wrong with having a bunch of inexpensive stuff to fill up the living room, the kitchen, and the refrigerator. Among its other definitions, "freedom" means an escape from necessity, so having an abundance of material goods empowers people far more than it suffocates or satiates them. Wal-Mart's retail revolution has made it possible for hundreds of millions of people around the world to buy the necessities of life far more cheaply than ever before. The realm of "distribution" no longer constitutes the uncharted and precarious economic continent about which Peter Drucker once wrote; it has been globalized, computerized, and occupies the strategic center of our economic life.

The retail revolution was a lot more than bar codes and satellite uplinks, good roads, powerful trucks, and distribution center conveyor belts. Walton's success was also connected to the rightward shift in politics, social policy, and culture. Wal-Mart's era of enormous growth coincided with the rise to power and influence of Ronald Reagan, Milton Friedman, Jerry Falwell, Newt Gingrich, Bill Clinton, and the Bushes, father and son. These were the years of a global free trade unfettered by any social or environmental constraints, stagnation in the living standards for most American families, the rise of both evangelical Protestantism and a post–Cold War triumphalism in the United States, and the destruction of both trade union power and much of America's manufacturing economy.

Although the retail revolution has brought us cheap goods, it has also generated risk and insecurity for millions, both at home and abroad. During their heyday, manufacturers thought economic efficiency and profitable operation demanded long production runs, standardized products, and steady employment. Government policy, trade union clout, and business school scholarship encouraged stable business relationships and lifetime careers, even for hourly workers. High wages and pensions were all part of the bargain. But the big-box retailers have thrived on risk and instability, for their employees and suppliers, if not for those at the corporate headquarters. They churn their workforce, whipsaw their vendors, and have turned retirement pay and health provision into a financial lottery for millions of workers. The forty-hour workweek hardly exists; for salaried managers and professionals, lean staffing on the sales floor has kept them on the job for many an extra hour, even as hourly workers find that their schedules and pay track the unpredictable ebb and flow of the customer stream.

All this was exacerbated by the sharp recession that began in 2008. Retail sales took their biggest nosedive in thirty-nine years, with department stores, apparel shops, and luxury emporiums posting the worst results. Circuit City, Mervyn's, Linens 'n Things, and Whitehall Jewelers went bankrupt, while Bon-Ton Stores, Dillard's, Talbots, Pier 1, Cost Plus, Eddie Bauer, and Rite Aid lost upwards of 90 percent of their stock value.[95] Wal-Mart-style health insurance, with its high deductibles, numerous out-of-pocket costs, and low monthly premium, spread from retail to well-established companies like Nissan and Delta Airlines, where it became the single take-it-or-leave-it option when it came to company-provided medical coverage.[96]

In this dismal economy, millions of shoppers traded down, so Wal-Mart held its own, with respectable sales increases posted at most stores and a bump in the stock price. "This is Wal-Mart time," said H. Lee Scott to a meeting of analysts and investors. "This is the kind of environment that Sam Walton built this company for."[97] And as in the impoverished, rural Arkansas of the company's early days, many Americans were now desperate to make ends meet. Thus the search for Wal-Mart bargains generated an early morning frenzy on Black Friday, the post-Thanksgiving sell-a-thon, when eager crowds literally broke down the entrance doors at some stores, and at Valley Stream, New York, actually trampled a company employee to death.

But if this was an economy that enabled Wal-Mart to forge ahead of the retail competition, these Depression-like conditions were obviously untenable, for the company as well as the nation. Wal-Mart executives knew this as well: the company scaled back its construction of new stores in the United States and looked abroad for new customers, stores, and acquisitions, a strategy ratified by the selection of Michael Duke as the Wal-Mart executive who would succeed H. Lee Scott as CEO. Duke, who had moved up through corporate logistics after leaving Federated Department Stores in 1995, became responsible for all of Wal-Mart's international operations in the new century. Duke forecast that Wal-Mart would devote more than half of its international spending to new markets like Brazil and India, up from a third in the previous five years. In China, Wal-Mart planned to double the number of new stores within five years, while it searched for retail partners in Russia and eastern Europe.[98]

But Wal-Mart's greatest challenge, as always, lay not in the realm of economics but in that of politics. The financial crisis, the recession, and the newfound power of the Democrats in

November 2008 have shifted the nation toward policies that envision a far more active role for government and a transformation and regulation of many business practices. The administration of Barack Obama is certain to adopt policies and push for legislation that will have an immediate impact on the Wal-Mart business model. A rise in the minimum wage and a crackdown on corporate violations of the wage and hour law will raise labor costs at Wal-Mart and thereby reduce its competitive advantage over other retailers and grocers. Even more important, the Obama administration's determination to finally do something about health insurance will have a radical impact not only on the lives of low-wage workers but on the businesses that employ them. Wal-Mart, long seeking to shift the health insurance burden elsewhere, has applauded any federal effort to expand government-subsidized programs. But the company has also been adamantly hostile to liberal Democratic initiatives that might require big businesses to bear a portion of the cost per employee or that set standards for the health insurance such businesses offer, limiting for example, the high deductibles that are a Wal-Mart favorite. Should Wal-Mart lose this battle, the three-dollars-per-hour labor-cost advantage it now enjoys over unionized grocery chains will largely disappear.

Wal-Mart and the rest of the retail industry are ready to bargain with Obama and the Democrats when it comes to finding an acceptable health insurance scheme. But when it comes to reform of the labor law that makes unionization possible, Wal-Mart and its business allies are intransigent. "We like driving the car," H. Lee Scott told a business audience, "and we are not going to give the steering wheel to anybody but us."[99] Scott feared what Obama and most Democrats support: the Employee Free Choice Act, which would enable the NLRB to certify a trade union and mandate collective bargaining when a majority of all employees have simply signed a card indicating their adherence to the union. This would enable unionists at Wal-Mart and elsewhere to circumvent the corporate propaganda onslaught that routinely accompanies a months-long, employer-dominated election campaign. With "card-check," Wal-Mart would have less opportunity to deploy its infamous home office labor team or to make use of its anti-union videos, captive audience meetings, and transfer or firing of pro-union workers in the days leading up to an NLRB election. Prospects for passage of this labor law reform seem uncertain, but whatever its chances the political environment has clearly shifted away from that to which two generations of Wal-Mart executives had become attuned.

The era of global laissez-faire and conservative governance is also on the wane. In much of Latin America and in East Asia, politics are shifting to the left. Globalization will continue, but in a reformed fashion that reshapes the supply chains that now hold much of the world economy together. Like Taiwan and South Korea two decades before, China is now in the midst of the kind of social turmoil that promises to boost wages, enhance citizenship rights, and make working conditions tolerable for millions of workers.[100] This not only will raise the prices of the toys and T-shirts that end up on the shelves of thousands of American and European big-box stores, but it may also force Wal-Mart and its vendors and subcontractors to recognize that the global reservoir of super-exploitable labor is vanishing and won't soon be replaced. A rise in Asian wages and world fuel costs is beginning to make it economical for companies to shorten their supply chains and manufacture locally many items once produced abroad.[101]

If this is our future, then companies like Wal-Mart will have to conform to a new set of social and political imperatives or find themselves on their own downward spiral, consigned to a shrunken and ghettoized portion of the retail economy. Perhaps the Wal-Marts of the world will change. As Sam Walton himself once put it, "constant change is a vital part of the

Wal-Mart culture itself. In fact one of the greatest strengths of Wal-Mart's ingrained culture is its ability to drop everything and turn on a dime."[102]

It has happened before. Dominant corporations have been forced to radically transform their business practices, sometimes prodded by public sentiment and customer preference, at other moments by an activist government and the unions it helped empower. Before the passage of antitrust legislation, muckraking journalists put John D. Rockefeller's Standard Oil on notice that it would have to curb its predatory pricing strategy. U.S. Steel was forced to abandon the punishing twelve-hour-day in 1924 after clergy, reformers, and Commerce Secretary Herbert Hoover lobbied the autocrats who ran America's largest company. In the 1930s and 1940s the unions not only raised wages but ended the reign of the autocratic foreman on the assembly lines and in the mills of that era. IBM put its entire blue-collar workforce on salary in 1959 to avoid unionization in an era when organized labor seemed to be winning a guaranteed annual wage for factory workers. In the civil rights era and after, corporations enshrined "diversity" as a core principle in their hiring and promotion practices. And on the environmental front, public hostility and new government regulations brought a halt to the construction of nuclear power plants in the United States, while making almost every oil and chemical company spend real money in the search for products and processes that were both clean and green.

So Wal-Mart and its clones face a day of reckoning. Their relentless growth and Darwinian competitiveness have created a world that is increasingly inhospitable to their own success and to the well-being of countless people who make, sell, or buy the products that line their shelves. It is not just that the political winds are shifting against them. Rather, their own success and the future of the people who live in the conditions they have created now depend upon a revitalization of all those

twentieth-century institutions of economic regulation and social responsibility that Wal-Mart has fought against for so long
and with such energy. On the agenda is not so much a struggle
specifically against Wal-Mart, although that is well under way.
In the end, it is Sam's world, the one in which people are compelled to live under economic and psychological duress, that
needs to change. The contest ahead will determine not only the
fate of America's largest company but that of the rest of us as
well.

AFTERWORD

American consumers have failed to do their duty in recent years. Their reluctance to shop, spend, and max out the credit cards made 2008 and 2009 the most dismal retail sales experience in forty years, with department stores, apparel shops, and luxury emporiums posting the worst results. Thousands of stores, perhaps as many as 75,000, closed their doors in 2009.

In this horrible economy, one company did just fine. Wal-Mart, the nation's largest employer, posted healthy sales and a stock price that held up quite well throughout the long recession. "My dad built Walmart for these times," boasted Rob Walton, who serves as chairman of the company's board of directors.[1] Consumers were trading down, looking for bargains.[2] As in the impoverished, rural Arkansas of the company's founding days, many Americans were now desperate to make ends meet. An internal company survey found that the proportion of customers who thought that "Wal-Mart saves me money so I can do more for my family" jumped from 49 percent in 2006 to 71 percent in 2009.[3] Corporate income was $405 billion in 2009, putting Wal-Mart at the number-two spot on *Fortune* magazine's list of the nation's five hundred largest companies.

So Wal-Mart is still on top at the checkout counter. Although every other major retailer has adopted some version of the Wal-Mart system—sophisticated logistics, just-in-time inventory controls, massive imports from Central America and China, plus low wages and skimpy benefits—the Bentonville-headquartered giant still holds a competitive advantage. Despite a temptation to go upscale—the company actually took out a ten-page advertising spread in *Vogue* a few years ago—Wal-Mart has kept its eye on the nation's downscale consumer market, a massive demographic created by a decade of income stagnation and one which seems destined to shed few households as the job-destroying impact of the Great Recession that began in late 2007 continues to plague the nation.

But if the recession has given Wal-Mart an unforeseen boost, what about the political aftershocks that still reverberate from the Democratic tide that swept Barack Obama into the White House and Democratic majorities into both houses of Congress? The retail revolution pioneered by Wal-Mart has always been based on a lot more than bar codes and satellite uplinks, good roads, powerful trucks, and distribution center wizardry. Founder Sam Walton linked his company's fortunes to the rightward shift in U.S. politics, social policy, and culture. Wal-Mart's era of enormous growth coincided with the rise to power and influence of Ronald Reagan, Milton Friedman, Jerry Falwell, Newt Gingrich, Bill Clinton, and the Bushes, father and son. These were the years of global free trade unfettered by any social or environmental constraints, a minimum wage that shrank by a third from its 1968 high, the rise of evangelical Protestant-ism—to which the company linked its distinctive work culture—and the destruction of both trade union power and much of American manufacturing capacity.

In this environment, Wal-Mart and the rest of the big box retailers have thrived on the risk and instability that has been foisted onto their employees and suppliers. They churn their workforce, whipsaw their vendors, and have turned retirement pay and health provisions into a financial lottery for millions of workers. The forty-hour work week hardly exists because the retail economy relies on millions of part-time workers. Indeed, at Wal-Mart hourly workers often found their lunch breaks and overtime pay stolen by hard-pressed store managers determined to make their labor budget hit the target generated by Bentonville's computers.

If this is our future, then the stakes are huge. The company employs more than 1.4 million workers in the United States, more than any other entity except the federal government. And the retail/restaurant/hospitality sector, which has increasingly adopted so many of the employment innovations advanced by Wal-Mart, now employs upward of 27 million workers, far more than in mining, agriculture, manufacturing, and construction, the "goods producing" industries that once constituted the core of the U.S. economy.[4]

But now the political environment seems to be turning against the Wal-Mart business model, whatever its sales success in the Great Recession. With the election of Barack Obama, a new generation of legislators and reformers has come into power determined to regulate the market, raise working-class incomes, and protect employees from the unfettered exercise of managerial authority. Wal-Mart's own surveys show that about 10 percent of all Americans refuse to shop there for essentially political reasons, and the company has been stymied in its effort to put a new generation of supercenters in coastal California, in Chicago, and in liberal cities like Boston, Washington, and New York.

Thus the company is looking abroad for new customers, a strategy ratified by the selection of Michael Duke to succeed H. Lee Scott as Wal-Mart CEO. Duke, who had been responsible for all of Wal-Mart's international operations, is gambling that even in today's unstable world economy, the company can find an increasingly larger proportion of its sales abroad. Duke therefore forecasts that Wal-Mart will devote more than half of its international spending to new markets like Brazil and India. In China, Wal-Mart has plans to double the number of new stores within five years, while it also searches for retail partners in Russia and Eastern Europe.[5]

However, the company can hardly abandon North America. Nor has it chosen to adopt a bunker mentality when it comes to most issues in U.S. politics and social policy. Wal-Mart executives have indeed chosen to hang tough on labor and liberal efforts to reform America's basic labor law. Along with virtually every other large company and business association, not to mention the Republican Party and many red-state Democrats, Wal-Mart has successfully stymied liberal efforts to advance the Employee Free Choice Act, which would enable the National Labor Relations Board to certify a trade union and mandate collective bargaining when a majority of all employees have simply signed a card indicating their adherence to the union. This would enable unionists at Wal-Mart and elsewhere to circumvent the corporate propaganda onslaught that routinely accompanies a months-long, employer-dominated election campaign. Although Wal-Mart has some dealings with trade unions in countries such as Mexico, Argentina, and China, where the government deploys a heavy hand in control of a single, official union, no such arrangement seems in the offing in North America, even in those Canadian provinces where EFCA-like laws are now in effect. There Wal-Mart stalls, litigates, and where necessary, closes stores that have gone union. Should a meaningful reform of the American labor law make progress in the U.S. Congress—and this is a daunting prospect—it seems certain that Wal-Mart will fight it with all the political, organizational, and propagandistic resources at its command.

But Wal-Mart has chosen to make a strategic retreat on other government regulations that impact the way the company does business. In the latter category are the state wage and hours laws that the company has long subverted, if only because store managers have been under such intense pressure to shave labor costs so as to ensure their own sizable end-of-the-year bonus. The violations have been rampant and systematic. Thus a Minnesota judge cited the company for more than two million infractions when he delivered a 2008 judgment covering just his state. The lawbreaking was all but encouraged by the Bush-era Labor Department, which boasted that it devoted 13 percent fewer hours to enforcement of the wage and hour laws in 2007 than in 2002.[6] Not unexpectedly, workers, lawyers, and unions stopped looking to the government for justice. Instead they filed a barrage of class-action lawsuits against Wal-Mart, a total of seventy-six as of December 2008. The company fought them all, appealing the losses and boasting of its victories, no matter how partial.

But with Obama's choice of Hilda Solis as Secretary of Labor, Wal-Mart's intransigence threatened to become an embarrassing liability. The Labor Department does not have all that much policy clout in the Obama Administration, but it can enforce existing law, and Solis, a pro-union Latina congresswomen from Southern California, has made it clear that she will do just that. "There is a new sheriff in town," Solis told cheering unionists shortly after her confirmation by the Senate. She soon shifted money and personnel to the numerous employer illegalities that have generated a pervasive culture of wage theft among thousands of firms in the American service sector.[7]

Wal-Mart quickly recognized that an era of political indulgence and regulatory neglect had come to an end, so on December 23, 2008 the company announced that it was resolving sixty-three wage-and-hour lawsuits in forty-two states to settle accusations that it forced employees to skip lunch breaks, work off the clock, and sidestep overtime laws. The cost: somewhere between $352 and $640 million, depending on the number of plaintiffs that can be found covered by each lawsuit.[8] Wal-Mart accompanied the announcement with a pledge to install electronic monitors on cash resisters, computers, and other tools to precisely record hours of actual work and adherence to legally mandated breaks. Not all the suits were settled, however, most notably the giant *Dukes v. Wal-Mart* gender discrimination class-action lawsuit, which sought not just monetary compensation for more than a million women, but a fundamental reform of the company's entire system of promotion and pay.

Wal-Mart did not trumpet its about-face on these wage and hour law cases, but it has loudly advertised its efforts to become the world's largest and most environmentally friendly company. Late in 2008 Wal-Mart began to rebrand all its stores with a new logo that dropped the hyphen/star, instead offering the rounded, lowercase "Walmart," followed by an asterisk-like design that resembles either a flower or a yellow sunburst. Image aside, Wal-Mart executives announced the next year that the company would create a Sustainability Index, which green activists soon dubbed "The Walmart Index," much to the company's satisfaction. To create this universal sustainability rating system for products sold in Wal-Mart stores, the company is "asking" tens of thousands of supplier firms to survey their energy consumption, waste production, greenhouse gas emissions, water use, and other environmentally measurable activities and send the information to Bentonville. Wal-Mart will then use its famed technological prowess to measure the environmental competence of thousands of suppliers and then display the results on every product it carries. One can be certain that manufacturers who long remain on the bottom of the index will soon be looking for a new retailer to sell their products. This Wal-Mart initiative is a significant innovation, a massive effort to ameliorate and regulate the environmental impact of a supply chain involving thousands of factories and millions of workers on every continent. But it is also classic Wal-Mart: use the company's tremendous buying power to foist as many costs as possible onto its vendors, discard those who fail to measure up, and then take credit for the low prices, or in this case for the environmental friendliness of the product when it finally gets to a Wal-Mart retail shelf.[9]

Wal-Mart also surprised its critics on the health insurance front. Wal-Mart has long known that its skimpy health insurance offerings were an embarrassment to the company and a ready target for its critics. Even after the company opened its health insurance rolls to new hires and offered its employees a variety of low-premium plans, it managed to boost the proportion of its employees who signed up for one of the company's own health insurance plans by just 5 points, to just under 52 percent of all employees. Wal-Mart has often claimed that more than 90 percent of all employees were covered by some form of health insurance, but this seemed merely to confirm that either the federal government or some other employer was actually paying for the health insurance that America's largest company had failed to make affordable for its own employees. Thus even before the Democrats had the White House in their sights, Wal-Mart executives were telling the press that America's health care mess could only be solved by government action.

When the Democrats took over in 2008, Wal-Mart hired its share of them. The company, which spent $6.6 million on governmental affairs in 2008, up from $4 million in 2007, added two lobbyists with Democratic histories to its Washington team. Jason Hill, who worked on health care issues for Democratic Senator Carl Levin of Michigan, became a point man for Bentonville as the health care debate heated up in early 2009. Likewise, Wal-Mart also hired Bruce Harris, a policy adviser for House Democrats on energy policy, who became the company's director of federal relations for sustainability issues, a new position. Neither Hill nor Harris had much real clout, but they were indicative of the company's new determination to be a player when it came to the Obama agenda. Lee Culpepper, the conservative, Georgia-born lobbyist who had given the Wal-Mart government affairs operation new influence, was kicked upstairs to Bentonville, and replaced as de facto head of the Washington office by Leslie Dach, the Yale-educated New Yorker and one-time Democratic Party presidential campaign strategist who was now an executive vice president of the company. Dach's rise signified Wal-Mart's determination to put its best foot forward when it came to mollifying some of the company's blue-state critics.

This put the company at cross-purposes not only with its traditional allies in the Republican Party, but also with other business lobbies in the capital, especially the Chamber of Commerce and the National Retail Federation, both of which were in sync with an increasingly intransigent GOP. Wal-Mart's Linda Dillman, whose transfer from head of company technology to executive vice president in charge of benefits signified just how important this human resources job had become, told reporters on Capitol Hill, "We're willing to take a stand independently and not just do it through our associations."[10]

That independence shocked other business lobbyists late in June 2009 when Wal-Mart president Michael Duke joined with trade union leader Andrew Stern and John Poseda of the liberal Center for American Progress to send a letter to the White House endorsing one of the key ideas advanced by liberal Democrats in the health care legislative fight. This was the employer mandate, which would require that all large corporations either provide health insurance or pay a mandated fee—$750 was then the ballpark figure—to the government for every employee who was not covered. This "pay or play" plan put Wal-Mart on the side of the unions and the liberals, but it immediately evoked a virtual declaration of war from the National Retail Association, whose officers reported themselves "flabbergasted" at what they considered Wal-Mart's "catastrophic" endorsement of a government mandate that most retailers, once including

Wal-Mart, have long considered anathema. The retail lobbying group labeled the Wal-Mart initiative a "job killer" and
"quite possibly the most unwelcome development to date of the
health care reform debate for us."[11] The sense of betrayal carried over to the Chamber of Commerce, whose senior manager
for health care policy denounced the Wal-Mart initiative as
"the worst incarnation" of the mandate idea, "the most dangerous policy."[12]

Wal-Mart's big switch was based on the same kind of calculation it had made when it decided to settle many of the wage
and hour lawsuits that had been hanging fire and damaging its
reputation. Company executives calculated, first, that the across-
the-board imposition of an employer mandate would actually
"level the playing field" in the retail sector and thereby reduce
the competitive advantage enjoyed by some of Wal-Mart's regional rivals whose health insurance benefits were now less generous than those of the mega retailer.[13] And second, Bentonville
executives strategized that even if Wal-Mart did incur additional health benefit costs, these would be more than made up
as the company enhanced its reputation and as it became an
inside player in the epic legislative negotiations that ultimately
framed the law whose impact on low-wage, low-benefit employers was so enormously consequential.

The *Wall Street Journal* concurred. Under the July 2009
headline "Retailer's Image Moves from Demon to Darling,"
reporter Ann Zimmerman marveled at Wal-Mart's "stunning
metamorphosis," which took it "from whipping boy of the political left to corporate leviathan now welcomed with open
arms by a Democratic White House."[14] Indeed, Michael Duke
was soon among the handful of friendly executives President
Obama invited to lunch just a week later.[15] That fall, when most
of the key provisions in the health care bill had been put in
place, Leslie Dach looked back with satisfaction. The new respect Wal-Mart had earned from politicians "has enabled us to

continue to be part of this debate in a far more effective way than we have ever been on the sidelines."[16]

· But Wal-Mart is hardly out of the political or economic woods. It is today a mature company that can no longer grow at a pace much greater than that of the entire U.S. economy. Because big city municipal governments and union-backed civic organizations have been so successful in blocking Wal-Mart from entering many of the most lucrative markets in the United States, the company has slashed by a third the number of stores it opens in the United States each year and by more than half the additional square footage these new stores represent. Instead, Wal-Mart has inaugurated an ambitious program of store renovation and remodeling that will make the shopping experience a more pleasant one for the customer and probably more lucrative for the company.[17] Good merchandising, but hardly expected to make the company grow on par with the exciting, transformative era when Wal-Mart was increasing revenue by 40 percent a year.

The company has inadvertently broadcast its predicament to tens of millions of Americans. In one of its most recent advertisements, Wal-Mart boasts, "In today's economy, nobody's more committed to helping family budgets go further than Walmart. Walmart saves the average family about $3,100 a year, no matter where they shop. Save money. Live better. Walmart."[18]

What can this possibly mean? "No matter where they shop." Wal-Mart's claim that the average family saves $3,100 a year is based upon a study that Wal-Mart commissioned from the economic research firm Global Insight. Its report concluded that if one takes 1985 as a baseline, then Wal-Mart's remarkable innovations in logistics, its famous squeeze on vendors and manufactures, and the downward pressures it exerts on the prices charged by competitors have led, over a twenty-two-year period, to a 3.6 percent decline in U.S. consumer prices as measured by the government. This does not sound like much, but in a multitrillion dollar economy it comes to real money, and if you do the arithmetic, it is $3,100 per family.[19]

This is indeed something to celebrate. Food, clothing, electronics, and appliances: they all cost less than before the retail revolution. Unfortunately for Wal-Mart, this price decline has hardly been confined to the Bentonville-based merchant. It has seeped into every nook and cranny of the retail economy. Target, Kroger, Sears, and most other retailers have appropriated Wal-Mart's innovations. Just as every auto company soon installed a version of the assembly line first deployed by Henry Ford, so too have the Wal-Mart innovations become standard operating procedure in retail. Wal-Mart may still sell some products at a price lower than its competitors, but the difference is not radical and it is likely to shrink as these retail rivals figure out how Wal-Mart does it.

If Wal-Mart is losing its competitive edge at home, so too is the giant retailer facing new challenges throughout its famed supply chain, where an era of global laissez-faire and rock-bottom labor costs may well be on the wane. For the better part of a decade, the world economy has been dominated by a symbiotic relationship between export-led development in China and overconsumption in the United States. Niall Ferguson and other commentators have taken to labeling this embrocated relationship "Chimerica."[20] To keep the yuan (and hence Chinese exports) competitive, authorities in Beijing consistently intervened to halt the appreciation of their own currency against the dollar. The result was a vast accumulation of dollar-denominated securities in the reserves of the People's Bank of China. Had it not been for the Chinese willingness to fund America's borrowing habit this way, interest rates and inflation in the United States would have been substantially higher, making it far more difficult for Wal-Mart and the other big-box retailers to brag so loudly that they had kept prices in check and saved American consumers so much money.

But the Great Recession of 2007–2009 has generated a severe crisis in an economic partnership that has been so vital to the Wal-Mart business model. Big-box imports from China have declined sharply in the last two years, likewise the propensity of the Chinese government to artificially undervalue its currency and thereby subsidize U.S. consumer demand. Because China is recovering from the global recession far more rapidly than the United States, China's revaluation of its currency, to the detriment of the dollar, is certain. This will make Chinese-made toys, clothing, shoes, and electronics more expensive for both American retailers and their consumers.

Meanwhile, coastal China, which anchors the supply chains upon which the Wal-Marts of the world depend, is now in the midst of the kind of chronic social turmoil that promises to boost wages, enhance citizenship rights, and make working conditions tolerable for tens of millions of workers.[21] While some production will undoubtedly shift to Vietnam, Bangladesh, and other low-wage counties, China is so big and so productive that it is unlikely to be replaced as the twenty-first-century workshop of the world. Combined with the revaluation of the yuan, these upward wage pressures will increase the prices of all the goods that end up on the shelves of thousands of American and European big-box stores. These social and financial transformations reshaping China will also force Wal-Mart and its vendors to recognize that the global reservoir of super-exploitable labor is vanishing and won't soon be replaced. The greater attention that the Obama administration is placing on labor and environmental standards in its trade diplomacy indicates that the construction of a global New Deal, with higher labor standards and protections, is no longer a leftist pipe dream. Under such conditions, it may even become economical for companies to on-shore the production of many items once purchased abroad.[22]

If this is the world of our future, then companies like Wal-Mart will be forced to purge themselves of their cheap-labor ethos. "Constant change is a vital part of the Wal-Mart culture," Sam Walton once remarked. "In fact one of the greatest strengths of Wal-Mart's ingrained culture is its ability to drop everything and turn on a dime."[23] It might happen.

NOTES

INTRODUCTION

1. Jeff Glasser, "Boomtown, U.S.A.," *U.S. News and World Report*, June 25, 2001, 17–20; Anne D'Innocenzio, "Wal-Mart Suppliers Flocking to Arkansas," *State* (Columbia, S.C.), September 21, 2003; author's interview with anonymous Bentonville resident, April 29, 2005, Bentonville, Ark.
2. Joseph Y. S. Cheng, *Guangdong: Preparing for the WTO Challenge* (Hong Kong: Chinese University Press, 2003); Michael Enright, Edith Scott, and Ka-mun Chang, *Regional Powerhouse: The Greater Pearl River Delta and the Rise of China* (Singapore: John Wiley, 2005); latest GDP figures taken from Olivia Chung, "China's Richest Province Wants More," *China Business*, November 27, 2007.
3. Thomas A. Stewart, "A New 500 for the New Economy," *Fortune*, May 15, 1995, 166–67.
4. Retail and manufacturing employment data taken from 2008 Bureau of Labor Statistics Web page at http://www.bls.gov/; Exxon Mobil employment data from http://www.exxonmobil.com.
5. Peter Drucker, *The Concept of the Corporation*, 2nd ed. (New York: John Day, 1972), 12, 149.
6. Glenn R. Pascall, "It's a Wal-Mart World, and Boeing Isn't Immune," *Puget Sound Business Journal*, July 24, 2003.
7. Brooks Blevins, *Hill Folks: A History of Arkansas Ozarkers and Their Image* (Chapel Hill: University of North Carolina Press, 2002), 147–78; Ben Johnson, *Arkansas in Modern America, 1930–1999* (Fayetteville: University of Arkansas Press, 2000), 200–202.
8. Bob Ortega, *In Sam We Trust: The Untold Story of Sam Walton and How Wal-Mart Is Devouring America* (New York: Random House, 1998), 86–90; see also the revealing Sandra Vance and Roy Scott, *Wal-Mart: A History of Sam Walton's Retail Phenomenon* (New York: Twayne, 1994), 44–47.

9. Wal-Mart Stores, Inc., *1980 Annual Report*, 29.
10. Jared Bernstein and Isaac Shapiro, "Nine Years of Neglect: Federal Minimum Wage Remains Unchanged for Ninth Straight Year; Falls to Lowest Level in More than Half a Century," *Economic Policy Institute*, August 31, 2006, 6, at http://www.epi.org/issuebriefs/227.
11. The Wal-Mart public relations offensive has not just targeted a mass audience of potential consumers but seeks to influence opinion-making liberals and intellectuals as well. Thus the company has become a sponsor of National Public Radio, and in April 2005 it published an open letter to readers of the *New York Review of Books*, "Wal-Mart's Impact on Society: A Key Moment in Time for American Capitalism."
12. The best statement of Wal-Mart's view is offered by CEO H. Lee Scott, "Wal-Mart and California: A Key Moment in Time for American Capitalism," speech at Los Angeles Town Hall, February 23, 2005, at http://www.walmartfacts.com.

CHAPTER ONE: SAM WALTON'S WORLD

1. C. H. Wilson, "The Economic Decline of the Netherlands," *Economic History Review* 9, no. 2 (May 1939), 112.
2. Glenn Porter and Harold Livesay, *Merchants and Manufacturers: Studies in the Changing Structure of Nineteenth-Century Marketing* (Chicago: Ivan R. Dee, 1971), 29–34.
3. Sven Beckert, "Merchants and Manufacturers in the Antebellum North," in *Ruling America: A History of Wealth and Power in a Democracy*, ed. Steve Fraser and Gary Gerstle (Cambridge: Harvard University Press, 2005), 116–17.
4. Gary Fields, *Territories of Profit: Communications, Capitalist Development, and the Innovative Enterprises of G. F. Swift and Dell Computer* (Stanford, Calif.: Stanford University Press, 2004), 91–135 passim.
5. Susan Strasser, *Satisfaction Guaranteed: The Making of the American Mass Market* (Washington: Smithsonian Books, 1989), 78–79.
6. Ibid., 81.
7. Alfred Chandler Jr., *Strategy and Structure: Chapters in the History of American Industrial Enterprise* (Garden City, N.Y.: Doubleday, 1962), 158–99 passim; Louis Galambos and Joseph Pratt, *The Rise of the Corporate Commonwealth* (New York: Basic Books, 1988), 167–69.
8. See Richard S. Tedlow, *New and Improved: The Story of Mass Mar-

keting in America (New York: Basic Books, 1990), for studies of Coca-Cola, Sears, A&P, and the automobile companies.

9. Strasser, *Satisfaction Guaranteed*, 207–10.
10. Tedlow, *New and Improved*, 270–77.
11. Charles Silberman, "The Department Stores Are Waking Up," *Fortune*, August 1962.
12. Donald Katz, *The Big Store: Inside the Crisis and Revolution at Sears* (New York: Viking, 1987); John Koten, "Upheaval in Middle Class Market Forces Changes in Selling Strategies," *Wall Street Journal*, March 13, 1987.
13. Jean Maddern Pitrone, *F. W. Woolworth and the American Five and Dime: A Social History* (Jefferson, N.C.: McFarland, 2003), 71–80.
14. Sandra S. Vance and Roy V. Scott, "Butler Brothers and the Rise and Decline of the Ben Franklin Variety Stores: A Study in Franchise Retailing," *Essays in Economic and Business History* 11 (1993), 259–61.
15. Sam Walton with John Huey, *Made In America: My Story* (New York: Bantam Books, 1992), 5.
16. Wal-Mart Stores, Inc., *Annual Report for the Year Ending January 31, 1972*, 5.
17. Blevins, *Hill Folks*, 176.
18. James Gregory, *American Exodus: The Dust Bowl Migration and Okie Culture in California* (New York: Oxford University Press, 1989), 6–7.
19. Blevins, *Hill Folks*, 208.
20. Walton with Huey, *Made in America*, 18.
21. Ibid., 22.
22. Quoted in Richard Tedlow, *Giants of Enterprise: Seven Business Innovators and the Empires They Built* (New York: HarperBusiness, 2001), 329.
23. Walton with Huey, *Made in America*, 28; Census State Data Center, Institute for Economic Advancement, University of Arkansas at Little Rock, at http://www.aica.ualr.edu/census/other/City1910–70 .html.
24. Butler Brothers, *The Butler Way System Book* (New York, 1916), 170–71.
25. U.S. Bureau of the Census, "Retail Trade: Arkansas," in 1958 *Census of Business* (Washington: Department of Commerce, 1959), 5. Statistics are for the year 1954. In Jackson County only 67 of 143 stores outside Newport, the county seat, paid taxes on any sort of payroll. In Benton County the proportion was slightly higher, but even there

more than half of the 229 county stores did not have a payroll in 1958. These statistics for Jackson and Benton counties are also found in "Retail Trade: Arkansas," 8–12.

26. Walton with Huey, *Made in America*, 38–39.

27. Arkansas Resources and Development Commission, "Arkansas Retail Sales Exceeded One Billion Dollars in Past Year," 1948, in Vertical File, Special Collections, University of Arkansas.

28. Tracy Deutsch, "Untangling Alliances: Social Tensions Surrounding Independent Grocery Stores and the Rise of Mass Retailing," in *Food Nations, Selling Taste in Consumer Society*, ed. Warren Belasco and Philip Scranton (New York: Routledge, 2002), 156–74.

29. Ibid., 203.

30. Peter Drucker, "The Economy's Dark Continent," *Fortune*, April 1962, 103.

31. Robert Sobel, *When Giants Stumble: Classic Business Blunders and How to Avoid Them* (Paramus, N.J.: Prentice Hall, 1999), 30–32.

32. Isadore Barmash, *More Than They Bargained For: The Rise and Fall of Korvettes* (New York: Lebhar-Friedman Books, 1981), 8–10.

33. Ibid., 9.

34. Sobel, *When Giants Stumble*, 37.

35. Charles Silberman, "The Revolutionists of Retailing," *Fortune*, April 1962, 264; Sobel, *When Giants Stumble*, 38.

36. Vance and Scott, *Wal-Mart*, 40–41.

37. Ortega, *In Sam We Trust*, 111–19.

38. Marcia Layton Turner, *Kmart's Ten Deadly Sins: How Incompetence Tainted an American Icon* (New York: John Wiley, 2003), xi–xii; Walton with Huey, *Made in America*, 243–44.

39. Vance Trimble, *Sam Walton: The Inside Story of America's Richest Man* (New York: Dutton, 1990), 100.

40. Wal-Mart Stores, Inc., *Annual Report, Year Ending January 31, 1971*, 5.

41. Vance and Scott, *Wal-Mart*, 47; author's interview with Larry English, June 7, 2006, Diamond Head, Ark.; Walton with Huey, *Made in America*, 226.

42. Lynda Schuster, "Wal-Mart Chief's Enthusiastic Approach Infects Employees, Keeps Retailer Growing," *Wall Street Journal*, April 20, 1981.

43. Hank Gilman, "Rural Retailing Chains Prosper by Combining Service and Sophistication," *Wall Street Journal*, July 2, 1984.

44. *DSN Retailing Today*, August 2002, 7; Jim Cory, "Up Against Wal-Mart," *Chilton's Hardware Age*, February 1988, 31–35.

45. Sobel, *When Giants Stumble*, 43–44. In addition to all the usual financial problems faced by retailers in the inflationary 1970s, Ferkauf committed the greatest discount sin: he went upscale and tried to compete with Lord & Taylor, Brooks Brothers, and the like.
46. Isadore Barmash, "The Hot Ticket in Retailing," *New York Times*, July 1, 1984.
47. Quoted in John Huey, "Wal-Mart: Will It Take Over the World?" *Fortune*, January 30, 1989, 53.
48. Ortega, *In Sam We Trust*, 110–11.

CHAPTER TWO: SUPPLY AND COMMAND

1. Ortega, *In Sam We Trust*, 63.
2. Walton with Huey, *Made in America*, 112.
3. "Mid '70s Marketing Changes Put Wal-Mart on the Road to Success," *Arkansas Gazette*, March 6, 1983.
4. Andrea Lillo, "Wal-Mart Gains Strength from Distribution Chain," *Home Textiles Today*, March 24, 2003 (Web edition).
5. Turner, *Kmart's Ten Deadly Sins*, 147–49.
6. Vance and Scott, "Butler Brothers and the Rise and Decline of the Ben Franklin Variety Stores," 262.
7. Roy Mayer, "To Our Shareholders . . . ," in Wal-Mart Stores, Inc., *1975 Annual Report*, 1.
8. Wal-Mart Stores, Inc., *1978 Annual Report*, 2.
9. Thomas O. Graff and Dub Ashton, "Spacial Diffusion of Wal-Mart: Contagious and Reverse Hierarchical Elements," *Professional Geographer* 46 (February 1994), 19–29.
10. Author's interview with Charles Gainus, former Harding College president, June 6, 2006, Searcy, Ark.
11. Wal-Mart Stores, Inc. *1980, 1981, 1982 Annual Reports*; and Wal-Mart Facts Web page.
12. These descriptions of a Wal-Mart distribution center are taken from the author's interview with Bill Lynn, June 6, 2006, Searcy, Ark.; Dan Scheraga, "Wal-Mart's Muscle," *Chain Store Age*, June 2005 (Web edition); and Thomas Friedman, *The World Is Flat* (New York: Farrar, Straus and Giroux, 2005), 128–29.
13. "Mid-70s Marketing Changes Put Wal-Mart on the Road to Success."
14. John P. Walsh, *Supermarkets Transformed: Understanding Organizational and Technological Innovations* (New Brunswick, N.J.: Rutgers University Press, 1993), 94–95.

15. "Wal-Mart Tests UPC," *Discount Store News*, June 15, 1992, 83; author's conversation with Wal-Mart cashier, June 6, 2006, Newport, Ark.

16. David Smith, "Satellite Scans Wal-Mart Empire," *Arkansas Democrat*, December 3, 1989; Christopher Sullivan, "Wal-Mart's Folksy Smile Belies Electronic Brain," *Northwest Arkansas Morning News*, September 27, 1993.

17. Author's telephone interview with Scott Nelson, May 2, 2007. In 1992 and 1993 Nelson worked as a telecommunications network consultant for Dylex Corporation, a Toronto retailer then phasing in a system derived from Wal-Mart's experience. Today he is an award-winning historian of southern labor at William & Mary.

18. Ortega, *In Sam We Trust*, 131–33.

19. Smith, "Satellite Scans Wal-Mart Empire."

20. Stephen A. Brown, *Revolution at the Checkout Counter* (Cambridge: Harvard University Press, 1997), 15–17.

21. Emily Nelson, "Retailing: Why Wal-Mart Sings, 'Yes, We Have Bananas!'" *Wall Street Journal*, October 6, 1998.

22. Ibid.

23. Quoted in Lou Pritchett, *Stop Paddling and Start Rocking the Boat* (New York: HarperCollins, 1995), 25.

24. Walton with Huey, *Made in America*, 66.

25. Davis Dyer, Frederick Dalzell, and Rowena Olegario, *Rising Tide: Lessons from 165 Years of Brand Building at Procter & Gamble* (Boston: Harvard Business School Press, 2004), 312.

26. Walton with Huey, *Made in America*, 237.

27. Dyer et al., *Rising Tide*, 315.

28. "P & G Rewrites the Marketing Rules," *Fortune*, November 6, 1989.

29. Dyer et al., *Rising Tide*, 316.

30. Ibid., 319.

31. Sarah Ellison, Ann Zimmerman, and Charles Forelle, "Sales Team—P&G's Gillette Edge: The Playbook It Honed at Wal-Mart," *Wall Street Journal*, January 31, 2005.

32. Ibid.

33. Constance Hays, "What's Behind the Procter Deal? Wal-Mart," *New York Times*, January 29, 2005; Davidowitz quoted in Jeremy Grant and Dan Roberts, "P&G Looks to Gain Strength Through Unity," *Financial Times*, January 31, 2005.

34. "Testimony by Manufacturers' Agents National Association," U.S. House of Representatives Committee on Small Business, *Impact of Discount Superstores on Small Business and Local Communities*,

August 10, 1994, in Wal-Mart Vertical Files, Food and Allied Service Trades Department, AFL-CIO.

35. Karen Blumenthal, "A Few Big Retailers Rebuff Middlemen—Manufacturers, Agents Say Trend May Spread," *Wall Street Journal,* October 21, 1986.

36. Quoted in John Huey, "Wal-Mart: Will It Take Over the World?" *Fortune,* January 30, 1989, 52.

37. "Chain Begins Servicing Own Racks"; "Vendor Rep Move Stirs Debate," *Discount Store News,* June 15, 1992, 68, 135.

38. "Vendor Rep Move Stirs Debate."

39. Andrea Harter, "New Group to Wage War on Wal-Mart," *Arkansas Democrat Gazette,* March 12, 1992.

40. "Testimony by Manufacturers' Agents National Association, August 10, 1994.

41. Steve Weinstein, "Brokers: Up the Creek?" *Progressive Grocer,* December 1992, 63.

42. Charles Fishman, *The Wal-Mart Effect* (New York, Penguin Press, 2006), 95.

43. Paul Westerman, *Data Warehousing: Using the Wal-Mart Model* (San Francisco: Morgan Kaufman Publishers, 2000), 179–80.

44. Sam Hornblower, "Always Low Prices," at PBS *Frontline* Web site, "Is Wal-Mart Good for America?"

45. Constance Hays, "What They Know About You," *New York Times,* November 14, 2004.

CHAPTER THREE: THE CORPORATE CULTURE

1. Or as *Fortune's* Jerry Useem put it on the eve of the Iraq war: "Wal-Mart in 2003 is, in short, a lot like America in 2003; a sole superpower with a down-home twang. As with Uncle Sam, everyone's position in the world will largely be defined in relation to Mr. Sam. Is your company a 'strategic competitor' like China or a 'partner' like Britain? Is it a client state like Israel or a supplier to the opposition like Yemen? Is it France, benefiting from the superpower's reach while complaining the whole time? Or is it . . . well, a Target? You can admire the superpower or resent it or—most likely—both. But you can't ignore it." Jerry Useem, "One Nation Under Wal-Mart," *Fortune,* March 3, 2003, 66.

2. Script, *Grapes of Wrath,* at http://www.script-o<->rama.com/movie_scripts/g/grapes-of-wrath-script-transcript.html.

3. Ibid.

4. Bethany Moreton, "It Came from Bentonville: The Agrarian Origins

of Wal-Mart Culture," in *Wal-Mart: The Face of Twenty-First-Century Capitalism*, ed. Nelson Lichtenstein (New York: New Press, 2006), 68; Nancy MacLean, *Behind the Mask of Chivalry* (Chapel Hill: University of North Carolina Press, 1994), 203.

5. Daniel Scroop, "The Anti–Chain Store Movement and the Politics of Consumption," *American Quarterly* 60, no. 4 (December 2008), 931.

6. Susan Strasser, "Woolworth to Wal-Mart: Mass Merchandising and the Changing Culture of Consumption," in *Wal-Mart*, ed. Lichtenstein, 49; Richard Schragger, "The Anti–Chain Store Movement, Localist Ideology, and the Remnants of the Progressive Constitution, 1929–1940," *Iowa Law Review* 90, no. 3 (March 2005), 1057–70.

7. Moreton, "Agrarian Origins," 77.

8. Sam Walton, "Message to Associates," *Wal-Mart World*, June 1989, 5, 3.

9. Author's interview with Larry English, June 7, 2006, Diamond Head, Ark.

10. Brad Seligman, "Patriarchy at the Checkout Counter: The *Dukes v. Wal-Mart, Inc.* Class Action Suit," in *Wal-Mart*, ed. Lichtenstein, 231–42. And about 80 percent of all store managers had names that were Anglo-Saxon, Scandinavian, or German in derivation, reflecting the south-central origins of the Wal-Mart workforce. Simon Head, "Letter to the Editor," *New York Review of Books*, April 28, 2005.

11. Author's interview with Chuck Webb, May 31, 2007, Bentonville, Ark. The bonus plan for store managers was "5-10-5" in the 1970s and 1980s. A manager earned 5 percent of the net profit on the first $25,000, 10 percent on the next $25,000, and 5 percent on everything above that.

12. Wal-Mart Visitors Center, *Making the Difference: The Story of Wal-Mart* (Bentonville, Ark.: Wal-Mart Stores, 1990), 17. See also the photo of a large group of young men who are attending a management training session in Bentonville in 1975. On the wall above is a banner: WELCOME! ASSISTANT MANAGERS AND WIVES. This photo appears in Wal-Mart Stores, Inc., "Wal-Mart People," *1975 Annual Report*, 7.

13. Declaration of Laverne Jones in support of plaintiffs' motion for class certification, case no. 01-2252, *Dukes v. Wal-Mart Stores, Inc.*, 2003, found at Impact Fund Web site. Laverne's declaration was but one of several score "life stories" generated by Impact Fund lawyers. Although a federal judge has certified some 1.5 million current and

former female employees as a "class," no resolution has yet been reached in the *Dukes v. Wal-Mart* lawsuit. Therefore, while they generally portray repeatedly noted patterns at Wal-Mart that have been widely reported, as a legal matter the life stories, and all such unresolved claims reproduced in this book and elsewhere, remain no more than allegations in the *Dukes* action and other still-pending suits.

14. Deposition of John Sherman, *Dukes v. Wal-Mart Stores, Inc.*, case no. 01-2252, August 9, 2002, Impact Fund files, 14 and 18–59 passim.
15. Ibid., 60.
16. Ibid., 109.
17. Ibid., 72–100 passim.
18. Jane Adams, *The Transformation of Rural Life: Southern Illinois, 1890–1990* (Chapel Hill: University of North Carolina Press, 1994), 185–98, quotation on p 185.
19. Blevins, *Hill Folks*, 211.
20. Chamber of Commerce, "You'll Like Rogers," 1947, Vertical File, "Benton County," archives, University of Arkansas; Blevins, *Hill Folks*, 184–211.
21. "Munsingwear . . . A Big Name in Rogers" (1956), Vertical File, Rogers Historical Society; Cass S. Hough, *It's a Daisy!* (Rogers, Ark.: Victor Comptometer Corp., 1976), 153–54, 158–68, found in Rogers Historical Society.
22. Kristy Ely, "'One of the Good Ones'—Miss Jackie Recalls Early Days," *Wal-Mart World*, May 1990, 5.
23. Edyth Lammey, store reporter, "Twenty Years AT #1!" *Wal-Mart World*, June 1989, 12.
24. Wal-Mart Stores, Inc., *Annual Report for the Year Ending January 31, 1973*, 7.
25. Ibid., 3.
26. Christopher Leonard, "Wal-Mart Employees Stick with Tradition: Pin Trading," *Northwest Arkansas News*, June 4, 2005.
27. Don Soderquist, *The Wal-Mart Way* (Nashville: Thomas Nelson, 2005), xvii.
28. Tracy Neal, "Thriving Black Community Once Supported a School, Church, and Lodges," *Northwest Arkansas News*, January 26, 2003.
29. Patrick Huber, "Southwest Missouri Riots, 1894–1906," *Encyclopedia of American Race Riots*, forthcoming; James Loewen, *Sundown Towns: A Hidden Dimension of American Racism* (New York: New Press, 2005), 36–37.

30. Loewen, *Sundown Towns*, 48, 408; Darryl Fears, "In Tulsa, Keeping Alive 1921's Painful Memory," *Washington Post*, May 31, 2005.

31. Ted Ownby, *American Dreams in Mississippi: Consumers, Poverty, and Culture, 1830–1998* (Chapel Hill: University of North Carolina Press, 1999), 148–58.

32. Author's telephone interview with Michael Honey, January 13, 2006.

33. Austin Teutsch, *The Sam Walton Story: An Inside Look at the Man and His Empire* (New York: Berkley Publishing Group, 1992), 114–15.

34. Ownby, *American Dreams in Mississippi*, 163.

35. "Wal-Mart Stores, Inc. EEO-1 Data," 2005, 2006, at Wal-Mart Facts Web site, 7–8.

36. Wal-Mart Stores, Inc., *Annual Report for the Year Ending January 31, 1973*, 3.

37. See Loewen, *Sundown Towns*, 73, where Loewen has constructed a striking map showing the extent of racial exclusion in southern Missouri, eastern Oklahoma, and northern Arkansas; Wal-Mart Stores, Inc., *Annual Report for the Year Ending January 31, 1975*, 5.

38. Todd Mason and Marc Fons, "Sam Walton of Wal-Mart: Just Your Basic Homespun Billionaire," *BusinessWeek*, October 14, 1985, 142.

39. Mary Jo Schneider, "The Wal-Mart Annual Meeting: From Small-Town America to a Global Corporate Culture," *Human Organization*, 57, no. 3 (1998), 295.

40. Mary Wagoner, "The Long-Term Commitment: How Service Longevity Can Reap Big Rewards in Profit Sharing," *Wal-Mart World*, April 1990, 20.

41. Tosha D. Cobbs, "A Man Called Sam," *Wal-Mart World*, June 1989, 9.

42. Soderquist, *The Wal-Mart Way*, 59–60. Today this innovation has been copied by many larger employers. Hence the "team members" at Target, the "partners" or "baristas" who work at Starbucks, and "the cast" employed by Disney theme parks.

43. Walton with Huey, *Made in America*.

44. Picture caption: "At Store #119 in Batesville, Ark., store manager Paul Folhoffer . . . dressed as a baby and was pulled around the store asking for donations," *Wal-Mart World*, January 1990, 9; "Christmas Activities," *Wal-Mart World*, April 1990, 11; Moreton, "Agrarian Origins," 81.

45. Michael Bergdahl, *The Ten Rules of Sam Walton* (Hoboken, N.J.: John Wiley, 2006), 145–46.

46. Schneider, "The Wal-Mart Annual Meeting," 295.
47. Author's telephone interview with Al Zack, UFCW organizer, August 12, 2005.
48. Debra H., certified assistant in the Wal-Mart Legal Department, . Bentonville, Ark., "The aisles were full of smiles and warm welcomes," June 15, 2006, "Life at Wal-Mart," Wal-Mart Facts Web page.
49. Charles R., manager, Powder Springs, Ga., "I love Wal-Mart, and I am Wal-Mart," May 22, 2006, "Life at Wal-Mart."
50. Stephen Arnold, Robert Kozinets, and Jay Handelman, "Hometown Ideology and Retailer Legitimization: The Institutional Semiotics of Wal Mart Flyers," *Journal of Retailing* 77 (2001), 257; George Anderson, "Wal-Mart's Super Sticky," *RetailWire*, July 28, 2005 (http://www.retailwire.com).
51. Jennifer Negley, "Wal-Mart Customer Connection Is Truly Something Special," *Discount Store News*, May 6, 1996, 5.
52. "Vox Populi: Focus Group 1," *Discount Store News*, May 6, 1996, 119–20, 124.
53. Billie Letts, *Where the Heart Is* (New York: Warner Books, 1995), 362–63. Letts is quoted in the Oprah's Book Club edition of the novel.
54. Ibid., 101.
55. Associated Press, "Baptists Have Highest Divorce Rate," December 30, 1999, at http://www.sullivan-county.com/; National Center for Health Statistics, table 25, "State Rankings by Divorce Rate, Out-of-Wedlock Birth Rate and Teen Birth Rate, 1998" (Web edition); and see Garance Franke-Ruta, "Remapping the Culture Debate," *American Prospect*, February 2006, 44.
56. Alan Raucher, "Employee Relations at General Motors: The 'My Job Contest,' 1947," *Labor History* 28, no. 2 (Spring 1987), 221–32.
57. Tammy F., financial analyst, Transportation Finance, Bentonville, Ark., "My husband is currently deployed in Iraq," April 24, 2006, "Life at Wal-Mart."
58. Virdia J., Store 601, San Angelo, Tex., "If it wasn't for Wal-Mart, I'd be dead!" April 21, 2006, "Life at Wal-Mart."
59. Suzanne H., financial planner, Bentonville, Ark., "There was an outpouring of love that came from my Wal-Mart family," July 7, 2006, "Life at Wal-Mart."
60. Matt L., Store 855, Union City, Ga., "I stand by my Wal-Mart," June 20, 2006, "Life at Wal-Mart."
61. Laurie, merchandising call center, Bentonville, Ark., "Thank you, Lee Scott," March 9, 2006, "Life at Wal-Mart."

62. Vance and Scott, *Wal-Mart*, 108–9.
63. David Kirkpatrick, "Shaping Cultural Tastes at Big Retail Chains," *New York Times*, May 18, 2003; Liza Featherstone, "As It Eyes Cities, Wal-Mart Has No Plan B," *Women's News*, June 26, 2005 (Web edition).
64. Soderquist, *The Wal-Mart Way*, 45.
65. Walton with Huey, *Made in America*, 161–82.
66. David Chidester, *Authentic Fakes: Religion and American Popular Culture* (Berkeley: University of California Press, 2005); Kimon Sargeant, *Seeker Churches: Promoting Traditional Religion in a Nontraditional Way* (New Brunswick, N.J.: Rutgers University Press, 2000); Christian Smith, *American Evangelicalism: Embattled and Thriving* (Chicago: University of Chicago Press, 1998); Zig Ziglar, *Secrets of Closing the Sale* (Grand Rapids, Mich.: Fleming H. Revell, 2003).
67. Gordon Bigelow, "Let There Be Markets: The Evangelical Roots of Economics," *Harper's*, May 1, 2005.
68. Alan Wolfe, *The Transformation of American Religion: How We Actually Live Our Faith* (Chicago: University of Chicago Press, 2003), 32, 36.
69. Wal-Mart Stores, *Sam's Associates Handbook*, 3, in Vertical File, Food and Service Trades Department, AFL-CIO.
70. Wal-Mart Stores, Inc., *Annual Reports*, 1990, 1991, 1992; Jack Kahl, *Leading from the Heart: Choosing to be a Servant Leader* (Austin, Tex.: Greenleaf Book Group, 2004), 107–9. Kahl was for many years owner and CEO of Manco, which supplied duct tape to Wal-Mart.
71. Mike Troy, "Scott, Coughlin Set to Lead Wal-Mart," *Discount Store News*, January 25, 1999, 48. See also James A. Autry, *The Servant Leader: How to Build a Creative Team, Develop Great Morale, and Improve Bottom-Line Performance* (New York: Three Rivers Press, 2001). Robert K. Greenleaf, a secular management consultant, coined the phrase "servant leader" in 1970, but it has been heavily Christianized since then. See in particular Ken Blanchard, *The Servant Leader* (Nashville, Tenn.: J. Countryman, 2003).
72. Walter Kiechel, "The Leader as Servant," *Fortune*, May 4, 1992, 121; Larry Spears, "Reflections on Robert K. Greenleaf and Servant-leadership," *Leadership and Organization Development Journal* 17, no. 7 (1996), 336.
73. Mark Roberts in reel F942970 (1994), tape transcription document, Flagler Productions, Lenexa, Kans.

74. Harry Miller in reel 930199 (1993), tape transcription document, Flagler Productions.

75. James Hoopes, e-mail to author, August 31, 2007.

76. *Wal-Mart Associate Handbook*, 1993, 19, found in files of *Savaglio v. Wal-Mart*, case no. 835687-7, the Furth Firm, San Francisco.

77. Kris Maher and Kris Hudson, "Wal-Mart to Sweeten Bonus Plans for Staff," *Wall Street Journal*, March 22, 2007.

78. *Wal-Mart Associate Handbook*, 1999, 7, found in files of *Savaglio v. Wal-Mart*.

79. *My Benefits: 2005 Associate Guide*, 11-12, found in files of *Savaglio v. Wal-Mart*.

80. Thomas O. Graff and Dub Ashton, "Spatial Diffusion of Wal-Mart: Contagious and Reverse Hierarchical Elements," *Professional Geographer*, February 1994, 19–29; "About Wal-Mart: Senior Officers," found at http://www.walmartstores.com.

81. Marc Bendick, "The Representation of Women in Store Management at Wal-Mart Stores, Inc.," January 2003, found on Impact Fund Web page under *Dukes v. Wal-Mart*.

82. Brent Schlender, "Wal-Mart's $288 Billion Meeting," *Fortune*, April 18, 2005, 97.

83. Author's telephone interview with Jon Lehman, June 7, 2005, and see Seligman, "Patriarchy at the Checkout Counter."

84. Michael Bergdahl, *What I Learned from Sam Walton: How to Compete and Thrive in a Wal-Mart World* (Hoboken, N.J.: John Wiley, 2004), 150–52; Carol Hymowitz, "Program Puts Students on the Leadership Path," *Wall Street Journal Online*, January 15, 2003. Unless otherwise noted, all information on SIFE is taken from its Web site: http://www.sife.org.

85. Mike Jackson, "Dallas Business Leader William H. Seay Dies," *Dallas Morning News*, April 13, 1997; Mac Roy Rasor, formerly public relations officer at Southwestern Life, e-mail to author, August 7, 2007.

86. See the Leadership Institute Web page at http://www.leadershipin stitute.org. Morton C. Blackwell refounded the group in 1979 and has remained the key figure ever since.

87. Harold F. Boss, *How Green the Grazing: 75 Years at Southwestern Life, 1903–1978* (Dallas: Taylor, 1978), 284–86.

88. "SIFE History" at Students in Free Enterprise Web site; SBU self-description at http://www.sbuniv.edu/aboutsbu.

89. SIFE, "Special Report: Expo 2004 Yearbook," in author's possession.

90. Quoted in Bethany Moreton, "Six Flags over Capitalism: Wal-Mart,

Students in Free Enterprise, and the Conservative Ascendancy" (unpublished essay).

91. Laurie Dempster, " 'Changing the World' and Other Funny Things I Have Heard as a Student Entrepreneur," e-mail to author, February 6, 2008.

92. See the Wal-Mart Stores Web site at http://www.walmartstores .com. Among the top Wal-Mart executives who have served on the SIFE board are Jack Shewmaker and Tom Coughlin.

93. Stephanie Armour, "While Hiring at Most Firms Chills, Wal-Mart's Heats Up," USA Today, August 25, 2002.

94. John Kerr, "Pass It On," Inc. Magazine, December 1995; author's telephone interview with Curtis DeBerg, June 1, 2005; information on SIFE expansion found at http://www.sife.org. Although Wal-Mart is careful to keep the relationship between its buyers and their vendor clients a highly formal one in Bentonville, SIFE provides a venue that is far less regulated. Indeed, the contributions so readily made by SIFE's Wal-Mart vendors purchase the kind of goodwill that might be quite remunerative.

95. Nicole Biggart, Charismatic Capitalism: Direct Selling Organizations in America (Chicago: University of Chicago Press, 1989), 170.

CHAPTER FOUR: BEAT YESTERDAY

1. Dale L. Stiles, "Low Pay Every Day," Arkansas Times, September 3, 1992.

2. Ibid., 16–17.

3. Ibid., 19.

4. Barry Bluestone et al., The Retail Revolution: Market Transformation, Investment and Labor in the Modern Department Store (Boston: Auburn House, 1981), 30; Pankaj Ghemawat, Wal-Mart Stores' Discount Operations, 1989 (Harvard Business School, 9-387-018), 7.

5. Strasser, "Woolworth to Wal-Mart," in Wal-Mart, ed. Lichtenstein, 31.

6. Walton with Huey, Made in America, 162–63.

7. Jerold Waltman, The Politics of the Minimum Wage (Urbana: University of Illinois Press, 2000), 36–38.

8. "Wage-Hour Fight a Test of Lobbies," August 19, 1960; Joseph Loftus, "Goldwater Leads Assault on Broadening Wage Law," August 11, 1960; "Goldwater to Receive Retail Group's Award," October 12, 1961; all in the New York Times.

9. Waltman, The Politics of the Minimum Wage, 37–41. The exemp-

tion of retail workers proved the most contentious issue in every legislative conflict over the minimum wage during the 1950s and 1960s. See Tom Wicker, "Minimum Wage: Congress Shows Power," *New York Times*, March 26, 1961.

10. Author's interview with Larry English, June 7, 2006, Diamond Head, Ark.

11. See Wal-Mart Stores, Inc., *2006 Annual Report: Building Smiles*, 51. As of the end of the fiscal year 2006, Wal-Mart reported that there were 2,640 Discount Stores, 2,396 Supercenters, 670 Sam's Clubs, and 435 Neighborhood Markets, each with one true manager.

12. Ortega, *In Sam We Trust*, 30–31, 59–60.

13. "Plaintiffs' Memorandum of Points and Authorities in Support of Motion for Class Certification," *Daniel Sepulveda v. Wal-mart Stores, Inc.*, U.S. District Court, Central District of California, January 14, 2006, 7.

14. David Levine and David Lewin, "The New 'Managerial Misclassification' Challenge to Old Wage and Hour Law or What Is Managerial Work?" 2006, 9, available at Lewin's Web page, MIT, Sloan School of Management; author's telephone interview with David Levine, May 22, 2006. Levine teaches in the Haas School of Business, University of California, Berkeley.

15. Kevin Helliker, "Sold on the Job: Retailing Chains Offer a Lot of Opportunity, Young Managers Find They Can Advance Rapidly, But Be Demoted Rapidly If They Fail to Produce," *Wall Street Journal*, August 25, 1995, 1.

16. Quoted in Fishman, *The Wal-Mart Effect*, 24.

17. Ellen Rosen, "The Quality of Work at Wal-Mart," unpublished paper for delivery at the conference "Wal-Mart: Template for 21st Century Capitalism," University of California, Santa Barbara, April 12, 2004, 7; Helliker, "Sold on the Job."

18. Rosen, "The Quality of Work at Wal-Mart," 7–8.

19. Ellen Rosen, "How to Squeeze More Out of a Penny," in *Wal-Mart*, ed. Lichtenstein, 244–45.

20. "Declaration of Joseph D. Hawkins," 15–16, *Barnett v. Wal-Mart*, case no. 01-2-24553-8 SEA, Washington Superior Court, January 23, 2004.

21. Rosen, "How to Squeeze More Out of a Penny," 245–46.

22. Chris Maher, "Wal-Mart Seeks New Flexibiity in Worker Shifts," *Wall Street Journal*, January 3, 2007; author's telephone interview with anonymous personnel manager, Pacific Northwest Wal-Mart store, July 7, 2008.

23. Mark Gimein, "Sam Walton Made Us a Promise," *Fortune*, March 18, 2002.
24. "Deposition of Ramona Benson Muzingo," October 3, 2002, in *Dukes v. Wal-Mart Stores, Inc.*, U.S. District Court, Northern District of California, 16–54. And see the "careers" section of the Wal-Mart Stores Web site for the story of Pat Curren, a regional vice president who oversees 520 stores in the southeastern U.S. She began her career twenty-two years before as an hourly associate in the pet department of her local Wal-Mart.
25. Douglas Shuit, "People Problems on Every Aisle," *Workforce Management*, February 2004, 32.
26. Author's telephone interview with Stephanie Haynes, February 24, 2006.
27. Ibid.
28. Coleman Peterson, "Employee Retention: The Secrets Behind Wal-Mart's Successful Hiring Policies," in *Human Resource Management*, Spring 2005, 85, 87–88.
29. Frank Tobias Higbie, *Indispensable Outcasts: Hobo Workers and Community in the American Midwest, 1880–1930* (Urbana: University of Illinois Press, 2003), 8.
30. Barry Bluestone, Patricia Hanna, Sarah Kuhn, and Laura Moore, *The Retail Revolution: Market Transformation, Investment, and Labor in the Modern Department Store* (Boston: Auburn House, 1981), 84–85.
31. "Declaration of Joseph D. Hawkins," *Barnett v. Wal-Mart*, January 23, 2004.
32. See Wal-Mart Facts, Texas Community Impact, at http://www.walmartfacts.com, for the number of stores and employees as of March 2008.
33. "Texas Workforce Commission Employer Tax System, H.B. 118 Rate Statistics," at http://www.twc.state.tx.us/tax/.
34. Jennifer Davies and Keith Darce, "Going Through the Checkout Line," *San Diego Union-Tribune*, February 25, 2007.
35. Coleman Peterson, "Employee Retention," *Human Resource Management*, 1994; Shuit, "People Problems on Every Aisle," 27.
36. "Wal-Mart: Increase Minimum Wage," *Times-Picayune*, October 26, 2005.
37. Robert Levering and Milton Moskowitz, "The 100 Best Companies to Work For," *Fortune*, January 24, 2005, 72. *Fortune* reports that it chose the top hundred companies by evaluating the policies and culture of each company, and the opinions of the company's own

employees. "We give the latter more weight: Two-thirds of the total score comes from employee responses to a 57-question survey created by the Great Place to Work Institute in San Francisco. The survey goes to a minimum of 350 randomly selected employees from each company and asks about things such as attitudes toward management, job satisfaction, and camaraderie. The remaining one third of the score comes from our evaluation of each company's demographic makeup, pay and benefits programs, and the like." It is possible that Wal-Mart chose not to cooperate with the Fortune survey, but in that case it may well have feared the well-publicized results.

38. Bergdahl, What I Learned from Sam Walton, 126.
39. Jill Seskin, "Production and Reproduction of Wal-Mart Workers: A Study of Spatial, Social and Economic Relations," unpublished master's thesis, Department of Geography, University of Arizona, 1992, 11; Barbara Ehrenreich, Nickel and Dimed: On (not) Getting By in America (New York: Metropolitan Books, 2001), 124.
40. "Wal-Mart Uses CBLs to Cut Turnover," HFN: The Weekly Newspaper for the Home Furnishing Network, 1995.
41. "Long Term Assistant Manager" to H. Lee Scott, April 24, 2003, exhibit 3, in Andrea Savaglio et al. v. Wal-Mart Stores, Inc., case no. C-835687-7, Superior Court of California, September 21, 2004.
42. "Co-Manager, USA, 3/2000–6/2004," in Wal-Mart Workplace Surveys, at http://www.vault.com/companies.
43. Julie Pierce, "The Wal-Mart Way, Not Sam's Way," 2006, unpublished manuscript in author's possession.
44. Ibid.
45. Ibid.
46. Bergdahl, The Ten Rules of Sam Walton, 206.
47. "Programmer/Analyst, Bentonville, 1/1997–3/2001," in Wal-Mart Workplace Surveys, at http://www.vault.com/companies/.
48. "Manager, Bentonville, 6/1998–11/2005"; "Network Administrator, Bentonville, 1/1999–8/2002"; both in Wal-Mart Workplace Surveys, at http://www.vault.com/companies/.
49. "Home Office Manager, 10/2003–5/2005," in Wal-Mart Workplace Surveys, at http://www.vault.com/companies/.
50. Mike Troy, "Wal-Mart Celebrates 40 Years, Pays Tribute to Founding Principles," DSN Retailing Today, July 29, 2002.
51. Declaration of Steven Quiriconi in Support of Plaintiff's Motion for Certification, Barnett v. Wal-Mart Stores, Inc., case no. 01-2-2-24553-8, Washington Superior Court, October 4, 2002, 8, 10. In Barnett and

similar wage and hour cases, Wal-Mart long took the position that individual store managers were responsible for breaking the law, not Wal-Mart Stores, Inc. However, in a settlement announced December 23, 2008, Wal-Mart agreed to pay at least $352 million, and possibly as much as $640 million, to settle wage and hour claims in *Barnett* and sixty-two cases pending in federal and state courts in forty-two states.

52. Ibid., 8.
53. Ibid., 4–5.
54. Ibid., 3.
55. "Declaration of Joseph Hawkins," January 23, 2004 in *Barnett v. Wal-Mart*; author's telephone interview with Stan Fortune, former Wal-Mart manager, January 17, 2006.
56. "Declaration of David L. Levine," in *Sepulveda v. Wal-Mart*, January 14, 2004.
57. "Declaration of John Hiser," October 1, 2002, in *Barnett v. Wal-Mart*; "Declaration of Keith Edwards," September 29, 2002, in *Barnett v. Wal-Mart*.
58. "Declaration of Keith Edwards"; Greenhouse interview with Peterson, from NOW transcript, "Off-the-Clock," November 8, 2002.
59. Steve Painter, "2 Pay Bills with Wal-Mart Tapes," *Arkansas Democrat-Gazette*, July 6, 2008.
60. T. A. Frank, "Everyday Low Vices," *Washington Monthly*, April 2006; Steven Greenhouse and Stephanie Rosenbloom, "Wal-Mart Settles 63 Lawsuits Over Wages," *New York Times*, Decemer 24, 2008, C1.
61. Ann Zimmerman, "Labor Pains: After Huge Raid on Illegals, Wal-Mart Fires Back at U.S.," *Wall Street Journal*, December 19, 2003; Charles Toutant, "Have Wal-Mart Plaintiffs Lawyers Found a 'Smoking Gun'?" *New Jersey Law Journal*, November 18, 2005, at http://www.law.com.
62. Zimmerman, "Labor Pains"; Greta McCaughrin to David Glass, December 5, 1999, letter found at http://www.walmartjanitors.com. Greta McCaughrin was a Russian-speaking academic at Washington and Lee University who, through friendship and diligence, penetrated the world of those Russian illegals who worked at the local Wal-Mart in Lexington, Va. She found that some of the Russian workers were "small time crooks" while others were "altruistic" and "honest." After detailing the exploitation of these workers in a letter to Wal-Mart executives, she reported that the police arrest of one group was followed by their replacement with yet another. Greta McCaughrin, telephone interview with author, August 7, 2005.

63. Steven Greenhouse, "Workers Assail Night Lock-Ins by Wal-Mart," *New York Times*, January 18, 2004.

64. Richard Hollinger and Lynn Langton, "Final Report: 2004 National Retail Security Survey," Department of Criminology, Law and Society, University of Florida, 2005, at http://www.crim.ufl.edu/research/spr/.

65. James Lee, "An Academic Approach to LP," *Loss Prevention*, January 1, 2005, at http://www.losspreventionmagazine.com/.

66. Keith Aubele, "Bottom Line: Loss Prevention Has Successful Track Record," *Wal-Mart Today*, January 2000, 8.

67. Walton with Huey, *Made in America*, 172.

68. "Shrinkettes," *Wal-Mart World*, June 1988, 19; the quote is in Paul Carter, "The Hard Facts About Shrink," *Wal-Mart World*, January 1990, 17.

69. "To Helen, Bud and Rob Walton from More than 100 Sam's Club Management Members," February 19, 1993 in Unprocessed Files, Impact Fund, Berkeley, Calif.

70. Lamon K. Griggs, *$8,500,000 Judgment Day* (Victoria, B.C.: Trafford, 2005), 45–67, Griggs quoted on p. 59. Griggs won an $8.5 million personal damage award from Wal-Mart in 2002. The company is appealing.

71. Author's telephone interview with Lamon Griggs, April 19, 2006; author's telephone interview with Stan Fortune, January 12, 2006.

72. Michael Barbaro, "Bare-Knuckle Enforcement for Wal-Mart's Rules," *New York Times*, 2007; Harold Meyerson, "Open Doors, Closed Minds; How One Wal-Mart True Believer Was Excommunicated for His Faith in Doing What He Thought the Company Expected of Him: Crying Foul," *American Prospect*, December 2005.

73. Ann Zimmerman and Gary McWilliams, "Inside Wal-Mart's 'Threat Research' Operation," *Wall Street Journal*, April 4, 2007.

74. Ibid.; Ann Zimmerman and Gary McWilliams, "Fired Wal-Mart Worker Speaks Out," *Wall Street Journal*, March 9, 2007; Marcus Kabel, "Wal-Mart Recruits Intelligence Officers," *BusinessWeek*, April 24, 2007.

75. Michael McIntyre, "The Real Deal; As President and CEO of Wal-Mart's U.S. Operations, Cleveland Native Tom Coughlin Guides the Biggest Company in the World," *Cleveland Plain Dealer*, Sunday magazine, April 28, 2002.

76. Anthony Bianco, *The Bully of Bentonville: How the High Cost of Wal-Mart's Everyday Low Prices Is Hurting America* (New York: Doubleday, 2006), 82; McIntyre, "The Real Deal," 14.

77. Mike Troy, "A Tribute to Tom Coughlin, a Legacy of Leadership," *Drug Store News*, February 14, 2005.
78. Bianco, *Bully of Bentonville*, 268–69; "A Guilty Plea in Wal-Mart Case," *New York Times*, February 1, 2006.

CHAPTER FIVE: UNIONS: KEEP OUT!

1. Sam Walton, "Keeping Our Partnership Strong," *Wal-Mart World*, October 1989, 3.
2. Author's interview with Larry English, June 7, 2006, Diamond Head, Ark.
3. Gilbert Gall, *The Politics of Right to Work: The Labor Federations as Special Interests* (New York: Greenwood Press, 1988); Martin Halpern, *Unions, Radicals, and Democratic Presidents: Seeking Social Change in the Twentieth Century* (Westport, Conn.: Praeger, 2003), 147–76. This chapter is titled "Arkansas and the Defeat of Labor Law Reform in 1978 and 1994."
4. David Brody, *Labor Embattled: History, Power, Rights* (Urbana: University of Illinois Press, 2005), 143.
5. James Brudney, "Neutrality Agreements and Card Check Recognition: Prospects for Changing Paradigms," *Iowa Law Review* 90 (2005), 868–73.
6. Jacoby, *Modern Manors*, 203; "Statement of Albert Cummings Beeson," *Hearings, National Labor Relations Board*, U.S. Senate Committee on Labor and Public Welfare, 83rd Congress, 2nd Session, 22.
7. Alan Story, "Employer Speech, Union Representation Elections, and the First Amendment," *Berkeley Journal of Employment and Labor Law* 16 (1995), 451–62.
8. Steve Jordon, "Anti-Union Attorney Took 'Golden Rule' to Wal-Mart," *Omaha World-Herald*, May 5, 1991; Ortega, *In Sam We Trust*, 87–88.
9. Jordon, "Anti-Union Attorney." For a time in the early 1950s Tate worked for H. L. Hunt, the right-wing Texas oilman, who paid him ten thousand dollars a year to serve as the Omaha head of Facts Forum, an organization that fought fluorination of drinking water and demanded that the House Committee on Un-American Activities hold additional hearings in the Midwest.
10. "My Name Is John Tate," before Federal Communications Commission Hearing, Omaha, 1962, in the folder "Midwest Employer's Council, Inc." (hereafter cited as MEC folder), box 219, Group Research Collection, Rare Book and Manuscript Library, Butler Library, Columbia University.

11. "Excerpts from Mid-West Employers Council Bulletins, February 19, 1963," in MEC folder.
12. *Midwest Employers Council Bulletin,* February 19, 1960, in MEC folder.
13. UPI, Nebraska AFL-CIO Convention, September 26, 1963, in MEC folder.
14. See generally Thomas Geoghegan, *Which Side Are You On? Trying to Be for Labor When It's Flat on Its Back* (New York: Farrar, Straus and Giroux, 1991); and Paul Weiler, *Governing the Workplace: The Future of Labor and Employment Law* (Cambridge: Harvard University Press, 1990); Kate Bronfenbrenner, "Raw Power: Plant-Closing Threats and the Threat to Union Organizing," *Multinational Monitor* 21 (December 2000), 24–30.
15. Author's telephone interview with Duane Acklie, May 29, 2007.
16. Speech transcript, dated June 1, 1959, in MEC folder.
17. *Wal-Mart Stores, Inc. and Retail Store Employees' Union, Local No. 655, affiliated with Retail Clerks International Association, case no.* 14-CA-6721, 201 *NLRB,* no. 35, 250–54.
18. Ortega, *In Sam We Trust,* 89.
19. John Tate, 1992 Wal-Mart Manager's Meeting, reel 121, Flagler Productions.
20. Ortega, *In Sam We Trust,* 89–90.
21. Walton with Huey, *Made in America,* 165.
22. Jacob Hacker, *The Great Risk Shift* (New York: Oxford University Press, 2006), 116–21. The individually controlled private retirement account—today as ubiquitous as the 401(k)—would not come into legal existence until 1978.
23. Author's telephone interview with Duane Acklie.
24. Jacoby, *Modern Manors,* 108–9.
25. Ortega, *In Sam We Trust,* 349.
26. Debbie Cambell, "Wal-Mart Associates Receive Largest Company Contribution Ever!" *Wal-Mart World,* April 1990, 17.
27. "Still the Darling of Wall Street," *Discount Store News,* June 15, 1992, 137.
28. Ibid., 18.
29. Quoted in "Lee's Garage," April 1, 2005, from http://www.ntimes.com/business, accessed February 17, 2006. See also Steven Greenhouse and Michael Barbaro, "On Private Web Site, Wal-Mart Chief Talks Tough," *New York Times,* February 17, 2006.
30. "Fall of 59," *Arkansas Gazette,* November 8, 1976; author's telephone interview with Ronald Heath, August 22, 2006; Shane Hamilton,

Trucking Country: The Road to America's Wal-Mart Economy (Princeton: Princeton University Press, 2008), 190–224.

31. Walton with Huey, *Made in America*, 156.
32. Author's telephone interview with Ron Heath, Teamster organizer, August 22, 2006.
33. Ortega, *In Sam We Trust*, 106.
34. Ibid.
35. Ibid.; author's interview with Ron Heath; Trimble, *Sam Walton*, 230.
36. Ortega, *In Sam We Trust*.
37. Quoted in Trimble, *Sam Walton*, 230.
38. Author's interview with Joe Bare, June 5, 2006, Little Rock, Ark.
39. "Delivering Low Prices," *Discount Store News*, October 1999, 4.
40. Michael Belzer, *Sweatshops on Wheels: Winners and Losers in Trucking Deregulation* (New York: Oxford University Press, 2000).
41. "Delivering Low Prices," 4.
42. *Daryal T. Nelson and Tommy Armstrong v. Wal-Mart Stores, Inc.*, case no. 2:04-CV-00171-WRW, "Order Granting in Part and Denying in Part Plaintiff's Motion for Class Certification," May 16, 2007.
43. "Paving the Way for Logistics: Wal-Mart's H. Lee Scott," *Supply Chain Management Review*, January 2003 (Web edition); "Wal-Mart Boss's Unlikely Role: Corporate Defender-in-Chief," *Wall Street Journal*, July 26, 2005.
44. "Supply Chain Power Heart of EDLP Success," *MMR*, December 17, 2001.
45. James Held, "Distribution Center Site Selection," *Economic Development Journal* (Summer 2003), 31–36. Although Missouri soon had three times as many stores as Arkansas, Wal-Mart avoided putting one of its distribution centers in that state until 1995, almost certainly because of the higher average wage level there, a historic product of the strong Teamster locals in St. Louis and Kansas City.
46. M. C. Associates, "Wal-Mart's Expansion in Missouri: Past Strategies, Future Plans," prepared for UFCW Local 88, St. Louis, July 1989, in files of FAST-AFL-CIO. Until 1983 Missouri had more Wal-Mart stores than any other state.
47. Orson Mason, "Labor Relations and You at the Wal-Mart Distribution Center #6022," September 1991, 7, copy in author's possession.
48. Erin Johansson, *Wal-Mart: Rolling Back Workers' Wages, Rights, and the American Dream* (Washington, D.C.: American Rights at Work, 2006), 15–16.
49. Tedlow, *New and Improved*, 220–21.

50. Roger Horowitz, *"Negro and White, United and Fight!"*: A Social History of Industrial Unionism in Meatpacking, 1930–1990 (Urbana: University of Illinois Press, 1997), 265–75.

51. Ibid.

52. Robert Brenner, "Wal-Mart Is Eating Everybody's Lunch," *BusinessWeek*, April 15, 2002, 43.

53. Julie Rawe, "Supermarket Smackdown," *Time*, May 3, 2004.

54. Abigail Goldman and Nancy Cleeland, "An Empire Built on Bargains Remakes the Working World," *Los Angeles Times*, November 23, 2003.

55. Patricia Callahan and Ann Zimmerman, "Price War in Aisle 3— Wal-Mart Tops Grocery List with Supercenter Format," *Wall Street Journal*, May 27, 2003; Anthony Bianco and Wendy Zellner, "Is Wal-Mart Too Powerful?" *BusinessWeek*, October 6, 2003, 100.

56. Tim Ferguson, "Food Union Tastes Gains Even as Trends Eat at Base," *Wall Street Journal*, February 16, 1993.

57. Bianco, *The Bully of Bentonville*, 130; author's interview with Al Zack, August 24, 2005.

58. Ann Zimmerman, "Butchers Claim Victory in War with Wal-Mart. But Battle in Texas Is Far From Over," *Wall Street Journal*, April 16, 2000.

59. John Logan, "The Union Avoidance Industry in the United States," *British Journal of Industrial Relations* 44, no. 4 (December 2006), 653–54.

60. Kris Maher, "Unions' New Foe: Consultants," *Wall Street Journal*, August 15, 2005, 1.

61. Rick Fantasia and Kim Voss, *Remaking the American Labor Movement* (Berkeley: University of California Press, 2004), 34–77 passim.

62. "A Manager's Toolbox to Remaining Union Free" (Bentonville: Wal-Mart Stores, Inc., 1997), on file at Food and Allied Service Trades Department, AFL-CIO.

63. Meeting notes from Eddie Lindsey to Don Harris (March 24, 2000), located in unprocessed files of the Impact Fund, Berkeley, Calif.

64. Wal-Mart, "You've Picked a Great Place to Work," copy in author's possession.

65. Jacoby, *Modern Manors*, 111–13; Logan, "The Union Avoidance Industry," 664.

66. "1998 Grass Roots Survey"; "History of Grass Roots," January 29, 2001; e-mail note, Katherine Ali to Al Zack, April 4, 2003, all in files of Impact Fund, Berkeley, Calif.

67. Al Zack to Roger Doolittle, December 11, 2003; Laura Pope to Tom Coughlin, "Wal-Mart Stores Grass Roots Results," May 7, 2001, both in Impact Fund files.

68. Complaint by "Drop," December 12, 1998, in Impact Fund files.

69. Christopher Hayes, "Symbol of the System," *In These Times*, November 6, 2005.

70. Wal-Mart, "A Manager's Toolbox to Remaining Union Free."

71. Conrad B. MacKerron, As You Sow Foundation et al., to H. Lee Scott, March 20, 2006, letter in author's possession.

72. Human Rights Watch, *Discounting Rights: Wal-Mart's Violation of US Workers' Right to Freedom of Association*, May 2007 at http://www.hrw.org, 92.

73. Ibid., 145–68; author's telephone interview with Tony Kuc, former assistant manager at Kingman, August 31, 2007; *Wal-Mart Stores, Inc. v. UFCW Local Union 99R*, February 28, 2003, case no. 28-CA-16832, NLRB.

74. Ibid., 154; Vicky Dodson, voice-mail transcripts, September 1, 5, 2000, exhibit 50, case no. 28-CA-16832, NLRB.

75. *Wal-Mart Stores, Inc. v. UFCW Local Union 99R*, supplemental decision, March 30, 2007, case no. 28-CA-16832.

76. Before the NLRB, Region 11, Wal-Mart Stores, Inc. and UFCW, case no. 11-CA-19105-1, hearing transcript, February 3, 2003, 459–61. Williams later quit Wal-Mart to become a labor relations executive for Honeywell.

77. Human Rights Watch, *Discounting Rights*, 146, 151; author's telephone interview with Tony Kuc.

78. Kirk Williams, voice-mail transcript, September 6, 2000; Human Rights Watch, *Discounting Rights*, 153.

79. Reported in "U.S. Newswire," November 2, 2000.

80. Human Rights Watch, *Discounting Rights*, 147, 152.

81. Ibid., 151.

82. Bianco, *The Bully of Bentonville*, 119–20, 235.

83. Vicky Dodson/Kirk Williams, voice-mail transcripts, September 6, 13, 25, 28, October 2, 3, 7, 9, 11, 2000. The labor team made a total of eighty-four reports to Bentonville, all within less than two months.

84. Wal-Mart Stores, Inc., 2003 NLRB Lexis 86 (2003).

85. Human Rights Watch, *Discounting Rights*, 203.

86. A portion of this speech is reported in Brian Ross, Maddy Sauer, and Rhonda Schwartz, "Clinton Remained Silent as Wal-Mart Fought Unions" (transcript), *ABC News*, January 31, 2008, at http://

abcnews.go.com. A more complete version is found in the Wal-Mart archive housed at Flagler Productions.

CHAPTER SIX: WAL-MART'S LONG MARCH TO CHINA

1. David Dollar, "Why Does One Country Draw More Investment Than Another?" *YaleGlobal* Web site, October 10, 2003.
2. Philip Goodman and Philip Pan, "Chinese Workers Pay for Wal-Mart's Low Prices," *Washington Post*, February 8, 2004.
3. Edna Bonacich with Khaleelah Hardie, "Wal-Mart and the Logistics Revolution," in *Wal-Mart*, ed. Lichtenstein, 163–88.
4. In the academy, the sociologist Emmanuel Wallerstein had first developed the idea of a "commodity chain" as part of his world systems schema. Such channels of world commerce were not new, not even a product of the industrial era, and as a consequence, they had something close to an organic, naturalistic provenance. Then in the 1980s, business consultants like Bain and Company coined the phrase "value chain management" or "supplier rationalization" to describe how components and materials were purchased and transformed into salable goods. The industrial relations scholars Frederick Abernathy and John Dunlop used the phrase "commodity channels" as recently as 1999 to describe the way apparel moved from Asian and Central American suppliers to North American retailers. In the twenty first century, however, the artful "supply chain" has become the pervasive terminology, especially in the hands of theorists such as Gary Gereffi and Gary Hamilton, who have emphasized the market-making potential of the contemporary buyer-driven supply networks in order to more clearly evaluate the hierarchy of power and profitability that characterizes contemporary global trade. For an overview of this literature see Jennifer Bair, "Global Capitalism and Commodity Chains: Looking Back, Going Forward," *Competition and Change* 9, no. 2 (June), 129–56; Frederick H. Abernathy, John T. Dunlop, Janice Hammon, and David Weil, *A Stitch in Time: Lean Retailing and the Transformation of Manufacturing—Lessons from the Apparel and Textile Industries* (New York: Oxford University Press, 1999); Gary Gereffi and Miguel Korzeniewicz, eds., *Commodity Chains and Global Capitalism* (Westport, Conn.: Praeger, 1994), 95–122. Author's telephone interview with former Bain and Company consultant, November 15, 2005.
5. Major Van Hart (retired), "Logistics: The Art of Doing War," at http://www.chuckshawks.com/logistics.htm.

6. Marc Levinson, *The Box: How the Shipping Container Made the World Smaller and the World Economy Bigger* (Princeton, N.J.: Princeton University Press, 2006), 171–88; Bahar Barami, "Productivity Gains from Pull Logistics: Tradeoffs of Internal and External Costs," paper presented at the Transportation Research Board Conference on Transportation and Economic Development, Portland, Ore., September 22–25, 2001.

7. Misha Petrovic and Gary Hamilton, "Making Global Markets: Wal-Mart and Its Suppliers," in *Wal-Mart*, ed. Lichtenstein, 107–42; see also Gary Hamilton, "Remaking the Global Economy: U.S. Retailers and Asian Manufacturers," hearing on "China and the Future of Globalization" before the U.S. China Economic and Security Review Commission, May 20, 2005; Naomi Klein, *No Logo: Taking Aim at the Brand Bullies* (New York: Picador, 1999).

8. Walton with Huey, *Made in America*, 83–84.

9. John Horan, "Wal-Mart Expects Sales of $1B Within 4 Years," *Women's Wear Daily*, April 18, 1977.

10. "Wal-Mart Buying Office Telephone Directory," November 5, 1976, in author's possession, courtesy of Chuck Webb; author's interview with Brent Berry, May 30, 2007, Rogers, Ark.

11. Walton with Huey, *Made in America*, 202.

12. Horan, "Wal-Mart Expects Sales of $1B Within 4 Years."

13. Walton with Huey, *Made in America*, 308.

14. Melina Lai, "A Glimpse at the People's Republic of China," *Wal-Mart World*, January 1982, 22.

15. Phyllis Overstreet, "Wal-Mart's Import Program—Sharpening Our Merchandise Strategy," *Wal-Mart World*, June 1989, 18; author's interview with Brent Berry.

16. Hamilton, "Remaking the Global Economy."

17. Sam Hornblower, "Wal-Mart in China: A Joint Venture," on PBS *Frontline* Web site, "Is Wal-Mart Good for America?"

18. Dana Frank, *Buy American: The Untold Story of Economic Nationalism* (Boston: Beacon Press, 1999), 131–38.

19. Ibid., 137.

20. Ibid., 187–97.

21. Eric Barton, "Life Without Wal-Mart," *Kansas City Pitch*, December 7, 2006.

22. "Wal-Mart Boasts 'Made in USA,'" *Discount Store News*, June 15, 1992, 127.

23. Ortega, *In Sam We Trust*, 208.

24. Ibid., 206; Stacey Duncan, "Merchandising Profiles: What It

Takes to Make a Conversion," *Wal-Mart World*, June 1989, 22. Although Wal-Mart never put out its own import figures, it is possible that the Buy American program briefly slowed the import rush, at least from Hong Kong and China. Using data from the U.S. *Journal of Commerce*, the Food and Allied Service Trades Department of the AFL-CIO found that the weight of Hong Kong and Chinese imports shipped by Wal-Mart increased only by 15 percent between 1988 and 1989 and by 5 percent the next year. But that was it. Thereafter South China imports exploded, doubling between 1990 and 1991 and then doubling again the next year as well. "Quantity of Wal-Mart Stores, Inc. Direct Imports of All Product Categories from the People's Republic of China and Hong Kong, January 1984–July 1992," found in FAST archive, Washington, D.C.

25. Bill Clinton speaking at 1986 Wal-Mart managers meeting, in Flagler Productions, reel MGR86LR.

26. Duncan, "Merchandising Profiles," 22.

27. Author's interview with Brent Berry.

28. Hornblower, "Wal-Mart in China."

29. Bill Bowden, "PREL CEO Says Wal-Mart's Policy Is No Sweat," *Northwest Arkansas Business Journal*, June 25, 2001.

30. Ibid.

31. Ortega, *In Sam We Trust*, 206.

32. Michael Barrier, "Walton's Mountain," *Nation's Business*, April 1988, 64.

33. Duncan, "Merchandising Profiles," 22–23.

34. "Wal-Mart Boasts 'Made in the USA,'" 127.

35. "Wal-Mart Campaign Brings Jobs," *Arkansas Democrat-Gazette*, March 14, 1985; Barrier, "Walton's Mountain."

36. Peggy Harris, "First 'Buy American' Firm Defends Wal-Mart Credo," *Morning News* (Ark.), December 24, 1992.

37. Caroline Mayer, "Wal-Mart Flies the Flag in Import Battle; Prods U.S. Producers with Favorable Terms," *Washington Post*, April 21, 1985; *Farris Fashions, Inc. and Amalgamated Clothing and Textile Workers Union*, Southwest Regional Joint Board, case nos. 26-CA-14258 and 26-RC-7323, September 30, 1993, 550; Richard Hurd, *Assault on Workers' Rights* (Washington, D.C.: Industrial Union Department, AFL-CIO, 1994), 39; author's telephone interview with Joan Suarez, former regional director for International Ladies' Garment Workers' Union, August 30, 2005; author's observations in Brinkley, Ark., June 5, 2006.

38. Bianco, *The Bully of Bentonville*, 187.

39. Clay Chandler, "The Great Wal-Mart of China," *Fortune*, July 25, 2005, 116.

40. Sarah Schafer, "A Welcome to Wal-Mart," *Newsweek International*, December 20, 2004, Web edition.

41. Ibid.

42. Xue Hong, "Wal-Mart's Ethical Standards Program: Public Relations vs. Sweatshops," paper delivered at the "Wal-Mart in China" workshop, Peking University, Beijing, June 30, 2007.

43. Ibid.

44. Eric Clark, *The Real Toy Story: Inside the Ruthless Battle for America's Youngest Consumers* (New York: Free Press, 2006), 217.

45. *The Hindu Business Line*, January 7, 2005.

46. Quoted in Xue Hong, "Wal-Mart's Ethical Standards Program."

47. Ibid.

48. Information in this paragraph is based on the discussions held at the "Wal-Mart in China" workshop, Peking University, Beijing, July 1, 2007.

49. Clark, *The Real Toy Story*, 194–95.

50. Yu Xiaomin, Pun Ngai, Chen You-Chung, and Chan Wai-ling, "Wal-Martization and Labor Practices of Toy Factories in South China," paper delivered at the "Wal-Mart in China" workshop.

51. Xue Hong, "Wal-Mart's Ethical Standards Program."

52. Steve Fraser, *Labor Will Rule: Sidney Hillman and the Rise of American Labor* (New York: Free Press, 1991), 27.

53. David Von Drehle, *Triangle: The Fire that Changed America* (New York: Atlantic, 2003).

54. Quoted in William Greider, "After the WTO Protest in Seattle, It's Time to Go on the Offensive," *Global Agenda*, January 31, 2000, from Global Policy Forum Web site.

55. Eileen Boris, "Consumers of the World Unite!: Campaigns Against Sweating, Past and Present," in Daniel Bender and Richard Greenwald, eds., *Sweatshop USA: The American Sweatshop in Historical and Global Perspective* (New York: Routledge, 2003), 203–5.

56. Ibid., 206–11.

57. NBC, *Dateline NBC*, December 22, 1992, prepared by Burrelle's Information Services.

58. Wendy Zeller, "O.K., So He's Not Sam Walton," *BusinessWeek*, March 16, 1992, 56–58.

59. Ortega, *In Sam We Trust*, 225–26.

60. Ibid., 225.

61. Ibid., 227.
62. David Glass, "Message to Associates," *Wal-Mart World*, February 1993, 4–5.
63. Ellen Neuborne, "Ad Support for Wal-Mart Swells," *USA Today*, January 12, 1993.
64. M. E. Freeman, "Wal-Mart Vendors Rally Behind Retailer with Ads," *Arkansas Democrat-Gazette*, December 24, 1992.
65. Phyllis Rice, "War on the Home Front," *Northwest Arkansas Times*, December 24, 1992.
66. "Wal-Mart: 2004 Report on Standards for Suppliers," at Wal-Mart Stores Web site, 2005.
67. Kyle Johnson and Peter Kinder, "Wal-Mart Stores, Inc.," Domini 400 Social Index Decision Series, No. 3, May 16, 2001; Molly Selvin, "Wal-Mart Faces Suit by Labor Group," *Los Angeles Times*, September 14, 2005.
68. Author's interview with Billy Han, SACOM, September 14, 2005, Hong Kong; author's interview with Dick Ambrocio, senior director, Reebok, September 13, 2005, Zhongshan.
69. Ibid.
70. Liu Kai-ming, "Research Report on Global Purchasing Practices and Chinese Women Workers" (Shenzhen: Institute of Contemporary Observation, 2003).
71. H. Lee Scott, "Twenty First Century Leadership," October 24, 2005, Wal-Mart Stores Web site.
72. Toh Han Shih, "Wal-Mart Dictates China Suppliers' Success on Its Terms," *South China Morning Post*, February 25, 2004.
73. Author's interview with Tom Mitchell, *South China Morning Post*, September 17, 2005, Hong Kong; author's interview with Liu Kai-ming, September 14, 2005.
74. Melina Lai, "Orient Offices—Strong Support Arm," *Wal-Mart World*, February 1982, 3; author's interview with Brent Berry, formerly of Wal-Mart international purchasing.
75. Author's interview with Brent Berry.
76. As quoted in Pun Ngai, "Global Production, Company Codes of Conduct, and Labor Conditions in China: A Case Study of Two Factories," *China Journal* 54 (July 2005), 101–13.
77. Hornblower, "Wal-Mart in China."
78. Richard Appelbaum organized this trip as part of his exploration of global supply chains. Eileen Boris and Karen Shapiro were also participants in the trip and did almost all the interviews.
79. Yue Yuen Industrial Holdings is the principal source of Pou Chen's

shoe production; as of June 2004, Pou Chen held 50.1 percent of the stock in Yue Yuen (http://www.yueyuen.com).

80. Sales data from Hoover's Web site. And see Yue Yuen's Web site at http://www.yueyuen.com for a more complete business profile.

81. Jeroen Merk, "Nike's Mirror Image: Yue Yuen and the Implementation of Labour Codes," paper presented at the forty-seventh ISA Convention, March 22–25, 2006, San Diego. Other clients include Polo Ralph Lauren, Kenneth Cole, Calvin Klein, and NBA Properties. About 60 percent of Yue Yuen's footwear production is for Nike, Reebok, and Adidas-Salomon.

82. Author's interview with Tiger Wu, Nike manufacturing manager, September 12, 2005, Dongguan; author's interview with Dick Ambrocio.

83. Associated Press, "Nike Ventures into Discount Shoe Business," *Clarion-Ledger* (Jackson, Miss.), April 23, 2005.

84. Author's interview with Tiger Wu.

85. Liu Kai-ming, "Global Purchasing Practices and Chinese Women Workers."

86. David Barboza and Louise Story, "Dancing Elmo Smackdown: In China, Mattel Toys Go Through the Wringer to Ensure Safety," *New York Times*, July 26, 2007; David Barboza, "Owner of Chinese Toy Factory Commits Suicide," *New York Times*, August 14, 2007.

87. Ortega, *In Sam We Trust*, 257.

88. Author's interview with Jenny Jiangheng, Research Center on Transnational Corporations, Ministry of Commerce, Beijing, June 29, 2007; *Annual Report on Social Responsibility of China Textile and Apparel Industry* (Beijing, 2006), 6.

89. Pun Ngai, *Made in China: Women Factory Workers in a Global Workplace* (Durham, NC.: Duke University Press, 2005), 46–48; author's interview with Pun Ngai, September 15, 2005, Hong Kong.

90. Murray Scot Tanner, "Chinese Government Responses to Rising Social Unrest," testimony presented to the US-China Economic and Security Review Commission, April 14, 2005; John Pomfret, "Labor Unrest in China Reflects Increasing Disenchantment," *Guardian Weekly*, May 4, 2000, 37.

91. Andrew Ross, *Fast Boat to China: Corporate Flight and the Consequences of Free Trade* (New York: Pantheon Books, 2006), 16.

92. Jim Yardley and David Barboza, "Help Wanted: China Finds Itself with a Labor Shortage," *New York Times*, April 3, 2005; Howard A. French, "Workers Demand Union at Wal-Mart Supplier in China," *New York Times*, December 16, 2004.

93. David Barboza, "China Drafts Law to Empower Unions and End Labor Abuse," *New York Times*, October 13, 2006.
94. Jonathan Adams, "New Labor Regulations Designed to Protect China's Workers Are Already Having an Impact," *Newsweek*, February 14, 2008, at http://www.newsweek.com.
95. Tim Costello, Brendan Smith, and Jeremy Brecher, "Labor Rights in China," *Foreign Policy in Focus*, December 21, 2006, at http://www.fpif.org.
96. Olivia Chung, "Last Call for Guangdong Shoemakers," *China Business*, February 5, 2008.
97. IHLO, "Sackings at Wal-Mart: Global Restructuring or Avoiding the New Contract Law?" December 2007, at http://www.ihlo.org.
98. Some reports indicate that the Chinese government favors workplace reforms that would facilitate unionization and end some labor abuses in the coastal districts. Intense opposition from U.S. and other foreign companies in China suggests that these labor law proposals may contain a few teeth. Barboza, "China Drafts Law to Empower Unions and End Labor Abuse."

CHAPTER SEVEN: DISCOUNT STORES IN EVERY CLIME?

1. "Wal-Mart International Operations," at http://www.walmartfacts.com.
2. Soderquist, *The Wal-Mart Way*, 17.
3. Bethany Moreton, "The Soul of Neoliberalism," *Social Text* 25, no. 3 (Fall 2007), 103.
4. Bill Saporito, "Inside the World's Biggest Store," *Time International*, January 20, 2003, 46.
5. Neil M. Coe and Martin Hess, "The Internationalization of Retailing: Implications for Supply Networks Restructuring East Asia and Eastern Europe," *Journal of Economic Geography*, 5 (April 2005), 450.
6. David Glass speaking at 1994 Wal-Mart manager's meeting, reel: MG94–142, Flagler Productions.
7. Alan Freeman and Marina Strauss, "Wal-Mart—What's to Hate?" *Toronto Globe and Mail*, February 19, 2005; "Canadian Fact Sheet," March 2008, at http://www.walmartstores.com/international.
8. Dana Flavelle, "Union Okays Loblaw Revamp," *Toronto Star*, October 17, 2006.
9. Barrie McKenna, "Unions Starting to Make Inroads at Wal-Mart," *Toronto Globe and Mail*, August 23, 2004.
10. Roy Adams, "Organizing Wal-Mart: The Canadian Campaign,"

Just Labour 6 and 7 (Autumn 2005), 2–3. However, in June 2005 the Liberals won control of Ontario again and restored to the labor board the power to automatically certify a union in the face of unlawful employer conduct.

11. John Stout and Jo-Anne Pickel, "The Wal-Mart Waltz in Canada: Two Steps Forward, One Step Back," *Connecticut Law Review* 39, no. 4 (May 2007), 1495–511. In October 2008, Wal-Mart also closed its Tire-and-Lube garage at a store in Gatineau after a Quebec arbitrator imposed a collective agreement on the company. "Wal-Mart Closes Shop Where Union Contract Imposed," Web site: CBS News, October 16, 2008.

12. Corporate Watch UK, "ASDA/Wal-Mart: A Corporate Profile," at http://www.corporatewatch.org.uk.

13. Steve Burt and Leigh Sparks, "ASDA: Wal-Mart in the United Kingdom," in *Wal-Mart World: The World's Biggest Corporation in the Global Economy,* ed. Stanley D. Brunn (New York: Routledge, 2006), 247–51; Bill Saporito, "Inside the World's Biggest Store," *Time International,* January 20, 2003, 46–47.

14. George Monbiot, "Economic Cleansing," *Guardian* (U.K.), June 17, 1999.

15. Burt and Sparks, "ASDA: Wal-Mart in the United Kingdom," 255–60. The Wal-Mart executive who met with Blair was Robert Martin, who resigned from the company just as soon as Wal-Mart announced the ASDA purchase. One can speculate that in contrast to the rest of the Bentonville high command, he was not certain that the regulatory climate in the United Kingdom was sufficiently accommodating.

16. Author's interviews with Martin Smith, GMB, June 19, 2007, London; and with Jeff Goswell, GMB, June 22, 2007, London.

17. Author's interview with Jeff Gosswell; press release, "Talks Tomorrow with ASDA on Bargaining Rights and Bonus in ASDA Depots," March 8, 2006 at http://www.gmb.org.uk.

18. Author's interview with Martin Smith; press release, "GMB ASDA Wal-Mart Depots National Strike Ballot Following ASDA Refusal to Deliver Deal of 11th April 2006," May 4, 2006, at http://www.gmb.org.uk.

19. Heather Timmons, "ASDA Settlement May Signal Shift in Wal-Mart Union Policy," *International Herald Tribune,* June 29, 2006; Eoin Callan and Jonathan Birchall, "Union Deal with Wal-Mart's Asda Unit," *Financial Times,* June 29, 2006.

20. Andreas Knorr and Andreas Arndt, "Why Did Wal-Mart Fail in

Germany (so far)?" unpublished paper available from Institute of World Economic and International Management, University of Bremen.

21. "Wal-Mart's Long Road of Self-Imposed Suffering in Germany," April 12, 2005, posted at http://www.union-network.org/unisite/sectors/commerce.

22. "Wal-Mart's Informant Hotline Reminds Many Europeans of Years of Communist Repression and East German Stasi," March 17, 2005, posted at http://www.union-network.org/unisite/sectors/commerce.

23. William Holstein, "Why Wal-Mart Can't Find Happiness in Japan," Fortune, August 6, 2007, 73–78.

24. Ibid., 74.

25. Chris Tilly, "Wal-Mart and Its Workers: NOT the Same All Over the World," Connecticut Law Review 39 (May 2007), 1815 17.

26. Elizabeth Malkin, "Mexican Retailers United Against Wal-Mart," New York Times, July 9, 2004.

27. Chris Tilly, "Wal-Mart in Mexico: The Limits of Growth," in Wal-Mart, ed. Lichtenstein, 201–9; Antonia Juhasz, "What Wal-Mart Wants from the WTO," AlterNet, December 13, 2005 at http://www.alternet.org/story/29464/.

28. Clay Chandler, "The Great Wal-Mart of China," Fortune, July 11, 2005.

29. Robert Slater, The Wal-Mart Triumph (New York: Penguin, 2003), 153–54; Dorinda Elliott and Bill Powell, "Wal-Mart Nation," June 19, 2005, at http://www.time.com.

30. David J. Davies, "Wal-Mao: The Discipline of Corporate Culture and Studying Success at Wal-Mart China," China Journal 58 (July 2007), 1–2.

31. Author's observations from tour of Beijing Wal-Mart, June 28, 2007.

32. Davies, "Wal-Mao," 10–15.

33. Author's interview with David Davies, June 28, 2007, Beijing.

34. Mark Williams, "Wal-Mart in China: Will the Regulatory System Ensnare the American Leviathan?" Connecticut Law Review 39, no. 4 (May 2007), 1361–82.

35. Ibid.

36. "China Fact Sheet," March 2008, at http://www.walmartstores.com/international.

37. Don Lee, "Big Boxes Battle in China," Los Angeles Times, July 2, 2006.

38. Lan Xinzhen, "Wal-Mart Presence: Can the Retail Giant Maintain Its Success in China?" *Beijing Review,* August 31, 2005, at http://www.bjreview.com.cn/En-2005/05-31-e.

39. Author's interview with Marshall Ma, general manager of a Wal-Mart store in Beijing, June 28, 2007.

40. Eileen Otis, "Working in Walmart, Kunming: Technology, Outsourcing, and Retail Globalization," paper presented at the conference "Wal-Mart in China," June 30, 2007.

41. Author's interview with Marshall Ma; this internal outsourcing is not alien to the retail industry in the United States. In the 1960s and early 1970s, before Wal-Mart developed its celebrated replenishment/distribution system, Sam Walton's company also rented out space for shoe, jewelry, and pharmacy departments to other firms.

42. Otis, "Working in Walmart, Kunming"; author's interview with Marshall Ma.

43. Anita Chan, "Realities and Possibilities for Chinese Trade Unionism," in *The Future of Organized Labour: Global Perspectives,* ed. Craig Phelan (Bern: Peter Lang AG, 2006), 286–87.

44. Ibid.

45. "Some Transnationals Go Seriously Against Trade Union Law, All China Workers Union," *People's Daily Online,* October 27, 2004; "Wal-Mart President Rushed to China to Conduct Urgent Crisis Management," *Beijing Times,* translated and posted November 3, 2004.

46. David Barboza, "Wal-Mart Bows to Trade Unions at Stores in China," *New York Times,* November 2, 2005.

47. Anita Chan, "Organizing Wal-Mart: The Chinese Trade Union at a Crossroads," *Japan Focus,* http://www.japanfocus.org, posted September 8, 2006.

48. Ibid.

49. Tim Johnson, "Wal-Mart Unions in China to be Controlled by Government, Lack Free Elections," *San Jose Mercury News,* August 15, 2006.

CHAPTER EIGHT: HOW WAL-MART MAKES THE RULES

1. Hugh Sidey, "The Two Sides of the Walton Legacy," *Time,* April 20, 1992, 50.

2. Karen Blumenthal, "Arrival of Discounter Tears the Civic Fabric of Small-Town Life," *Wall Street Journal,* April 14, 1987.

3. Kevin Helliker, "Advertising: Small-Town Newspapers Retaliate

When Wal-Mart Cuts Advertising," *Wall Street Journal*, October 14, 1992.

4. Julie Morris, "Store Shuts Doors on Texas Town," *USA Today*, October 11, 1990; Lisa Belkin, "Wal-Mart, Once Again, Shakes Up Texas Town," *New York Times*, December 14, 1990.

5. Steve Bishop, "Wal-Mart Killed Hearne, Texas—Twice," *Dallas Morning News*, November 22, 1992.

6. Author's telephone interview with Margaret Gardner, president of Gardner Construction in Chicago, January 29, 2008.

7. Paul Kaplan, "Battles over Wal-Mart Stir Passions," *Atlanta Journal-Constitution*, December 27, 2004.

8. *1990 Wal-Mart Annual Report; 1995 Wal-Mart Annual Report*.

9. Kenneth Stone, "Impact of Wal-Mart Stores and Other Mass Merchandisers in Iowa, 1983–1993," *Iowa State University, Economic Development Review*, Spring 1995.

10. Quoted in Andrew Rowell, "The Wal-Martians Have Landed," *Ecologist* 29 (August–September 1999), 308.

11. Transcript, "Up Against the Wal-Mart," *60 Minutes*, April 30, 1995, in FAST Wal-Mart archive.

12. Author's telephone interview with Al Norman, February 12, 2008.

13. Anita French, "Wal-Mart Rolls On Despite Opposition," *Morning News* (Ark.), June 27, 2006.

14. Evan Halper, "Orange County: Thinking Outside Big-Box Zoning" *Los Angeles Times*, April 29, 2002.

15. Paul G. Lewis, "Retail Politics: Local Sales Taxes and the Fiscalization of Land Use," *Economic Development Quarterly* 15, no. 1 (February 2001), 24–28.

16. Rachel Torres interview with Carl Morehouse, May 8, 2007, Ventura, Calif., in author's possession.

17. Kathie Sutin, "Revenue from Wal-Mart, Sam's Is Allowing Maplewood to Grow," *St. Louis Post-Dispatch*, June 23, 2005.

18. Stacy Mitchell, *Big Box Swindle: The True Cost of Mega-Retailers and the Fight for America's Independent Businesses* (Boston: Beacon Press, 2006), 166.

19. Philip Mattera and Anna Purinton, *Shopping for Subsidies: How Wal-Mart Uses Taxpayer Money to Finance Its Never-Ending Growth* (Washington: Good Jobs First, 2004), 22.

20. Ibid., 14.

21. Stacey Duncan, "The Wal-Mart Touch," *Wal-Mart World* (May 1990), 20.

22. Betty Feng and Jeff Krehely, "The Waltons and Wal-Mart: Self-Interested Philanthropy," National Committee for Responsive Philanthropy (September 2005), at http://www.ncrp.org.

23. Associated Press, "Wal-Mart Is Top Corporate Charity," March 27, 2007, at http://www.msnbe.msn.com/id/17803920.

24. Walton with Huey, *Made in America*, 306.

25. Richard C. Halverson, "A Grass-Roots Approach to Charity," *Discount Store News*, December 18, 1989, 221.

26. Duncan, "The Wal-Mart Touch," 20.

27. Betsy Reithemeyer speaking at the 2004 managers meeting in Dallas, reel MGR04DAL, Flagler Productions.

28. Target Foundation, "2005 Grants," November 27, 2006, at http://www.targetcorp.com/.

29. "The Wal-Mart Foundation," 990-PF (tax return of private foundation), 2005, found at the Foundation Center Web site.

30. "Community Comes First," *Discount Store News*, October 1999.

31. Liza Featherstone, "On the Wal-Mart Money Trail," *Nation*, November 21, 2005.

32. Testimony of Jason Jackson, director of business continuity global security, Wal-Mart Stores, Inc., at Senate Homeland Security and Governmental Affairs Committee, November 16, 2005; see also Devin Leonard, "The Only Lifeline Was the Wal-Mart," *Fortune*, October 3, 2005, 77–78.

33. Halverson, "A Grass-Roots Approach to Charity," 221.

34. Michael Barbaro and Justin Gillis, "Wal-Mart at Forefront of Hurricane Relief," *Washington Post*, September 6, 2005.

35. Leonard, "The Only Lifeline Was the Wal-Mart," 76.

36. Quoted in Philip Mattera, "Disaster Relief: How Wal-Mart Used Hurricane Katrina to Repair Its Image," Corporate Research E-Letter no. 55, September–October 2005, at Corporate Research Project Web page, http://www.corp-research.org/archives/sept-oct05.

37. Ibid., 2.

38. John Tierney, "From FEMA to WEMA," *New York Times*, September 20, 2005.

39. Ibid., 3.

40. Carol J. Loomis, "Helen Walton's Will," *Fortune*, May 14, 2007, 18.

41. Jill Barshay, "Trying to Hold On for the Walton Family Foundation," *CQ Weekly*, November 7, 2005, 2978.

42. Walton with Huey, *Made in America*, 302.

43. Featherstone, "On the Wal-Mart Money Trail."

44. "The Walton Family Foundation, Inc." at http://www.wffhome

.com/program_focus.html, accessed October 22, 2005; Joanee Jacobs, "The Carnegie of School Choice," *Philanthropy Roundtable*, September 1, 2005, at http://www.philanthropyroundtable.org.

45. Michael Barbaro and Stephanie Strom, "Conservatives Help Wal-Mart and Vice Versa," *New York Times*, September 8, 2006.

46. Andy Serwer, "The Waltons: Inside America's Richest Family," *Fortune*, November 15, 2004, 88.

47. Dan Lips, "John Walton's Real Legacy," *Heritage Foundation*, September 22, 2005, at http://www.heritage, org/Press/Commentary/ed.

48. Featherstone, "On the Wal-Mart Money Trail."

49. Serwer, "The Waltons," 89; see also Glen Ford and Peter Gamble, "Wal-Mart Prepares to Bury the Left Under a Mountain of Money," *Black Commentator*, March 31, 2004, at http://www.blackcommen tator.com.

50. Fishman, *The Wal-Mart Effect*, 240–41.

51. Arindrajit Dube and Ken Jacobs, "The Hidden Cost of Wal-Mart Jobs: Use of Safety Net Programs by Wal-Mart Workers in California," University of California Berkeley Labor Center, Briefing Paper Series, August 24, 2004.

52. Jesse Eisinger, "Best and Worst: Health Care Benefits Vary Widely from Industry to Industry," *Wall Street Journal*, October 24, 1996.

53. AFL-CIO, "Wal-Mart: An Example of Why Workers Remain Uninsured and Underinsured," October 2003, 11.

54. Center for a Changing Workforce, "Wal-Mart and Health Care: Condition Critical," October 26, 2005, at http://www.cfcw.org. CFCW is a Seattle based nonprofit health research and policy analysis organization.

55. Human Rights Watch, *Discounting Rights*, 206.

56. Ibid., 43.

57. Bernard Wysocki and Ann Zimmerman, "Bargain Hunter: Wal-Mart Cost-Cutting Finds a Big Target in Health Benefits," *Wall Street Journal*, September 30, 2003.

58. Human Rights Watch, *Discounting Rights*, 47–48.

59. Jason Roberson, "Wal-Mart Touts High Deductibles," *Dallas Morning News*, May 24, 2007.

60. Steven Malanga, "What Does the War on Wal-Mart Mean?" *City Journal*, Spring 2004.

61. Theo Francis and Ellen Schultz, "Health Accounts Have Benefits for Employers," *Wall Street Journal*, February 3, 2006.

62. Barbara T. Dreyfuss, "Cheap Trick: Bush's Health-Savings Accounts

Are a Bargain—Provided You Never Get Injured or Sick," *American Prospect*, September 2004, 25–26.

63. Ricardo Alonso-Zaldivar, "Healthcare Overhaul Is Quietly Underway," *Los Angeles Times*, January 31, 2005.

64. Steven Greenhouse and Michael Barbaro, "Wal-Mart Memo Suggests Ways to Cut Employee Benefit Costs," *New York Times*, October 26, 2005.

65. Reed Abelson and Michael Barbaro, "The Public Face of Wal-Mart's Health Care Program," *New York Times*, November 13, 2007.

66. Ann Zimmerman, "Wal-Mart Insured Ranks Rise; Half of Employees Take Retailer Plans," *Wall Street Journal*, January 23, 2008.

67. Greenhouse and Barbaro, "Wal-Mart Memo."

68. Associated Press, "Wal-Mart Increases Starting Pay, Adds Wage Caps," *USA Today*, August 7, 2006.

69. Steven Greenhouse and Michael Barbaro, "At Wal-Mart, a Push to Cut Worker Costs," *New York Times*, October 2, 2006.

70. Greenhouse and Barbaro, "Wal-Mart Memo."

71. Mark Fefer, "Attention Wal-Mart Workers: Please Do Not Report Injuries," *Seattle Weekly*, April 18, 2001.

72. *Wal-Mart Stores, Inc. v. Lee Douglass, Insurance Commissioner of Arkansas*, CA 95-34, Court of Appeals of Arkansas, opinion delivered May 8, 1996.

73. Valerie Smith, "State Sues Wal-Mart Over Workers' Comp," *Arkansas Gazette*, August 23, 1991.

74. Ellen Rosen, "Adding Insult to Injury: Wal-Mart's Workers Compensation Scam," *New Labor Forum* 17, no. 1 (Spring 2008), 58–59.

75. Author's telephone interview with Edward White, January 22, 2008.

76. Christie Toth, "The NOC on Wal-Mart," *Portland Phoenix*, June 3–9, 2005. "NOC" stands for Notice of Controversy, which Wal-Mart files when it contests a workers' compensation claim.

77. Washington State Department of Labor and Industries, "Wal-Mart's Privilege to Manage Workers' Comp Benefits Revoked," December 6, 2000.

78. Washington State Department of Labor and Industries, "L&I Settles Wal-Mart Decertification Case; Workers Win Protections," February 14, 2002.

79. *State of Maine Workers' Compensation Board Office of Monitoring, Audit & Enforcement v. Claims Management, Inc.*, "Consent Decree" found on Maine Workers' Compensation Board Web page;

author's telephone interview with Steve Minkowsky, deputy director of benefits administration, January 25, 2008.

80. Ibid.

CHAPTER NINE: WAL-MART VERSUS THE WORLD IT HAS CREATED

1. Frank Norris, *The Octopus: A Story of California* (1901; reprint, New York: Viking Press, 1986), 616–17.

2. Ida Tarbell, *The History of the Standard Oil Company* (New York: McGuire, Philips and Co., 1904).

3. Quoted in Stephen Meyer III, *The Five Dollar Day: Labor Management and Social Control in the Ford Motor Company, 1908–1921* (Albany: State University of New York Press, 1981), 164.

4. Wake-Up Wal-Mart press release, "MSNBC Democratic Presidential Debate Asks the Question 'Is Wal-Mart a Good Thing or Bad Thing for America?'" April 27, 2007, at http://www.earthtimes.org; Dennis Roddy, "John Edwards on Campaign Trail Again, This Time Against Wal-Mart," *Pittsburgh Post-Gazette*, August 5, 2006.

5. Pallavi Gogoi, "Can Barack Wake Up Wal-Mart?" *BusinessWeek*, November 16, 2006.

6. Quoted in Floyd Norris, "Swiping at Industry from Atop the Stump," *New York Times*, August 20, 2006.

7. Wal-Mart Facts, at http://www.walmartfacts.com.

8. Statistics taken from ibid.

9. Joel Jordan, "With Such Victories, Who Needs Defeats?" *New Labor Forum* 13, no. 3 (Fall 2004), 50.

10. Martin Zimmerman and Ronald D. White, "Ralphs to Pay $70 Million for Illegal Hiring Scheme," *Los Angeles Times*, July 1, 2006.

11. Jordan, "With Such Victories, Who Needs Defeats?" 47–56.

12. Ken Jacobs, Arindrajit Dube, and Felix Su, "Declining Health Coverage in the Southern California Grocery Industry," University of California, Berkeley, Labor Center, January 2007.

13. Steve Fraser, "The 'Labor Question,'" in Steve Fraser and Gary Gerstle, *The Rise and Fall of the New Deal Order, 1930–1980* (Princeton, N.J.: Princeton University Press, 1989), 55–84; see also Nelson Lichtenstein, *State of the Union: A Century of American Labor* (Princeton: Princeton University Press, 2002), 12–16.

14. An excellent summary article, focusing on the Los Angeles region, is Scott Cummings, "Law in the Labor Movement's Challenge to Wal-Mart: A Case Study of the Inglewood Site Fight," *California Law Review* 95 (2007), 1927–98.

15. Bianco, *The Bully of Bentonville*, 155.
16. Ibid., 156.
17. Nancy Cleeland and Debora Vrana, "Wal-Mart CEO Takes His Case to California," *Los Angeles Times*, February 24, 2005.
18. Cummings, "Law in the Labor Movement's Challenge to Wal-Mart."
19. John Wagner, "Maryland Legislature Overrides Veto on Wal-Mart Bill," *Washington Post*, January 13, 2006.
20. Liza Featherstone, "Race to the Bottom," *Nation*, March 28, 2005, at http://www.nation.com.
21. Lorene Yue, "Daley Vetoes Big-box Ordinance," *Chicago Business*, September 11, 2006, at http://www.chicagobusiness.com; Monica Davey and Michael Barbaro, "Chicago Minimum Wage Ordinance Fails," *New York Times*, September 14, 2006.
22. Edward Zelinsky, "Maryland's Wal-Mart Act: Policy and Preemption," *Cardozo Law Review*, 28, 847–90.
23. Orly Lobel, "Big Box Benefits: The Targeting of Giants in a National Campaign to Raise Work Conditions," *Connecticut Law Review* 39, no. 4 (May 2007), 1708.
24. Author's telephone interview with Al Norman, February 12, 2008.
25. Kate Ackley, "Wal-Mart, Under Fire, Builds a Lobbying Team Befitting a Giant," *Roll Call*, June 6, 2005.
26. Michael Barbaro, "A New Weapon for Wal-Mart: A War Room," *New York Times*, November 1, 2005.
27. Bianco, *The Bully of Bentonville*, 293.
28. Adam Nagourney and Michael Barbaro, "Eye on Election, Democrats Run as Wal-Mart Foe," *New York Times*, August 17, 2006.
29. Ann Zimmerman and Kris Maher, "Wal-Mart Warns of Democratic Win," *Wall Street Journal*, August 1, 2008, A1.
30. "Wal-Mart to Begin Voter Registration Campaign with Public Service Announcement on In-Store TV Network," at http://walmartstores.com, September 11, 2008; Zogby Interactive, "McCain Wins Wal-Mart Shoppers, but Obama Prevailed at Target, Macy's, Costco & JC Penney," at www.zogby.com, December 8, 2008.
31. "For Most of the Country, a Blue Shift," *New York Times*, November 6, 2008, P1.
32. NWAnews.com, April 24, 2006.
33. Michael Barbaro, "Wal-Mart's Detractors Come in from the Cold," *New York Times*, June 5, 2008, C1.
34. Philip Mattera, "Is Wal-Mart Going Soft? The Giant Retailer Embraces Style and Social Responsibility—Up to a Point," Corporate

Research E-Letter no. 60, July–August 2006, at http://www.corp-research.org/archives.
35. Robert Reich, *Supercapitalism: The Transformation of Business, Democracy, and Everyday Life* (New York: Alfred A. Knopf, 2007), 187.
36. Joshua Green, "The New War Over Wal-Mart," *Atlantic Monthly,* June 2006, 38–39.
37. Cleeland and Vrana, "Wal-Mart CEO Takes His Case to California."
38. "Wal-Mart's Impact on Society: A Key Moment in Time for American Capitalism," an Open Letter to readers of the *New York Review of Books* from Lee Scott, President and CEO, Wal-Mart Stores, April 2005.
39. Michael Crittenden and Rebecca Adams, "Mr. Sam Comes to Washington," *CQ Weekly,* November 7, 2005.
40. Don Soderquist, "Wal-Mart Sees New Rules as Threat to Workforce Stability," *Discount Store News,* May 16, 1994.
41. Data taken from http://www.opensecrets.org, a Web site that summarizes and archives PAC contributions and expenditures.
42. Emily Miller, "Wal-Mart in Washington," at PBS *Frontline* Web site, "Is Wal-Mart Good for America?"
43. Michael Forsythe, "Washington Presence Pays off for Wal-Mart in Medicare Bill," *Los Angeles Business Journal,* December 15, 2003.
44. "Remarks by the Vice President to Employees of the Wal-Mart Distribution Center," May 3, 2004, at http://www.whitehouse.gov/news/releases/2004/05/.
45. Jim Snyder, "From Restaurants to Wal-Mart," *The Hill,* June 14, 2005.
46. Shawn Zeller, "Wal-Mart Gets Protective Cover in Retail Trade Group," *CQ Weekly,* May 1, 2006; *RILA Report,* April 24, 2008, at RILA Web site.
47. Alex Daniels, "Bush Nominee Quizzed by Panel," http://www.nwanews.com, August 2, 2006.
48. Michael Barbaro, "Image Effort by Wal-Mart Takes a Turn," *New York Times,* May 12, 2006.
49. "Working Families for Wal-Mart," from SourceWatch: A Project of the Center for Media and Democracy, at http://www.sourcewatch.org/index.
50. Abigail Goldman, "Young to Quit Wal-Mart Group After Racial Remarks," *Los Angeles Times,* August 18, 2006; Anne Kornblut and Jim Rutenberg, "Tennessee Controversy Shaped by Spin Expert," *New York Times,* October 27, 2006.
51. Jeffrey Goldberg, "Selling Wal-Mart," *New Yorker,* April 2, 2007, 32–38.

52. Marc Gunther, "The Green Machine," *Fortune*, August 7, 2006, 44, 48.
53. Abigail Goldman, "Wal-Mart Goes 'Green,'" *Los Angeles Times*, November 13, 2006.
54. Kim Chipman and Lauren Coleman-Lochner, "Wal-Mart Warms to Democrats," *International Herald Tribune*, December 4, 2006.
55. Josephine Hearn, "Corporate Executives Played Key Role in Passage of the VRA," *The Hill*, July 28, 2006.
56. Reich, *Supercapitalism*, 186.
57. Anne D'Innocenzio, "The Week's Business: Is Wal-Mart Really Changing?" *Pittsburgh Post Gazette*, October 31, 2005; Peter Flaherty of the National Legal and Policy Center offered his critique of Wal-Mart appeasement at the company's 2007 annual shareholders' meeting. Author's observations and notes.
58. "Citizen's Groups Blocked 47 Wal-Mart Supercenters Last Year," at http://www.sprawl-busters.com, March 10, 2007.
59. George Will, "Democrats vs. Wal-Mart," *Washington Post*, September 14, 2006.
60. Steven Malanga, "What Does the War on Wal-Mart Mean?" *City Journal*, Spring 2004.
61. Michael Barbaro and Steven Greenhouse, "Wal-Mart Chief Writes Off New York," *New York Times*, March 28, 2007.
62. Author's interview with Kevin R. Elliott, senior vice president, Hill & Knowlton, April 28, 2005, Bentonville, Ark.
63. "Attention: All Store Managers," October 31, 2005, as reproduced at http://www.walmartmovie.com, which was the Robert Greenwald Web page for *Wal-Mart: The High Cost of Low Price*.
64. Alan Murray, "Labor Tries Political Tack Against Wal-Mart," *Wall Street Journal*, August 10, 2005.
65. "Wal-Mart's Impact on Society: A Key Moment in Time for American Capitalism."
66. Women, children, and older citizens have composed a majority of the workforce in many employment sectors, including the garment trades, food processing, secondary-school teaching, and the old department stores. But these industries were not template enterprises at the core of the American political economy.
67. These estimates are by the consulting firm Global Insight, as reported in Jared Bernstein, L. Josh Bivens, and Arindrajit Dube, "Wrestling with Wal-Mart: Tradeoffs Between Profits, Prices and Wages," *EPI Working Paper*, June 15, 2006, 2.
68. "Wal-Mart and California: A Key Moment in Time for American

Capitalism," an address by H. Lee Scott, President and CEO, Wal-Mart Stores, Inc., Los Angeles Town Hall, February 23, 2005, at http://www.walmartfacts.com; Bradford C. Johnson, "Retail: The Wal-Mart Effect," *McKinsey Quarterly* 1 (2002), 40–43.

69. Andrew Leonard, "Obama's New Pro-Wal-Mart Economist," Salon .com, June 12, 2008.

70. John Tierney, "The Good Goliath," *New York Times*, November 29, 2005.

71. Quoted in Jeffrey Goldberg, "Selling Wal-Mart," *New Yorker*, April 2, 2007, 38.

72. David Barboza, "China Inflation Exacting a Toll Across the U.S.," *New York Times*, February 1, 2008.

73. Bernstein, Bivens, and Dube, "Wrestling with Wal-Mart," 6.

74. Ibid., 6.

75. H. Lee Scott, "Wal-Mart: Twenty-First Century Leadership," October 24, 2005, 13–14, found at Wal-Mart Facts Web site.

76. Liza Featherstone, "Wal-Mart Helps Defeat Minimum Wage," the *Nation's* blog, "The Notion," June 22, 2006, at http.//www.the-nation.com/blogs/notion.

77. Meg Jacobs, *Pocketbook Politics: Economic Citizenship in Twentieth-Century America* (Princeton, N.J.: Princeton University Press, 2004).

78. U.S. Department of Labor, *Handbook of Labor Statistics*, Bulletin 2217, Washington, D.C., 1984, 201–3.

79. Anthony Bianco, "Wal-Mart's Midlife Crisis," *BusinessWeek*, April 30, 2007.

80. Wal-Mart, *1992 Annual Report*, 5. Sales rose 35 percent over the previous year, to $44 billion.

81. Sprawl-Busters, "Citizen Opposition Forces Wal-Mart to Apply Brakes on Growth," June 2, 2007, at http://www.sprawl-busters. com; author's interview with Al Norman, February 12, 2008.

82. Bianco, "Wal-Mart's Midlife Crisis."

83. Target Corporation, at http://http://sites.target.com.

84. Laura Rowley, *On Target: How the World's Hottest Retailer Hit a Bull's-Eye* (New York: John Wiley, 2003), 9.

85. George Anderson, "Target's Tactics Called Heavy Handed," March 31, 2006, *Retailwire*, at http://www.retailwire.com.

86. Kari Lydersen, "Target: Wal-Mart Lite," April 20, 2006, at Corp-Watch (http://www.corpwatch.org).

87. Edna Bonacich and Jake B. Wilson, *Getting the Goods: Ports, Labor, and the Logistics Revolution* (Ithaca, N.Y.: Cornell University Press, 2008), 137.

88. Steven Greenhouse, "How Costco Became the Anti-Wal-Mart," *New York Times,* July 17, 2005; Walton with Huey, *Made in America,* 102.
89. "A Rich Man Wants to Share the Wealth," *Multinational Monitor* 16, no. 12 (December 1995), 143–44, 27–28.
90. Stanley Holmes and Wendy Zeller, "The Costco Way," *Business-Week,* April 12, 2004, 76–77; Ann Zimmerman, "Costco's Dilemma: Be Kind to Its Workers, or Wall Street?" *Wall Street Journal,* March 26, 2004; Michael Forsythe and Rachel Katz, "Retailers in Political Battle," *National Post* (Canada), July 21, 2004.
91. Moira Herbst, "The Costco Challenge: An Alternative to Wal-Martization?" the Labor Research Association online, accessed August 11, 2005, at http://www.laborresearch.org.
92. Morris Newman, "Nobody Plays the Redevelopment Game Better than Price Club," *California Planning and Development Report,* August 1991, 10, in files of FAST, AFL-CIO; Greenhouse, "How Costco Became the Anti-Wal-Mart."
93. Impact Fund, "National Class Action Gender Bias Suit Filed Against Costco," August 17, 2004, at http://www.genderclassactionagainstcostco.com; Marc Lifsher, "Costco's Petition Drive Violates Law, Union Says," *Los Angeles Times,* March 30, 2004. (The threat that the initiative would appear on the ballot proved pressure enough to force a compromise with pro-labor Democrats in the state legislature.)
94. Herbst, "The Costco Challenge."
95. Andrea Chang, "Picture Gets Fuzzy for Circuit City," *Los Angeles Times,* November 11, 2008, 11.
96. Milt Freudenheim, "Employers Offer Workers Fewer Health Care Plans," *New York Times,* November 15, 2008.
97. Stephanie Rosenbloom, "Wal-Mart Stands Apart as a Holiday Contender," *New York Times,* November 6, 2008, B1.
98. Miguel Bustillo and Ann Zimmerman, "Wal-Mart View: Big Plans Abroad, Small U.S. Stores," *Wall Street Journal,* October 29, 2008, B8; Parija Kavilanz, "Wal-Mart Names New CEO," CNNMoney .com, November 21, 2008.
99. As quoted in Wal-Mart Watch, *Weekly Update,* November 12, 2008, at WalmartWatch.com.
100. Tom Mitchell, "Wal-Mart in Pay Deals with Chinese Unions," FT .com, July 24, 2008.
101. Ajay Goel, Nazgol Moussavi, and Vats Srivatsan, "Time to Rethink Offshoring?" *McKinsey Quarterly,* September 2008.
102. Walton with Huey, *Made in America,* 216.

AFTERWORD

1. Rob Walton, Wal-Mart 2009 Annual Report, 12.
2. Stephanie Rosenbloom, "Wal-Mart Outpaces a Weak Economy," *New York Times*, February 18, 2009.
3. Powerpoint Exhibits, Wal-Mart Stores, Inc. 16th Annual Meeting for the Investment Community, Day 1, Session 1, October 21, 2009, at www.walmartfacts.com.
4. Data taken from 2008 Bureau of Labor Statistics Web page at www.bls.gov/.
5. Miguel Bustillo and Ann Zimmerman, "Wal-Mart View: Big Plans Abroad, Small U.S. Stores," *Wall Street Journal*, October 29, 2008, Parija Kavilanz, "Wal-Mart Names New CEO," CNNMoney.com, November 21, 2008.
6. U.S. Department of Labor, Employment Standards Administration Wage and Hour Division, "2007 Statistics Fact Sheet," at http://www.dol.gov/esa/whd/statisitcs/.
7. "Labor Secretary Solis Pledges To Put Enforcement Back at DOL," *Daily Labor Report*, March 3, 2009.
8. Steven Greenhouse and Stephanie Rosenbloom, "Wal-Mart Settles 63 Lawsuits Over Wages," *New York Times*, December 24, 2008.
9. "Sustainability Index," at www.walmartstpres.com.
10. Chris Frates, "Wal-Mart Lends Muscle to Health Reform," *Politico*, March 17, 2009 at www.politico.com.
11. Pamela Lewis Dolan, "Wal-Mart Backs Employer Mandate for Health Coverage," *American Medical News*, July 27, 2009.
12. Janet Adamy and Ann Zimmerman, "Wal-Mart Backs Drive to Make Companies Pay for Health Coverage," *Wall Street Journal*, July 1, 2009.
13. Only about 40 percent of all retailers provide health benefits, compared to 63 percent of all employers. Small companies, those with fewer than 200 employees, are much less likely to offer such benefits.
14. Ann Zimmerman, "Retailer's Image Moves from Demon to Darling," *Wall Street Journal*, July 16, 2009.
15. Don Davis, "NRF/RILA Bust-up: Small Fry Find It Hard To Make Common Cause With Retailing Industry's Great White Sharks," *Internet Retailer*, September 2009 at www.internetretailer.com.
16. Final Transcript, Wal-Mart Stores, Inc. 16th Annual Meeting for the Investment Community, Day 2, Session 3, 5, October 22, 2009, at www.walmartstores.com.
17. "Walmart U.S. Capital Expenditures," (Powerpoint) in Final Transcript,

Wal-Mart Stores, Inc. 16th Annual Meeting for the Investment Community, Day 1 Session 1, 43, October 21, 2009, at www.walmartstores.com.

18. "Prices—TV Commercial," May 11, 2009, at www.walmartstores.com.

19. Global Insight, "The Price Impact of Wal-Mart: An Update Through 2007," at www.walmartstores.com.

20. Niall Ferguson and Moritz Schularick, "The End of Chimerica," Working Paper 10 037, Harvard Business School, October 2009.

21. Tom Mitchell, "Wal-Mart in Pay Deals with Chinese Unions," FT.com, July 24, 2008.

22. Ajay Goel, Nazgol Moussavi, and Vats Srivatsan, "Time to Rethink Offshoring?" McKinsey Quarterly, September 2008.

23. Sam Walton with John Huey, Sam Walton, Made in America: My Story (New York: Doubleday, 1992), 216.

ACKNOWLEDGMENTS

It would be an exaggeration to claim that this book had its origins in 1959, when I first clerked in my father's dime store, located right on Main Street in Frederick, Maryland, a still-Southern town not all that different from those in which Sam Walton was putting his first generation of retail stores. I disliked "waiting" on customers, sorting the merchandise, and keeping an eye out for shoplifters. When my father sold out in 1962— the very year that Walton opened his first true discount store in far-off Arkansas—the family was relieved. Certainly, neither my brother nor I wanted to grow up in order to run Dad's three-store, small-town chain.

But for decades afterward, some retail resonance reverberated in the far recesses of my mind. I never quite forgot the long car drives to the Baltimore wholesale houses where we could pick up a deal on ten dozen blouses or sneakers; the visiting salesmen, some refugees from Hungary or Poland, whose banter had already become half-Americanized; the lucrative excitement of the holiday rush as well as the growing competition from the suburban shopping centers; and the increasingly difficult racial terrain, which found my father stocking a set of dolls, both "colored" and white, even as he wrote small checks to the more militant civil rights organizations. Sam Walton confronted and transformed this same retail culture, which may well have made this study of his empire not quite such an alien enterprise after all.

Unlike established companies such as Ford or defunct ones like the Pennsylvania Railroad, Wal-Mart has no readily available corporate archive, so I had to scurry about to find materials on the company, its competitors, its suppliers, its executives, and its employees. For almost twenty-five years, ever since a 1985 issue of *Forbes* celebrated Sam Walton as the richest man in America, the company has been the subject of a wide variety of investigative reports in the *Wall Street*

Journal, the *Financial Times, Discount Store News,* the *New York Times,* the *Los Angeles Times,* and the *Northwest Arkansas News.* Indeed, the company is so big and so controversial that for some reporters Wal-Mart is their near-exclusive "beat." Nancy Cleeland, Abigail Goldman, Steven Greenhouse, Ann Zimmerman, Sam Ortega, and Jonathan Birchall are among the reporters with whom I have exchanged information and ideas and whose reportage, past and present, I have avidly mined.

But journalism can take the historian only so far. Wal-Mart's many opponents, within the labor movements, in numerous communities, and at the class-action bar, have been extraordinarily busy trying to figure out what makes the company tick. Jeff Fiedler of the AFL-CIO's Food and Allied Service Trades Department maintains a big archive exclusively devoted to Wal-Mart; likewise Brad Seligman and his associates at the Berkeley-based Impact Fund have used the "discovery" process to put into the public domain hundreds of depositions and thousands of internal company documents, many of which bear on subjects well beyond the scope of the gender discrimination suit the fund now has in litigation. Guided by Carol Pier, Human Rights Watch has also assembled a large collection of documents and interviews bearing on Wal-Mart's employment policies. And, finally, Flagler Productions of Lenexa, Kansas, has developed an extraordinary video archive covering many aspects of Wal-Mart's internal governance. Until two years ago, Flagler was a Wal-Mart vendor that enjoyed a long-standing commercial relationship with the company. It produced the Wal-Mart annual meeting; taped hundreds of internal management conclaves in Kansas City, Dallas, and Bentonville; and maintained a large file of other materials. When Wal-Mart severed their relationship, Flagler opened much of this material to the public, and I've used a slice of it.

This book is also based on more than fifty interviews with Wal-Mart workers, managers, and executives, as well as with those who have encountered the company as community leaders, vendors in the Wal-Mart supply chain, and state officials who have sought to exercise their regulatory authority. I've interviewed Wal-Mart managers and unionists in the United Kingdom, Canada, and China, as well as in the United States. Some of these people are mentioned in the footnotes, the rest wish to remain anonymous.

Research for this book was supported by grants and fellowships from both the Academic Senate at the Santa Barbara campus of the University of California and from the UC Office of the

President. Among the academic friends who have read and commented upon sections of the manuscript, I thank Richard Appelbaum, Sven Beckert, Jennifer Blair, Anita Chan, Peter Coclanis, George Cotkin, David Davies, Leon Fink, Dana Frank, John French, Gary Gerstle, Shane Hamilton, Xue Hong, Meg Jacobs, Laura Kalman, Jennifer Klein, Bethany Moreton, Alice O'Connor, Eileen Otis, Katie Quan, Jonathan Rees, Ellen Rosen, Elizabeth Shermer, Kaxton Sin, Susan Strasser, and Christine Williams. Riva Hocherman proved a skillful and insightful editor as the manuscript neared its tardy completion. All the while, the enthusiasm of publisher Sara Bershtel never flagged.

An enormous debt goes to Steve Fraser. He has been an editor of my books and articles for almost thirty years and in this case, as in the past, he has deployed his great energy and intellect to help me sharpen my argument, texture my scholarship, and tell the reader what I really want to say. His example, as an accomplished historian and forceful essayist, has provided a standard to which this book aspires.

As always my spouse, Eileen Boris, has been an insightful reader of draft after draft of this work, keeping the larger picture in perspective even as I sometimes waxed overenthusiastic about Arkansas farming, bar code economics, health insurance politics, and Chinese consumption patterns.

INDEX